THE LIBRARY
ST. MARY'S COLLEGE OF MARYLAND
ST. MARY'S CITY, MARYLAND 20686

D1474109

Cambridge in the age of the Enlightenment

Cambridge in the age of the Enlightenment

Science, religion and politics from the Restoration to the French Revolution

JOHN GASCOIGNE

Lecturer, School of History
The University of New South Wales

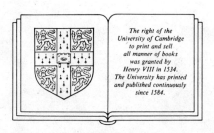

The right of the
University of Cambridge
to print and sell
all manner of books
was granted by
Henry VIII in 1534.
The University has printed
and published continuously
since 1584.

CAMBRIDGE UNIVERSITY PRESS

Cambridge
New York *New Rochelle* *Melbourne* *Sydney*

Published by the Press Syndicate of the University of Cambridge
The Pitt Building, Trumpington Street, Cambridge CB2 1RP
32 East 57th Street, New York NY 10022, USA
10 Stamford Road, Oakleigh, Melbourne 3166, Australia

© Cambridge University Press 1989

First published 1989

Printed in Great Britain at the University Press, Cambridge

British Library cataloguing in publication data
Gascoigne, John
Cambridge in the Age of the Enlightenment.
1. Religion related to science, 1660–1800
1. Title
215

Library of Congress cataloguing in publication data
Gascoigne John.
Cambridge in the age of the enlightenment: science, religion, and
politics from the restoration to the French Revolution / John
Gascoigne.
p. cm.
Bibliography
Includes index.
ISBN 0 521 35139 1
1. Cambridge (England) – Intellectual life. 2. England –
Intellectual life – 18th century. 3. England – Intellectual
life – 17th century. 4. Science – Study and teaching (Higher) –
England – Cambridge – History. 5. Religion – Study and teaching
(Higher) – England – Cambridge – History. – 6. Political science – Study and teaching
(Higher) – England – Cambridge History. – 7. University
DA690.C2G37 1989
942.6'5906 – dc19 88–21413 CIP

ISBN 0 521 35139 1

To my parents

Contents

vii

Acknowledgements

Donne's maxim, that 'No man is an island, entire of itself', is as true of the writing of history as of most other fields of human endeavour. In writing this book I have benefited from the advice of a number of historians to whom I wish to record my thanks. In the first place to Professor Lawrence Stone who first suggested the topic and took a continuing interest in its progress. To Professors J. H. Plumb and A. R. Hall who, in its early stages, watched over the Cambridge Ph.D. thesis on Cambridge intellectual life, 1660–1727, out of which this book grew and to Dr R. S. Porter who did much to help pilot this thesis across stormy seas and into port through his tactful criticism and warm encouragement. The book has also benefited much from Dr Porter's continued interest and helpful comments. I am grateful, too, to Dr M. Hunter for his close interest in the project and his valuable suggestions. I also wish to thank Dr P. Jenkins, Professor D. Oldroyd, Dr P. Turnbull, and Dr R. Yeo for taking the trouble to read, and comment on, an earlier draft of some of my chapters and Dr J. Twigg for looking over the work as a whole. I have benefited, too, from discussions with Dr J. C. D. Clark, Dr D. Cressy, Dr E. Duffy, Dr M. Feingold, Professor M. C. Jacob, the late Dame Lucy Sutherland, Dr S. Taylor and Professor D. Whiteside. The usual caveat applies: my mistakes are my own.

I am grateful to the master and fellows of Gonville and Caius College for the award of a Gonville Studentship which made possible my stay in Cambridge while a Ph.D. student and to the dean of the Faculty of Arts, University of New South Wales, for grants to cover travel, photocopying and typing expenses which enabled me to finish this book. For permission to quote from manuscripts in their custody I acknowledge the kind cooperation of the Bodleian Library, the British Library, the Cambridge University Archives, the syndics of the Cambridge University Library, the masters and fellows of Clare College, Emmanuel College, Gonville and Caius College, King's College, Magdalene College (Cambridge), St

John's College (Cambridge), Sidney Sussex College, and Trinity College (Cambridge), the earl of Clarendon (for permission to quote from the Clarendon MSS held in the Bodleian), the duke of Grafton (for permission to quote from the Grafton MSS held in the Suffolk Record Office), the archbishop of Canterbury and the trustees of Lambeth Palace Library, Leeds Public Library and the West Yorkshire Archive Service, Manchester Public Library and the City of Manchester Leisure Services Committee, Northamptonshire Record Office, Nottingham University Library and the Mellish Trustees, the Public Record Office and Dr Williams's Library (the last-named also ask that those using its MSS state that the Library is not responsible for the selection made by authors and that control of the copyright remains with the Library). To the editor of the *Historical Journal* I express my thanks for permission to incorporate much of the material from an article published in that journal (Gascoigne, 1984b).

Closer to home, I am glad to be able to have an opportunity to express my gratitude to my parents for their support, both moral and financial, throughout my education in divers lands (and to my father for ungrudgingly providing his services as proof-reader and copy-editor), to my brother, Robert, for sharing my interests over many years, and to my wife, Kate, and my children, Robert and Catherine, for living so long and so patiently under the shadow of 'the book'.

Abbreviations

Add.	Additional manuscripts
BL	British Library
BMNH	British Museum of Natural History
Bodl.	Bodleian Library, Oxford
CSPD	M. A. E. Green *et al.* (eds.), *Calendar of state papers, domestic series, 1660–1704*. 38 vols. London, 1860–1938
CUA	Cambridge University Archives
CUL	Cambridge University Library
DNB	*Dictionary of national biography*
DSB	*Dictionary of scientific biogrpahy*
DWL	Dr Williams's Library
GM	*Gentleman's Magazine*
HMC	Historical Manuscripts Commission
LRO	Leicestershire Record Office
MCL	Manchester Central Library
MR	*Monthly Review*
NRO	Northamptonshire Record Office
NU	Nottingham University
PRO	Public Record Office
RGO	Royal Greenwich Observatory, Herstmonceux
RS	Royal Society
SCL	Sheffield City Library
SM	L. S. Sutherland and L. G. Mitchell (eds.), *The history of the University of Oxford. Vol. V: The eighteenth century*. Oxford, 1986
SRO	Suffolk Record Office

NOTE

Quotations are cited verbatim except that contractions have been spelled out. Up to 31 December 1751 dates are given in old style except that the calendar year is taken as beginning on 1 January.

Introduction

Despite recent attempts (Porter, 1981; A. M. Wilson, 1983; Pocock, 1985a) to lay claim to the Enlightenment as being, at least in part, English territory, the conjunction of the terms 'English' and 'Enlightenment' still seems almost a solecism: no less an historian than R. R. Palmer has gone so far as to write that 'the term "English Enlightenment", would be jarring and incongruous if it were ever heard' (1976: 608). Was not the Enlightenment essentially a French phenomenon, albeit with pale reflections in Germany and Scotland and even paler reflections elsewhere? In any case what need had eighteenth-century England of an enlightenment when it had achieved many of the goals for which the French *philosophes* were striving? Influential accounts of the Enlightenment such as those by Hazard or Gay concede the importance of such major English thinkers as Bacon, Newton or Locke in the prehistory of the movement and cite examples drawn from eighteenth-century England, but their views of the Enlightenment are largely framed in terms of debates within France. Since in France the clash between the *philosophes* and a powerful and privileged ecclesiastical establishment assumed special significance, they emphasise the anti-clerical and even irreligious character of the Enlightenment (Gilley, 1981) – what Hazard (1965) refers to as the phenomenon of 'Christianity on trial' and Gay terms 'The rise of modern paganism' (1970). Intellectual historians, like political or military historians, are naturally drawn to the heat and smoke of past battles where the sources of conflict and the identity of the opposing sides are clear-cut. But, as Plumb remarks in his *Growth of political stability in England 1675–1725* (1969: 12–14), it is important for historians to examine the sources of stability as well as conflict – an admonition which applies to historians of ideas as well as of politics.

In its intellectual as well as its political life Hanoverian England appeared to foreigners to have achieved a remarkable degree of stability. As always, such calm was more evident to the outsider than to those on the inside who were more conscious of continuing sources of division; but, for all that, there was nothing like the same gulf in England as there was in France between a group of self-consciously enlightened thinkers and the defenders of established tradition. Underlying this relative harmony was the *rapprochement* that had been achieved between secular learning, notably science, and the established Church of England – an institution which, as J. C. D. Clark (1985) has recently emphasised, remained fundamental to the workings of society during the eighteenth century. In France science was often a weapon to be used in an attack on the privileges of the clerical estate and the political order with which it was inextricably intertwined; in England, however, science formed part of the established Church's own armoury – in large part thanks to the type of education offered to intending clergymen at Cambridge and, to a lesser extent, at Oxford. Though the highly clerical universities of England (and, in particular, Oxford) were in some respects more impervious to Enlightenment values than their Scottish counterparts, Sher's comment about the character of the Scottish Enlightenment also has some relevance to the English situation: 'If the Enlightenment in France developed outside of, and sometimes in opposi-tion to, the clergy and the schools, the Enlightenment in Scotland, along with less spectacular instances in parts of Germany and other Protestant countries, was largely an ecclesiastical and academic phenomenon' (Sher, 1985: 151).

While in France Bacon and Newton were invoked by the encyclopedists in their campaign to 'écraser l'infâme', in England both men still formed part of the Anglican pantheon. The origins of this marriage between the new science and Anglicanism can be traced back to the foundation of the Royal Society in 1660, an organisation which owed much to the work of Anglican clergymen such as Wilkins, Ward and Sprat. However, the alliance achieved its most permanent and public expression in the 'holy alliance' between Newtonian natural philosophy and Anglican apoli-getics, which was forged at the turn of the seventeenth century and remained an important landmark on the English intellectual horizon until the mid-nineteenth century. Indeed, the use of the term 'holy alliance' to describe the bond between science and religion dates from the early Victorian period when the phrase had been popularised in the very different context of the diplomacy of Metternich. Thus in his review of Robert Chambers's *Vestiges of the natural history of creation* (1844) – a work which prompted a virtual dress rehearsal of the debates about the relation-ship between religion and science engendered by the publication of Darwin's *Origin of species* (1859) – the prominent Scottish physicist, former clergyman and biographer of Newton, David Brewster, wrote that 'we did not expect that this holy alliance would be disturbed either by the philosopher or the divine' (Yeo, 1984: 11).

As the example of the Presbyterian Brewster's comments on a work largely concerned with natural history suggests, the bond between science and religion in Britain was not restricted to Anglicanism nor to Newtonian natural philosophy, though these form the focus of this study where the phrase 'holy alliance' is used as a convenient way of referring to the association between the apologetics of the Church of England and the popular understanding of Newton's achievement. By charting the fortunes of this 'holy alliance' from the late seventeenth to the end of the eighteenth century this book seeks to illuminate the nature of the English Enlightenment more generally. In particular, it aims to provide some corrective to the largely Francocentric view of the Enlightenment, which views it largely as a clash between the apostles of reason and the clerical defenders of tradition, by indicating the ways in which religious and ecclesiastical developments helped shape eighteenth-century English intellectual life generally. Like Gaul, the book is divided into three parts, which are intended to correspond to three different phases in the development of the 'holy alliance'; each part is in turn further divided into three chapters – the first being devoted to political and ecclesiastical developments, the second to theology and the third to science. Part One, which covers the period from the Restoration to the Revolution of 1688, describes the development of the theological and scientific concepts which lay behind the 'holy alliance' together with a discussion of some of the influences which impeded the earlier development of that alliance; Part Two, which extends from the Revolution of 1688 to the accession of George III in 1760 (and, in deference to the importance of the duke of Newcastle as chancellor of Cambridge, with a further extension to 1768 when that great master of whig patronage died) describes the formation and dissemination of the 'holy alliance'; and, lastly, Part Three, which deals with the period from 1768 to the end of the century, examines the way in which it was questioned by a number of developments which were to become more pronounced in the nineteenth century when the 'holy alliance' was finally dissolved. Among such developments in the late eighteenth century was the growth of political and religious radicalism which in England (and in Scotland) challenged the accepted view that Enlightenment values supported rather than disturbed the existing order (Porter, 1981: 16; Sher, 1985: 304).

In order to discuss intellectual developments over nearly a century and a half it is necessary to employ some analytical categories: two which loom particularly large in this book are 'Newtonianism' and 'latitudinarianism', both of which need to be used with some caution. The term 'Newtonianism', as R. E. Schofield (1978) has shown, can be subdivided into a number of different species, particularly in its Continental manifestations. The variety of Newtonianism with which this work is primarily concerned is what Schofield calls 'theological Newtonianism' which used a selective form of Newtonian natural philosophy in order to provide support for the argument from design. As he remarks, it was a form of Newtonianism which 'differed but little from the earliest scientific Newtonianism represented, at first, by the Edinburgh–Oxford coterie of David Gregory, John and James Keill, John Freind, and Archibald Pitcairne'. The main characteristics of both the early theological and scientific followers of Newton were a strong hostility to Descartes, a conviction that scientific certainty could be achieved through the use of mathematics and the quantification of observational and experimental data, a corpuscular view of matter combined with a belief in attractive and repulsive forces, and an assumption (largely theologically based) that space and time were absolutes (R. E. Schofield, 1978: 177–8).

In common with many terms that originate in religious controversy the work 'latitudinarian' is difficult to define with precision. Like the term 'puritan' it was used for polemical effect and was employed only reluctantly as a term of self-description. But, though terms such as 'puritan' or 'latitudinarian' may not be sharp-edged tools of historical analysis, they are none the less sanctioned by contemporary usage and provide a possible key to understanding the religious mentality of our predecessors. The term 'latitudinarian' originated in the debates about the nature of the Restoration Church to describe those who had conformed both to the parliamentary regime and to the restored Church and King and who favoured a widening of the established Church's theological boundaries to include as many English Protestants as possible. Since those seeking such ends tended to emphasise those doctrines on which the majority of Protestants were agreed, rather than the theological points that were likely to cause divisions, the word 'latitudinarian' (or its synonym 'latitude-man') was coined to suggest theological breadth or vagueness; as one critic put it, a latitudinarian was 'a Gentleman of a wide swallow' (E. Fowler, 1670: 10).

The failure of proposed schemes for theological comprehension and the widening gulf between Anglican and dissenter after 1662 are indications of the marginal position of those with latitudinarian views within the Restoration Church. Such churchmen were, however, to play a more significant role in the decades following 1688 when the divisions within the Church which the term 'latitudinarian' reflects became even more acute. Though the Restoration Church had regarded it as its particular mission to instil the doctrine of passive obedience, most Anglican clerymen arrived at some compromise with the post-revolutionary order which followed the overthrow of James II's rule. None the less, many of the clergy were hostile to those of their estate who acted as apologists for the new regime, particularly as such churchmen – to whom the term 'latitudinarian' was frequently applied – were often appointed to sees vacated by the nonjurors. As the political and religious divisions prompted by the Revolution of 1688 slowly subsided the word 'latitudinarian' was less likely to be used to describe a particular ecclesiastical party (Rupp, 1986: 32–3), though it never entirely lost its partisan character since latitudinarian opinion never won over the Church as a whole (Mather, 1985: 282). However, it was sufficiently widely diffused, particularly in the period before the reign of George III, to call into question the view that 'the Georgian [ecclesiastical] norm' was 'profoundly conservative, theologically orthodox and devotionally viable' (J. C. D. Clark, 1986: 109). Norman Sykes correctly points out that latitudinarianism as a 'theological temper' could transcend 'differences of political persuasion' (1934: 343) but, in practice, latitudinarianism was generally associated with whig political principles. After all, the tory party, the traditional defender of the Church's privileges, was unlikely to be the natural haven for those who wished to widen the doors of the Church to accommodate at least some of the dissenters. This association between whiggery and latitudinarianism is reflected in a complaint made in 1729 by a member of the predominantly tory University of Oxford that he 'suffered . . . as a Whig and Hoadleian' (a follower of the arch-latitudinarian Bishop Hoadly) (W. R. Ward, 1958: 118). In 1733 a whig apologist alleged that if the tories 'had Power, they would shew all *Freethinkers*, *Latitudinarians*, and *Dissenters* too, that they did not much regard the Tenderness of their Consciences' (*GM*, 1733: 540) – such suspicions being further heightened by comments like those made by the tory *Jackson's Oxford Journal* during the hotly contested Oxfordshire election of 1754 that 'The principles of whiggism, at the best are lax and latitudinarian . . . they are for introducing a wild medley of all sorts of impieties from Judaism down to Quakerism' (Colley, 1982: 131).

However, such overtly partisan connotations of the term 'latitudinarian' declined in the course of the eighteenth century, in part because the definition of 'whig' itself became more elastic and inclusive. The term 'latitudinarian' was given renewed prominence in the late eighteenth-century controversy prompted by the abortive attempts to abolish clerical subscription to the Thirty-Nine Articles and the word continued to be used into the nineteenth century to describe churchmen who tended to emphasise individual interpretation of Scripture rather than the doctrinal traditions of the Church, and natural as against revealed

theology. Without the word 'latitudinarian', then, it is difficult to draw
attention to the way in which the theological developments of the
Restoration period continued to shape the outlook of a significant group of
eighteenth-century Anglican clergy who were particularly active in
fostering the 'holy alliance'. In the late eighteenth century Anglican clergy
who were described by contemporaries as 'latitudinarians' still proclaimed
themselves as followers of late seventeenth-century theologians like
Tillotson – an intellectual continuity which was strengthened by institutional and personal links in an age when ecclesiastical life was dominated
by patronage.

THE CHARACTER OF UNREFORMED CAMBRIDGE

The importance of patronage in helping to maintain the continued
existence of a latitudinarian tradition within the eighteenth-century
Church underlines the importance more generally of locating intellectual
developments in a political and institutional context – hence the focus on
Cambridge University, the *alma mater* both of Isaac Newton and of most
of the prominent latitudinarian theologians. Moreover, it seemed probable that a university which produced men like Newton and Bentley was
not as devoid of interest as was commonly thought – the general view of
post-Restoration Cambridge being summed up by Westfall, Newton's
latest, and most complete, biographer who writes of 'the catastrophic
decline of the university after the Restoration [which] left it an intellectual
wasteland as the Cambridge Platonists died off' (1975: 194). The purpose
of this section is, then, firstly, to outline some of the chief features of
Cambridge's institutional life before it was reshaped by the reforms of the
nineteenth century in order to provide some background to the intellectual
and political developments which are the chief focus of this book; and,
secondly, to compare Cambridge with other major eighteenth-century
British institutions of higher education, notably Oxford, the dissenting
academies and the Scottish universities.

As is the case with many aspects of the English old regime, the
conventional view of the eighteenth-century universities owes much to
the nineteenth-century reformers who naturally tended to emphasise the
faults and failings of the traditional order in Church and State in order to
underline the need for change. Not that these reformers were altogether
wrong; even the most enthusiastic advocate of unreformed Cambridge
would find it difficult not to agree with the would-be university reformer,
Mr Heywood, who in 1850 moved in the House of Commons: 'That in
the ancient English and Irish Universities, and in the Colleges connected
with them, the interests of religious and useful learning have not advanced

to an extent commensurate with the great resources and high position of these bodies' (C. H. Cooper, 1842–1908, v: 10). But in their preoccupation with exciting public outrage at the manifold imperfections of Oxford and Cambridge, the reformers paid little attention to those aspects of university life which indicated that these institutions were something more than dry husks of a bygone age – an example that subsequent historians have largely followed.

Thus it is not often acknowledged that the end of the seventeenth and beginning of the eighteenth century was a period when Cambridge (and, to a lesser extent, Oxford) almost totally reshaped its curriculum, breaking with a tradition of scholasticism that stretched back to the high Middle Ages. At Cambridge (unlike Oxford) classical logic – traditionally the chief preoccupation of the curriculum – gave way to mathematics and the study of Locke's epistemology, and at both universities scholastic natural philosophy was supplanted by 'the new philosophy'. Indeed, by the early eighteenth century Cambridge retained little from its academic past except the study of the classics, which had largely been grafted onto the university's traditional curriculum in the sixteenth century. Moreover, at Cambridge (again in contrast to Oxford) such humanistic studies were increasingly overshadowed by the mathematical sciences as the eighteenth century progressed. The scholastic curriculum at Cambridge (as at many other European universities (Gascoigne, 1989a)) had been coming under increasing strain in the course of the seventeenth century as it became more and more difficult to assimilate the developments associated with the Scientific Revolution into intellectual categories largely derived from Aristotelian thought, but it was not until the late seventeenth century that the traditional scholastic order was almost totally abandoned. Undergraduates were at first exposed to a new system of natural philosophy based on the work of Descartes though, by the early decades of the eighteenth century, this had given way to a study of Newton's work – a further illustration of the university's capacity for change. The scale of this virtual academic revolution was somewhat camouflaged by the fact that the university continued to pledge allegiance to the same set of Elizabethan statutes and still maintained many of the outward and visible signs of the old order in the form of disputations – exercises which were preserved at Cambridge until about 1830, even though their original function of testing a student's mastery of classical logic was now outmoded.

The declining pedagogical importance of disputations – the traditional method of assessing students – helps account for the growth of another distinctive, and relatively unacknowledged, feature of unreformed Cambridge, namely the Senate House examination which eventually became known as the mathematical tripos. This rigorous and highly competitive examination gradually took shape during the eighteenth century, though its basic form was established by 1753 when students were first classed as wranglers and senior and junior optimes, a system that laid the basis for subsequent systems of honours. It was the mathematical tripos which provided the nineteenth-century reformers with a model for competitive examinations which would provide an alternative to the deeply entrenched practices of 'Old Corruption' and appointment by patronage (Roach, 1971: 12–13).

Given the pre-eminence of the mathematical sciences within eighteenth-century Cambridge – something which the importance of the mathematical tripos reflects – it is ironic that the university is sometimes contrasted with the dissenting academies and the Scottish universities as a bastion of clerical obscurantism which was impervious to mathematics and science. Hill, for example, writes of the dissenting academies that 'They trained men for business and the professions with a far wider and more up-to-date curriculum than that of grammar schools and universities; it included mathematics and science . . . The cultural split between Anglican universities and middle-class Dissenting Academies extended to a rigid distinction between the arts and the sciences' (1961: 293–4). It is true that at Cambridge so much attention was paid to mathematics (including 'mixed' or applied mathematics) that the experimental and observational sciences were relatively neglected, though even in these areas there was more activity than is commonly thought. Moreover, although the dissenting academies were to be of scientific importance in the late eighteenth century in the age of Priestley and Dalton, they naturally at first offered a curriculum very similar to that traditionally provided by the universities since their staff had themselves been trained at either pre-1662 Oxford or Cambridge (W. A. L. Vincent, 1950: 118). Gradually the dissenting academies developed their own academic traditions though these did not always favour scientific education – at Attercliffe academy (which existed from 1690 to 1720), for example, mathematical studies were forbidden 'as tending to scepticism and infidelity' (McLachlan, 1931: 32). With the growing theological liberalism of the dissenting community such cases became more and more rare and these institutions provided an increasingly broad range of secular subjects including the sciences. So broad, indeed, was the range that students often acquired little more than a superficial acquaintance with any single discipline; as one contemporary nonconformist wrote: 'The grand error in almost every dissenting academy has been the attempt to teach and to learn too much' (*ibid.*: 40).

A similar criticism was levelled at the Scottish universities which, wrote Dr Johnson, gave everyone a mouthful and no one a bellyful of learning (McDowell and Webb, 1982: 120). Cambridge with its mathematical myopia went to the other extreme, though its best graduates could claim to have been exposed to a more rigorous, albeit more narrow, training than their Scottish counterparts. In 1805 a young Scot remarked about a friend who had been second wrangler at Cambridge: 'To take such a degree requires reading that in Scotland we have hardly any notion of. If there are greater instances of idleness in English seminaries, there are likewise more astonishing proofs of application' (Winstanley, 1935: 228).

Where the Scottish universities clearly surpassed Oxford and Cambridge was in the encouragement they provided for original work in what have become known as the natural[1] and the social sciences. Part of the reason for this difference probably lies in the continuing vitality of the professorial system in Scotland which allowed an individual to concentrate his energies on a single discipline even though, ironically, his students might be expected to master a wider range of subjects than their English counterparts. Though Cambridge's professoriate expanded from 7 to 21 in number in the period 1660 to 1800 and its ranks included some men of distinction (quite apart from Newton) – 65% of incumbents, for example, were thought to be sufficiently important to be accorded an entry in the *DNB* – it had little impact on a university where teaching was almost exclusively a preserve of the colleges, hence the number of professors who treated their posts as sinecures. Undergraduate instruction was dominated by college tutors who were generally expected to teach the full range of the university curriculum through a system of 'catechetical' lectures which had to cater for all levels of ability; consequently, those aspiring to high honours generally employed a private coach. Such a system did little to encourage a don to identify closely with one particular branch of learning and to take an interest in its advancement.

Another area where the Scottish universities were clearly superior to their eighteenth-century English counterparts was in the provision of lay professional education, something which reflects the lay, civic control of

---

[1] Morrell (1971: 159) has made the following calculations based on Hans's sample of 680 scientists from the seventeenth and eighteenth centuries:

	% Oxford-educated	% Cambridge-educated	% Edinburgh-educated
1726–1745	11	18	20
1746–1765	16	13	24
1766–1785	8	12	17

Given the relative sizes of Edinburgh and the English universities, the figures reveal the clear superiority of Edinburgh as a centre of scientific research. These statistics also underline Cambridge's declining scientific importance as the eighteenth century progressed.

the Scottish universities in contrast to the clerical nature of Oxford and Cambridge. Holmes has recently (1982) drawn attention to the great increase in the size of the professions in late seventeenth- and early eighteenth-century England, the membership of which, he calculates, expanded by about 70% from 1680 to 1730 (p. 17). This development had little effect on Oxford and Cambridge where the faculties of law (by which was meant civil law) and medicine were little more than vestigial forms – between 1660 and 1727, when about 11,200 BA degrees were awarded at Cambridge, only 373 graduated LL B and only 356 with an MB; there were also 144 LL Ds awarded and 252 MDs. As a proportion of total degrees, then, qualifications in law or medicine formed only 9% of degrees awarded (excluding the largely nominal MA) (Borlase, 1800). The situation at Oxford was similar: in 1804 there were 638 MAs studying divinity and a mere five taking medicine and either eight or fifteen law (Sutherland, in SM: 488n). Part of the reason, Holmes suggests, for the ease with which the professions expanded in the eighteenth century was that professional training could be supplied relatively cheaply through a system of apprenticeship. By contrast legal or medical training at the university was long and expensive: at Cambridge the statutes stipulated six years' residence for those taking either an MB or an LL B. Though in practice students generally remained at Cambridge for only three years and returned at the end of six to fulfil the prescribed academic exercises (Winstanley, 1935: 58), it was still an expensive, complex and often ineffective means of training.

Moreover, the general costs of a university degree had greatly increased by the early eighteenth century: in 1732 Daniel Waterland (who had matriculated in 1699) wrote to Dr Bishop that 'expenses are almost doubled within my memory' (Magdalene College, Cambridge, Waterland MSS).[2] Gone was the early seventeenth-century practice of undergraduates sleeping in a truckle bed in their tutor's room; undergraduates now had to meet the cost of more lavish accommodation. In the eighteenth century undergraduates also had to pay increasing fees to their tutors as the traditional system of college lectures fell into decay; those wishing to excel in the late eighteenth-century tripos also had to employ a private tutor. The sizar system, whereby poor students paid reduced fees in return for menial duties, was in decline, thus further limiting the opportunity for those with slender means to attend university. At St John's in March 1715 fellows were urged to observe 'a very antient and laudable custom of the said college that every Fellow and all others who

---

[2] Stone (1974: 43) writes that 'The cost of an Oxford education thus appears to have increased five or sixfold from the early seventeenth to the mid-nineteenth century, although the general cost of living index had risen by only two and a half times.'

are in Fellows commons [i.e., the wealthy student fellow-commoners] should entertain a sizar . . . [since] by neglect of this good Custom many poor scholars have been depriv'd of that support which they should have had' (St John's Admonition book). Needless to say, such admonitions had little effect: the number of sizars at St John's fell from about 33 in the 1660s and 1670s to about 13 in the 1760s (E. Miller, 1961: 60); servitors also largely disappeared in late eighteenth-century Oxford (Doolittle in SM: 257).

In Scotland, by contrast, the costs of a university education were considerably reduced by the fact that residency was not compulsory; in many cases undergraduates could have lived at home and those coming from outside the university town could use the six-month long vacation to return home to earn money for the coming year. In the mid-eighteenth century, it was possible to survive on as little as five pounds a year at one of the Scottish universities in contrast to fifty pounds or more necessary at Oxford and Cambridge (O'Day, 1982: 276). The Scottish universities, then, were in a better position to provide a relatively cheap form of education in professions such as law or medicine which in England were largely provided outside the universities. The Scottish universities of the big cities, Glasgow and Edinburgh, unlike Oxford and Cambridge, also had access to major hospitals and courts.

It was probably the Scottish universities' involvement in professional education which accounts for their considerable growth in the course of the eighteenth century, in contrast to the enrolments at Oxford and Cambridge which, for much of the century, were in decline. Overall, the enrolments at Scottish universities increased from about 1,000 in 1700 to 2,700 in 1800. Edinburgh had about 300 students at the beginning of the century, a figure which had risen to 1,279 by 1800; of these, 660 were studying medicine (O'Day, 1982: 274–7). Glasgow's enrolments doubled during the same period (Emerson, 1977: 473). The Scottish universities' involvement in professional education also provided a stimulus for research. The law faculty helped to provide the institutional setting for the Scottish pioneering work in the social sciences; thus as professor of moral philosophy at Glasgow from 1752 Adam Smith lectured on a range of subjects including jurisprudence while his pupil, John Millar, author of a number of important works of sociological history, was professor of law at Glasgow from 1761. Similarly the medical faculty acted as a catalyst for scientific research, notably in chemistry: the chemist William Cullen held both medical and chemical professorships at Edinburgh, an example emulated by his more famous pupil, Joseph Black.

In the wake of the controversy generated by Sir William Hamilton's less than tactful comparison of the achievements of the Scottish and the

English universities in the *Edinburgh Review* of 1831 the Cambridge polymath, William Whewell, sought to counter criticisms of his university's relatively meagre research record by arguing that the English universities' 'primary function is that of institutions for the purpose of education; and their being seats of science is a character which belongs to them mainly as connected with and resulting from the other [i.e., their educational function]'. Consequently, he continued, 'it is mere folly to look upon such persons [as college fellows] as men whose office is *discovery*, or to make demands upon them as if their duty were to produce *new* truths' (*British Critic*, 1831: 71–2). The force of this defence is weakened, however, when one considers that in fact only a small proportion of fellows were directly involved in teaching since undergraduate instruction was virtually monopolised by the tutors. The 1796 *Cambridge University calendar* reveals that all colleges had only one or two tutors apart from Queens' (which had three), St John's (three senior tutors and four junior tutors) and Trinity (two tutors and four assistants). Thus only a small fraction of the university's approximately four hundred fellows were involved in teaching in any permanent capacity. The tutors, as Heberden wrote in 1792, 'form[ed] the most respectable part of the society' and it was often from their ranks that future masters were chosen. Heberden went on to add that the pre-eminence of the tutors was 'an additional proof, if any such were wanting of the efficacy of employment on the mind and character, and of the necessity of rubbing off the corroding rust of inactivity; a rust with which the resident Fellows of Universities are too frequently incrusted' (pp. 46–7).

What, then, did the fellows who were not tutors do? As Heberden's comments suggest it is difficult to find any tangible record of many of the fellows' activities. John Venn calculated that of the 158 fellows elected at Caius between 1707 and 1777 only eleven are listed as authors in the British Library's catalogue (1901: 157). As the eighteenth century progressed, however, a growing proportion of the fellows – possibly even the majority – were nonresident, coming into college only at special times in the year such as the audit dinner or the election of fellows. Nonresidency had been frowned upon in the seventeenth century except in special circumstances, for example when a fellow was given leave to accompany a genteel pupil on the grand tour. There were still residues of such attitudes in the eighteenth century: in 1721 Caius reminded a fellow who was practising as an advocate in the Court of Arches that there was an 'order, of above twenty years' date, that every Fellow is required to reside one quarter of every year'. A similar order was repeated in 1734 though, by 1751, there were signs that the college was slowly giving way, for it reduced the requirement to 'one month in each half-year, and that in term time'. However, it did not finally concede defeat until 1809 when it was agreed 'not to require for the present any residence in College from the junior Fellows' (*ibid.*: 196–7). The same pattern was also evident at Queens' where William Sedgwick (president, 1732–60) regarded large-scale nonresidency as only having become a problem after he first came to the college in 1716. Sedgwick decried the growing extent of nonresidency since one of the purposes of a fellowship was to make its incumbent 'more fit to go out into the World by the advantages of a Learned Conversation' (Twigg, 1987: 186). Despite such objections, by the end of the eighteenth century a fellowship was regarded as a prize for past accomplishment (which from the 1760s was increasingly measured by success in the tripos (Gascoigne, 1984a: 561)) rather than as an office entailing duties or even residence. A fellowship, then, was often considered as a subsidy for those beginning in a profession; consequently, many junior fellows acted as curates and a lesser number might study for the bar or for membership of the College of Physicians. One remained entitled to a fellow's income until marriage or until appointed to a substantial living (though this latter provision was subject to exceptions (Winstanley, 1935: 234)). Apart from these provisions, and cases of flagrantly criminal behaviour, a fellowship was an absolute freehold; even William Frend who was expelled from the university on political and religious grounds in 1793 continued to draw his income as a fellow of Jesus until his marriage in 1808.

Though there were a few fellowships specifically allocated for the study of law or medicine which could be held by laymen, about 87% of fellowships (CUL, Mm.1.48: 455) required their incumbents eventually to take orders. For most fellows, then, the chief merit of their fellowship was that it offered the chance of a benefice in the gift of the college and hence the possibility of married life. The colleges' clerical patronage was particularly important for those fellows without connections who otherwise had little hope of gaining a living, particularly in the late eighteenth century when the landed classes began to place their offspring in increasing numbers in clerical posts – a trend apparent in the growing number of well-born bishops (Ravitch, 1966: 120–1). College livings were allocated according to seniority and the remark made by the mid-nineteenth-century Oxford University Commission – that by the time some fellows were finally given a living they were 'fit neither for the post they have coveted, nor for any other' (Haig, 1980: 323) – no doubt applied with equal force in the eighteenth century. The livings in the gift of the Cambridge colleges were generally more valuable than the normal run of benefices and, not surprisingly, most were in the vicinity of Cambridge.[3]

[3] It is not until the Ecclesiastical Commission of 1835 that we have the first systematic survey since the Reformation of the nature and income of all clerical posts (including college

The majority of Cambridge livings were relatively close to the university, but in practice it must have been difficult to maintain any regular contact with the university once one had accepted a living, given the often inadequate nature of pre-railway transport. Unreformed Cambridge was, then, an institution which lost most of its more able fellows to college livings or to posts in the gift of influential patrons. Those who remained as life-fellows were often those without the necessary connections, abilities or political skills to acquire a living. Such fellows often led embittered existences, a fact which helps to explain the vehemence of internal college disputes. A system which encouraged fellows to regard their college posts as generally but a prelude to a living offered little institutional incentive to undertake original enquiry. Those fellows who did use their time waiting for a living to produce original work found it difficult to continue their investigations once they were given a living and found themselves intellectually isolated in a rural rectory. There were some cases like that of Stephen Hales, who continued his scientific work, begun at Corpus, after being appointed perpetual curate of Teddington (near London), but probably more typical was the experience of his promising young colleague, Robert Danny – the friend and scientific collaborator of Cotes – who, in February 1725, wrote thus to his former pupil, the antiquary William Stukeley, from a living in distant Yorkshire:

you must . . . look upon me as a Lover of Learning, destitute of some of the principal means of Improvement, & consequently rusting in a Desert . . . That Mr. Hales has obliged the Curious, is a matter of great joy to me; & I wish that I was capable of doing any thing, which might either increase Knowledge, or receive your Approbation. (Bodl., MS Eng. Misc. c.113: 140v)

For the fortunate few who became heads of colleges it was possible to combine matrimony and college life. Most heads remained in their posts

livings) but its findings probably provide a fairly good guide to the situation at the end of the eighteenth century. Overall, college livings were more valuable than the normal run of benefices: 18% were worth up to £151 per annum (in contrast to a national average in 1873 of 28.4%), 24% between £151 and £300 (as against a national figure of 37.2%) and 21% over £600, in glaring contrast to a general average of 8.1%. Most college livings were located in the diocese of Ely (of which Cambridge formed a part) or the adjoining dioceses of Lincoln, Norwich or London (which included much of Essex): the number of livings in each of these dioceses were 42 (15%), 50 (18%), 72 (26%) and 23 (8%) respectively out of an overall total of about 300 individual livings (which is reduced to a figure of 272 when livings held in plurality are taken into account). The only other dioceses which included more than 10 Cambridge livings were York with 22 (8%) and Winchester with 13 (5%). (Figures for incomes of Cambridge benefices have been derived from *The report of the commission of inquiry into the ecclesiastical revenues of England and Wales*: Parliamentary papers, vol. XXII, 1835: 15–1,060. The national figures are given in Haig, 1980 (Appendix: Table 8) – since the latter are from 1873 and the former are from 1835 the contrast between the value of Cambridge livings and those in the country at large was probably even greater than these figures suggest.)

until they died, this being true of 86% of heads appointed from 1689 to 1800 at Cambridge and about 80% of eighteenth-century Oxford masters of colleges (Doolittle in SM: 230). For a small minority, however, a mastership could provide a stepping-stone into the lofty heights of the episcopate. A greater number were advanced to bishoprics during the period from the Restoration to the Revolution of 1688 than thereafter – a reflection of the universities' importance in the process of re-establishing the Church of England and of the general shortage of those with unimpeachable Anglican credentials. Thus from 1660 to 1688 11 out of the total of 49 masters appointed (22%) were made bishops in contrast to a figure of 13 out of 93 (14%) in the period 1689 to 1800. The greater eminence of those appointed in the period 1660 to 1688 (and, to a lesser extent, from 1689 to the accession of George II in 1727) is also reflected in the percentage of masters listed in the *DNB*: for these two periods the figures are 69% and 51% respectively; for the remainder of the eighteenth century the figure drops to 38%. The composition of the heads from 1660 to 1800 again emphasises the clerical nature of the university: the only laymen were the heads of Trinity Hall, a foundation that specialised in civil law, and four of the seven heads of Gonville and Caius, a college with a strong medical tradition. Like the masters, professors could generally marry – but their stipend was not sufficient to support a family and such posts were generally held in conjunction with a fellowship or some other source of income.

For the great majority of fellows obliged to wait for a living if they wished to marry, the period of waiting appears to have increased during the eighteenth century. At Queens' the average length of a fellowship was about six or seven years in the period 1500 to 1640 but had risen to nearly twelve in the period 1660 to 1778 (Twigg 1987: 185). The same trend is apparent at Clare, where the average of fellows rose from twenty-seven in 1600 to thirty-one in 1700 and thirty-two in 1750 (Harrison, 1958: 85).[4] This increasing length of tenure of fellowships was probably the result both of a bottleneck in the supply of livings and the increasing value of the fellowships which made fellows less inclined to give up their posts for more minor positions. Both at Oxford (Dunbabinin in SM: 277) and at Cambridge the colleges benefited greatly from the general increase in landed incomes during the eighteenth century which were particularly spectacular during the period of the Napoleonic wars. By 1815, Clay suggests (1980: 157), some clerical landowners may have benefited from an increase in revenue of some several hundred per cent – though this was

---

[4] Professor Lawrence Stone points out that such average figures may be distorted by a number of life-fellows.

lessened by the increasing burden of wartime taxation and (in the case of some colleges) the costs of instituting enclosures.[5] The growing value of college fellowships is reflected in the mounting size of the total dividend at St John's – the dividend being the income derived from fines (money paid for the renewal of leases on college estates) which was used to supplement the increasingly nominal stipend paid to fellows under the terms of the college's statutes. At St John's the annual dividend for the fellowship as a whole rose from an annual average of £493 in the 1660s to £900 in the 1730s (over a period when the cost of living had actually declined) and thereafter increased apace: in the 1740s it was £1,110, a figure that had risen to £7,711 by the 1840s (Howard, 1935: 303–25) – nearly a sevenfold increase over a century when the cost of living increased only about twofold (Phelps Brown and Hopkins, 1956). The total dividend was divided among the college fellows according to seniority and, needless to say, the largest shares went to the senior fellows. Indeed, C. Brooke (1985: 184) suggests that one of the reasons for the increasing nonresidency of eighteenth-century junior fellows was that the size of their dividend made it difficult for them to survive without an additional source of income – though, if this is true, it reflects the rising expectations of eighteenth-century fellows since even junior fellows were considerably better off than their seventeenth-century counterparts.

What did the colleges do with their increasing wealth? One thing they did not do was to appoint many more fellows to share in the dividend. In 1672 the total number of Cambridge college fellowships was about 395; by 1796 this figure had risen only to 408 (Wordsworth, 1874: 640–2).[6] Some college funds went into improving college buildings, the eighteenth century being an important age architecturally for Cambridge (and Oxford (Colvin in SM: 831–56)). Another area of expenditure – which was particularly close to the hearts of most fellows – was the purchase of more advowsons, thereby increasing the number of livings in the college's gift. The number of Cambridge livings appears to have risen from about 250 early in the eighteenth century (CUL, MS Mm.1.48: 454) to about 300 by 1796 (*Cambridge University calendar*, 1796). By this time, then, the overall proportion of college livings to fellowships was about 75% and only at two colleges (Catharine Hall and Magdalene) did this figure fall below 50%. The number of livings would probably have been even higher but for the Mortmain Act of 1736 (discussed in chapter 4) which was enacted by anti-clerical whigs who were afraid of the Church gaining too much wealth and independence.

[5] I owe this last point to Dr John Twigg.
[6] Since Wordsworth does not give the size of the Pembroke and Sidney Sussex fellowships in 1672, figures listed by the Cambridge antiquary Dr Warren in the early eighteenth century (CUL, Mm.1.48: 455) have been used in these cases.

The high level of anti-clericalism in post-Restoration England may go some way towards explaining one of the most striking features of both Oxford and Cambridge during this period: the marked decline in student numbers. Sending one's son to the predominantly clerical universities entailed a large degree of acquiescence in the views and goals of the clerical estate. Before the Civil War, when a greater proportion of Englishmen were receiving a university education than was to be the case until the period following the First World War (Stone, 1964: 68), both the laity and the clergy shared the same sense of urgency about the great issues of grace and salvation which the Reformation had brought to the fore. The laity were therefore prepared to entrust the education of their sons to the clergy and viewed a university education as of value for any future career, even though it was intended primarily for aspiring clergy. By the early eighteenth century, however, the values and intellectual presuppositions of the laity and the clergy had so far diverged that universities were commonly regarded as of little value to anyone not intending to embark on a clerical career. Though an Oxford graduate himself, Frederick Leigh commented to a friend in 1704 that 'for my part I doe not think of sending my eldest son to either of them [the universities], nor any of my Youngest but such whom I design for the Church in which case 'tis absolutely necessary to qualify them for orders, by taking Degrees there' (NRO, MS Dryden (Canons Ashby) 354: 51). Sir William Chaytor came to the same conclusion when discussing his sons' education in 1701, writing, 'We must not think of the University unless they will study divinity' (E. Hughes, 1952: 367). Elements of the elite still most inclined to favour the clerical universities – some sections of the lesser gentry and the clergy themselves – were largely identified with the tories and hence were more likely to send their sons to predominantly tory Oxford rather than Cambridge which, after about 1730, was clearly in the whig camp. Thus 269 of the 617 tory MPs who entered parliament between 1715 and 1760 were Oxford alumni as against 76 from Cambridge (Colley, 1982: 85). Cambridge, moreover, had the further disadvantage of providing a generally unpopular mathematically based curriculum while at Oxford greater attention was paid to the classics. Such factors help to explain why Cambridge's enrolment appears to have been significantly below that of Oxford throughout the eighteenth century.[7]

After the religious turmoil which accompanied the Civil War and the Interregnum there were many in England (including, perhaps, Charles II)

---

[7] According to J. A. Venn (1908: 58) enrolments at eighteenth-century Oxford were 60% higher than those at Cambridge. However, this figure may be somewhat misleading since there were a considerable number of eighteenth-century Cambridge students who were admitted to a college without being listed in the matriculation register (Stone and Stone, 1984: 262–3).

who viewed the clergy with some suspicion and who were particularly wary of those bastions of clerical influence, Oxford and Cambridge. Hobbes went so far as to write that 'the Universities have been as mischievous to this Nation, as the Wooden Horse was to the Trojans' (Richardson, 1928: 16). Even the Cavalier gentry, the backbone of political Anglicanism, were determined to prevent the clergy laying claim to the level of legal and political power to which Laud had aspired. Anti-clericalism was further heightened by the clergy's close identification with the tories during the Exclusion Crisis of 1679–81 and still more by the ambivalent attitude of the clergy to the Glorious Revolution and the Hanoverian succession, with the result that hostility to the clergy reached its peak in the reign of George II (when the Mortmain Act was passed). 'Since the day of the Lollards', wrote Mark Pattison, 'there had never been a time when the established ministers of religion were held in so much contempt as in the Hanoverian period, or when satire upon churchmen was so congenial to general feeling' (Best, 1964: 94). Eighteenth-century English anti-clericalism differed, however, from the French variety in that – apart from the early eighteenth-century deists who attracted few followers – it rarely extended to an attack on the principle of an established Church or to a general assault on Christianity. Indeed, English anti-clericals often regarded themselves as the defenders of Protestant Christianity against the popish tendencies of some of the clergy.

It is probably never difficult to collect examples of clerical paranoia but outrage at 'the contempt of the clergy' does appear to have been particularly marked among the pastors of the post-Restoration Established Church. In 1699 the low churchman White Kennett declared that 'the contempt of the clergy is the sin and shame of this latter age' (Overton, 1885: 302), a situation that had changed little by 1750, to judge from a sermon by Henry Hubbard, a tutor at Emmanuel, who bemoaned the fact 'that, in this Age, every attempt to magnify the office of a clergyman is looked upon as invidious' (1750: 16). Such views were also echoed by lay writers: Edward Chamberlayne in his *Angliae notitia* (first ed., 1669) remarked that the English clergy are 'less respected generally than any in Europe' while Defoe commented that 'the ecclesiastical power has lost its credit' (Overton, 1885: 302–3). The strength of this anti-clericalism has also left a more tangible record in the way in which clerical landed incomes fell significantly behind their lay counterparts up to the mid-eighteenth century – a result, in part, of the refusal of lay tenants (often broad-acred members of the governing classes) to permit clerical landowners to extract the same rents and conditions that they themselves demanded (Best, 1964: 101; Clay, 1980).

As the recovery of clerical incomes after about 1750 suggests, however, anti-clericalism was less marked in the second half of the century. Less and less was the Church perceived as a threat to the existing political order; on the contrary, the Church was seen as a bulwark of a social and political system increasingly under attack – an attitude reflected in the growing number of clergymen acting as JPs (Best, 1964: 71). One indication of the generally more favourable attitude to the clergy by the end of the eighteenth century was the repeal in 1805 of those sections of the Mortmain Act which restricted the colleges from purchasing more advowsons (C. H. Cooper, 1842–1908, IV: 482–3). Moreover, the rising value of clerical livings – which reflected the increase in landed incomes generally, including college fellowships and livings[8] – made the clerical estate a more inviting career for the sons of the governing classes, thus weakening the class prejudice that lay beneath much anti-clericalism. As early as 1752 Bishop Warburton remarked: 'Our grandees have at last found their way back into the church. I only wonder they have been so long about it' (N. Sykes, 1934: 157).

The general pattern of anti-clericalism – a steady increase from the Restoration which reached its peak in the reign of George II and thereafter declined – largely matches (in reverse) the overall pattern of student enrolments at both English universities. At Cambridge the number of those matriculating increased in the 1660s (with an average annual enrolment of 304) as compared with the troubled 1650s (when the figure was still remarkably high: 254) but thereafter the picture is one of general decline: 290 in the 1670s, 226 in the 1680s, 191 in the 1690s. There was a slight improvement in the decade 1700–9 (with a figure of 204), when the staunch Anglican, Queen Anne, was on the throne, but this only briefly halted the downward trend which reached its nadir in the 1760s with a figure of 112. From the 1760s, however, the number of matriculants generally increased, reaching 162 by the 1790s (Stone, 1974: 92). Lucas has shown that the level of student enrolments at the Inns of Court also improved in the late eighteenth century, something he attributes to an 'aristocratic resurgence', 'firming up the faith of the "Establishment" in its existing legal order' (1742: 242) – an argument that can also be advanced (as Lucas suggests) to account for the increasing popularity of the universities in this same period. This rising support for the universities towards the end of the eighteenth century is also reflected in the growing proportion of MPs who had attended a university: in the general elections between 1734 and 1761 the proportion was about 45% rising to about half in the period 1768–1812 and almost 60% in 1818–31 (Judd, 1955: 42). Ironically, one of

---

[8] Ecton, 1742, gives the current value of fifty-one Cambridge livings which, on average, had an annual income of £53. The same livings in 1832, according to the parliamentary commission of that year, had an average income of £242.

the best indexes of the number of sons of the elite attending the universities is the proportion of students who did not graduate after matriculating, since a degree had no particular value to those whose future was assured. At Cambridge the percentage ratio of those graduating with a BA to those matriculating was 71 in the period 1636 to 1666, 73 between 1667 and 1699, 79 between 1700 and 1733, 80 between 1734 and 1766 and 75 between 1767 and 1799.[9] Though the variation is small, these figures suggest declining enrolments by the sons of the gentry from the Restoration down to about 1760 with a slight increase thereafter. It is arguable, then, that university enrolments were something of an index of lay sympathy with clerical aspirations. Before the Civil War the laity shared many of the clergy's preoccupations and were prepared to entrust their offspring to clerical educators, but from the Restoration onwards there was a growing degree of lay suspicion of clerical ambitions – an animosity which diminished in the late eighteenth century in the face of threats to the established order in both Church and State.

Educational treatises of the post-Restoration era exhibit the same reaction against clerical control of education. Locke suggested that a tutor should not be university-trained but rather be 'well bred, and understand the Ways of Carriage, and Measures of Civility in all the Variety of Persons, Times and Places' (Axtell, 1968: 190) – a recommendation for a man of the world rather than a scholarly divine. John Aubrey was less diplomatic in expressing his distrust of the clergy as educators: the universities, he claimed, catered for future divines but not for 'the right breeding up of Gentlemen of Qualitie' (Bodl., Aubrey MS 10: 7); moreover, he feared that his proposed educational reforms would be prevented by 'a black Squadron marching from Oxford, led up by a Crozier staffe' (*ibid.*: 146). In his *Letters to a student at the university* (1716) Shaftesbury was equally hostile to the clerical estate, bidding his correspondent to guard himself against 'the narrow Principles, and contagious Manners of those corrupt Places the universities, whence all noble and *free* Principles ought to be propagated' (p. 7); furthermore, he urged anyone aspiring to become a clergyman to recognise that the dignity of this profession derived entirely from the 'Public', 'all other pretensions of Priests being Jewish and Heathenish' (p. 44). By contrast, Burke, in his *Reflections on the revolution in France* (1790) indicates the growing sympathy for the clergy in the late eighteenth century since he argued for the advantages of a young gentleman having a clerical tutor: 'By this connexion', he writes, 'we conceive that we attach our gentlemen to the

---

[9] Matriculation figures are derived from Ball and Venn, 1913–16, 1: 10–12. Graduation figures are given in Ball, 1889: 249.

church; and we liberalize the church by an intercourse with the leading characters of the century' (Best, 1964: 73-4).

Despite the indications towards the end of the eighteenth century of some renewed interest in the English universities as finishing-schools for the sons of the governing classes, for most of the century Oxford and Cambridge principally attracted those intending to take orders – though after about 1760 this included an increasing number of the well-born. Thus the decline in student numbers seems also to have been accompanied by a contraction in the function of the universities. In the late sixteenth and early seventeenth centuries, Curtis (1959) has argued, the universities gained a more assured position in national life since they were regarded as providing an education which could serve as a useful prelude to any career, clerical or lay; by the eighteenth century, however, Oxford and Cambridge appear to have reverted more and more to their traditional role as seminaries for the clergy. Cressy notes that the one group to expand significantly in early eighteenth-century Cambridge was the sons of clergy (1973: 273), most of whom would have been destined for the Church; Oxford in the same period seems to have followed the same trend: 58% of those matriculating in 1690 were ordained, a figure that had risen to 69% by 1700 though it dropped slightly in 1710 to 65% (Bennett in SM: 392). At the end of the century Cambridge still remained predominantly a clerical seminary: 60% of alumni in the period 1752 to 1799 took orders, a figure that rose slightly to 62% between 1800 and 1849 but fell markedly to 38% in the second half of the nineteenth century (Jenkins and Jones, 1950: 99).

Linked with the universities' traditional role as seminaries for the clergy was another important clerical function: that of the universities as defenders of the Anglican faith. For Oxford and Cambridge were expected to repel those intellectual assaults which endangered the Established Church and, with it, the whole political and social order that rested on the traditional assumption that, as Burke put it, 'the Church and the State' were 'one and the same thing, being different integral parts of the same whole' (E. N. Williams, 1960: 325). The willingness of many Cambridge dons to define the boundaries of acceptable theological and intellectual debate in a very inclusive manner did much to open the eighteenth-century Church, and the English Establishment more generally, to the currents of thought to which the term 'the Enlightenment' refers. By doing so Cambridge helped to absorb the Enlightenment into the main stream of English life rather than leaving it to become a potentially subversive and even revolutionary movement (Porter, 1981: 17–18; Sullivan, 1982: 266). On the other hand, Oxford's less hospitable attitude to the Enlightenment served another, complementary, purpose: that of providing an institutional source of religious and intellectual renewal by preserving older theological traditions which had been overshadowed by the widespread eighteenth-century emphasis on the need to stress the accord between reason and religion. Thus it was Oxford which produced Methodism and which kept alive the high church tradition which, in the nineteenth century, manifested itself in the Oxford Movement.

Though Oxford and Cambridge were more exclusively concerned with the education of intending clergymen in the eighteenth century than they had been before the Civil War they also continued to educate important sections of the lay elite. Thus all the eighteenth-century prime ministers (if one takes Walpole as the first of that line), apart from the duke of Devonshire and the earl of Bute, spent some time at either Oxford or Cambridge, as did just under a half of MPs (Judd, 1955: 42). The proportion of peers attending the universities more than doubled during the eighteenth century, an increase that was particularly marked during the reign of George III (Beckett, 1986: 101). The Stones' sample of landed heirs also indicates an increasing proportion proceeding to the universities in the course of the eighteenth century, particularly in the second half of the century: 34% in the period 1650–99, 43% in 1700–49 and 49% in 1750–99 (the last percentage actually surpassing the figure (44%) for the period 1600–49). Their figures for the more numerous younger sons, however, indicate the more general decline in lay attendance at the universities, when compared with the pre-Civil War period, since the eighteenth-century high-water mark of 28% for the period 1750–99 was well below the figure for 1600–49 of 36% (Stone and Stone, 1984: Table 7.4). The relatively low figures for younger sons also underline Oxford's and Cambridge's slight importance as centres of lay professional education since it was particularly from the younger sons of landed families that many such professionals were drawn (Holmes, 1982: 16).

The substantial difference in the proportion of landed heirs, as against younger sons, attending the universities, together with the expansion of the number of peers at a time when lay enrolments generally were falling, also suggests a more general closing of ranks within the eighteenth-century oligarchy. Like the exercise of political power (Stone, 1980: 84–5), university places became more the preserve of a smaller and socially more elevated section of the lay elite than had been the case before the Civil War. Such a concentration of a substantial portion of an increasingly exclusive governing class in two universities – a situation which had no parallel elsewhere in Europe – may go some way towards explaining the cohesion of the eighteenth-century English Establishment, for a considerable pro-portion of it was linked by a common education and, in many cases, first-hand acquaintance – particularly since the well-born tended to be concentrated at particular colleges: Christ Church at Oxford and Trinity and St John's at Cambridge (Beckett, 1986: 101).

Eighteenth-century Oxford and Cambridge, then, became identified with an increasingly restricted portion of society, both because their traditional function as clerical seminaries was reinforced and because the lay students to whom they catered were largely drawn from a socially narrow band of the Anglican landowning classes. By the end of the century both universities were remote from the trading and manufacturing classes who, after gaining political power in the nineteenth century, were to look with considerable hostility on Oxford and Cambridge as citadels of an Anglican oligarchy (Green in SM: 358). But, like the institutions of the old regime more generally, the universities were to survive the storms the nineteenth century had in store largely because, as the example of eighteenth-century Cambridge illustrates, such institutions were often more flexible and open to change than their outward veneration of traditional practice might suggest. Though maintaining its public deference to its seemingly immutable Elizabethan Statutes, eighteenth-century Cambridge poured new wine into these old bottles by developing a new curriculum which helped to lessen a potentially explosive gap between the Enlightenment and the religious bases of the eighteenth-century political and social order. It also transformed its traditional system of disputations into a demanding and highly competitive examination which, in the long term, provided the model for competitive examinations throughout the British world – a development which, though it originally derived from one of the pillars of the old regime, did much to provide a meritocratic alternative to the system of appointment through birth and connection which underlay the old regime.

In France, writes Brockliss, the universities 'were indissolubly identified with the administrative and legal institutions of the *ancien régime*. When these institutions were destroyed, so too were the universities' (1987: 15). In England, too, the universities were inextricably linked with the old regime – though more with the Church than with the bureaucratic apparatus of a centralised State which, in any case, was less well developed in England than in France. But in England the old regime and, with it, the universities, avoided the fate of its French counterpart, largely because it proved more elastic and capable of change than its critics – or even its more diehard defenders – were prepared to concede. Though the pace of change in such traditional institutions had generally been slow during the eighteenth century there had been enough movement – as the example of unreformed Cambridge suggests – for the old regime not to be suddenly shattered when sudden acceleration was demanded to avoid the tremors produced by the French and Industrial Revolutions.

Part One

The 'holy alliance' in gestation, 1660–88

1

Restoration, religion and reaction

Oxford's reputation has never quite recovered from Matthew Arnold's description of his beloved *alma mater* as a 'home of lost causes and forsaken beliefs, and unpopular names and impossible loyalties' (Arnold, 1962 ed.: 290). While in popular stereotype Oxford is associated with such movements as the Laudians, the jacobites and the tractarians, Cambridge, by contrast, is seen as the home of more radical and reformist creeds: the puritans, the Cambridge Platonists and the broad churchmen. Consequently, we are predisposed to think it unremarkable that Cambridge proved to be fertile ground for the growth of latitudinarianism – a variety of theology which sought to minimise doctrinal discord by emphasising the role of natural rather than revealed theology and which therefore placed considerable emphasis on the apologetical uses of the 'new philosophy'.

Yet Restoration Cambridge was at least as wedded as Oxford to traditional ideals which left only limited room for theological experimentation or, indeed, to intellectual innovation more generally. At the Restoration, Cambridge's royalist credentials were far less noteworthy than those of its sister university. Oxford had been the university of Laud, the former headquarters of the King, and it had surrendered to the parliamentary forces only after a long and stubborn siege. In recognition of its loyalty the House of Commons resolved in 1665 'That the thanks of this house be given to the Chancellor, Scholars, and Fellows of the famous University of Oxford, for their eminent loyalty to his Majesty and his Father of ever-blessed memory during the late rebellion' (Cobbett, 1806–20, IV: 328). By contrast Cambridge's loyalty seemed less exemplary: the university was remembered as a breeding-ground for puritans and, however unwillingly, it had been under parliamentary control virtually since the beginning of the Civil War. Cambridge, then, was under some pressure to demonstrate its loyalty to the restored regime; thus Henry Newcome, a young student of dissenting sympathies, decided to go to

Oxford rather than Cambridge in 1666 because of the 'greater exactness to Conformity there to expiate for their defects in loyalty in the war: whereas Oxford that had stood to the last for the King needed no such expiatory methods & so was accounted more moderate' (Diary, MCL, MS 922.3 N21: 7).

The impact of the Restoration within Cambridge is naturally bound up with the larger question of the character of the Restoration Church settlement in the nation as a whole, a question that has been subject to some debate. To Bosher (1951) the settlement was the work of an organised group of 'Laudians' who manipulated key episcopal appointments with the connivance of Clarendon and the King and so ensured that the Presbyterians were excluded from the Church as finally established. I. M. Green (1978), on the other hand, has argued that the King favoured a comprehensive church settlement as a means of unifying the nation and that the more restrictive ecclesiastical order which finally emerged was the result of 'the zeal of the gentry for the episcopal Church of England both in the counties and at Westminster' (p. 200); for Bosher, by contrast, the role of parliament 'had been merely negative – the refusal, after a prolonged internal struggle, to take a hand in the church settlement' (p. 216). Furthermore, Green takes the view that there is not the evidence to substantiate the existence of such concerted and programmatic activity in the critical period before and immediately after the Restoration as is implied by the phrase, 'Laudian party' – a term which, in any case, properly refers to the pre-Civil War period (pp. 22–3).

While Green's interpretation of the Restoration Church may better explain events at the national level Bosher's analysis does correspond more closely with the course of events within the university where the role of parliament, and of the laity more generally, was relatively small and the clergy's influence was strong. The character of Restoration Cambridge was indeed largely shaped by a group of restored royalist churchmen acting with the support of the King and of Clarendon. Such churchmen were described by Baxter as being 'of the New Prelatical way' (1931: 84) since they regarded episcopacy as being of the essence of the Church rather than being simply a convenient form of church government (Packer, 1969: 48). Such clerics were subsequently described as 'high churchmen' though the term did not gain wide currency until after the Glorious Revolution. However, it was used before 1688, particularly in the highly charged political and religious climate that followed the Exclusion Crisis; thus in 1681 a critic of the theological views of William Saywell (master of Jesus, 1679–1701) refers to those who 'commonly pass by the Name of *High-Church-Men*' and a pamphlet in the following year contrasts those who are 'counted Moderate Men and Friends to Dissenters' with those who 'are branded as Popishly Affected, Persecutors and High Church Men' (Spurr, 1985: 314, 317).[1] Moreover, as early as the Restoration there are indications that contemporaries regarded some of the newly restored clergy as forming a distinct grouping within the ecclesiastical politics of the day. Thus Henry Hickman (who was ejected at the Restoration) argued in his pamphlet, *Laudensium apostasia . . .* (1660), that within the restored Church of England there was a group of 'Laudians' or 'Canterburians' who had 'unchurched all the [Protestant] Transmarine Churches' through their emphasis on the importance of episcopacy (Packer, 1969: 127). Similarly, Baxter referred to those who followed Hammond and Bramhall as 'High Prelatists' and the 'high and swaying party' at the Restoration (Spurr, 1985: 314). Such clerics, who are most conveniently referred to as high churchmen, had been foremost in preserving Anglicanism during the Interregnum (Bosher, 1951). After the Restoration they sought to mould the universities to the task of training a new generation of clergy committed to the goal of revitalising the doctrine and discipline of the Church of England. Of the eighteen new heads of colleges appointed in the 1660s eight had been ejected from their fellowships by the parliamentary visitors (Twigg, 1983a: 523) and all (with the possible exception of Spencer of Corpus) had been conspicuously loyal to the King during the days of royalist adversity.

Within Restoration Cambridge, too, the term 'Laudian' is not altogether misplaced since some of the dominant figures had had close personal ties with Laud. Thus Matthew Wren (bishop of Ely from 1638 to 1642 and from 1660 to his death in 1667), who exercised considerable influence over appointments within Restoration Cambridge, had been closely associated with Laud – with the result that after Laud's impeachment Wren was committed to the Tower. Wren's successor as bishop of Ely, Benjamin Laney (master of Pembroke from 1630 to 1644 and from 1660 to 1662), was also identified with Laud before the Civil War; Prynne denounced him as 'one of the professed Arminians, Laud's creatures to prosecute his designs in the university of Cambridge' (I. M. Green, 1978: 93). Moreover, though the Restoration laity would no longer tolerate Laud's ambitions for the expanded temporal power of the Church, his vision of the Church as an active partner of the State with a revitalised adminstration, a well-educated and disciplined clergy and an ordered and uniform liturgy witnessing to 'the beauty of holiness' still remained the

---

[1] These examples precede the *Oxford English Dictionary*'s first recorded usage of the term in 1687. It should be added that Spurr (1985), from whom these examples are drawn, plays down the theological significance of such terms as 'latitudinarian' and 'high churchman' though he concedes that they 'can serve the historian of attitudes towards the new science, philosophy and the contest of the Ancients and Moderns as useful organizing categories' (p. 326).

ideal of the high churchmen (Bennett, 1975: 295) who set the tone for the post-Restoration university.

Naturally, such aims clashed with the views of those members of the university who were committed to the anti-episcopal church order which had prevailed during the Interregnum. Few in Cambridge, however, refused to conform to the restored Church of England: between 1660 and 1662 only 47 were ejected: 6 heads of colleges, 32 fellows, 7 students and 2 college chaplains (Matthews, 1934: xiii). At Oxford the figure was higher: 66, including 14 heads of colleges. This difference partly reflects the greater number of parliamentary ejections at the older university – 575 at Oxford as against 254 at Cambridge (Matthews, 1947: xiii). But Cambridge's stronger nonconformist character is evident in the fact that of the total clergy who refused to conform after the Restoration 733 were Cambridge graduates and 513 were from Oxford (Matthews, 1934: lxi). Most of those ejected from Restoration Cambridge had come up as undergraduates during the Interregnum and the basis of their nonconformist beliefs had been laid during that period;[2] of the 32 fellows ejected only 3 matriculated before 1642. While relatively few were ejected there was considerable tension between the high churchmen who, after 1660, dominated the university's upper echelons and the many dons who were prepared to accept both the Church of the Interregnum and the Restoration but who lacked the new appointees' zeal for the restored episcopal church order.

Thus throughout the university there was conflict about the restoration of the pre-Civil War liturgical ceremonies, as George Dunte, a fellow of Corpus, reported to the Secretary of State in January 1661 (*CSPD*, 1660–1: 488). At Emmanuel (formerly the pre-eminent puritan college) such tensions were particularly acute – Thomas Smith, a fellow of the college, reported to Sancroft in November 1660 that 'In your college half the society are for the Liturgy, and half against it, so it is read one week, and the Directory used another' (CUL, Mm.1.45: 127). Two months earlier John Ray, a fellow of Trinity, described the return of the 'old gang' (the master, Henry Ferne and about fourteen royalist fellows) who 'have brought all things here as they were in 1641: viz., services morning and evening, surplice Sundayes and holydays, and their eves, organs, bowing, going bare and fasting nights' (Gunther, 1928: 17). Though he remained in lay communion with the Church of England John Ray refused to conform and lost his fellowship – a decision based more on his dislike of oaths and the overbearing ways of the high churchmen than because of any deep-rooted theological objections to the Restoration Church. Ray's dislike of

---

[2] For a discussion of developments within Interregnum Cambridge, see Twigg, 1983b and Gascoigne, forthcoming.

the methods of the newly appointed high churchmen was shared by others among his contemporaries: Pepys recorded after a visit to Cambridge in 1661 that he had been told 'how high the old [restored] Doctors are in the University over those found, there, though a great deal better schollers than themselfs – which I am very sorry – and above all, Dr. Gunning' (Latham and Matthews, 1970–83, II: 147).

As Pepys's comments suggest, perhaps the most active of these new appointees was Peter Gunning, who had resolutely defended the Anglican cause during the Interregnum (Bosher, 1951: 37, 39) and who, in Baxter's words, was the Church of England's 'forwardest and greatest speaker' at the Savoy Conference of 1661. Indeed, the conspicuous role that Gunning was permitted to play at the Conference is possibly an indication that the bishops did not really wish to achieve a compromise (Lloyd Jukes, 1964: 229) since to dissenters like Baxter Gunning was an example of a churchman 'vehement for his high imposing principles, and . . . over-zealous for Arminianism and formality and church-pomp' (Baxter, 1931: 169). Within Cambridge Gunning was rapidly advanced to positions of influence. After being appointed to the mastership of Corpus and the Lady Margaret professorship of divinity in 1660 by royal mandate he was advanced in the following year to the more prestigious posts of master of St John's and Regius professor of divinity. He had been chosen for the latter post as 'the fittest man . . . to settle the university right in their principles again, after many corruptions had crept in there by means of the rebellion' (Wood, 1813–20, IV: 142). Gunning's reputation for militant opposition to nonconformity also accounts for his appointment at St John's where 'it was necessary to bring in such a man as would effectively rout out the old leaven and restore it [the college] to its former lustre' (Baker, 1879, I: 233). So effectively did Gunning and his successors, Turner and Gower, inculcate high church principles within St John's that it was to produce three times as many nonjurors as any other Oxford or Cambridge college (Findon, 1979: 51).

After Gunning became bishop of Ely in 1674 the position of Regius professor of divinity passed to his close friend, Joseph Beaumont, who had been appointed master of Peterhouse in 1663 by Bishop Matthew Wren (a relative by marriage) contrary to the wishes of the fellows (Mullinger, 1873–1911, III: 663). Beaumont shared Gunning's determination to exorcise Cambridge's past lapses from the royalist and Anglican cause. Both men (along with Sparrow, president of Queens' from 1662 to 1667) were described by Gilbert Burnet, after he visited the university in early 1662, as carrying 'things so high that I saw latitude and moderation were odious to the greater part even there' (Foxcroft, 1902: 464). The bulky question-books which survive from Beaumont's tenure of office as Regius professor (CUL, Add. 697–9) reflect his determination to use the post to train his students thoroughly in the defence of Anglican doctrine by using the traditional means of scholastic debate to refute Calvinists, papists, Socinians and Arians. For example, students were expected to defend the freedom of the will against the claims of orthodox Calvinists and to show that the Church had the right to regulate 'rituals and ceremonies of divine worship' (Add. 697: 41, 39). The Calvinists are also attacked in Beaumont's lectures on the epistle to the Romans (CUL, Kk.3.1) which display the thorough grounding in patristics and philology which characterised the high church theology which dominated the divinity faculties of both Restoration Cambridge and Oxford (Bennett in SM: 10). It would appear, too, that Beaumont was disturbed at the increasing role that reason was playing in the work of theologians such as the Cambridge Platonists since his students debated such topics as 'The human reason is not an adequate measure of revealed religion' (CUL, Add. 697: 109).

After Gunning's brief tenure of office as Lady Margaret professor the office passed to John Pearson who, like Gunning, held two masterships in rapid succession – Jesus from 1660 to 1662 and then Trinity where he remained until he was made bishop of Chester in 1673 (when he also relinquished the Lady Margaret chair). Pearson had joined Gunning in publicly defending Anglican doctrine during the Interregnum (Bosher, 1951: 39) and the two men also joined forces at the Savoy Conference – though (according to Baxter) 'Dr. Pearson was their true logician and disputant without whom . . . we should have had nothing from them but Dr. Gunning's passionate invectives' (1931: 169). Gilbert Burnet, who was not given to praising high churchmen, described Pearson as 'in all respects the greatest divine of the age' (1839: 442); his *Exposition of the creed* (1659) long remained a classic textbook of Anglican doctrine while his *Vindiciae epistolarum S. Ignatii* (1672) helped to shore up high church claims that episcopacy had been a feature of the Church since the first century.

Like Beaumont, he believed in training students in the traditional methods of scholastic debate and in his inaugural lectures as Lady Margaret professor he acknowledged that he drew his method from the schoolmen and, in particular, Aquinas (Mullinger, 1873–1911, III: 587). Pearson's theological work, like that of the high churchmen generally, was characterised by a strong emphasis on the role of the Fathers and of the tradition of the Church as a means of resolving the doctrinal disputes which arose so readily from the study of Scripture; thus, in the dedication to his *Exposition*, he wrote that 'in Christianity there can be no concerning truth which is not ancient; and whatsoever is truly new, is certainly false' (McAdoo, 1965: 387). Gunning, according to Gilbert Burnet, was even more zealous in his admiration for the early Church and 'formed many in

Cambridge upon his own notions' (Burnet, 1897–1900, 1: 321). The influence of the high churchmen therefore helped to strengthen a commitment to scholarship and academic rigour but their strong emphasis on tradition did little to promote intellectual innovation.

The lectures of the Regius and Lady Margaret professors of divinity were, however, intended for postgraduate divinity students rather than for the student body as a whole. To judge from the tutorial accounts of Samuel Blythe (tutor at Clare from 1658 to 1684) (Clare College, Cambridge, Bursary) the theological training received by undergraduates was commonly of a considerably more eclectic and uncontroversial character. The high churchmen are well represented but chiefly by works of devotion rather than of controversy. The principal theological primer for Blythe's students was *The practical catechism* (1645) of the Laudian Henry Hammond (1605–60), a work which aimed to present an outline of doctrine common to all Christian churches rather than highlighting the differences between them. The enormously influential *Whole duty of man* (c. 1658) – which was probably written by the staunch royalist, Richard Allestree (Regius professor of divinity at Oxford, 1663–79) – was also a standard author for Blythe's students. This work assumes the discipline and ritual of the Church of England but concentrates on Christian ethics rather than doctrine. Other works by the author of the *Whole duty* prescibed by Blythe were the *Causes of the decay of Christian piety* and the *Gentleman's calling* which were both directed against the abuses of the age, and aimed particularly at encouraging the social elite to set a better example than hitherto (J. E. Mason, 1935: 148–9). Blythe's students were also frequently set the irenical works of Grotius and of John Hales and William Chillingworth (both of whom were associated with the Tew circle). Thus, although the high churchmen dominated the upper echelons of the university, their impact on the common run of students could vary according to the sympathies of the college tutors many of whom (like Blythe) had been appointed before the Restoration.

However, as the careers of Gunning, Beaumont and Pearson illustrate, the most influential posts within the Restoration university were held by men who were determined to remove from Cambridge the taint of past nonconformity. At seven out of the eleven colleges where the mastership changed hands at the Restoration the ousted royalist master was reinstated – though three of these new masters died shortly afterwards while the remainder (Cosin, Sterne, Laney and Rainbowe) were soon made bishops and so played little direct part in university affairs. More influential within Cambridge were the heads who were elected or appointed to office in the 1660s. Of these eighteen men one half had been ejected from their fellowships by the parliamentary visitors and all (except Spencer of Corpus) had been conspicuously loyal to the King during the days of adversity. This last group included some of the major figures of the Restoration Church – Gunning, Pearson, Sparrow, Fleetwood, Ferne and, most importantly, Sancroft – who, having displayed their zeal for the revitalisation of the Church within the university, were subsequently elevated to the episcopal bench. They, in turn, were succeeded as masters of colleges by protégés whom they had trained to share their ideals; thus the mood of Anglican reaction against the upheavals of the Interregnum remained strong within Cambridge from the Restoration to the Glorious Revolution.

A whole generation of students and young dons had been reared on Calvinist theology and the liturgy of the Directory and, though only a few were prepared to go into the clerical wilderness, there must have been many both within the universities and in the Church at large who accepted the new ecclesiastical order only under sufferance. Yet by 1688 the national religious climate had changed to such an extent that one of the largest problems faced by William and his advisors was to wean the clergy away from their over-zealous loyalty to the Stuarts and the divine-right theory of monarchy. In effecting this transformation the universities played an enormous part since it was they who trained a whole new generation in the principles of passive obedience – an indication of the energy and determination with which the high churchmen harnessed Oxford and Cambridge to the goal of revitalising the newly restored episcopal church. One important result of these endeavours was the fact that in the 1670s and 1680s 'the ministry of the Church of England became almost wholly a graduate profession' (Bennett in SM: 12).

In winning the universities over to their ends the high churchmen were not, however, without allies – the most notable of whom was the King. Charles was well aware of the importance of the universities in securing a stable settlement: as the duke of Newcastle reminded him, it was they which had produced the puritan lecturers who 'preached your Majesty out of your kingdoms' (Stone, 1974: 54). Following the Restoration Charles used his influence to aid those whom he felt he could trust to keep the universities loyal to the restored Crown and Altar; thus between 1660 and 1669 the King overrode customary practice by issuing at least seven royal mandates to ensure the election of proven royalists as heads at Emmanuel, Queens', Caius and Corpus as well as exercising his right to appoint the master of Trinity and provost of King's.

Emmanuel, with its reputation as a breeding-ground for puritans, was singled out for special attention. After the removal of Dillingham, the former master, for nonconformity Sancroft was appointed head by royal mandate in 1662 and was assured by Bishop Sheldon that 'the King hath promised you a liberty (not withstanding any letter he shall send) to do what you thinke best for the promoting of piety and learninge there, and if you need any assistance from him, you shall have it' (BL, Harleian MS 3784: 77). In the same year Sancroft was granted a doctorate by royal mandate as a reward for his 'loyalty and good affection . . . during the late unhappy and unnaturall commotions' (CUA, Lett. 13: 43). Sancroft acted with vigour to purge the college of its nonconformist traditions and on at least four occasions used royal mandates to ensure the election of suitable fellows, presumably because of internal opposition to their appointment. Sancroft's successor, John Breton (master from 1665 to 1676), another firm royalist who had been ejected during the Interregnum, was also appointed by royal mandate – the cowed mood of the college at the time of his appointment being evident in a letter to Sancroft of one Emmanuel fellow, Alfounder, who wrote that 'the Royall choyce . . . is the only way to preserve unity among us . . . it is easier to obey than to chuse' (BL, Harleian MS 3784: 276). So successfully was Emmanuel purged of its puritanism that it became a bastion of high churchmanship throughout the late seventeenth and eighteenth centuries.

If necessary, the King and his ministers were prepared to intervene more vigorously in Cambridge affairs to strengthen the position of their clerical sympathisers. In 1662 the fellows of Queens' attempted to exercise their traditional right of electing their own president, choosing Simon Patrick rather than the high churchman Sparrow, whom the King had nominated. The court responded by sending a *mandamus* to the vice-chancellor instructing him to form a commission to suspend the disobedient fellows (*CSPD*, 1662: 365). When Patrick and his allies persisted in taking legal action they were confronted by a Commission which included the Lord Chancellor and the bishops of London, Winchester and Ely – the eminence of the commissioners indicating the gravity with which the King regarded the matter. Nothing was resolved though Clarendon attempted to browbeat Patrick and his allies into submission and ordered that they should have their names noted as 'factious fellows' (CUL, Add. 20: 26v). Soon afterwards Patrick withdrew from the contest, having been offered the benefice of St Paul's, Covent Garden, by William Russell, earl of Bedford, a former parliamentarian who had no personal ties with Patrick but perhaps sympathised with him as a victim of royalist reaction. Though legally inconclusive, the Queens' College affair indicated the lengths to which the King and his ministers were prepared to go to defend the interests of the high churchmen within the university. Indeed, the case convinced Ray that 'the old and new University will never kindly mingle, or make one piece' (Gunther, 1928: 29). Nor was the Queens' College case an isolated incident. The King acted with similar vigour in 1666 to overrule internal opposition at Trinity Hall to the appointment in 1664 of a fellow by royal mandate – an affair which, like that at Queens', appears to have been regarded by the high churchmen as a trial of strength. When Sparrow of Queens' (then vice-chancellor) attempted to intervene in the dispute the young fellows of Trinity Hall put out a petition objecting that Sparrow was prejudiced against them (CUA, Lett. 13: 256(17)) while Beaumont in a letter to Sancroft about the 'great stirrs at Trinity Hall' remarked that 'This much it will gain us, that we shall discover the temper of the University' (BL, Harleian MS 3785: 90). Ultimately, in 1666, a commission consisting of the Lord Chancellor, the archbishop of Canterbury and other dignitaries enforced the royal prerogative following which the Crown used its influence to increase the number of clerical fellows in what had previously been primarily a lay foundation (Malden, 1902: 152–7).

But once firmly established in Cambridge the high churchmen had less cause to look to the King for assistance and their once-cordial relationship with the monarchy became somewhat strained as the university attempted to assert its autonomy. In doing so the university needed allies who could act as something of a buffer between it and the King. One of the most obvious protectors was Archbishop Sheldon, to whom the university successfully looked to overturn a royal mandate ordering the reinstatement of Daniel Scargill of Corpus who, in 1669, had been deprived of his fellowship on account of his 'Hobbist' opinions (Axtell, 1965; Twigg, 1983b: 201). Thanks to its chancellor, the duke of Monmouth, the university gained an even more important victory in 1674 when the King sent a letter absolving it from the need to comply with further royal mandates for the appointment of scholarships or fellowships (C. H. Cooper, 1842–1908, III: 563). However, this concession plainly did not quieten the university's fears about the extent of royal interference since in 1682 another royal letter stipulated that mandates need only be accepted if they were approved by the archbishop of Canterbury (Churchill, 1922: 312). Even after this the university had to be on its guard and royal appointments to fellowships continued under weak masters, such as John North (1677–83) and John Montagu (1683–99) at Trinity (Bodl., Tanner MS 35: 96; Manuel, 1968: 103). Cambridge's opposition to James II's attacks on its autonomy can therefore be seen as a continuation of its efforts during the reign of Charles II to reduce the power of the central government in its internal affairs – though James's Catholicising policies made the previously largely unnoticed conflict a matter of national importance.

However, such strains in the cordial relationship between the monarchy and the high churchmen developed after the latter had been firmly entrenched in university officialdom in the 1660s. During this critical period another influential ally of the Cambridge high churchmen was Matthew Wren. As bishop of Ely he had the right to nominate the master of Jesus and he appointed a series of staunch royalists – Pearson (1660–2), Beaumont (1662) and his chaplain, Edmund Boldero (1663–79). At Peterhouse, where he was visitor (and a former master) he ensured the election of Beaumont as head in 1663 and he probably used his influence at Pembroke (where he had been a fellow) to ensure the election of Robert Mapletoft (later one of his executors in 1664). Naturally, Wren was highly sympathetic to Sancroft's plans to remove from Emmanuel 'the taint of disaffection', assuring him in a letter of April 1664 that 'Either for the University, or for the Colledg, whatsoever (at any time, & in any kind) lies within my power, you may assuredly promise yourself, shall never be wanting' (BL, Harleian MS 3784: 158).

Most active of all in moulding Cambridge to the needs of the restored Church was William Sancroft, both during his term as master of Emmanuel from 1662 to 1664 and in his subsequent career, which culminated with his appointment as archbishop of Canterbury in 1678. As primate his zeal for the reform and revitalisation of the Church of England was reminiscent of Oxford's famous son, William Laud (Bennett, 1975: 6) – whose *Memorials*, appropriately, were published by Sancroft. Though, naturally, Sancroft's links were strongest at his old college of Emmanuel he had a wide acquaintance throughout the university at large; in his copious correspondence there are letters to, or at least mention of, some twenty of the heads of Cambridge colleges in the period between the Restoration and the Glorious Revolution.

Though the King's most loyal subject and a virtual martyr to the principle of passive obedience, Sancroft's concern for the welfare of Cambridge and the Church more generally led him on occasions to act as a buffer between the university and the monarchy – most spectacularly during the reign of James II but also, albeit more discreetly, during the reign of Charles. As early as 1665 when Sancroft was dean of St Paul's his colleagues at Emmanuel successfully asked him to have a royal mandate (obtained by the chancellor, the earl of Manchester) for a fellowship revoked on the grounds that the candidate was insufficiently qualified and was suspected of nonconformity (BL, Harleian MS 3784: 261). As archbishop of Canterbury Sancroft was regarded as Cambridge's most powerful ally at court because (as the provost of King's put it in 1679) of 'his Majesties accustomed deference to your integrity and prudence in all concernes wherein you are pleased to appeare; particularly such as relate to Church and Universities' (Bodl., Tanner MS 155: 196). In July 1679

Francis Turner, then vice-chancellor, urged Sancroft to 'move speedily' to prevent a royal mandate for an unsuitable candidate for a doctorate 'or my Lord Sunderland will send us thunder and lightning' and when, in August 1685, Cambridge's chancellor (the duke of Albemarle) left the court for a time it was Sancroft whom the vice-chancellor asked to act as the university's 'Noble Patron at Court' (Bodl., Tanner MS 158: 61, 59).

Sancroft, then, used his considerable influence at court to help protect the rights and privileges of his *alma mater*. But this influence was purchased by his loyalty to the Stuart cause, particularly during the Exclusion Crisis when the archbishop used the newly created Commission for Ecclesiastical Promotions to advance only those whose loyalty to the doctrine of passive obedience was unquestioned (Beddard, 1967). Until James II broke with his faithful Anglican allies, Cambridge followed Sancroft's lead in loyally co-operating with the monarchy in most major appointments (even if it sometimes did its best to oppose some of the more minor letters of mandate). From 1660 to 1688 Cambridge continued the long-established tradition of choosing courtiers as its chancellors, a post that changed hands as Charles's favour waxed and waned. In 1660 Edward Montagu, earl of Manchester, was restored to the office and held the post until his death in 1671 when the loose-living royal favourite, George Villiers, second duke of Buckingham, was appointed. At the royal command he was replaced in 1674 by the royal bastard, Monmouth, who in turn was ousted in 1682 by royal decree and succeeded by the compliant Christopher Monck, duke of Albemarle, who died just before the Glorious Revolution. During Charles's reign the university also elected MPs amenable to the King's will and hence opponents of any moves to exclude James from the throne (Henning, 1983, I: 148–50). Sancroft probably played a part in ensuring the election of such MPs – the extent of his influence within the university was so considerable that Sir Robert Sawyer remarked that he would not stand for election as the university's MP in 1688 without Sancroft's 'approbation' (Bodl., Tanner MS 28: 178).

Cambridge also followed Sancroft's example in supporting James's claim to the throne. During a visit of the King to Cambridge in 1681 the vice-chancellor, Humphrey Gower, responded to the enemies of the duke of York by delivering a classic statement of Anglican passive obedience – a doctrine which Restoration Cambridge and Oxford did much to revive and inculcate (Bennett in SM: 10). Gower saw it as 'the great Honour of this your University' to maintain steadfastly, despite the 'Reproaches of Factious and Malicious Men', that 'our Kings derive not their Titles from the People, but from God; that to Him only they are accountable' (C. H. Cooper, 1842–1908, III: 589). Initially, too, Cambridge, long accustomed to royal interference in its affairs (Churchill, 1922: 315), complied with James's demands. In 1686 Sidney Sussex College dutifully elected Joshua

Basset as master despite his obvious Roman Catholic sympathies. Once in office the traditional anti-popery oaths were dispensed with and Basset declared himself a Roman Catholic; he also had the statutes altered to allow his co-religionaries to be elected fellows. But even passive obedience had its limits and a royal mandate of 8 February 1687 ordering the university to allow the Benedictine, Alban Francis, to take a master's degree without the customary anti-popery oaths stirred the university into action.

As in the country at large, prominent among the leaders of the opposition to James's Romanising policies were the high churchmen who had been the main supporters of James until he turned against the interests of the Established Church. Sancroft's intimate friend, Francis Turner, bishop of Ely since 1684, had been particularly influential in mustering Anglican support for James during the Exclusion Crisis (Beddard, 1965: 18–19) but in a letter of 25 February 1687 he praised Gower (his successor as master of St John's) for his 'most glorious part' in opposing the royal mandate in favour of Alban Francis and reported that 'The good Archbishop [Sancroft] is mightily revived by this account' (Vellacott, 1924: 93). Cambridge emphasised its support for Sancroft's stand against James II's religious policy by inviting him to become chancellor when Albemarle died in November 1688 in a letter in which the vice-chancellor described the archbishop as 'the Ornament of our University as well as the support of our whole Church' (Bodl., Tanner MS 28: 265); James's recommendation that Lord Dartmouth be made chancellor was ignored (Tanner, 1917: 19n).

Sancroft was elected as chancellor on 15 December 1688, four days after James's flight from Whitehall, and, given his divided loyalties, it is not surprising that he declined the honour despite the university's urging. Reluctantly the university bowed to political realities and in March 1689 finally elected as chancellor Charles Seymour, duke of Somerset, who had been an unequivocal supporter of William throughout the Glorious Revolution. But even after Sancroft's ejection from his see in 1690 there were many in Cambridge who remained committed to the ideals which he had done so much to implant in the university. Restoration Cambridge had been successfully purged of its past nonconformity and had been transformed into a seminary for young high churchmen: only gradually was the imprint left by Sancroft and his allies on the university dispelled by the whigs' astute use of patronage after the Glorious Revolution. While Restoration Oxford may have gloried in its reputation for loyalty to the Martyred King it was in fact Cambridge which displayed greater allegiance to the principle of passive obedience to the Lord's Anointed after the Glorious Revolution: while Oxford produced twenty-six nonjurors, at Cambridge forty-one members of the university followed Sancroft into the ecclesiastical wilderness (Wordsworth, 1874: 603–5).

2

Cambridge and the latitude-men

Both within Cambridge and in the Church at large the restored high church clergy directed particular animosity at those divines who justified their past allegiance to the Church of the Interregnum and their present loyalty to the restored Church of England by maintaining that they were remaining true to the basic tenets of Christianity even though they might compromise on inessentials. The high churchmen's label for such divines was the 'latitude-men' or 'latitudinarians', a word (as the sympathetic Glanvill put it) 'that signifies compass or largeness, because of their opposition to the narrow stingy Temper then called Orthodoxness . . . But afterward among them that knew not those persons, it came to be taken in a worse sense, and Latitudinarian went for one of a large Conscience and Practice' (Cope, 1954: 273).

While an apologist for the latitudinarians like Gilbert Burnet could describe them as a new sect of men who 'loved the constitution of the church, and the liturgy, and could well live under them: but they did not think it unlawful to live under another form' (G. Burnet, 1897–1900, 1: 335), to their opponents they appeared to be a Trojan horse within the citadel of restored Anglicanism: as late as 1755 the nonjuror, George Smith, characterised them as 'men, who though they enjoyed her [the Church of England's] Preferments were never truly of her, being only bodily within her Walls, but in Heart and Wish in the Camp of the Adversary' (1755: 10). Nor were accusations that the latitudinarians were not wholehearted members of the Church as restored altogether without foundation, despite Burnet's advocacy: even a latitudinarian sympathiser like Tillotson's pupil, John Beardmore, conceded that they 'had no great liking for the liturgy or ceremonies, or indeed, the government of this church' even though they 'had attained to such a largeness and freedom of judgement, as that they could conform, though without any warmth or affection for these things' (Birch, 1752: 407).

Contemporaries were agreed that the latitudinarians were closely associated with Cambridge. Simon Patrick in his *Brief account of the new sect of latitude-men* (1662)[1] commented that one of the few things that was definite about the latitudinarians was that they 'had their rise at Cambridge' (p. 3), while Hearne later remarked with customary acerbity that 'the word was first hatch'd at Cambridge' (Hearne, 1885–1921, I: 92). Though the term first gained currency in Cambridge 'something before his Majesty's most happy Return' (Grove, 1676: 25), being used 'in opposition to that hide-bound, straight lac'd spirit that did then prevail' (Patrick, 1662: 5), it did not become widespread until after the Restoration when it was used by the high churchmen to characterise those within the university and the Church generally who were thought to be conforming out of expediency rather than conviction. Indeed, Simon Patrick's defence of the latitude-men was probably a response to the attacks made on him after his abortive election as president of Queens' in 1662.

In this pamphlet Patrick sets out to refute the view that the latitude-men were 'a party very dangerous both to the King and the Church as seeking to undermine them both' (p. 3). He concedes that they were largely men who were educated in Cambridge 'since the beginnings of the unhappy troubles of this Kingdom' and received preferment without 'much troubling themselves to enquire into the Titles of their Electours' but adds that they 'were always looked on with an evil eye by the successive usurping powers' (p. 5). Despite Patrick's conciliatory tone he does reveal that there were some substantive differences between the theology of the latitude-men and that of many of the restored Anglican clergy. He concedes, for example, that it was with some cause that 'these men are generally suspected to be for liberty of Conscience' and declares that 'I shall always think him most conscientious who leads the most unblameable life, ʳˊ ough he be not greatly scrupulous about the externals of Religion' ᵗp. 11). Such a view was quite at variance with that of many of the restored clergy who still harboured hopes of achieving Laud's goal of a united national church witnessing to the 'beauty of holiness' through uniform ritual and an ordered theology and able, if necessary, to call on the coercive power of the State (Bennett, 1975: 295).

For the Cambridge high churchmen, with their high hopes of dispelling the stigma of puritanism which was attached to their *alma mater*, the latitude-men must have appeared a particularly vexing problem. The most eminent of the latitude-men, the Cambridge Platonists Ralph Cudworth (master of Clare from 1645 to 1654 and of Christ's from 1654

---

[1] The author of this pamphlet is simply given as 'S. P. of Cambridge'. J. A. Birrel in his preface to the Augustan Reprint Society edition of this work (Publication No. 100; Los Angeles, 1963) summarises the very strong case that exists for attributing the pamphlet to Patrick as well as outlining the circumstances of its composition.

until his death in 1688) and Henry More (fellow of Christ's from 1639 until his death in 1687), were prominent and influential members of the university and yet they neither joined the dissenters nor were prepared to co-operate wholeheartedly in the task of re-establishing a uniform Anglican liturgy and discipline within the university – to More, 'none of these things were so good as to make men good, nor so bad as to make men bad' (Foxcroft, 1902: 463).

While Cudworth and More were too old and too firmly ensconced in Cambridge to move, younger latitude-men like Patrick who found Restoration Cambridge uncongenial sought advancement in London. Though most of this younger generation of latitude-men, which included Patrick, Tillotson, Stillingfleet, Tenison, Sharp and Moore, were Cambridge-educated, all left the university and became prominent as preachers rather than academics. The term 'latitudinarian' has since become more closely associated with this group of London preachers rather than with the Cambridge Platonists whose mystical and metaphysical theology was quite different from the common-sense appeal to the experience of their congregations which characterised the Cambridge Platonists' younger admirers – even though both groups shared a common desire to distinguish the inessentials from the irreducible bases of Christianity in order to reduce religious discord.

The most prominent of the latitudinarians, John Tillotson, left Cambridge in 1660 when Gunning had insisted on depriving him of his Clare fellowship on the grounds that it was the same fellowship from which Gunning himself had previously been ejected by the parliamentary visitors (a claim which Tillotson vainly contested) (Birch, 1752: 401–2). Benjamin Whichcote and John Worthington, whose work had more in common with the Cambridge Platonists than with the younger latitudinarians, were both ejected from the masterships of their colleges (King's and Jesus respectively) to make way for royalist claimants. Similarly, John Wilkins – whose *Principles and duties of natural theology* (1675) is perhaps the clearest statement of latitudinarian principles – lost his mastership to the royalist Ferne, Ray's *bête noire* (though Wilkins was appointed to the deanery of Ripon soon after).

Though Wilkins was master of Trinity for little more than a year he none the less had an effect on the religious and scientific life of the university. During his time at Cambridge Wilkins came to know Cudworth, More, Worthington, Whichcote and Hezekiah Burton, a fellow of Magdalene who (after becoming chaplain to Lord Keeper Bridgeman) was actively involved with Wilkins in attempting to achieve greater comprehension within the Established Church; in fact, Wood reports that a club formed by Wilkins to promote such aims used to meet at the 'chamber of the great trimmer and latitudinarian, Doctor Hezekiah Burton' (1813–20, IV: 513). It was this circle of Cambridge acquaintances (along with Trinity scientists like Ray, Willughby and Barrow) which Burnet presumably had in mind when he wrote of Wilkins: 'But at Cambridge he joined with those who studied to propagate better thoughts, to take men off from being in parties . . . [and] from narrow notions . . . He was also a great observer of natural; and a promoter of experimental philosophy' (1897–1900, I: 332–3).

With the departure of Tillotson, Patrick, Whichcote, Worthington and Wilkins the only prominent latitude-men who remained in Cambridge permanently after the Restoration were More and Cudworth – both of whom were attacked for their past compliance with the parliamentary authorities and for their alleged lack of loyalty to the restored Church and Crown. In 1660 there was an attempt to deprive Cudworth of the mastership of Christ's on the grounds that his election during the Inter-regnum had been irregular (Crossley and Christie, 1847–55, I: 203). Later, an internal dispute led by Ralph Widdrington (a man who was particularly anxious to establish his royalist credentials since he had benefited from Cromwellian patronage) resulted in public accusations that as master Cudworth 'hath been more scandalously complying with the rebels, and more notoriously disaffected to the royal cause and more disserviceable to the interest of the King and the Church and the College and the University'; he was also charged with justifying his actions by appealing to 'the old plea for liberty of conscience' (Nicolson, 1929a: 46). In a letter to Lady Conway of 1663 More described such accusations as part of a more general campaign by those who '*feigne* so great zeal against Heresy' against anyone whom 'they would brand with the name of Latitudemen' (Nicolson, 1930: 220).

In the same year, Mark Frank, the newly installed master of Pembroke, wrote to Sancroft to express his concern at the prevalence of Socinianism within the university and reported that at a recent disputation a student had quoted 'Socinus noster', 'with which the Bishop of Ely [Matthew Wren] was much offended'. Frank added that Sparrow had witnessed a similar performance at Queens' and concluded with the warning: 'And how farr Dr. More's whimseys have prevailed in the university, you need not be told: though on the perusal of his Books we are likely to find strange things. And time it is, we sleep not till all is past the remedy' (CUL, MS Mm.1.45: 119). Sparrow evidently saw More as being responsible for the spread of heterodoxy for, in a letter to Boyle of 1665, More commented that Sparrow had been reported as saying that 'he would prosecute my opinions as long as he lived' (Nicolson, 1930: 264).

The high churchmen were not slow to confront More publicly, for in

1665 Beaumont published a work entitled *Some observations upon the apologie of Dr. Henry More for his Mystery of Godliness*. Beneath all of Beaumont's minute and carping criticisms of More there was a more fundamental point at issue, for Beaumont wrote that someone 'that is acquainted with Dr. More's theology will easily perceive that the drift of his desperate and blasphemous opinion is chiefly, if not solely, to usher in this Liberty of Conscience' (p. 13). More welcomed the restoration of the Church of England – indeed, in the work which Beaumont attacked he emphasised the need to maintain 'the Peace and Authority of the Church' (Gabbey, 1982: 229). But he viewed religion as primarily an individual relationship between God and the believer: rituals and creeds were a useful stimulus to devotion but were of secondary importance. For a high churchman like Beaumont, by contrast, true Christian practice involved the corporate worship of the nation as a whole and required an established church capable of regulating religious ceremonies and ensuring uniformity of belief. To Beaumont, then, More's willingness to tolerate, and even encourage, individual variations in religion served to undermine the mission of the restored Church. Beaumont's attack, together with a petition by one of his colleagues at Christ's to Archbishop Sheldon 'against the Colledge as a seminary of Heretics' (Nicolson, 1929a: 51), prompted More to complain to Lady Conway in July 1665: 'They push hard at the Latitude men as they call them, some in their pulpitts call them sons of Belial, others make the Devill a latitudinarian, which things are as pleasing to me as the raillery of a jack-pudding at one end of a dancing rope' (Nicolson, 1930: 243).

But after the onslaughts of the early 1660s both More and Cudworth led quieter lives: both retained their positions at Christ's and continued to publish, though More's works became less philosophical and more apologetical in character (Gabbey, 1982: 236). The fall of Clarendon and the death of Matthew Wren in 1667 may have cooled the ardour of some of the more militant high churchmen; in any case, the uncompromising mood of the early Restoration seems to have given way to more moderate counsels as the political and religious order began to function normally once again. Sancroft, for example, who, at the Restoration, had advocated the most uncompromising policies towards the dissenters, came to look sympathetically on moves for comprehension when archbishop of Canterbury (Sykes, 1959: 82), and his influence within Cambridge may have helped reconcile the high churchmen and the latitude-men. By 1675 the theological atmosphere within Cambridge was sufficiently relaxed for the fellows of Catharine Hall to elect as their master John Eachard, the author of the impish *Grounds and occasions of the contempt of the clergy and religion* (1671) – a work which prompted the venerable high churchman Barnabas

Oley to criticise Eachard's facetious treatment of the clergy (Ure, 1958: xv).

Moreover, More, and to a lesser extent Cudworth, came to enjoy the patronage of the powerful Sir Heneage Finch, first earl of Nottingham and lord chancellor from 1674 until his death in 1682. While always a staunch Anglican, Finch gradually mellowed and retreated from his uncompromising stance against nonconformists at the Restoration to become the latitudinarians' chief patron. The unworldly Henry More was reluctant to break with his scholarly life and is said to have declined Finch's offer of a bishopric, though in 1675 he was persuaded to accept a prebend's post at Gloucester which, however, he promptly resigned in favour of his protégé, Edward Fowler (BA Oxford 1653; MA Trinity College, Cambridge, 1656) (R. Ward, 1710: 59). Five years previously Fowler had published a defence of the latitudinarians entitled *The principles and practices of certain moderate divines of the Church of England, abusively called latitudinarians . . .* in which he had argued 'that the grand designe of the Gospel is to make men good: not to intoxicate their brains with notions, or furnish their heads with a systeme of opinions' (p. 18). Cudworth's *True intellectual system of the universe* (1678) opens with a dedicatory letter to Sir Heneage Finch in which he refers to the 'many favours I have formerly received from you'; in the same year he was installed as a prebend of Gloucester, presumably at Finch's instigation.

But though they were not as forceful in their opposition as in the early 1660s, there were still high churchmen in Cambridge who remained suspicious of the latitude-men. In a sermon preached before the King in 1675 John Standish attacked 'those false Apostles . . . That would supplant Christian Religion with Natural Theologie . . . that preach up Natural and Moral Religion, without the Grace of God' (1676: 24–5). Five years later he received his DD from Peterhouse where More's old adversary, Beaumont, was still master. In the same year as Standish's attack on latitudinarian theology, Miles Barne – like Standish a fellow of Peterhouse and a royal chaplain – delivered a Whitehall sermon in which he sought to discredit the latitude-men by commenting that 'Latitudinism in Principles is ever accompanied with Libertinism in Practice.' He also criticised 'The *Patrons of liberty*' for 'despis[ing] their Ecclesiastical Superiors' (1685: 2, 4). Earlier, in a university sermon of 1683, Barne had castigated Calvinism for undermining passive obedience to the Lord's Anointed and, true to his principles, he was ejected in 1688 as a nonjuror.

Two years after Standish's and Barne's sermons, John Warley (a fellow of Clare where Gunning and his former teacher, Barnabas Oley, exercised considerable influence (Wardale, 1903: 82, 98)) echoed Standish's unflattering description of the latitudinarians in his *Reasoning apostate: or modern latitude-men consider'd* . . . (1677). In this work he accused them of imagining that 'there were to be virtuosos in Religion as well as Philosophy, and that this age made new discoveries of Doctrines as the Astronomers have of the Stars, and that new Creeds in Divinity are as necessary as new Systems of the World' (Jacob, 1976: 48). Neither Standish, Barne nor Warley had directly attacked any prominent Cambridge latitude-man but in 1685 John Turner (who received his BA at St John's, Cambridge's high church seminary, before becoming a fellow of Christ's, in 1673) bluntly accused Cudworth of heresy in his *Discourse concerning the Messias, to which is prefixed a large preface, ascertaining and explaining the Blessed Trinity, against the late writer of The intellectual system.* In this work Turner wrote of Cudworth that 'no severity [is] too great to be used towards him, who hath made use of a great, however ill deserved reputation, to *undermine* the great *Pillar* and *Corner Stone* of the *Christian Religion* [the Trinity]' (pp. clxii–clxiii). Turner also directed his polemic against Cartesianism (with which Cudworth was associated) as an ally of materialism. Significantly, Barne, Warley and Turner all took up fellowships after the Restoration and their zeal for orthodoxy is an indication of the success of the restored high churchmen in winning over a new generation to their principles.

Was there also a band of youthful latitude-men within Restoration Cambridge? Despite Cambridge's reputation for theological liberalism and even radicalism, between the Restoration and the Glorious Revolution latitudinarian activity within the university was very limited. Isaac Barrow, master of Trinity from 1672 until his death in 1677, was on friendly terms with latitudinarians like Patrick, Wilkins and Tillotson (who edited his theological works) and in some of his sermons emphasised the reasonableness of Christian doctrine and ethics in the manner of the latitudinarians, choosing titles such as 'The Pleasantness of Religion' or 'The Profitableness of Godliness'. He also defended the latitudinarians against their critics and wrote approvingly of their policy of comprehension (Napier, 1859, IX: 584). However, Barrow had been a staunch royalist during the Interregnum and a youthful protégé of the Laudian Henry Hammond; he was also a friend of Gunning and admired the work of Beaumont as Regius professor of divinity (Osmond, 1944: 211).

These differing personal allegiances are also reflected in his theology. Some of Barrow's sermons resemble those of Tillotson in their emphasis on the prudential nature of Christian ethics and the consonance between natural and revealed religion, but Barrow also stressed the doctrinal aspects of Christianity in a manner which set him apart from Tillotson – particularly in some of his university addresses. Indeed, it is in his university setting that we see Barrow at his most clerical: an attempt to obtain a dispensation from taking orders for Newton's friend Aston, a fellow of Trinity, in 1674 was met by Barrow with the answer that this would lead 'to the subversion of the maine design of our foundation, which is to breed Divines' (Napier, 1859, I: xlv). Barrow was also extremely cautious of countenancing anything which challenged the alliance between the restored monarchy and the Church. When, in 1677, Daniel Skinner, a fellow of Trinity, attempted to edit the *State letters* of John Milton, Barrow sent him a letter peremptorily ordering him to refrain from publishing 'any writing mischievous to the Church or State' (Masson, 1859–94, VI: 804). Though Barrow's work exhibits some latitudinarian leanings his conservatism in interpreting his duties within the university is an indication of the prevailing mood of reaction against the events of the Interregnum within Restoration Cambridge. It is significant, too, that despite Barrow's friendship with several prominent London latitudinarians there is little evidence that his influence encouraged the growth of latitudinarianism within the university.

Nor did Cudworth and More attract many disciples from within Restoration Cambridge – perhaps because of high church opposition or because their theology was thought to be inappropriate to the concerns of post-Restoration England. Henry More did use his connection with the Finch family to advance his young colleague, John Sharp, to the position of domestic chaplain to Sir Heneage Finch (Sharp, 1825, I: 15). It is possible, too, that Henry More helped John Moore gain a similar post in the Finch household since the Cambridge Platonist admired Moore sufficiently to leave him a funeral ring (Nicolson, 1930: 483).

While a fellow of Clare, from 1667 to 1677, Moore delivered a number of sermons which must have been regarded with suspicion by young high churchmen like Warley. Like Tillotson (a former fellow of Clare) Moore talked of 'the reasonableness of our religion' (CUL, MS Dd.14.9: 38) and emphasised the ethical character of Christianity rather than its doctrines. To Moore 'the excellence of the Christian religion above the heathen philosophy consists in this, that it has not only given more clear and distinct notices of virtue and naturall laws, but also powerfully enforced our obedience thereunto' (*ibid*.: 59). Sharp was more of a theological traditionalist than Moore but in natural philosophy, at least, he was influenced by his theologically *avant-garde* colleague at Christ's, Thomas Burnet (Sharp, 1825, I: 10) and in London Sharp became closely involved with latitudinarian clergy, particularly in their opposition to James II's Catholicising policies.

Both Sharp and Moore, then, were young Cambridge latitudinarians who had links with Henry More though there is no clear evidence of any theological debt to the Cambridge Platonists. Although More and Cudworth were tolerated (perhaps because of their influential connections) the influence of the high churchmen within Cambridge was too strong to allow the formation of a latitudinarian school, as might have occurred if new graduates like Sharp or Moore had gained advancement within the university. Before the Glorious Revolution the centre of latitudinarian activity was not Cambridge, though most of the latitudinarians had been educated there, but London where they went as a result of high church intolerance (as in the cases of Tillotson or Patrick) or to seek the advancement that was lacking within Cambridge for men of their theological bent.

In London there were many livings that were controlled by the secular arm, making it possible to move up the ecclesiastical ladder despite opposition from the high churchmen. The fact that there were a number of sympathetic lay patrons within the capital meant that London came to provide a geographical focus for the latitudinarians, reinforcing their personal ties and giving the group a greater cohesion. The Finch family was particularly conspicuous as patrons of the latitudinarians: John Moore, John Sharp and William Wotton (BA Catharine Hall, 1679), an ally of Bentley in the Ancients versus Moderns debate, all served as chaplains to the family and Heneage Finch entrusted John Sharp with the recommendations to livings in the gift of the lord keeper (Sharp, 1825, 1: 24) – hence Gilbert Burnet's praise for Finch's clerical appointments. Among Finch's protégés were Tillotson, who was made a prebend at St Paul's; Simon Patrick, who was given the living of St Martin-in-the-Fields (but recommended Tenison in his place); and Richard Kidder (BA Emmanuel, 1652), who was appointed a prebend at Norwich Cathedral despite high church attacks on his writings.

Though the Finches were the most outstanding of the latitudinarians' patrons there were other laymen – and, in particular, other lawyers – who also helped advance their careers. It is possible that some members of the legal profession favoured the latitudinarians since their conciliatory views on church authority naturally appealed to a profession which had long contested the power of the church courts and which must have looked upon the high churchmen's plans for a revival of ecclesiastical discipline with some alarm. Certainly, it is striking how many latitudinarians owed their advancement to prominent lawyers. Tillotson, for example, was chaplain to Sir Edmund Prideaux, a barrister at the Inner Temple, before the Restoration and later became a protégé of another lawyer, Sir Robert Atkyns, a bencher of Lincoln's Inn, through whom he was advanced to a preachership there in 1663. The same Sir Robert Atkyns also assisted John Wilkins and other moderate churchmen associated with the duke of

Buckingham in their attempt to draw up a bill allowing for greater theological comprehension within the Church of England (Shapiro, 1969: 170). Wilkins himself also benefited from the patronage of the legal profession since in 1661 he was made a preacher at Gray's Inn.

Another prominent latitudinarian, the Scottish Gilbert Burnet, was protected from hostile criticism by a prominent lawyer with the Dickensian name of Sir Harbottle Grimston (master of the rolls from 1660 to 1685) (T. E. S. Clarke and Foxcroft, 1907: 139). In contrast to Heneage Finch, who was always a strong churchman, Grimston had been, in Oldmixon's words, 'a zealous *Parliamentarian*, Presbyterian and Covenanter' (1730–9, II: 465), and had been elected speaker of the Convention Parliament. Grimston's past associations perhaps made him sympathetic to those who opposed the high churchmen; he was active, for example, in advancing the career of Richard Kidder (like Grimston a graduate of Emmanuel) who, despite having been ejected in 1662 as a nonconformist, subsequently conformed and was made a preacher at the Rolls through Grimston's agency. Another latitudinarian appointed by Grimston to the same office was Stillingfleet, who, like Kidder, was raised to the episcopate after 1688.

Within London the focus of latitudinarian activity was the Church of St Lawrence Jewry. Wilkins was appointed to this living in 1662 by the King and it thereafter acted as a forum for the latitudinarians: symbolically the two most prominent latitudinarians, Wilkins and Tillotson, were both later buried within its walls. In 1664 Wilkins appointed Tillotson as Tuesday lecturer at St Lawrence Jewry (Stillingfleet being among those whom he chose to preach (Stillingfleet, 1707–10, I: 24)), and, after Tillotson's appointment as dean of Canterbury in 1672, he largely left the task of selecting preachers to his friend Thomas Firmin, a prominent philanthropist of Unitarian beliefs. When Wilkins was made bishop of Chester in 1668 both he and Tillotson used their influence to have Whichcote appointed as his successor at St Lawrence Jewry, possibly with the assistance at court of the lord keeper, Orlando Bridgeman (BL, Harleian MS 7045: 82). Whichcote, in turn, chose Sharp as one of his Friday preachers (Sharp, 1825, I: 31). After Whichcote's death in 1668 the living passed to Benjamin Calamy (BA Catharine Hall, 1664) who was among those praised by Gilbert Burnet for 'rescu[ing] the church from those reproaches that the follies of others drew upon it' (1897–1900, II: 221). Calamy was succeeded at his death in 1686 by John Mapletoft (MA Trinity, 1655) who held the post until his death in 1721. Mapletoft was an old school-friend of Locke who, through Mapletoft, came to know many of the more prominent latitudinarian divines including Tillotson, Patrick and Whichcote (Fox-Bourne, 1876, I: 212). Mapletoft, formerly a professor of physick at Gresham, had finally taken orders in 1683, having put to rest his scruples about subscribing to the Thirty-Nine Articles, a matter on which he consulted Simon Patrick (BL, Add. 5878: p. 151).

Though St Lawrence Jewry was the most prominent of latitudinarian livings, other London parishes were also colonised by the latitude-men. Thus when Wilkins's friend, William Lloyd, was made bishop of St Asaph in 1680 he recommended to Heneage Finch (in whose gift the living lay) that Simon Patrick should succeed him as vicar of St Martin-in-the-Fields. Though Patrick himself declined the position he was able to pass it on to Thomas Tenison (MA Corpus, 1660), a fellow Cambridge latitudinarian. Such close personal and institutional links within London were strengthened by the hostility of the high churchmen which naturally drew the latitudinarians closer together. A pamphlet by Tillotson on private judgement in matters of faith led to an attack on both Tillotson and Patrick in the House of Lords in 1680. Likewise Stillingfleet was attacked along with his friend Tillotson (whose work Stillingfleet had defended) in 1685 by Simon Lowth (MA Clare, 1660), a firm upholder of the doctrine of episcopal succession. Stillingfleet's reply caused Lowth to widen his attack to include Gilbert Burnet as well, and both Burnet and Robert Grove (MA St John's, 1660) were moved to reply to Lowth. Earlier, Grove had published a *Vindication of the conforming clergy* . . . in which he refers to ill-founded fears of some of 'this fearful Bugbear of latitudinarianism' (second ed., 1676: 25).

The latitudinarians, then, formed a relatively cohesive group within the world of London ecclesiastical politics. These close personal ties help explain their organised activity in opposing James II's Catholicising policies. Tillotson, Patrick and Stillingfleet were particularly prominent in the pamphlet war against popery in the years before James finally pushed the Anglican hierarchy into active defiance over his order of May 1688 insisting that the Declaration for Liberty of Conscience be read in all churches. When matters finally came to this crisis it was the latitudinarian clergy who helped to strengthen the resolve of those Anglican clergy who were wavering in their intention to defy the King. At a meeting of concerned clergy Edward Fowler, Tillotson and Patrick forcefully overcame the opposition of those high churchmen who were afraid that refusal to obey the King would lead to a schism. Patrick and Tenison were then appointed by the meeting to canvass the London clergy; they later met Grove, Stillingfleet and Tillotson at Lambeth, along with Sancroft and five other bishops, whereupon it was finally agreed that they should petition the King in the name of the archbishop of Canterbury and the other bishops present (A. Taylor, 1858, IX: 132; Thomas, 1961).

Though the majority of latitudinarians were Cambridge graduates it was in London, not Cambridge, that they formed themselves into something approaching an ecclesiastical party with close personal ties and a common theological purpose. During the Restoration period their influence within the Church was too weak to allow them any significant influence over the universities which were dominated by high churchmen who, in some cases, had been adversaries of the latitudinarians. But after the Glorious Revolution, when many of the latitudinarians were advanced to the episcopate, they were able to play an important part in shaping the intellectual and religious character of their *alma mater*: those once without recognition in Cambridge were to become corner-stones of a new ecclesiastical order.

3

Restoration Cambridge
and the 'new philosophy'

When the high churchmen were restored to their positions at Cambridge after the Restoration they were returning to a university where the intellectual climate had changed in their absence. Sancroft said as much in a letter to his old tutor, Ezekiel Wright, in 1663 in which he lamented that the 'old genius and spirit of learning' he had known and admired at Emmanuel before the 'age of sorrow' were no longer diligently pursued, 'the Hebrew and Greek learning being out of fashion everywhere . . . and the rational learning they [now] pretend to being neither the old philosophy nor steadily any one of the new' (D'Oyly, 1821, I: 128).

Largely thanks to Henry More, Interregnum Cambridge had become known for its interest in the work of Descartes (Webster, 1975: 134) – thus Glanvill, who graduated from Oxford in 1655, later 'lamented that his friends did not first send him to Cambridge, because that new philosophy [Cartesianism] and art of philosophizing were there more than here in Oxon' (Webster, 1969: 360). The study of Descartes led in turn to a more general debate about the fundamentals of natural philosophy which continued to be a part of the university's intellectual milieu after the Restoration, leaving its mark on Newton's early studies (McGuire and Tamny, 1983; Gascoigne, 1985).

Sancroft himself had shown an early interest in Cartesianism and the study of mathematics (Nicolson, 1929b: 357; Feingold, 1984: 64) but after the Restoration such pursuits seemed to be something of a distraction from the more fundamental task of re-establishing the Church of England. Moreover, the growing interest within the university in recent developments in natural philosophy which, in comparison with the stability of the traditional Aristotelianism, appeared transitory and uncertain, seemed to Sancroft and his high church colleagues to be more and more of a diversion from the most basic concerns of university scholars: the study and exegesis of the basic texts of the Christian tradition, above all Scripture and the

Fathers, which rested on a knowledge of 'the Hebrew and Greek learning' which Sancroft saw as in decline within the university.

Like Sancroft other high churchmen, while not necessarily hostile to the 'new philosophy', tended to subordinate such academic innovations to their first priority: the re-establishment of the universities as clerical seminaries committed to reviving the doctrines and discipline of the Church of England after its time of trouble. The rather guarded attitude of such high churchmen to the study of recent scientific developments was summed up by Archbishop Sheldon, a token member of the Royal Society, who told Henry More that he approved of the new 'free method of philosophizing' provided 'the faith, the peace and the institution of the Church were not thereby menaced' (Mullinger, 1873–1911, III: 646).

Moreover, some of the restored clergy took a more overtly hostile view of the 'new philosophy', seeing it as a danger to orthodoxy since it challenged the cosmology with which Christian theology had long been intertwined. In his *Brief account of the new sect of latitude-men* (1662) Patrick specifically set out to counter such arguments which were evidently gaining ground within Restoration Cambridge. Thus Patrick endeavoured to refute the view that 'all innovations are dangerous; *Philosophy* and *Divinity* are so interwoven by the School-men, that it cannot be safe to separate them; *new Philosophy* will bring in *new Divinity* and freedom in the one will make men desire liberty in the other' (p. 22). Patrick added that attempts by the Presbyterians to forbid the study of the 'new philosophy' during the Interregnum had resulted in its being 'more eagerly studied and embraced' (p. 23) – an indication that traditionalist divines in both the Presbyterian and Anglican camps saw an assault on scholastic natural philosophy as an attack on the theology with which it had long been associated. As an early eighteenth-century life of John Wallis forcefully put it: around the time of the Restoration the new philosophy 'increased, and began to prevail very much at Cambridge', its followers being a 'bug-bear not only to the sour and narrow soul'd Presbyterians, but also to the bigotted zealots of the Church of England' (BL, Add. 32601: 60). But during the Interregnum the Presbyterians did not have the support of the State in the way that the high churchmen did after the Restoration, and so had less power to prevent the spread of the 'new philosophy'. High churchmen and Presbyterians may have had similar reservations about Cartesianism but at the Restoration it was the 'Church of England men' who were in the best position to attempt to stem this new intellectual tide.

In the decade following the Restoration there are indications that there was in fact a number of attempts to discourage the study of the 'new philosophy' and, in particular, Cartesianism. The 'new philosophy' tended to be equated with Cartesianism since that philosophical system was considered the most dangerous rival of traditional scholastic natural philosophy. Like scholasticism, Cartesianism offered an all-embracing philosophical and scientific schema which proceeded from an underlying metaphysics to a theory of matter and thence to detailed explanations of particular natural phenomena. But while scholastic natural philosophy, following Aristotle, depicted matter and spirit as integrated and complementary, Cartesianism emphasised their duality. Scholastic· natural philosophy regarded nature as being intrinsically purposeful so that all phenomena were directed towards purposeful ends while, by contrast, Cartesianism described nature as a machine composed of particles whose size, shape and motion were sufficient to explain physical phenomena without reference to final causes.

Even dons with scientific inclinations like Covel or Barrow criticised Descartes. Covel in his MA oration of 1663 jocularly remarked that Cambridge students learnt the works of French philosophers like Gassendi and Descartes along with their alphabet and, with a wry comment on the French disease, suggested that the proponents of the new philosophy had been unfair and ungenerous in their criticisms of Aristotle whom he praised as a bulwark against Hobbism (BL, Add. 22910: 13–15). Barrow, who in his MA oration of 1652 had referred to Descartes with respect while taking issue with some of his conclusions, now satirised the French philosopher in a speech delivered in 1661 in which he sharply contrasted Aristotle's philosophy as a discipline for youth with 'a new fashioned one which blunts the apprehension with too much Meditation' (Osmond, 1944: 95). Barrow's former tutor, James Duport (a royalist in and out of season who was master of Magdalene from 1668 to 1679), held Descartes' work in contempt and was never reconciled to the Copernican system which he regarded as contradicting Scripture. He was also suspicious of the Royal Society even though it included among its members some of his former pupils such as Barrow and Ray (Monk, 1826: 695). Fears of the materialistic overtones of Cartesianism help account for the decision by the vice-chancellor, Edmund Boldero (another staunch royalist), to issue a decree in November 1668 forbidding undergraduates and BAs from basing their disputations on Descartes' work and stipulating that Aristotle's writings be used instead (Bodl., Rawlinson MS C.146: 37). In the same period John North, an undergraduate at Jesus from 1667 to 1669, found that his study of Descartes led some to accuse him of having 'impugned the very Gospel. And yet', he continued, 'there was a general inclination, especially of the brisk part of the University, to use him' (North, 1890, III: 15).

Nevertheless, despite such objections, Cartesianism appears to have gradually become part of the undergraduate curriculum in natural philosophy. By 1686 there was such a demand for Cartesian texts that the university press reprinted Schuler's *Exercitationes ad principorum Descarti primam partem* (Kearney, 1970: 151), a work, moreover, which emphasised Descartes' controversial metaphysical premises. When Joshua Barnes (a fellow of Emmanuel from 1678 to 1701) revised Holdsworth's 'Directions for a student at the universities' (written in the 1640s) he left in place most of Holdsworth's scholastic texts but added that 'because the course of Philosophical studies is now altered' a student 'may make use of Des Cartes his Book of Meteors, also his De Passionibus and etc.; as also of Le Grand, Regius and other Cartesians e.g. Rohault and others' (Emmanuel College, Cambridge, MS 179: 56).

The high churchmen, then, were no more successful than the Presbyterians in halting the spread of Cartesianism. Natural philosophy was too well-established a part of the curriculum and the objections to Aristotelian physics too widely known for novel scientific developments to be ignored. Moreover, like the textbooks of scholastic natural philosophy, Cartesian works offered the pedagogical advantages of a highly systematic and deductive structure. John North (master of Trinity from 1677 to 1683) had discouraged his brother, Roger, from the study of Cartesianism in the 1660s but later conceded that, although Descartes might not be correct in every particular, this was not a reason for students to be 'kept back so much from the highway, as to spend time on Aristotle when Cartes keeps as good a Method, and for an Hypothesis doth as well and better than this, that he comes nigh the true Method' (BL, Add. 32514: 190v).

The early Royal Society, with its strong emphasis on experiment, raised few of the religious problems provoked by an all-embracing philosophical schema like that of Descartes or, *a fortiori*, that of Hobbes, a long-standing critic of both the clerical order and the universities (Shapin and Schaffer, 1985: 311–12). None the less, the Royal Society did meet with opposition from a number of the high churchmen, largely because it seemed a possible challenge to the universities' monopoly on higher education (if Gresham College is excepted) and perhaps, too, because it revived memories of the radical sectaries' programmes for the reform of Oxford and Cambridge – especially as some of the most active of the Royal Society's foundation members had come into prominence during parliamentary rule (Syfert, 1950a and 1950b). At Oxford, with which many of the early members of the Royal Society were associated, the controversy between the 'Greshamites' and the high churchmen was particularly fierce. Thus in 1669 Wallis wrote to Boyle expressing his dismay at South's speech at the dedication of the Sheldonian Theatre in

Oxford, the first part of which 'consisted of satyrical invectives against *Cromwell*, fanaticks, the Royal Society and the new Philosophy' (R. F. Jones, 1965: 255).

In Cambridge the opposition was less vocal, perhaps because there were fewer members of the university directly involved in the Royal Society, but there, too, there were signs of high church distrust of the new organisation. The Royal Society's chief opponent within Cambridge was Gunning who, in 1669, prevented Peter du Moulin from publishing a poem in the Royal Society's honour. In the same year du Moulin lamented to Boyle that there was 'a feud between that noble Society and the Universities' (*ibid.*: 579). The irascible Henry Stubbe, the Royal Society's most determined opponent, also wrote to Boyle claiming that 'the two universities (especially that of *Cambridge*, which was most inclined to novelty) avow my quarrel; and they, that favoured experimental philosophy, judge those virtuosi unfit to prosecute it. The bishop of *Chichester* [Gunning] reads against them, and intends to hold his lectures a year or two, and that for this reason, to overthrow the esteem of them. The concurrence to hear him is such, as the university never saw before' (*ibid.*: 254). A further indication of the controversial nature of the Royal Society and its goals within the university in 1669 is that in that year a visiting Medici prince was present at a Cambridge disputation where the propositions 'De methodi philosophari in experimentis fundata, et contra systema [m] Copernicum' were 'very spiritedly and strenuously opposed by the professors and masters of arts' (C. H. Cooper, 1842–1908, III: 536).

Like Sancroft, who bemoaned the neglect of the 'Hebrew and Greek learning' which, he claimed, had flourished before the Civil War, a number of other Cambridge high churchmen were wary of the new science, not so much for its own sake but rather because it tended to overshadow the traditional scholarship which sought to establish the Church of England's claims to be a true embodiment of Scripture and Christian antiquity. The most lucid expression of such fears was Meric Casaubon's *Letter . . . to Peter du Moulin . . . concerning natural experimental philosophie, and some books lately set out about it* (published at Cambridge in 1669) – a work prompted by discussions between Casaubon and du Moulin on the effects of the new philosophy on traditional learning (R. F. Jones, 1965: 241–2). Du Moulin had given Casaubon Glanvill's *Plus ultra* and the high claims for the new experimental philosophy there, and in Sprat's *History of the Royal Society*, led Casaubon to take issue with those who 'cry down all other studies and learning, ordinarily comprehended under the title of *humane learning*' as being 'of little or no use, since this new light of *true* [experimental] *real knowledge*' (Spiller, 1980: 155). Casaubon was particularly concerned that advocates of the new science would 'make it the onely *useful*, true, solid learning, to which they would have all Schools and Universities fitted' (*ibid.*: 174).

These issues were also addressed in his unpublished tract (recently edited under the title *Of learning* (Spiller, 1980)) which was addressed to Francis Turner (Gunning's successor as master of St John's). Here Casaubon defended his ideal of a 'general Scholar' against those propagandists of the new science who took the view 'that all other learning is but uerball and useless' (*ibid.*: 197; Hunter, 1982a). Himself a loyal supporter of the Church of England in its days of adversity, Casaubon summed up the high church tradition of scholarship in his definition of a 'general Schollar' as a man 'by whome doubts and difficulties of Scripture must be resolued; the creditt and authorities of the Scriptures themselves, as the Word of God, against all opposers mainteined; controuersies in religion, by the exact knowledge of former tymes, decided' (Spiller, 1980: 213; Hunter, 1981: 155).

Since the Church of England argued in its debates with papists and dissenters that it was the Church which best conformed to both the purest traditions of the ancient Church and the Scriptures this led to a particular preoccupation with ecclesiastical history and biblical scholarship (Bennett, 1971/2: 63). The 'appeal to antiquity' was most strongly associated with the high churchmen, though latitudinarians like Stillingfleet and Patrick also stressed the importance of the Church Fathers. However, the latitudinarians approached the Fathers not so much as representatives of an authoritative historical tradition but rather as theologians whose works could be used to demonstrate the more general conformity between reason and Revelation (McAdoo, 1965: 389); moreover, some notable latitudinarians like Wilkins or Tillotson made little reference to patristic works.

The high churchmen's interest in ecclesiastical tradition encouraged the growth within both universities of historical and philological studies, especially those connected with the Church. Sancroft, 'a zealous if unproductive student of history' (Pocock, 1950–2: 193), encouraged the historical work of Brady and helped to found a readership in ecclesiastical history at Emmanuel (Bodl., Tanner MS 155: 76–82). William Cave and William Beveridge (both graduates of St John's) produced massive histories of the early Church and joined Pearson in attacking the Huguenot Jean Daillé who had rejected the authority of the Fathers. Though Newton was out of sympathy with the high churchmen's theology his absorbing interest in church history (Manuel, 1963) indicates that he was influenced by the intellectual milieu of Restoration Cambridge. He also studied closely the work of Cambridge scriptural scholars of whom the most prominent was John Spencer, master of Corpus from 1667 to 1693

(Manuel, 1974: 66, 87). Such an academic environment also favoured the growth of secular historical studies – some of the more notable being the work of Robert Brady and the histories of Anglo-Saxon England by Robert Sheringham (who was also a noted Hebrew scholar), Aylett Sammes, Thomas Smith and Thomas Gale (Douglas, 1939: 67–76).

However, an emphasis on such branches of scholarship did little to promote an interest in mathematical and experimental sciences. Though Restoration Cambridge was certainly not devoid of scientific activity (Gascoigne, 1985) there was, contrary to popular stereotype, less interest in Cambridge in the new science than at Oxford. Thus an attempt to found an equivalent to the Oxford Philosophical Society at Cambridge in 1685 foundered (as Newton reported) because of 'the want of persons willing to try experiments' (Turnbull *et al.*, 1959–77, II: 415). Hans's analysis of the careers of 680 scientists from 1660 to 1785 shows that Oxford consistently produced more scientists than Cambridge until the 1690s (Hans, 1951: 32–3). As Frank points out, on the basis of Hans's figures, in the cohort educated at Oxford in the period 1660 to 1688 there were four times as many future scientists as at Cambridge, while in the first three decades of the eighteenth century, by contrast, there were twice as many future scientists at Cambridge as at Oxford (Frank, 1973: 240). Cambridge's rather tepid interest in the experimental sciences is reflected in the university's tenuous involvement with the Royal Society. Of the 443 members elected between 1660 and 1688 only 76 (16%) were Cambridge graduates and of these 32 (42%) were physicians, most of whom had left Cambridge after graduation. In the same period a mere twenty fellows of the Royal Society held fellowships at Cambridge and, apart from the work of Newton and – to compare great things with small – that of Newton's young friends, Edward Paget and Francis Aston (both fellows of Trinity), who were active in the institutional life of the society, Cambridge contributed little to the society in this period (Hunter, 1982b).

The different levels of scientific activity at the two univesities can be partly accounted for by the earlier foundation of scientific chairs at Oxford: there the Savilian chairs of geometry and astronomy were established in 1619; by contrast the Lucasian professorship of mathematics and the Plumian professorship of astronomy and experimental philosophy were established at Cambridge in 1663 and 1704 respectively. However, the intellectual priorities of the Cambridge high churchmen with their emphasis on traditional scholarship and their reservations about the theological consequences of adopting the 'new philosophy' probably also played a part in retarding scientific activity within Restoration Cambridge. Though high churchmen like Fell were also active in cultivating traditional scholarship within Restoration Oxford (Hunter, 1975), their influence was possibly greater at Cambridge because of its eagerness to demonstrate its loyalty to the restored Throne and Altar after its less than exemplary record during the Interregnum. In any case, at Oxford the scientific tradition was better entrenched before 1660 and so was less likely to be overshadowed by the different, and in some respects competing, intellectual tradition to which the high churchmen saw themselves as belonging.

One exception to Restoration Cambridge's rather undistinguished record in the mathematical and physical sciences before the publication of the *Principia* in 1687 was the work of Isaac Barrow, the first Lucasian professor of mathematics whose published lectures (and, in particular, his geometrical lectures) gave him a European-wide reputation. However, Barrow is an exception that goes some way to proving the rule since he resigned the Lucasian chair in 1669 in order to devote himself more fully to theology and thereafter played little part in the scientific world. Barrow's motives for resigning the chair are evident in a Latin verse he sent to Tillotson in 1669: 'While you, my dear friend', he wrote, 'deliver the mysteries of sacred truth to the people in powerful eloquence . . . and carry on successful controversy for the law of God; I, as you perceive, am so unhappy as to be fixed to the [mathematical] books which you see here; and so waste my time and my power' (Napier, 1859, IX: xxxviii–xxxix). That even an accomplished mathematician like Barrow should regard mathematics as such a poor second to theology suggests how lowly a place science more generally had within Restoration Cambridge where the overriding concern was the re-establishment of the authority and influence of the Established Church.

Though the high churchmen did little to encourage the growth of the physical and mathematical sciences within the university they none the less viewed medicine and its related sciences in a rather more positive light. Medicine had a long-established place in the university curriculum and had traditionally been linked with the Church – many physicians, for example, were episcopally licensed, particularly after the Restoration (Holmes, 1982: 172–3). Moreover, though in fact changes in the biological sciences were linked with fundamental philosophical reorientations, the sciences associated with medicine appeared to make few of the overt metaphysical claims which made Cartesian physics, for example, a threat to the traditional amalgam of Christian theology and Aristotelian natural philosophy. Perhaps, too, the biological sciences were seen as a more obvious source of support for the argument from design than the physical sciences. Thus, although the loyally Anglican James Duport of Trinity was opposed to the 'new philosophy', he appears to have been interested in natural history since his library catalogue includes approximately twenty-nine books related to the biological sciences including the *Catalogue of plants around Cambridge* by his former pupil, Ray.[1]

Restoration Cambridge, then, continued to promote a tradition of activity in the biomedical sciences which had been well established before 1660. After his appointment as Regius professor of physick in 1636 Francis Glisson was active in furthering the Harveian research tradition and in encouraging his students to take as their topics for the statutory disputations theses at variance with the traditional Galenic physiology. In 1653, for example, Robert Brady (who succeeded Glisson as Regius professor in 1677) took for his MB disputation the overtly Harveian proposition that 'The Pulsation of the Arteries is Caused by the Impulsion of Blood from the Heart' (Frank, 1979: 74).

The medical faculty, in turn, helped to stimulate an interest in the biological sciences more generally. In the 1650s there was a flourishing circle of young Cambridge fellows who shared an enthusiasm for subjects which were closely related to medicine such as botany, zoology and chemistry (Raven, 1950; Webster, 1975: 150–3). While the most notable member of the group was the naturalist John Ray, its leader appears to have been the comparatively obscure John Nidd who became a fellow of Trinity in 1647 and whose primary interest – to judge by his library catalogue which lists 126 medical texts out of a total collection of 277 items (Leedham-Green, 1986: 577) – was medicine. Traditionally, the medical faculty had been the least significant of the higher faculties and had little impact on university life but (to quote Webster) 'during the interregnum the English universities could for the first time have claimed to possess fully effective medical schools' (1975: 143). One of the reasons for this was that in the troubled political and religious conditions of that era many students who would normally have gone on to higher studies in divinity or law chose the less controversial area of medicine. As Walter Charleton remarked (perhaps with some exaggeration) in 1657: 'our late Warrs and Schisms, having almost wholly discouraged men from the study of theologie; and brought the Civil Law into contempt: the major part of young Schollers in our Universities addict themselves to Physick' (Rattansi, 1962: 217). This surge of activity in medicine and its associated sciences during the Interregnum was particularly evident at Cambridge and was to leave its mark on the Restoration Royal College of Physicians which was dominated by Cambridge graduates, just as the early Royal

---

[1] Though Duport was an opponent of the 'new philosophy' he was not altogether ignorant of recent developments in natural philosophy since his library included Gassendi's *De motu impresso*, two works on Cartesian natural philosophy, two books on Boyles's experiments and Henry Power's *Experimental philosophy*. (See Trinity College, Cambridge, Add. a. 150: 332–427.)

Society was dominated by Oxford men largely thanks to the activities of the Wadham College circle (Frank, 1973: 263).

This predilection for the biomedical sciences continued to remain a feature of Cambridge after 1660. Malachi Thruston, a fellow of Caius from 1655 to 1701, continued the Harveian research tradition with work on the physiology of respiration (Frank, 1980: 241). His colleague, Robert Brady, who succeeded Glisson in 1677, largely owed his appointment to his services to the royalist cause during the Interregnum. Though more famous as an historian than as a clinician he was not altogether unworthy of the post since he helped to popularise the use of quinine and corresponded with Sydenham on the treatment of rheumatism. Other prominent Cambridge medical graduates of the period included Charles Goodall (MD 1670), four times censor of the Royal College of Physicians and its president from 1708 to 1712; William Briggs (fellow of Corpus, MD 1677) who wrote one of the first full accounts of the anatomy of the eye, a subject on which he corresponded with Newton (Turnbull *et al.*, 1959–77, II: 377–8, 381–5); Clopton Havers (who began his studies at Catharine Hall in 1668 but completed his MD at Utrecht in 1685), the author of the first treatise on the microscopic structure of bones; and the tory polemicist James Drake (BA Caius 1688, MB 1690), who, like Thruston (another Caius man), wrote on the problem of respiration as well as publishing a textbook of anatomy.

Far from opposing such interests, the high churchmen appear to have encouraged them, just as the Anglican royalists had promoted Harvey's work within Civil War Oxford (Webster, 1975: 130). St John's, the bastion of Cambridge high churchmanship, was the most active college in the teaching of medicine and produced more medical graduates than any other Cambridge college throughout the period from 1660 to 1760 (except that from 1680 to 1689 and from 1700 to 1709 it was surpassed by Caius) (Rook, 1969a; 111). Among its medical fellows was Henry Paman (MD 1658; FRCP 1687) who served as professor of physick at Gresham from 1679 to 1689 and was a close friend of Sydenham to whom he addressed a letter on the treatment of venereal disease; his high church sympathies are evident in his close association with Sancroft (in whose household he resided after 1677) and his refusal to take the oaths to William III after 1689. Paman was followed as professor of physick at Gresham by Edward Stillingfleet, another fellow of St John's. Another of Paman's colleagues, Thomas Short (MD 1668; FRCP 1675), was also a friend of Sydenham who dedicated to Short the *Treatise on gout and dropsy* (*ibid.*: 107–8).

St John's College's most distinguished scientist from this period, Martin Lister, though not a medical graduate, devoted himself to zoology and botany and later established himself as a medical practitioner (receiving an honorary MD from Oxford in 1684). Lister's royalist credentials were sufficient for him to be awarded a fellowship by royal mandate in 1660 which he resigned in 1669 while still maintaining contact with the university thereafter. His correspondence with Humphrey Gower, master of St John's from 1679 to 1711, indicates the sympathy that the high churchmen could have for natural history since Gower praised Lister's work in the highest terms and spoke enthusiastically of the importance of research into all branches of animate nature (Bodl., Lister MS 35: 38).

As the example of Lister suggests, the Cambridge medical school continued to act as a catalyst for work in natural history. To the dismay of Trinity which (according to Ray's colleague Stephen Scandrett) 'was peculiarly desirous to keep him in' (Raven, 1950: 59) Ray declined to take the oaths prescribed by the Act of Uniformity of 1662 and so lost his fellowship. Nevertheless, he remained in touch with Cambridge and his influence continued to stimulate work in natural history after the Restoration. Thus Ray warmly responded to Lister's first letter to him in 1667 (which was to be the first of many) thanking him for his additions to the *Cambridge catalogue* (of plants) and praising him for not confining 'Your Studies and Enquiries to Phytology only; but [for] tak[ing] in Zoology, and the whole Latitude of natural History' (Derham, 1718: 19). Ray also corresponded regularly on natural history matters with Peter Dent, a Cambridge physician who incorporated his Lambeth MB at Cambridge in 1680.

A mutual friend of Ray and Dent was John Covel (master of Christ's from 1688 to 1722) who studied medicine for a time before turning to theology. While in Constantinople as chaplain between 1670 and 1676 Covel corresponded with Dent on botanical matters, sending back samples which Dent used for teaching botany within Cambridge (HMC, Portland, II: 33) and some which were sent on to Ray (Raven, 1950: 215). Another peripatetic Cambridge don who supplied Ray with field material was William Vernon who, in 1697, obtained leave from Peterhouse to spend four years abroad 'to improve his Botanick Studies in the West Indies' (Wordsworth, 1877: 207). A friend of both Vernon and Ray was the naturalist Adam Buddle, a fellow of Catharine Hall from 1686 to 1691 when he was ejected as a nonjuror, who was described by Vernon as 'the top of all the moss-croppers' (Raven, 1950: 393n).

Like natural history, chemistry was also closely associated with medicine: Barrow, for example, when he turned to the study of medicine during the Interregnum because he found 'the times not favourable to men of his opinion in the affairs of Church and State', was said to have made 'great progress in the knowledge of Anatomy, Botanicks and Chymistry' (Napier, 1859, I: xli). The Nidd circle, to which Barrow was linked, conducted chemical experiments along with its work in medicine and natural history. Possibly some members of this group continued their chemical investigations after the Restoration; in any case, John Beale reported to John Evelyn in 1669 that there was a 'Club of Philosophical Chymists' at Cambridge.[2] The link between medicine and chemistry is also evident in the case of the Italian, Francis Vigani, Cambridge's first professor of chemistry, a post he held from 1703 to 1712. Vigani was primarily an iatrochemist – his only published work, the *Medulla chymiae* (1st ed. Danzig, 1682; London, 1683) was largely taken up with descriptions of pharmaceutical preparations (Coleby, 1952a: 53). His first patron within Cambridge, when he began to give private classes there in the early 1680s, was John Eachard, master of Catharine Hall from 1675 to 1697, an amateur physician (Robb-Smith, 1974: 353) and while at that college Vigani prescribed medicine for a number of students and probably offered a course of anatomy classes (W. H. S. Jones, 1936: 103). Vigani also gave private classes in chemistry to which Newton referred when he described Vigani as someone 'who has been here performing a course of Chymistry to several of our University much to their satisfaction' (Westfall, 1980: 339).[3]

The high churchmen, then, were more sympathetic to the less overtly metaphysical sciences associated with the medical faculty than to the physical sciences which had more obvious consequences for the traditional amalgam between Christian theology and Aristotelian philosophy and which were associated with what seemed to some the overweening claims of the Royal Society's propagandists. The latitudinarians, on the other hand, were known for their enthusiasm for the 'new philosophy'. As early as 1662 Patrick felt obliged to counter allegations that the latitudinarians were 'followers for the most part of the new Philosophy, wherewith they have so poisoned' the university (1662: 3). Sympathy for the 'new philosophy' tended to be equated with approval of Cartesianism, as John North's comment that 'It hath been observed that the Latitudinarians are generally Cartesians' (BL, Add. 32514: 176v) indicates (though in fact the latitudinarians viewed Cartesianism with rather more reservations than North's remark suggests).

The basis for this latitudinarian affinity for the 'new philosophy' surely lies in the character of their theology. The latitudinarians – in contrast to the high churchmen – emphasised natural rather than revealed religion and the study of the natural order rather than the tradition and teaching of the

[2] Christ Church College, Evelyn Correspondence, no. 79. I owe this reference to Dr M. Hunter.
[3] The above five paragraphs are based on material in Gascoigne, 1985: 400–1, 3.

Church. For the high churchmen Christianity was based on the scriptural record which was clarified through the history and teaching of the Church. To the latitudinarians, however, Scripture did not require such authoritative interpretation and, though inessentials might be obscure, the fundamentals were clear to men of good will and their truth could be confirmed by reflection on the natural order without any need for dependence on human authority.

Naturally, the latitudinarians' own circumstances helped shape their theology: most of the original latitudinarians had, to some degree, co-operated with the parliamentary regime and their loyalty to the restored Crown and Altar was under question. If, as the high churchmen advocated, conformity to traditional rites and observances was to be a hallmark of true Anglicanism, the latitudinarians would obviously have little place in the restored Church. But if, instead of history and tradition, theologians emphasised what were regarded as the eternal and unchanging verities of the natural order the problem of the latitudinarians' ecclesiastical waverings would seem far less important. Moreover, the study of the 'new philosophy' was a catalyst for change in theology. Traditionally, Christian theology had been intertwined with a Ptolemaic cosmology and an Aristotelian natural philosophy, raising fears (as the mathematician Edward Davenant had remarked as early as the 1640s) that 'if a new philosophy is brought in, a new divinity will shortly follow' (Aubrey, 1898, 1: 201). For men, like the latitudinarians, who felt under threat from the leaders of the restored Church, the corrosive effect of the 'new philosophy' on traditional theological systems and the church order which was associated with them could appear a positive advantage. There may, then, have been some justice in the remark reported by Glanvill to Oldenburg in 1669 that the 'new philosophy' was suspected of being 'a Lattitudinarian designe to propogate new notions in divinity' (Hunter, 1981: 118).

Furthermore, the latitudinarians wished to see the creation of a comprehensive national church which could accommodate the great bulk of English Protestants and thus reverse the effects of the Act of Uniformity. They were therefore advocates of a brand of theology which minimised areas of doctrinal debate and, like Grotius (whose *De veritate religionis Christianae* Patrick translated), they emphasised the conformity of Christianity with natural law in an effort to focus attention on the undisputed essentials of Christianity rather than on doctrines which caused divisions. While the high churchmen's emphasis on ecclesiastical tradition attracted them to historical scholarship, the latitudinarians' preoccupation with natural law and the revelation of God's handiwork in the natural order meant that they were naturally inclined to take an interest in developments in natural philosophy in the expectation that such findings could be put to good apologetical use.

All the major latitudinarians displayed some interest in recent scientific developments. Patrick in his *Brief account* praised the work of Tycho Brahe, Boyle, Bacon, Galileo and, with some reservations, Descartes. He also expressed his concern that, despite the Galileo affair, the Church of Rome with followers like Descartes and Gassendi had at present the lead in the study of the 'new philosophy' and urged Anglicans not to fall behind in the battle of ideas. Tillotson, the latitudinarians' most successful publicist, was said by his biographer, Birch, to have had a 'love for the real philosophy of nature' and to have believed that 'the study of it is the most solid support of religion' (Birch, 1752: 349). Like his close friend John Wilkins, who greatly influenced Tillotson's theology (*ibid.*: 6), he was a member of the Royal Society and a friend of such prominent Greshamites as Boyle, Halley, Hooke and Ray (the last of whom dedicated one of his books to Tillotson) (Birch, 1772, VI: 505; Raven 1950: 431; Jacob, 1976: 30). Stillingfleet devoted one whole section of his massive and erudite *Origines sacrae: or a rational account of the grounds of the Christian faith . . .* (1662) to illustrating the conformity between Scripture and the 'new philosophy', though his reservations about Cartesianism are evident in his comment that 'there is a great difference to be made between those who have proceeded in the way of *Experiments* which do great service as they go, and such as have form'd *Mechanical Theories* of the System of the Universe' (1707–10, II: 99*). By the 1697 edition Stillingfleet was able to contrast Descartes' natural philosophy unfavourably with that of Newton (*ibid.*: 116; Jacob, 1976: 32). The Scot, Gilbert Burnet (who, though not a Cambridge graduate, was linked with the latitudinarians) was also a keen student of the new philosophy – thus he recorded that in 1661 while a probationer of the Scottish Church, 'I applied myselfe to Philosophy and Mathematicks, and ran through Des Cartes and Gassendi' (Foxcroft, 1902: 461).

While Patrick, Tillotson and Stillingfleet lived and worked in London after the Restoration, there were a few younger Cambridge latitudinarians who became interested in science while at the university, though they subsequently moved to London where they gained positions through the influence of prominent lay patrons. John Sharp's biographer reports that while at Christ's, 'Besides the course of studies that he went through under the direction of his tutor, he heard lectures in natural philosophy from Dr. Thomas Burnet . . . who taught the Cartesian philosophy' (Sharp, 1825, I: 10). Sharp's undergraduate notebooks also include excerpts from botanical and chemical texts as well as records of some chemical experiments (*ibid.*). His continuing interest in recent developments in science is evident in the fact that later, while archbishop of York, he set out to master Newtonian natural philosophy 'of which he used frequently to discourse, and always spoke of with great delight, as setting forth the Creator in the most beautiful light that it was possible for us to conceive him in, with respect to external nature' (*ibid.*). Sharp's friend, John Moore, in his sermons as a fellow of Clare, used metaphors drawn from recent scientific works referring to the work of Helmont as well as 'the ingenious atomical hypothesis', for example, when discussing the resurrection of the body (CUL, MS Dd.14.9: 53). Like others at Cambridge, Moore's scientific interests were stimulated by his attention, while a student, to medicine – a subject which remained a lifetime preoccupation as the comprehensive holdings of sixteenth- and seventeenth-century medical literature in his vast library indicate (McKitterick, 1986: 90–1). Similarly, Thomas Tenison's interest in science probably originated in his study of medicine, which he had originally taken up when he graduated in 1657 because of the uncertain times (Carpenter, 1948: 7), though he subsequently turned back to theology. While vicar of Holywell in 1671 he corresponded with Oldenburg on the natural history of the area and expressed his 'reverence for your society' (Hall and Hall, 1965–86, VII: 494). Six years later he published his *Baconiana* (1677) in which he placed Bacon on a lofty pedestal above Copernicus, Galileo, Harvey and Gilbert.

Of all the Cambridge latitudinarians the one whose work in natural philosophy attracted most attention was that of Thomas Burnet, a fellow of Christ's from 1657 to 1678 and author of *The sacred theory of the earth*.[4] At Cambridge Burnet had close contact with the latitudinarians. At Clare, where he was an undergraduate, he came to know Tillotson who always remained a close friend and to whom he dedicated the first Latin edition of the *Telluris theoria sacra* (Birch, 1752: 277). Shortly after Cudworth became master of Christ's in 1654 Burnet followed him to his new college and thus, throughout the rest of his stay at Cambridge, Burnet was a colleague of both Cudworth and More. When Gilbert Burnet visited Cambridge in 1663 he praised the work of the two Cambridge Platonists and described his namesake, Thomas, as 'the most considerable among those of the younger sort' (Foxcroft, 1902: 463).

Burnet's *Sacred theory* was the most thoroughgoing attempt by a Cambridge latitudinarian to demonstrate the conformity of Scripture with the 'new philosophy'. Burnet's originality and intellectual daring lay in his attempt to construct a biblically based cosmogony explained by natural causes rather than by the direct intervention of the Deity. 'This theory being Chiefly Philosophical', Burnet wrote, 'Reason is to be our

---

[4] Burnet's work was published in two parts. The Latin first part appeared in 1681 and was translated in 1690 (Jacob and Lockwood, 1972: 265).

first Guide; and where that falls short or any other just occasion offers itself, we may receive further light and confirmation from the sacred writings' (1965: 26). Elsewhere Burnet warned against invoking miracles too readily, commenting that 'the course of Nature is truly the will of God' (*ibid*.: 221) – a view shared by Newton who, in his detailed and largely sympathetic correspondence with Burnet about the book, remarked that 'where natural causes are at hand, God uses them as instruments in his works' (Turnbull *et al*., 1959–77, II: 334).

Though the actual details of Burnet's scheme provoked considerable controversy, his attempted synthesis of the 'new philosophy' (and, in particular, Cartesianism) and Scripture exercised a considerable fascination over his contemporaries now that the old amalgam of Aristotelian natural philosophy and Christianity was breaking apart (Porter, 1977: 62–90). Some, while attempting to improve on Burnet's theory, paid him the compliment of imitation. In 1692 Ray published his *Miscellaneous discourses concerning the dissolution and changes of the world* which, like Burnet's work, was dedicated to Tillotson. More popular were John Woodward's *Essay towards a natural history of the earth* (1695) and Whiston's *New theory of the earth* (1696), the latter helping to popularise some of the conclusions of Newton's *Principia*.

Burnet's work was also significant since it marked such a definite break with the old scholastic learning: appropriately the *Sacred theory* was largely responsible for sparking off 'The Battle of the Books' between the advocates of ancient and modern learning. In his dedication to Charles II of the first English edition of his book Burnet criticised 'the dead Learning of the Schools'. This 'dry Philosophy', he argued, '. . . hath brought forth no Fruit, produc'd nothing good to God or Man, to Religion or human Society' (Jones, 1965: 342). Stung by Burnet's criticism of traditional learning Sir William Temple published his *Essay upon the ancient and modern learning* in 1690 and thus arose the long controversy between the defenders of ancient and modern learning which was to involve two prominent Cambridge men, Wotton and Bentley, as advocates for the Moderns.

But, though Burnet remained a fellow of Christ's until 1678 and stimulated students like Sharp to take an interest in scientific studies, it is interesting that his *magnum opus* was not published until 1681 when he had resigned his fellowship and left Cambridge. Similarly, although Tenison may have laid the foundations of his scientific interests while at Cambridge, he did not publish his pamphlet on Bacon nor begin his correspondence with Oldenburg until after he had left the university. It was in London, not Cambridge, that the latitudinarians had most hope of advancement and with the departure of men like Sharp, Moore, Tenison and Thomas Burnet (along with others like Patrick and Tillotson who were ousted soon after the Restoration) Cambridge lost a potential nucleus for scientific activity.

   Indeed, despite Newton's presence within the university, Restoration Cambridge showed few signs of the pre-eminence in physical and mathematical sciences for which it was later to be renowned. It was not until the early eighteenth century that Cambridge's curriculum began to stress the mathematical sciences to an extent that clearly distinguished it from Oxford, which had previously displayed the greater scientific promise. Though this intellectual metamorphosis followed the publication of Newton's *Principia* in 1687 the popularity of Newton's work in Cambridge was not foreordained. The first popular Newtonian textbook, John Keill's *Introductio ad veram physicam* (1701), was produced at Oxford, not at Newton's own university, and it is conceivable that Oxford could have assimilated Newton's natural philosophy into its curriculum in the way that Cambridge adopted the work of John Locke, an Oxford man. Newton's *Principia* was too forbidding a work to capture public imagination immediately – in Cambridge, as in Britain and Europe at large, Newton needed popularisers. As will be argued at length in the next section, the fact that such intellectual under-labourers were more forthcoming in Cambridge than in Oxford owes more to the changes in the political and religious views of those holding office in the university after the Revolution of 1688 than to the presence of Newton who, after the publication of the *Principia*, looked more towards public office in London than intellectual aggrandizement in the fens.

Part Two

The 'holy alliance'
proclaimed, 1689–1768

4

The creation and consolidation of whig Cambridge

By 1688 Cambridge had largely been remodelled in the image and likeness of the high churchmen who had dominated its counsels since the Restoration. It saw itself as an integral part of a revitalised Church which was distinguished by its insistence on passive obedience to the Lord's Anointed. Yet eighteenth-century Cambridge was to be known (particularly when compared to its obstinately tory sister university) as a breeding-ground for whigs. It was also widely praised by the supporters of the Hanoverian regime for its adherence to the Revolutionary Settlement which (in whig ideology at least) was characterised by those limitations on the power of kings which the advocates of passive obedience regarded as the province of God rather than man. How, then, to trace the way in which such a transformation took place in the four decades following the Glorious Revolution and how Cambridge's allegiance to the whig cause was still further strengthened during the reign of George II is the subject of this chapter.

Cambridge greeted the Glorious Revolution with unenthusiastic propriety; as William Wotton (a fellow of St John's) commented, the event 'was observed neither with much rejoycing, nor yet so coldly as to affront any body' (Bodl., MS Rawlinson D.1232: 63). The university's dutiful acquiescence in the new regime was also underlined by the unanimous election in 1689 of Charles Seymour, sixth duke of Somerset, as chancellor – Seymour having recommended himself to Cambridge on account of his 'moderate and prudent behaviour throughout the whole course of this wonderful Revolution together with his steddiness to the true Church of England' (CUL, MS Mm.6.50: 107–8). Somerset's claims to the gratitude of the Church of England were further emphasised by the vice-chancellor, John Covel, who praised his 'most admirable courage and concern for our distressed Church in the late unhappy times' (CUL, Mm.6.50: 135) – a reference to the fact that Somerset was removed from James II's court for refusing to take part in the papal nuncio's audience with the King (Anon., 1748: 58).

Cambridge was one of the first beneficiaries of the new regime. Eager to avoid any comparison with the high-handed treatment of the universities by his predecessor, William allowed Cambridge to assert its claim to greater autonomy after years of Stuart interference in its internal affairs. Thus it was agreed in 1689 that royal mandates for degrees should thereafter only be issued at the petition of the chancellor who would not make such a request unless he received a certificate signed by a majority of heads of houses that the applicant was a person of good learning (Winstanley, 1922: 161). At King's, the provostship of which was traditionally a royal appointment, the fellows took the opportunity to establish their right to elect the provost themselves when Dr Coplestone (provost, 1681–9) died soon after the Revolution. William vainly attempted to have one of his own nominees (among them Newton) appointed to the post but reluctantly accepted the election of Dr Roderick by the fellows following the intercession of the chancellor (Bloxam, 1886: 272–4). Thereafter King's was entitled to elect its own provost.

Superficially, then, Cambridge appeared to have accepted the new regime with a good grace but beneath the smooth surface which university officialdom attempted to present there were disturbing cross-currents. The confusion and uncertainty within Cambridge is evident in a petition drawn up by fifty-nine members of the university to the Commons and to William and Mary enquiring about the exact sense of 'allegiance' in the oath of 1689 and asking that in the meanwhile 'we may be excus'd from taking the said oath' (though the petition was probably never presented) (Bodl., MS Eng. Hist. b.114–15 (R); Findon, 1979: 44); of these fifty nine, twenty-six became nonjurors while the remainder conformed (Findon, 1979: 108). In August 1689 Pepys wrote that at Cambridge

Some will pray for the King and Queen but not by name. Some will not pray for them at all. Some will pray for them but not take the oaths. Some will pray for the Parliament as it is now assembled under King & Queen, that will not own them to be King & Queen so as to pray for them as such. (Findon, 1979: 109)

Even among the great majority of fellows who took the oaths and made all the appropriate obeisances towards the new monarchy there was a deep-seated disquiet at the need to abjure their loyalty to their former monarch. As Whiston wrote in his *Memoirs*:

Yet do I too well remember, that the far greatest part of those of the university and clergy that then took the oaths to the government, seemed to me to take them with a doubtful conscience, if not against its dictates. Nor considering the doctrines of passive obedience and non-resistance, they had generally been brought up in, and generally signed before, was it to be otherwise expected. (1753: 27–8)

Moreover, there was a significant minority within the university who resolutely refused to take the oaths – indeed, Cambridge produced far more nonjurors than Oxford, the reputed 'home of lost causes': at Cambridge there were 37 fellows and 4 scholars ejected as nonjurors while at Oxford there were a mere 25 fellows (and 1 scholar) (Wordsworth, 1874: 603–5). Furthermore, Cambridge alumni among the nonjurors more generally totalled 200 as against 157 from the older (and larger) university (Findon, 1979: Table 1). Sixty-four of Cambridge's nonjurors were graduates of St John's, which produced three times as many nonjurors as any other individual college at either university (*ibid.*: 51). Of the Cambridge nonjuring dons the majority (24) were members of St John's though many of these remained in residence until 1717 when 10 fellows of St John's were ejected for not taking the oath abjuring the claims of 'James III' to be rightful monarch (Mullinger, 1901: 215–16). Those nonjuring fellows, who were not ejected until 1717, were shielded for a time by Humphrey Gower (master of St John's, 1679–1711). Though Gower himself conformed he used his influence to protect his nonjuring colleagues and after some deft legal manoeuvring, which led to his being suspected of jacobitism, successfully evaded the *mandamus* requiring the nonjurors' ejection. St John's therefore remained a centre of nonjuring sentiment within the university and the uncompromising stand of some of its fellows acted as a continual rebuke to those members of the university who had conformed with wavering consciences. In October 1695 Pryme, an undergraduate at St John's, recorded in his diary that the nonjurors

were frequently exceedingly bold, and would talk openly against the government, which the government connived a little at, for fear of raising any bustle, knowing that they were inconsiderable by reason of their paucity. They set up separate meetings all over, where there was any number of them, at which meetings I myself have once or twice been in Cambridge, for we had above twenty fellows in our College that were non-jurors. The service they used was the Common Prayer, and always pray'd heartily for king James, nameing him most commonly; but in some meetings, they onely prayed for the king, not nameing who. (Wordsworth, 1874: 22–3)

The Glorious Revolution, then, left Cambridge divided and uncertain and its slow reconciliation to the Revolutionary Settlement was to colour the life of the university for some decades, affecting both the social relations and the intellectual sympathies of its members.

The ambivalent mood within Cambridge after the Glorious Revolution reflected, in miniature, the tensions within the Church more generally. For the Anglican clergy William's triumphant entry into London in

December 1688 was both a deliverance and a new cross to bear: on the one hand there was the sense of relief that England was now free from the danger of popish bondage, on the other their grief that they were required to abandon their sworn allegiance to a son of the martyred King. Some felt this conflict of loyalties less acutely than others: to Gilbert Burnet, for example, the Church's deliverance from James's popish proselytising was so welcome and even miraculous an event that it was clearly the work of Providence and thus justified allegiance to the new King. This theme he developed in the sermon with which he greeted William soon after his arrival in London which took as its text: 'It is the Lord's doing and it is marvellous in our eyes' (Straka, 1962: 650). But for many of Burnet's clerical brethren the divine will was not so evident as they wavered between the oft-repeated precepts of passive obedience and their joy at seeing a Protestant on the throne.

Naturally, many of the clergy waited for guidance from their primate, William Sancroft, who had so courageously led the opposition to James's assaults on the Church of England. But, after signing the Guildhall Declaration of 11 December 1688 which called on William to assist in procuring peace and a 'free parliament', Sancroft lapsed into an ominous silence as he saw that William would not be content with the role of regent or indeed with anything less than the throne itself. The archbishop's absence from the coronation and his seclusion within Lambeth Palace (where he bade his chaplain, Henry Wharton, to 'desist from offering prayers for the new king and queen . . . for so long as King James was alive no other persons could be sovereigns of the country' (D'Oyly, 1821, I: 435)) cast a dark shadow over the monarchy; inevitably he was finally deprived of his office (on 1 February 1690), along with five other bishops and about four hundred clergy.

William, a stranger to Anglican ways, was naturally less than sympathetic to the Church of England after this unhappy beginning to his reign and it was only through the tact and political adroitness of Daniel Finch, earl of Nottingham, that more harmonious relations were restored between Church and Crown (Bennett, 1966). In seeking religious leaders for the new regime Nottingham had to go outside the existing bench of bishops whose political outlook had been shaped by their antipathy to the events of the Great Rebellion and who, if not all nonjurors, were less than wholehearted in their support for the post-revolutionary order. Nottingham, then, turned to the circle of London clergy whom he had come to know through his chaplain, John Sharp, and who had been particularly active in the opposition to James II (*ibid.*: 109). From this group many of the new bishops were chosen: in 1689 Simon Patrick was made bishop of Chichester and Stillingfleet bishop of Worcester, replacing the nonjuring

John Lake and William Thomas (both of whom, however, had died before the sentence of deprivation was carried out).

But it was in 1691, with the replacement of still-living deprived nonjuring bishops by clergy loyal to the new regime, that William III and Nottingham broke decisively with the old order; as a high church pamphleteer put it in 1705, the bishoprics 'were filled up with Men of *Moderation*, for now that Name was in Fashion' (Stewart, 1978: 217). After much persuasion from Nottingham, Tillotson became archbishop of Canterbury in the place of Sancroft, Patrick was translated to Ely to replace Sancroft's lieutenant, Francis Turner, Richard Kidder was made bishop of Bath and Wells in the place of Thomas Ken, John Moore displaced William Lloyd as bishop of Norwich, and Edward Fowler became bishop of Gloucester – a post formerly held by Robert Frampton. In the same year John Sharp, who had provoked William's anger by his initial reluctance to take up episcopal office, accepted the archbishopric of York, though both at York and Lincoln (where Tenison was made bishop in 1691) the previous incumbents had died after conforming to the post-revolutionary order; hence Sharp and Tenison were spared the moral scruples of many of their episcopal brethren. Other newly created bishops who had links with Sharp's circle were Robert Grove (bishop of Chichester, 1691), who had joined with Patrick, Stillingfleet and Tillotson in urging Sancroft to defy James (A. Taylor, 1858, IX: 132); Richard Cumberland (bishop of Peterborough, 1691), a friend of Samuel Pepys and Hezekiah Burton (who was involved with Tillotson and Wilkins in the abortive plans for a new scheme of comprehension); and James Gardiner who assisted Patrick's historical investigations at Peterborough and who, at Tenison's recommendation, took his place as bishop of Lincoln when Tenison became primate in 1695. These men were all Cambridge graduates – indeed, the 1690s was the first decade since the Restoration when Cambridge alumni outnumbered Oxford graduates in their numbers on the episcopal bench. The new appointees had, however, all left the university to seek advancement in London – some, like Patrick and Tillotson, having made the move as a result of high church militancy. Their elevation to the episcopate consequently marked a new beginning both for the Church and for their *alma mater*.

The increasing importance of these Cambridge 'moderate' clergy in directing the fortunes of the post-revolutionary church had been previously underlined by the fact that they had figured prominently on the ecclesiastical commission which William had established in September 1689. Indeed, of the 20 divines on this commission 14 were Cambridge alumni, 2 were educated at both universities and a mere 4 were from Oxford. Furthermore, all Oxford's representatives (with one exception) were subsequently to walk out of the commission and proceeded to organise successful opposition to William's proposal for greater religious comprehension on the part of the Established Church; by doing so they prompted the King to look with increasing suspicion on a university which had long prided itself on being 'the friend of princes'. The beginning of this ebbing of Oxford's once-close ties with the monarchy – which was to be so notable a feature of the eighteenth century until the accession of George III – had already been foreshadowed by William's decision to pay a state visit to Cambridge rather than Oxford on 7 October 1689 when he presided at the granting of honorary degrees (recommended by Tillotson) to two prominent 'moderate' divines: Richard Kidder and John Williams (Bennett in SM: 26–9).[1]

Though contemporary usage sanctions the use of the term 'latitudinarian' to describe these 'moderate', largely Cambridge-educated clergy associated with the earl of Nottingham, it (like many party labels) should not be taken to imply a completely homogeneous group with uniform beliefs. The latitudinarians diverged on some theological issues and Sharp parted company with his former colleagues on political matters so that during the reign of Queen Anne Sharp and Tenison found themselves on either side of the party divide, with Sharp the leading tory prelate and Tenison his more ineffectual whig counterpart. The remainder of the latitudinarian bishops, however, sided with the whigs so that at the division of the House of Lords over the Occasional Conformity Bill, Sharp voted for the bill while Tenison, Lloyd, Burnet, Patrick, Moore, Cumberland, Gardiner and Fowler voted against it (N. Sykes, 1934: 35n). Sharp had indeed wandered so far from his former clerical allies both politically and theologically that White Kennett noted in 1712 that Tenison 'sometimes upbraided him [Sharp] . . . and told him it was a new Light; for he had been formerly a profest Latitudinarian; and says he, you were one of the Moderate Men, when I was thought a much higher Church Man at St. Martin's than You at St. Giles's' (BL, Lansdowne MS 1024: 372).

The word 'latitudinarian' was used abusively to suggest a lack of precision in theological matters since the latitudinarians wished to promote comprehension through divesting Anglicanism of what they felt were unnecessary doctrinal and ecclesiastical accretions. Their willingness to accept William as rightful monarch was of a piece with this position. As a group they emphasised the role of natural theology rather than Revela-

---

[1] Richard Kidder: BA, Emmanuel, 1652, fellow 1655; ejected from living in 1662, subsequently conformed; bishop of Bath and Wells, 1691–1703. John Williams: MA Oxford, 1658, incorporated Cambridge, 1660; Boyle lecturer, 1696; bishop of Chichester, 1696–1709.

tion and so, too, in the political realm the latitudinarians tended to favour theories of government based on natural law rather than the almost sacerdotal view of kingship held by their ecclesiastical opponents; similarly, in matters of church government the latitudinarians tended to view episcopal authority as a convenient form of administration rather than a divinely ordained institution. If the orderly government of the nation and the well-being of the Church demanded the deposition of the Lord's Anointed the latitudinarians, however reluctantly, were prepared to accept it in a way that many of their clerical brethren with a more transcendental understanding of both Christianity and the monarchy found impossible. In short, the latitudinarians had, in both their political outlook and their ecclesiology, largely accommodated themselves to the post-revolutionary order for, as Sullivan writes, 'By rejecting a sacred monarchy, Englishmen had virtually rejected a sacred episcopacy' (1982: 131).

Though the great bulk of Anglican clergy swore allegiance to William and Mary after the Glorious Revolution most did so not because they regarded James's actions as disqualifying him from remaining as monarch but rather because they viewed the victorious William as *de facto* King (Kenyon, 1977: 32–4). Consequently, their Filmerite assumptions that royal authority was ordained by God with its origins stretching back to Adam were left unchallenged. The latitudinarians, on the other hand, though they employed all available arguments (including the *de facto* and providentialist theories) to convince themselves and their clerical brethren of the validity of William's authority, none the less tended to place more emphasis than the clerical estate generally on the argument that James had forfeited his title because he had not observed the basic laws of the realm. This was a view advanced by Patrick (Bodl., MS Rawlinson D. 1232: 2–3), Gilbert Burnet and Stillingfleet (Kenyon, 1977: 22); Newton also employed the same line of argument when, as an MP for the university, he attempted to win over those who were wavering in their attitude to the Revolutionary Settlement (Turnbull *et al.*, 1959–77, III: 12). The fact that the latitudinarians envisaged such restrictions on the authority of the Lord's Anointed indicates that they were less inclined to emphasise 'the divinity that doth hedge about a king' than the many Anglican clergy still preoccupied with the cult of the Royal Martyr. This less exalted conception of kingship was of a piece with the latitudinarians' emphasis on natural rather than revealed theology which, in turn, was associated with their interest in recent developments in natural philosophy; their high church opponents, by contrast, gave more weight to the transcendental aspects of both Christianity and the monarchy.

Though the whole aim of Nottingham's ecclesiastical policy had been to avoid dividing the Church, the bishops who came into office in the wake of the Glorious Revolution, and particularly those who had replaced the ejected nonjurors, were inevitably regarded with some suspicion by the many members of the clergy whose consciences were still troubled over their change of allegiance, and with outright hostility by the nonjurors themselves. In the nonjurors' eyes the bishops who had replaced them were men who had broken their oath to their rightful king, and were now betraying the Church while the nonjurors themselves (as Francis Turner put it) steadfastly 'kept up [the Anglican Church] in a Remnant' (BL, Add. 29546: 106v). Ken bluntly described Kidder, his replacement as bishop of Bath and Wells, and Kidder's ecclesiastical allies as 'Latitudinarian Traditours, who would betray the baptismal faith' (N. Sykes, 1934: 332), though it was at Tillotson and Tenison, the post-revolutionary primates, that the nonjurors directed most of their vitriol. 'The congratulations to the new Archbishop', wrote Birch, Tillotson's biographer, 'were soon followed by a very opposite treatment from the Nonjuring party, the greatest part of whom, from the moment of his acceptance of the Archbishopric, pursued him with an unrelenting rage, which lasted during his life, and was by no means appeas'd after his death' (1752: 268). One of the most vehement attacks on Tillotson came from the nonjuror, George Hickes, who, in 1695, answered Gilbert Burnet's funeral sermon on Tillotson (which included an attack on the nonjurors) with a pamphlet in which he characterised Tillotson as a former puritan 'season'd with the principles of resistance and rebellion' (ibid.: 7). Another nonjuror, Charles Lesley, published a pamphlet in the same year (probably with the aid of Hickes) which included an attack on the whole drift of latitudinarian theology: Tillotson's sermons, he asserted, 'are all the genuine effects of Hobbism, which loosens the notions of religion, takes from it all that is spiritual, ridicules whatever is called supernatural: it reduces God to matter, and religion to nature . . . His politics are Leviathan, and his religion is Latitudinarian, which is none' (ibid.: 323–4).

Tenison, Tillotson's successor as primate, also incurred the wrath of the nonjurors, particularly on account of his laudatory oration at Queen Mary's funeral. This oration prompted a pamphlet (attributed to Bishop Ken though perhaps written by George Hickes) which criticised Tenison for not having pointed out Mary's impiety in assisting in her father's overthrow and assailed the archbishop for the 'ill example you have given to the Clergy'. Tenison, argued the pamphleteer, had 'given the World reason to conclude that your Conscience misgave you, being Sensible, that in reproving her, you must have reproved yourself' and Tenison's critic appealed to the judgement of 'my reverend brethren of the clergy who are untainted with latitudinarian leaven' (Carpenter, 1948: 405–6;

Benham 1889: 306). The nonjurors also dwelt on what they regarded as the irony of the appointment of an archbishop who did not believe in the importance of the Apostolic Succession. Tenison, wrote Hickes, was one of those 'Gentlemen of this averse Spirit to antiquity, who think Episcopacy not strictly necessary for the Being, but only most convenient for the Well-being of the Church' (Every, 1956: 116). Hearne, with customary malice, summed up the nonjurors' objections to Tenison: Tenison, he wrote, was 'the heavy archbishop of Canterbury', one of the 'virulent Enemies of the Church of England and Universities, such as are for bringing in a Comprehension and establishing everything that makes for the Whiggs and Presbyterians' (Hearne, 1885–1921, II: 115; Carpenter, 1948: 438).

Nor was this hostility to the newly created bishops restricted to the nonjurors. Among those clergy who conformed there was also considerable animus against their fathers-in-God who, it was felt, were not adequately protecting the purity of the faith or the privileges of the Established Church. Soon after the Revolution there are some indications of this hostility towards the latitudinarians on the part of many of the lower clergy: thus when Tillotson was proposed as the prolocutor of Convocation by Sharp in 1689 he gained fewer than a third of the votes and his rival Dr William Jane, canon of Christ Church, whose watchword was 'Nolumus leges Angliae mutari' (Let us not alter the laws of England), was overwhelmingly elected and proceeded to organise successful opposition to William's proposed plans for comprehension (Bennett, 1975: 47; Wordsworth, 1874: 32–3).

This clerical truculence remained latent for a time but, as William's counsels came to be more and more dominated by the pro-foreign war and pro-City 'junto' whigs after the election of 1695, the 'Country' party began to exploit the clergy's discontents and in 1696 came the manifesto of the high church revolt: Atterbury's *A letter to a Convocation man* (Bennett, 1975: 47–8). In this *Letter* Atterbury dwelt on the prevalence of irreligion and immorality which had been encouraged not only by deists and Socinians but also by an enemy within the gates: 'Latitudinarians, Denyers of Mysteries and pretended Explainers of them' (*ibid.*: 48). This suspicion of latitudinarian theology surfaced again when the Lower House of Convocation presented its formal complaint against Bishop Gilbert Burnet's *Exposition of the Thirty-Nine Articles* in 1701 – a book, it was claimed, which 'tends to introduce such a Latitude and Diversity of opinions as the Articles were fram'd to avoid' (Every, 1956: 101). Even a moderate tory layman like Harley joined in the chorus against the latitudinarians, warning Tenison in 1702: 'I must tell you what you have nobody else faithful enough to do it, you are entirely under the influence of those who have not only discharged themselves from al obligations of religion, but also have for many years been promoting, first Socianisme, then arrianisme & now deisme' (Holmes, 1967: 260).

To the latitudinarian-inclined bishops the disputes over Convocation appeared to be a deliberately orchestrated campaign to undermine their power within the Church and hence the Church's adherence to the Revolutionary Settlement. John Moore (to whom Hearne referred as a member of 'the low Church Party' (1885–1921, I: 200)) wrote to Tenison in 1700 to recommend that no licence be granted for holding Convocation business since 'if there should be, it will be thought the effect of Mr. Atterbury's book' (Carpenter, 1948: 251). Later Gibson, in a letter to Wake written in 1716, characterised the Convocation controversy as having been 'raised on purpose to render the archbishop, and that part of the bench which had distinguished itself in favour of the Protestant succession, odious to the nation; as if they were destroying the constitution of the Church and the liberties of the inferior clergy' (N. Sykes, 1935: 451).

The tension between the newly created bishops and many of the clergy was further exacerbated by the reforming spirit of some of the former. With considerable vigour and initiative these bishops set about instituting reforms which were meant to take account of the Church's changed position after the Toleration Act of 1689; instead of relying on the power of the State in the tradition of Laud and Sancroft they attempted to revitalise the Church's own administrative and disciplinary machinery. Thus Stillingfleet in his 'Proposals for Reformations in the Church' asked whether 'the Canons requiring the coming to Church, and the receiving the Sacrament, under a penalty should be altered', 'the Kingdom at present seeming inclinable to grant a Comprehension to some and in a manner a Toleration to all Persons' (Lambeth Palace Library, MS 1743: 111). The latitudinarian-inclined bishops were also closely identified with voluntary bodies such as the Societies for the Reformation of Manners which relied on individual initiative, rather than the power of the State, to lift the moral and religious tone of the nation; these societies were also associated with the goals of comprehension because of their openness to dissenters as well as Anglicans. Consequently, such bodies tended to be viewed with suspicion by high churchmen – Sacheverell, for example, claimed that the goal of the Societies for the Reformation of Manners was 'to overturn Its [the Church of England's] Ancient *genuine Constitution*' (Isaacs, 1982: 401; Bahlman, 1957).

In the year before the Glorious Revolution Gilbert Burnet wrote of the Church of England that it was lying 'yet in many great corruptions. The generall neglect of the duties of the Pastorall Charge, the Profanation of

Church discipline in those Corrupt Courts that are called the Spirituall Courts; pluralities and Nonresidence . . . have made me conclude long that wee lookt like a Church that was either to be quite cast off by God or that was to be purged by a firy triall' (J. J. Hughes, 1977: 224). Once appointed to the episcopate Burnet set about righting such wrongs with characteristic vigour. His book on *Pastoral care* (1692) – which was eulogised by Tillotson – reviewed the different aspects of church life and argued that wholesale ecclesiastical reform was required; he also included an historial survey, first of the growth of popish corruption and then of the slow loss of Protestant zeal which it was his life's ambition to rekindle. Not surprisingly, Burnet's biting criticism of the state of the Church of England provoked considerable animosity from many of the clergy; Burnet himself commented pugnaciously that the book 'helped not a little to heighten the indignation of bad clergymen against me; they looked on it as writ on design to expose them to the nation; for reformation and moderation are the two things that bad clergymen hate the most' (Clarke and Foxcroft, 1907: 314).

Though many of their opponents remained implacable, the latitudinarian-inclined bishops and their supporters among the lower clergy were none the less anxious to win over both clerical and lay opinion to their side. With considerable energy and ability they set about publicising their theological opinions and the church order which was associated with them, seeking new forms of expression which would capture public imagination. One of the most successful vehicles for popularising latitudinarian theology, at a time when it was fiercely opposed within the Church, was the Boyle lectures which were founded in 1691 under the terms of Robert Boyle's will with the object of defending Christianity against the attacks of 'Atheists, Theists [deists], Pagans, Jews, and Mahometans' (Jacob, 1976: 159). Without Tenison's aid this institution may have foundered since Boyle's endowment was inadequate, but Tenison supplemented it with 'a yearly stipend of £50 per annum for ever' (Carpenter, 1948: 34n); Tenison also had considerable say in choosing the lecturers, and Bentley and Clarke were among those he appointed. In an important work Jacob (1976: 143–61) has shown in detail how the Boyle lectures were colonised at their inception by the latitudinarians (with the support of the Finch family) and used to popularise their theological views. Newtonian natural philosophy (albeit of a highly simplified and selective form) was used by Bentley, Clarke, Harris and Derham (*ibid.*: 178) in their Boyle lectures as a means of demonstrating that the highest reaches of human reason were in accord with natural religion. The Boyle lectures, suggests Jacob, reflected the latitudinarians' determination not to let the Revolutionary Settlement become 'a victory for the "crafty and ill-principled"', and the theological opinions popularised by the Boyle lecturers were intended to 'forge among Protestants a consensus upon which the church's moral leadership would rest secure' (*ibid.*: 144); elsewhere Jacob describes the Boyle lecturers 'as the spokesmen of the church in this period [the 1690s]' (though conceding that the latitudinarians were under attack during the reign of Queen Anne) (*ibid.*: 157).

But though the Boyle lectures were certainly intended to stem the tide of scepticism among the leisured classes the theological views they popularised did not command universal assent within the Church. It is symptomatic that Bentley, the first and perhaps most influential of the Boyle lecturers, was later involved in a long dispute over the epistles of Phalaris with Atterbury, the champion of the high church party, in the course of which Atterbury suggested that Bentley's critical methods led to scepticism about the divine inspiration of the Bible (Bennett, 1975: 42). Clarke and Whiston – the two other Boyle lecturers most actively involved in popularising Newton's work – also provoked considerable opposition from the high churchmen and both were censured by Convocation. The Boyle lectures may have been intended to help shore up the social and religious establishment, as Jacob suggests (*ibid.*: 179), but the choice of lecturers and the style of theological exposition (including the use of Newtonian natural philosophy) also reflect the deep divisions within that religious establishment. The Boyle lectures not only served Boyle's professed aim – 'for proving the Christian Religion against notorious Infidels' – but they were also another means of popularising the latitudinarians' understanding of divinity and church order and thus of winning over both lay and clerical support at a time when the authority of the 'moderate' or 'latitudinarian' bishops was under serious attack.

In their efforts to win support within the Established Church the newly consecrated latitudinarian bishops naturally gave special attention to the universities – 'the nurseries of the clergy' – and, in particular, to Cambridge, the *alma mater* of Tillotson, Sharp, Tenison, Stillingfleet, Patrick, Moore, Kidder and Grove. Just as Cambridge high churchmen like Matthew Wren and William Sancroft used their influence in the period between the Restoration and the Glorious Revolution to advance those of like mind within Cambridge, so too the latitudinarian bishops used their powers of patronage to gain influential positions for those within the university holding political and religious views similar to their own. Such latitudinarian clients were frequently in conflict with those who had gained office within the university before 1688 and in Cambridge, as in the country as a whole, the period following the Glorious Revolution was characterised by acrimonious religious and political debate.

Since the archbishop of Canterbury was in a position to play a particularly influential role within the university, the ejection of Sancroft, the chief patron of the Cambridge high churchmen, and his replacement by Tillotson in 1691 had special significance for Cambridge – particularly since Tillotson had been compelled to forfeit his Clare Hall fellowship in 1661 at the insistence of Gunning, one of Sancroft's episcopal colleagues. Tillotson, who was archbishop of Canterbury for only three years (1691–4), had less influence within Cambridge than his long-lived successor, Tenison, but his choice of clients indicated a significant departure from the policies that had hitherto prevailed within the university. Among those whom Tillotson 'was desirous to promote' after his appointment as primate was his former pupil from Clare Hall, Dr Thomas Burnet (Birch, 1752: 277), for whom Tillotson obtained the post of chaplain-in-ordinary to the King, and later that of clerk to the (royal) closet. Indeed, according to Oldmixon, Tillotson favoured Burnet as his successor and on Tillotson's death Burnet's name was proposed 'with some Prospect of Success, till upon a Representation of Certain Bishops, that some of this Writings were too Sceptical, another Divine [Tenison] was pitch'd upon, and made Archbishop of Canterbury' (Kubrin, 1968: 145–6). After Tillotson's death Burnet was no longer shielded from the hostility of those who regarded his works (particularly the *Archaeologia philosophica* (1692) which departed radically from the biblical account of the creation) as heretical and his advancement within the Church halted abruptly. Another of Tillotson's Cambridge acquaintances was John Laughton, the librarian of Trinity (and of the university as a whole), and one of Newton's few close friends within Cambridge. Like Newton, Laughton was active in promoting a more whole-hearted acceptance of the Glorious Revolution within the university and it was he who, on 14 February 1689, preached the university's thanksgiving sermon 'for the deliverance of the nation from Popery and arbitrary power' (C. H. Cooper, 1842–1908, IV: 2). Not surprisingly, then, the nonjuring Hearne regarded him as 'a rank Whig, a great Talker, and very violent in his aspersions of the true Church of England Men' (Hearne, 1885–1921, I: 53). Laughton attempted to use his influence with Tillotson to obtain for Newton the post of master of the Charterhouse in succession to Thomas Burnet. But Burnet's hopes of further advancement were dashed and the vacancy never eventuated; none the less it is significant that Laughton could report to Newton that the archbishop was his 'friend' (Turnbull *et al.*, 1959–77, III: 184). Whiston, a member of Tillotson's own college, Clare Hall, and an early disciple of Newton, also became a protégé of Tillotson. Whiston records in his *Memoirs* that after he became a tutor at Clare Archbishop Tillotson 'to encourage me in that employment' (1753: 24) sent his nephew to be one of Whiston's pupils. Tillotson also appointed Samuel Bradford, a graduate of

Corpus, as a tutor to his two grandsons and in 1693 collated him to the rectory of Mary-le-Bow in London. Bradford later served as a Boyle lecturer (1699) and as master of Corpus (1716–24), and his loyalty to the Hanoverian succession led to his elevation to the bishopric of Carlisle in 1718 and later that of Rochester in 1723.

Though Tenison was regarded by his contemporaries as being a 'heavy' bishop, lacking the preaching ability of Tillotson or the resolute adherence to lost causes of Sancroft, it was Tenison who did most to help steer the Church through the troubled waters of post-revolutionary politics. Gibson, who served as Tenison's chaplain and later attempted to continue his ecclesiastical policies, wrote of him in 1717 that the principle 'upon which he acted in the whole course of his administration' was the conviction 'that there was no way to preserve the Church but by preserving the present establishment in the State, and that there was far greater probability that the Tories would be able to destroy our present establishment in the State, than that the dissenters would be able to destroy our establishment in the Church' (N. Sykes, 1935: 451). These views Tenison actively set out to inculcate within his *alma mater* as well as in the Church as a whole.

Tenison, of course, had most influence within his own college of Corpus and he exercised close supervision over its affairs with the result that it came to be known (as Kerrick, a fellow of Corpus, claimed) for being 'remarkably attach'd to the Revolution and the succession in the House of Hanover' (Hartshorne, 1905: 53). When the mastership of Corpus became vacant in 1698 (three years after Tenison's appointment as primate) Tenison was actively involved in ensuring the election of Thomas Green, his domestic chaplain, as master and even after his resignation from the mastership in 1716 Green remained active in ensuring that the whig interest 'may always flourish in the college' (Nichols, 1817–58, VI: 789). Tenison also used his influence to advance promising younger fellows of Corpus. When he became bishop of Lincoln in 1691 he appointed as his chaplain Charles Kidman, a fellow of Corpus, who became well known within the university both on account of his abilities as a tutor and because of his strong whig sympathies. Tenison, writes Masters, did not retain Kidman's services when he became archbishop because of 'the clamour raised against him as a person of Latitudinarian principles, from a Sermon preached before the University, on "Private Judgement in Matters of Religion"' (1831: 372); but he continued to take an interest in Kidman's career and advanced him to a rectory in Essex in 1706, 'As soon as the Work he had undertaken [as tutor] could be safely committed to other Hands' (Hartshorne, 1905: 53). Tenison also acted as patron to Arthur Ashley Sykes, a former pupil of Kidman's, who became known as one of the arch-latitudinarians of the eighteenth century, being a zealous defender of both Samuel Clarke and Benjamin Hoadly. Sykes owed his first ecclesiastical appointment – a vicarage in Kent (1713) – to Tenison, and the archbishop, wrote Sykes's biographer, Disney (a late eighteenth-century Cambridge Unitarian), 'had a great personal regard for Mr Sykes; and, having been formerly fellow of Benet college [Corpus], was not only a very considerable benefactor to that society, but a very generous patron to several of its members' (1785: 5). Another such fellow of Corpus who benefited from Tenison's patronage was Benjamin Ibbot who, in 1707, was made the archbishop's chaplain and librarian and, through Tenison's influence, was appointed Boyle lecturer in 1713 and 1714. Ibbot later became a close friend of Samuel Clarke who, in 1726, published a posthumous edition of Ibbot's sermons.

Nor was Tenison's influence restricted to his old college. After the death of Queen Mary in 1694 William set up a commission to recommend suitable clerics for appointments to ecclesiastical offices within the royal gift. The members of this commission were the two archbishops (Tenison and Sharp) and Bishops Burnet, Patrick, Lloyd and Stillingfleet (and John Moore of Ely after Stillingfleet's death in 1699) – all of whom (with the exception of Lloyd) had been advanced to the episcopate after the Glorious Revolution and all of whom (save the Scottish Burnet) held Cambridge degrees. As primate Tenison naturally had considerable influence within this commission particularly as Sharp, his fellow archbishop, came more and more to side with the tories – in contrast to his colleagues – and so his recommendations were frequently ignored (Ravitch, 1966: 99; Carpenter, 1948: 167–76). Tenison was therefore closely involved in choosing candidates for appointments to royal benefices from 1694 until William's death in 1704. Quite apart from the authority this gave him (and his latitudinarian colleagues on the commission) in the Church at large it also increased his importance within Cambridge, particularly at Trinity, the mastership of which was in the royal gift. Thus Tenison appears to have used his influence to advance the career of John Montagu (master of Trinity, 1683–1700 and dean of Durham, 1700–28)[2] who, though undistinguished as master of Trinity, none the less had loyally supported the Revolutionary Settlement and, as the fourth son of Edward Montagu, first earl of Sandwich, came from an influential family with whig connections. According to Conduitt, after Montagu had resigned the mastership in 1700, Tenison offered the post to Newton if he would first take orders; when Newton declined the offer, writes Conduitt, 'Tennison pestered him to take any preferment in the Church saying to him "Why will you

---

[2] Thus in 1695 Montagu sent Tenison an effusive letter of thanks for nominating him to the position of clerk of the (royal) closet (Lambeth Palace Library, MS 942: 107).

not? You know more divinity than all of us together.'' "Why then", said Sir Isaac, "I shall be able to do you more service then if I was in orders"' (King's College, Cambridge, Keynes MS 130). In the event the Ecclesiastical Commission unanimously chose Richard Bentley as master of Trinity (Wordsworth, 1842, II: 448), a decision in which Tenison must have played an influential part. Tenison had earlier helped to secure Bentley's appointment as the first Boyle lecturer in 1692 (Jacob, 1976: 155), Boyle's trustees choosing Bentley 'principally because of Tenison's high opinion of him' (Monk, 1830–3, I: 38). Bentley and Tenison, then, had a long association and Bentley appears to have regarded the archbishop as closely involved in his appointment as master of Trinity: soon after taking up the post he wrote to Tenison to assure the archbishop that he was well received as master and that he hoped 'shortly to wait in person upon your Grace' (Wordsworth, 1842, I: 186).

Next to the archbishop of Canterbury the bishop with the most influence in Cambridge affairs was the incumbent of the see of Ely which, between the Restoration and the Glorious Revolution, had been ruled by a succession of Cambridge high churchmen – Matthew Wren, Benjamin Laney, Peter Gunning and Francis Turner. But in 1691 (after the ejection of the nonjuring Francis Turner) the office passed to Simon Patrick who, appropriately, had been forced to leave Cambridge in 1662 because of high church opposition. Like Tenison, Patrick took an active interest in Cambridge affairs and, naturally, was particularly sympathetic to those members of the university who shared his political and religious views. In 1701 Patrick appointed Bentley archdeacon of Ely and in the following year offered Whiston a prebend's post (though the offer later had to be withdrawn) (Whiston, 1753: 180). In the faction-fighting at Clare, Patrick intervened on the side of the whigs and, in response to a letter from Whiston, wrote to Samuel Blythe, the master, on 7 December 1697 recommending Richard Laughton[3] – a keen whig and one of the first in Cambridge to promote the study of Newtonian natural philosophy – for a foundation fellowship. Patrick added the warning that, if Laughton did not gain this position, 'it will not hear well among those who bear a respect to you, and to the Colledg' (Wardale, 1903: 128).

Patrick's successor as bishop of Ely was John Moore, who had served as bishop of Norwich from 1691 to 1708. Both at Norwich and Ely Moore attracted a number of promising young Cambridge graduates to serve as his chaplains. As a former fellow of Clare Moore naturally had particularly close ties with that college and among his chaplains were Richard

---

[3] Not to be confused with John Laughton, his namesake at Trinity.

Laughton, William Whiston and Charles Morgan (a keen Newtonian, elected master of Clare in 1726), all Clare graduates. Like Patrick, Moore attempted to intervene at Clare on the side of the whig Richard Laughton of whom he wrote to the master that 'the great piety, wisdom and learning of good Mr. Laughton have made him a blessing and ornament to all places he has been' (*ibid.*: 125). Later, Moore also wrote to Blythe 'earnestly to recommend' Charles Morgan, another of his chaplains, for a Clare fellowship (*ibid.*: 136).

However, Moore's most distinguished client – Samuel Clarke – was from Caius though he was recommended to Moore by Whiston (a fellow of Clare) who had become acquainted with Clarke through their common enthusiasm for Newtonian natural philosophy. Moore, wrote Hoadly in his introduction to Clarke's *Works*, 'fixed his eyes upon Mr. Clarke as a young man of genius much exalted above the common rank, and promising great things to the world in his riper years' (Moore, 1885: 20). Moore aided Clarke in obtaining a number of benefices, culminating in the influential living of St James's Church, Westminster, in 1709 (Ferguson, 1976: 40) and it was Clarke whom Moore chose as his executor. Also from Caius was Thomas Pyle – a staunch whig and a supporter of Hoadly in the Bangorian controversy.

Moore also aided the career of the historian, Dr Samuel Knight (MA Trinity, 1706) whom he made a prebend at Ely in 1714 and later presented to a rectory in Huntingdonshire (Nichols, 1812–15, V: 354). Knight's two major works – *The life of Colet* (1724) and *The life of Erasmus* (1726) – place strong emphasis on political and religious liberty and were both dedicated to Sir Spencer Compton, the whig Speaker of the House of Commons; he also wrote an admiring (but unpublished) life of Bishop Patrick (CUL, Add. 20). Peter Needham, a fellow of St John's from 1698 to 1716, also benefited from Moore's encouragement of his classical studies (McKitterick, 1986: 73) – something reflected in Needham's dedication to Moore of two of his works. Needham's *University sermon* of 1716 is a plea for religious toleration; it is not surprising, then, that Hearne regarded him as 'a most rash Whig' (1885–1921, III: 172).

Moore was praised by Clarke, in an introduction to his edition of Moore's sermons, for being 'so steady in his Adherence to the real Interest of his Country, through all Changes of Times; and Eminent in his Zeal for promoting, upon all Occasions, the true Spirit of the Protestant Religion' (J. Moore, 1715: i–ii). Indeed, even posthumously, Moore helped advance the cause of the Revolutionary Settlement since his widely renowned library was bought at the sale of his estate by the Crown and given to Cambridge as a reward for its loyalty (at least when compared with

Oxford) during the 1715 uprising – a gift which prompted an Oxford wit
to produce the oft-quoted epigram:

> The King observing with judicious eyes,
> The state of both his Universities,
> To Oxford sent a troop of horse; and why?
> That learned body wanted loyalty:
> To Cambridge books he sent, as well discerning
> How much that loyal body wanted learning.
>   (in Toynbee, 1927: 106)

The gift of Moore's library to Cambridge was an appropriate gesture since
throughout his episcopal career Moore, like his friends Tillotson, Tenison
and Patrick maintained an active interest in the affairs of his *alma mater* and
used his considerable influence to cultivate clients within the university as
a means of winning over Cambridge to a greater enthusiasm for the post-
1688 political order.

Appropriately, Tillotson, Tenison, Patrick and Moore were following the
lead of their patron, Nottingham, who, as early as 1689, had shown his
interest in Cambridge's internal affairs by helping to gain for King's the
right of a free election for its provostship (Leigh, 1899: 158). Although
Nottingham was himself an Oxford man he had family ties with Cambridge, particularly at Christ's where his uncle, Sir Henry Finch, had
established two fellowships which were generally held by members of the
Finch family. In 1721, nine years before his death, Nottingham received
the public thanks of the university for his answer to Whiston's attack on
the Athanasian Creed (Van Mildert, 1823, i: 24) – a work which Nottingham had published at the urging of Waterland, a resolute defender of
both orthodoxy and the Hanoverian succession, who was active in
promoting the Finch family's political interests within Cambridge (LRO,
Finch MSS, Lit.pap.10).

But in return for his devotion to the interests of the Church and the
universities Nottingham expected Cambridge's compliance with the
post-revolutionary regime. When in September 1691, the heads of colleges made a vague reply to the royal directive which required a list of all
persons who had refused to take the oaths he responded by tartly
describing their reply as 'expressed in such general and ambiguous terms
for the most part as gave little satisfaction' and made it clear that 'her
Majesty expects they [the heads] doe every one of them forthwith proceed
to fill up the vacant places in each College and Hall pursuant to the Act of
Parliament without any connivance' (CUA, Lett. 14.22.3). He also sought
to discourage the revival of high church claims about the authority of
Convocation which exacerbated conflict between Church and Crown; in

this he was supported by his episcopal allies and in 1701 Simon Patrick wrote to Nottingham that he was 'highly delighted . . . in your abhorrence of those contentions which now lamentably trouble & endanger our Church. I can but bewail them, but hope I shall never engage in them' (BL, Add. 29584: 86).

Just as Nottingham had only accepted William as his rightful monarch after much deliberation, it also took Archbishop Sharp's persuasion for him to abjure the claims of the Pretender and to acquiesce in the Hanoverian succession (Dickinson, 1977: 40); none the less, on 22 September 1714 he was among those who delivered Cambridge's loyal address to George I (C. H. Cooper, 1842–1908, IV: 122). Having accepted the Hanoverians as rightful monarchs Nottingham continued to use his influence to lead the Church (and with it Cambridge University) away from the sterile paths of nonjuring and nostalgia for the Stuarts. After his dismissal as president of the council in 1716 Nottingham learned the painful lesson that the future of the Church lay with the whigs (B. W. Hill, 1976: 159–60) – the new connection between the Finch family, the whigs and Cambridge being symbolised in February 1726 by the marriage of the whig Somerset (chancellor of Cambridge) to Nottingham's third daughter, Charlotte.

This political metamorphosis was at first too much for many in Cambridge to accept and Henry Finch (Nottingham's fourth son) was defeated when he stood as MP for the university in 1720 in the whig interest. This led Henry's brother, Lord Finch, to express his disappointment in a letter to Colbatch (a fellow of Trinity) that 'a son of my Lord Nottingham should be so very disagreeable to the University' and Lord Finch expressed his belief that though 'many may have led the Church party with better success and some with art may have betrayed them, but this I will pretend to affirm that no man living has ever served them with zeal and sincerity equal to My Lord Nottingham' (BL. Add. 22908: 104). But Cambridge soon learned greater political wisdom and in 1727 elected Edward Finch (Nottingham's fifth son) as one of its burgesses despite the fact that the Finch family was now closely identified with the whig cause – a transformation borne out by a letter of 1728 seeking the Finches' aid lest his fellowship at Peterhouse where 'the Tories have the majority' be taken by 'an Enemy to the Government' (NU, MS Mellish 155–94/52). Edward Finch became a willing tool of Newcastle, and his continual re-election until 1768 (three years before his death) indicates the political torpor that descended on Cambridge after the accession of George II.

It was the Nottingham circle, then, which, in Cambridge as in the Church at large, laboured most actively to reconcile a generation of clergy formed in the period of reaction to the Interregnum to the changed realities of post-revolutionary England. Somerset, Cambridge's chancellor, allied himself with the court whigs (apart from a few months in Harley's cabinet in 1710) (Holmes, 1967: 225–6) but his involvement in university affairs was relatively slight. In January 1695 he urged the university to hasten its publication of the customary verses on the death of the Queen – though he appears to have been prompted more by the fact that Oxford had already issued theirs than by any fears of disaffection at Cambridge (CUA, Lett. 14: 28*). Soon afterwards, in late 1695 and early 1696, Somerset was involved in reviving the Cambridge University Press though it appears to have been Bentley who played the most important role in those proceedings (McKenzie, 1976: 323) – Somerset did, however, contribute eight hundred pounds to the project (CUA, Lett. 14: 30*).

His most obvious intervention on behalf of the whig interest within Cambridge was his letters in support of his kinsman, the whig Henry Boyle, when he stood for election as MP for the university in 1692 and 1698 (*ibid.*: 24*, 35*). Boyle was elected on both these occasions and at the elections of 1698 and 1701, but at the 1705 election he moved to the seat of Westminster no doubt sensing that, despite Somerset's support, the tide of high church feeling was running too strongly within the university to permit the election of anyone but a tory candidate. In any case Somerset's scanty bestowal of patronage within the university meant that he commanded little electoral influence at Cambridge: the tory, Thomas Tudway, the professor of music, remarked apropos of Somerset's meagre record as a patron that 'the chancellor rides us all, without a bit in our mouths' (C. H. Cooper, 1842–1908, IV: 76). Moreover, Somerset was of such an imperious disposition that he found it extremely difficult not to offend the university's strongly developed sense of the sanctity of its own traditions. A tactful attempt by the vice-chancellor, Edward Lany, in 1708 to persuade Somerset that it was contrary to precedent for anyone except members of the Senate to draft the wording of a royal address led to a furious rejoinder from the chancellor who curtly informed Lany 'that if I was at Cambridge, you are nothing, whatever you may now fancy your self to be' (BL, Harleian MS 7030: 282). None the less, Somerset continued to be thwarted since the heads (with only Ellis of Caius dissenting) subsequently agreed with Lany that 'sending up the Address to the Chancellor, before It had passt into an Act by the 2 Houses, was a new practice, & not fit to be comply'd with' (*ibid.*: 282v). Somerset treated even his family and aristocratic neighbours with Olympian disdain (M. H. Black, 1984: 88) and his reputation for arrogance was such that at his death in 1748 Horace Walpole remarked that 'His whole stupid life was a series of pride and tyranny' (J. Cannon, 1984: 172n). One can imagine, then, his

contempt for those so far beneath him socially as Cambridge dons and his
rage at their reluctance to comply with his commands – all of which would
have further weakened his interest in university affairs. Somerset's already
small role within Cambridge faded to near insignificance after he withdrew into private life in 1715 following a violent disagreement with
George I (Anon., 1748: 61–2). Though Somerset remained chancellor
until his death in 1748 he was increasingly overshadowed on the Cambridge stage by the duke of Newcastle – particularly after Newcastle's
election as high steward in 1737 (Cook, 1935: 253).

Somerset, then, played little part in the creation of whig Cambridge and
even Nottingham only belatedly used his influence to help transform the
university's political loyalties, having reluctantly shed his attachment to
the tory party. Until some time after the accession of the Hanoverians it
was, then, former members of the Nottingham circle such as Tillotson,
Tenison, Patrick or Moore – together with their Cambridge clients – who
did most to lay the foundations for Cambridge's subsequent reputation as
the whig university. As the clash between the upper and lower houses of
Convocation became more heated such bishops and their supporters
became more and more convinced that the Church's future lay with the
whigs – the growing polarisation in both religion and politics being
evident in the remark of a pamphleteer in 1704 that 'all the noise about
High and Low Church . . . signifies no more than Whig and Tory' (Shapin,
1981: 205).

Within the university it was the protégés of the latitudinarian bishops
who formed much of the core of whig support. At the 1698 election
Tillotson's client, John Laughton, was active in promoting the candidature of the whig James Montagu (later one of Sacheverell's prosecutors) as university burgess though, in the event, he was defeated by the
tory, Anthony Hammond. In May 1702 Richard Bentley seized the
opportunity to demonstrate the university's (and his own) rejection of the
high church tactics in the Convocation debate by obtaining Cambridge
doctorates for William Nicolson, White Kennett and Edmund Gibson:
three Oxford clerics who had been denied degrees at their *alma mater*
because of their opposition to Atterbury and his claims (Bennett in SM:
64–5). It was Bentley, too, who, along with Daniel Waterland, ensured
the passage of a university grace in April 1716 congratulating the King on
the suppression of the jacobite uprising, despite concerted attempts to
have it vetoed (C. H. Cooper, 1842–1908, IV: 143). Bentley's action owed
much, as always, to his personal ambition for he hoped to ingratiate
himself with the whig politician, Townshend (W. R. Ward, 1958: 65),
who had prompted the King to give Bishop Moore's valuable library to
Cambridge in the previous year (HMC, Townshend MSS: 341) – a gift

which led to a courteous exchange of compliments between Waterland (who served as vice-chancellor in 1715) and Townshend (CUA, Lett. 17: 8). The aim of this royal largesse was to give support to those members of the university who actively defended the Hanoverian succession; such dons continued to face considerable opposition within the university: Bentley commented that as a result of the royal address of 1716 'the fury of the whole disaffected and Jacobite party here against me and Mr Waterland is inexpressible'. Bentley added that the ministry's treatment of himself and Waterland would help determine whether they 'make the University their own, or let the Jacobite party carry all here before them, and the King's present of books continue rotting in their baggs' (Wordsworth, 1842, II: 527). Waterland and Bentley were, however, duly rewarded in 1717 – the former with a royal chaplaincy and the latter with the Regius professorship of divinity (though he gained this post more through his own sharp political skills than through the good will of the court).

The gift of Bishop Moore's library to Cambridge in 1715 was part of a more general strategy on the part of the new Hanoverian regime to strengthen its support within the universities and the Church more generally. A number of influential figures – notably Archbishop Wake and Thomas Parker (from 1721 earl of Macclesfield) – took the view that the only way to achieve such an aim was to institute a governmental visitation of the universities. Rumours of this proposed visitation led Brook Rand to write to his Corpus colleague, Samuel Kerrick (Tenison's former protégé), on 26 December 1718 that 'A Vysitation general would be greatly to [be] wyshed since nothing would more tend to the good of the Nation in preventing so many malcontents to [be] Dispersed by the University all over England' (Corpus Christi, Cambridge, Hartshorne MS XI: 52). However, the proposed bill for establishing such a commission lapsed into political oblivion in 1719 following the defeat of the Peerage Bill, the whigs' chief legislative initiative (B. Williams, 1932: 403, 410).[4] None the less, Parker, who was a resolute foe of the high churchmen, as his involvement in the Sacheverell prosecution indicates, continued to devote considerable energy to attempting to win over the universities to the whig cause and among his most active agents in this endeavour were the clients of the latitudinarian bishops.

Parker's chief agent within Cambridge was Thomas Bell, a fellow of Trinity, Parker's old college, who energetically sought out other whiggishly inclined dons; in 1715 he could report to Parker that 'I have some very fast and worthy friends here, who bear a just sense of what is due to

---

[4] On the failure of this and other eighteenth-century attempts to instigate parliamentary reform of the universities see Gascoigne, 1989b.

his Majesty and his Ministers' (BL, Stowe MS 750: 165). Among these 'friends' was the formidable master of Trinity, Richard Bentley, though his overriding concern with advancing his own career made him an uncertain ally (*ibid.*: 155v, 219). More reliable was Richard Laughton, a former chaplain of Bishop Moore, to whom Parker entrusted the education of his son, George (a future president of the Royal Society), in 1715. Laughton provided Parker with reports on Cambridge's internal politics which Parker evidently valued since, in a letter of 29 December 1716, Laughton thanked him for 'entertaining so favourable an opinion of me, and of my poor endeavours to serve the publick' (BL, Stowe MS 799: 138). In the same letter Laughton praised Parker for his 'very generous and uncommon concern for the true interest of our University' (*ibid.*: 138), a clear indication of Laughton's strong whig sympathies. It was Laughton who recommended to Bell that he use Parker's influence to help ensure the election of the whiggish William Towers as master of Christ's in 1723 (BL, Stowe MS 750: 167). Towers (in the words of the antiquary, William Cole) subsequently 'always behaved himself steadily in the Hanoverian Interest, and that at a Juncture when it was most wanted' (BL, Add. 5821: p. 78)

Laughton was probably also involved in Bell's successful machinations at Queens' which resulted in the election of John Davies (another former chaplain of Bishop Moore and an ally of Bentley) as president in 1717. Davies dutifully acknowledged his indebtedness to Parker and promised to 'retain a lasting sense of your goodness, & [to] take it as an honour to receive your commands' (BL, Stowe MS 750: 252). Another of Moore's protégés who reported to Parker on the progress of whiggery within Cambridge was Peter Needham of St John's who, in February 1719, assured him that 'Disaffection to his Majesty's Person and Government . . . seems to wear off daily, [and] I much hope it will quite disappear in time' (PRO, State Papers 35/15: 134).[5] In November that same year the whiggish Brook Rand, after criticising the actions of Thomas Gooch, the tory vice-chancellor, added that he was pleased to hear from Kerrick 'that protestantism increases & that we may hope that one time or other to get the Majority of our side in Cambridge' (Corpus Christi College, Cambridge, Hartshorne MS XI: 60). Despite the optimism of Needham and Rand much of Cambridge remained obstinately tory for at least another decade. A whole generation of dons had been reared in a university which, until after 1688, was overshadowed by the cult of the Royal Martyr; they were reluctant, then, to abandon the high claims for both Crown and Altar with which the tory party remained associated – though, largely thanks to

[5] I owe this reference to Dr J. P. Jenkins.

the influence of the latitudinarian-inclined bishops and their clients, this was eventually achieved.

After the failure of the proposed parliamentary visitation of 1719 the whig ministers largely lost interest in direct intervention in the universities' affairs. As we shall see, the possibility of a visitation did surface again briefly in 1749 – prompted once again by a jacobite uprising which focused attention on the universities' ambivalent attitude to the Hanoverian regime (though it was Oxford that was the chief target of whig complaint) (W. R. Ward, 1958: 175) – but like its predecessor this planned visitation never eventuated. 'Ministries', as Porter succinctly put it, 'let sleeping dons lie' (1982: 178). Within the Church, however, some influential figures continued to hold the view that had prompted Archbishop Wake's involvement in the proposed visitation of 1719: that if the universities could be won over to a firmer adherence to the whig cause then this would help change the attitudes of the clergy more generally and thus gain for the Church a stronger position within the post-revolutionary order. Indeed, Bishop Gibson acknowledged that it was his hope of bringing 'the clergy and the two universities at least to be easy, under a whig administration' (N. Sykes, 1926: 95n) which prompted him to institute the system of Whitehall preachers in 1723. Under this scheme the duty of preaching in the King's chapel was to be performed by 'twenty-four persons who are Fellows of Colleges in the two Universities twelve from Oxford and twelve from Cambridge' (Firth, 1917: 4) – a transparent plan to reward dons loyal to the ministry from which whiggish colleges like Corpus benefited (Hartshorne, 1905: 153–4). Its effect, however, appears to have been more to reward the already converted than to win over new whig converts.

   As well as making the universities more effective as seminaries of the clergy Gibson also wished to make university studies better suited to the 'accurate understanding of publick affairs' (N. Sykes, 1926: 95) and to this end Gibson (with the support of Townshend) instigated the establishment in 1724 of the Regius chairs of history in the two universities. Along with the chairs of history there were also created positions at each university for two assistants to teach modern languages and twenty scholars who were appointed by the Crown – thus further strengthening whig patronage within the university. From these students, it was hoped, would be recruited future diplomats and tutors for young gentlemen on the Grand Tour. But the government soon lost interest in the project and after 1728 no more royal scholars were appointed and the Regius chairs of history, like other newly founded eighteenth-century professorships, soon lapsed into sinecures (N. Sykes, 1926: 94–107; Firth, 1917).

Gibson's concern to win over the universities and the clergy more generally to the whig cause is an indication of the extent to which the Church continued to be divided between a generally whiggish episcopate and a body of lower clergy who were still predominantly tory (Colley, 1982: 104–7). This had its analogue in early eighteenth-century Cambridge where the heads of colleges – who frequently looked to episcopal patrons for further ecclesiastical advancement – were (with important exceptions) more inclined towards whiggery than the mass of fellows. Thus in the 1705 general election Dixie Windsor, 'a virtually unknown tory zealot', was successfully elected though he did not receive a single vote from the head of a college (Bennett in SM: 76–7). This tension between the heads and the fellows probably accounts for the abortive attempt in 1712 to put forward a fellow of Pembroke (a stronghold of toryism) as a candidate for the vice-chancellorship (C. H. Cooper, 1842–1908, IV: 110), despite the fact that since 1586 the office had been a preserve of the heads of colleges. This move followed a successful motion in the Senate to prevent the election of Bentley as vice-chancellor, an action that appears to have been prompted by Bentley's address to the Queen earlier that year in support of the whig ministry and his declaration that the university supported the Hanoverian succession (Monk, 1830–3, I: 334–5). Post-revolutionary Cambridge, then, like the nation as a whole was characterised by the clash between whig and tory – a conflict which coloured all the university's activities including its intellectual life.

The most obvious manifestation of such partisan divisions was the conflicts which surrounded the election of the university's two burgesses – posts which carried a particular prestige within the House of Commons and which conferred special authority when discussing church affairs (Bennett in SM: 13). At the election for the Convention Parliament of 1689 Cambridge had the prudence to return two MPs – Isaac Newton and Sir Robert Sawyer – who were both warm supporters of the Glorious Revolution. Like Newton, Sawyer sought to persuade the doubtful within Cambridge that James's 'refusal to govern according to the Laws and Constitutions' of England was 'a generall refusal of the Government of that Kingdom, and therefore an Abdication' (Bodl., Rawlinson MS D.1232: fol. 7). When Sawyer died in 1692 he was replaced as MP by the whig Henry Boyle who was re-elected as MP for Cambridge University in five subsequent parliaments (1695, 1698, 1700/1, 1701 and 1702). But Boyle was generally accompanied to parliament by a member of the 'Church party' – in 1695 George Oxenden, master of Trinity Hall (whose election as MP was opposed by Newton (Turnbull *et al.*, 1959–77, VII: 395)); and in 1698 and 1701 Boyle was returned along with Anthony

Hammond, a client of Nottingham (Cook, 1935: 225). The election for the short parliament from December 1701 to July 1702 produced an unusual result since Boyle was returned along with the whiggish Isaac Newton (who defeated Anthony Hammond). But at the election held after the accession of Anne, Newton declined an offer to stand as Cambridge's burgess, probably fearing the revival of high church sentiment within the university now that a Stuart was back on the throne; he certainly had cause to do so to judge from a letter of Metcalfe Robinson (an undergraduate at Queens') of 10 March 1702 which spoke of 'the far greater part of the university' (and, in particular, St John's) exclaiming 'against the King's too much favoring the Dutch, and Dissenters'.[6] And indeed, Newton's place was taken by Arthur Annesley, 'a sound High Churchman' (Holmes, 1967: 278) who in 1710 became the fifth earl of Anglesey. Annesley served as MP for the university in 1702, 1705 and 1708–10 and in 1721 was unanimously appointed Cambridge's high steward by the Senate (BL, Add. 22908: 111), a post he held until his death in 1737 (when he was succeeded by the duke of Newcastle).

A particularly significant election was that of 1705 at which the long-serving Boyle, sensing the reviving power of the Cambridge tories, declined to stand for the university. Newton, however, did stand though he began to have misgivings before the election and commented to one correspondent (probably his patron, Halifax) that 'the opposition of W[indsor, a rival tory candidate] and the vogue against me of late have discouraged my friends and checkt and diminished my interest and inclined different persons against me' (Turnbull et al., 1959–77, VII: 437). Newton's fears were justified since both he and his fellow whig candidate, Francis Godolphin (MA King's 1705), were defeated and Cambridge returned two tories, Annesley and Dixie Windsor, a son of the earl of Plymouth, whom Newton described as 'being under firm obligations to A[nnesley]' (ibid.).[7] The election appears to have polarised university opinion markedly: Reneu, an undergraduate at Jesus, reported in 1705 that his fellow students were 'up to their ears in divisions about High Church and Low Church, Whig and Tory' (CUL, Add. 4: 152) and Simon Patrick, then bishop of Ely, expressed his concern 'at the heat and passion of the gentlemen there [in the universities], which they inculcated into their pupils . . . that at the election at Cambridge [of 1705], it was shameful to see a hundred or more young students, encouraged in hollowing like

[6] Leeds Public Library, Robinson Correspondence, VR6004.
[7] Bodl., MS Ballard 23: 114–16 gives the voting list for this key election. At Peterhouse, St John's, Clare, Jesus, Gonville and Caius, and Pembroke the two tory candidates received first and second places while only at Queens' and Sidney Sussex was this true of both whig candidates. Overall the total number of whig votes exceeded those for tory candidates only at Queens', Corpus, Sidney Sussex, Trinity Hall and, surprisingly, Emmanuel.

schoolboys and porters, and crying, No Fanatic, No Occasional Conformity against two worthy gentlemen [i.e. Newton and Godolphin] that stood candidates' (Edleston, 1850: lxxiv).

From 1705 till the accession of George II Cambridge's political life was dominated by the influential Annesley who used his university contacts to build up a 'connexion' of MPs from Cambridgeshire and beyond. Among the members of this 'connexion' were Dixie Windsor; Windsor's brother, Andrews; and, at least for a time, Thomas Paske, a fellow of Clare, who represented the university along with Windsor in 1710, 1713 and 1715 and was described as being 'the great favourite of the Church party, by his great acquaintance as agent to Mr. Annesley and Mr. Windsor' (HMC, Portland MSS, IV: 605; Holmes, 1967: 281n). In 1720 Paske died and was succeeded by the tory Thomas Willoughby who, along with Dixie Windsor, was returned in 1722 and thereafter both men were re-elected until 1727.

The political tensions apparent in the elections for university burgesses also caused divisions within individual colleges, and Clare was a college where such disputes were particularly evident. The leader of the whig interest at Clare was Richard Laughton, a friend of Whiston, Bentley and Samuel Clarke. In 1697 a number of Clare fellows had attempted to prevent Laughton's appointment as a foundation fellow of the college and Whiston, one of Laughton's allies within the college, successfully invoked the support of Simon Patrick, bishop of Ely, and John Moore, bishop of Norwich, in ensuring that Laughton gained the fellowship (Wardale, 1903: 124–9). Commenting on the Laughton affair in a letter to Blythe, the master of Clare, Whiston lamented 'The heats, and divisions; the censures and unchristian animosities which are at this time in our College' (*ibid.*: 111). In 1710 Laughton incurred the wrath of tories throughout Cambridge when as proctor he attempted to break up a drinking party which was celebrating Sacheverell's victory over his whig opponents (among those rejoicing was Dr Paske, one of Laughton's adversaries at Clare Hall and later an MP for Cambridge University in the tory interest) (CUL, Add. 7896: 28).

At Blythe's death in 1713 Laughton was one of the candidates for the mastership of Clare but the fellowship was so evenly divided that he received the same number of votes as his rival, and the college's visitor, the chancellor (the duke of Somerset), appointed his chaplain, William Grigg (a fellow of Jesus), master of Clare (Wardale, 1899: 148). Grigg helped to strengthen Clare's reputation as a centre of whiggery; by contrast, the fellowship of Jesus, Grigg's former college, appears to have remained predominantly tory since, soon after moving to Clare, Grigg complained to Bishop Moore that he had not been permitted to retain his fellowship at

Jesus along with the mastership of Clare because at Jesus ' 'Tis but calling a man Whig ... and this shall be sufficient to turn one out of a fellowship' (Wardale, 1903: 142).

Like Clare, King's was also divided by party strife. The election of Snape (an opponent of Hoadly) as provost in 1719 – despite the use of court influence on behalf of Snape's opponent, Waddington (Leigh, 1899: 178) – was a considerable victory for the tory faction within the college, prompting the nonjuror, Thomas Baker of St John's, to write to Hearne that 'though it [Snape's appointment] be a good choice, yet I doubt they may loose the Court by it, and their hopeful Expectations of a new building' (Hearne, 1885–1921, VII: 100). Snape appears to have done little to assuage party feeling within the college. In 1725 he expelled a member of the college by the name of Bushe for whiggish reflections on a college exercise; the college's visitor, the bishop of Lincoln (Richard Reynolds), however, reinstated Bushe and though the visitor's action was challenged 'in the end, the Whigs prevailed, and gave a turn to the political sentiments of the whole University' (Nichols, 1812–15, v: 399). In the same year the visitor also overruled Snape's demand that another fellow of King's, Mr Dale, apologise publicly for allegedly preferring 'the Puritans to the Members of the Church of England' and for suggesting that some members of the college 'were not well affected to the [Glorious] Revolution' (Bodl., Tanner 155: 172v).

Even Corpus, where Tenison and his clients had developed strong whig attachments, was not untouched by party disputes. In 1717 there was an appeal to the college visitor, Archbishop Wake, against the election of William Bradford as master in 1716 – a move which Brook Rand described, in a letter to Samuel Kerrick of 6 July 1717, as having been the work of a discontented tory faction within the college (Corpus Christi College, Cambridge, Hartshorne MS XI: 37). When Bradford's appointment was upheld with the support of the government the new master remarked to Kerrick in November 1718 that he could now congratulate the college on 'our late, happy deliverance from Toryism & Tyranny', adding that he hoped that 'this assistance afforded by a Gracious King & a Wise Ministry to a Private College is a good omen of what they [can] do for an whole University oppress'd by Faction' (*ibid.*: 138). Despite these internal disputes Corpus came to be regarded by the university tories as being a breeding-ground for whigs and heretics. Thomas Herring, a fellow of Corpus and a future archbishop of Canterbury, expressed his concern to Kerrick in 1725 that the college was being 'so much calumniated abroad' by those accusing it of 'the old Trumpery of Arrians, & Socinians, & Devils Incarnate'. Even some whigs looked on the college with suspicion 'because we are too Zealous in maintaining that Interest'.

Such accusations led Herring to ask rhetorically: 'Shall we endeavour to wipe out the polluted stains of Heresie, by turning good Orthodox Churchmen, & endeavour to reconcile ourselves to the Whigs, by condescending in great Compassion & Humility to let the Tories once more get upon our Books?' (*ibid.*: MS xii: 51).

Elections to university offices, and in particular the vice-chancellorship, were also influenced by 'the rage of party'. 'At this period', writes Masters in his eighteenth-century history of Corpus, 'political animosities were carried to a disgraceful height in the university; and the tory party, which was altogether predominant, determined upon depriving Dr. Bradford, who was known as a whig and a decided friend of the house of Hanover, of the accustomed honour of the vice-chancellorship' (1831: 223). Accordingly, at the vice-chancellorship election of 1717 Bradford (a former protégé of Tillotson) was opposed by the tory Gooch, master of Caius, who received almost double the number of votes cast for Bradford. In the following year Gooch was elected by an even greater majority, defeating the classicist, Dr Davies, president of Queens' (*ibid.*: 223–4), an ally of Bentley and a protégé of Bishop Moore. As vice-chancellor Gooch tolerated displays of undergraduate hostility to the whig administration – something on which Bradford commented in a letter to Kerrick of February 1719 when he remarked menacingly that the ministry knew of the vice-chancellor's actions which were 'only increasing his crime for which he will find the punishment increased' (Corpus Christi College, Cambridge, Hartshorne MS xi: 167). By 1729 the strength of the tory interest in Cambridge had considerably diminished and at the vice-chancellorship election for that year the tory candidate, Dr Lambert (master of St John's), defeated his whig rival, Dr Mawson (master of Corpus and a former protégé of Tenison) by only one vote. At this election Gooch, who had undergone a recent political conversion, abandoned his tory colleagues and 'was now the chief supporter of Dr. Mawson and the Whig interest against his former friends' (Masters, 1831: 230).

Though the tory Lambert narrowly won the 1729 vice-chancellorship the poll indicates the narrowing base of tory support within the university (Lunn, 1883: 20–1; BL, Add. 5841: p. 31). Of Lambert's 84 votes, 32 were a block-vote from his own college of St John's which, to a whig like Arthur Sykes, still appeared to be 'a nest of jacobites' (Disney, 1785: 371). The only other colleges where the tory interest was still clearly ascendant were King's (where 8 voted for Lambert and a mere 1 for Mawson), Jesus (2 to 0 in favour of Lambert), Emmanuel (6 to 1) and Pembroke (9 to 0). More qualified support came from Caius (5 to 2), Trinity Hall (3 to 2), Catharine Hall (4 to 2) and Peterhouse (5 to 2). In the following year the tories' knife-edge majority was blunted and the whig Mawson was elected as vice-chancellor; further salt was rubbed in the tory wounds by his re-election in 1731. The tories had one last brief taste of office in 1733 when the tory Long of Pembroke defeated the whig Towers of Christ's of whom Cole remarked that he 'was of too inflexible & rugged a Nature to push his Interest with any Party' (BL Add. 5841: p. 35); thereafter, however, the whigs were securely and unassailably at the helm. The lure of whig ecclesiastical patronage had done its work – as the tory Cole remarked sourly of the 1729 vice-chancellorship election, 'When party ran high, it was the harvest for preferment hungers. Dr. Mawson stood in the Whig interest, and got a bishoprick; Dr. Lambert was supported by the Tories, and got nothing' (Nichols, 1812–15, I: 551).

After the accession of George II in 1727 made it apparent that the Hanoverian dynasty was in England to stay and that nostalgia for the Stuarts and their style of monarchy was in vain, more and more Cambridge dons deserted the tory cause. Significantly, at the election for Cambridge's burgesses in 1727 the university returned Thomas Townshend and Edward Finch, both of whom stood in the whig interest and were actively supported by Bentley (Monk, 1830–3, II: 263) and by the ministry who won over a number of waverers by granting them honorary degrees (R. Sedgwick, 1970, I: 200–1). The final figures were 221 for Finch, 198 for Townshend and 176 for Windsor. Predictably the colleges which cast more votes for Windsor than for either Finch or Townshend were the familiar tory strongholds of King's, St John's, Caius, Pembroke and Emmanuel together with Catharine Hall (Anon., 1727: 13). Thereafter these two men were re-elected with monotonous regularity until 1761. Cole records that when, in 1727, the tory candidate, Dixie Windsor, visited Dr Gooch, master of Caius and one of Cambridge's leading tories, Windsor complained 'to the Doctor, whom he supposed to be the most hearty in his Cause, that he found the University much altered, and that if the Court Party would set up a Broom-stick, he believed they would vote for him, [but] to Mr. Windsor's no small Surprize, the Doctor turned about, and very gravely told him, and so must I too' (BL, Add. 5833: p. 233). Shortly afterwards Gooch's change of political allegiance was rewarded with a prebend's place at Canterbury: the age of 'political stability' (Plumb, 1969) had arrived.

Some of the traditional bastions of Cambridge toryism also began to disappear beneath the rising whig tide. When Lambert died in 1735 he was succeeded as master of St John's by the whig Newcome, a client of the duke of Newcastle (who obtained for him the deanery of Rochester). The importance of this election, even outside the university, is evident in the abortive attempt of Edward Harley, second earl of Oxford, to prevent Newcome becoming master (Nichols, 1812–15, 1: 480). Newcome's election did not, of course, mean that St John's deeply rooted toryism was immediately abandoned: Newcome, writes Cole, 'was often made uneasy by the difference of his politicks with those of his Fellows; especially during the former part of his government'; indeed, one of his opponents, Paulet St John, was rusticated 'for grossly abusing and affronting him, on political foundations'. Before his death in 1765, however, 'matters cooled; and he had time to make the College, in a long Prefecture of thirty years, according to his own system' (*ibid.*: 557–8).

At King's, by the latter years of Snape's provostship, writes Cole, 'the Management of the College was wholly wrestled out of his and his Friends' Hands and entirely governed by the Whigs' (BL, Add. 5817: p. 16). When Snape died in December 1742 he was succeeded by William George who, with the aid of Robert Walpole and other court whigs such as Newcastle and Thomas Townshend (Leigh, 1899: 196; BL, Add. 4251B: 1002), narrowly defeated his tory opponent, Chapman. Emmanuel, however, resisted the winds of change and continued to remain true to the ideals which Sancroft had so firmly implanted in the former 'nest of puritans' after the Restoration: in 1736 it elected the tory William Richardson as master who, in 1775, was followed by Richard Farmer, another old-school tory. Caius also showed some signs of independence since after the death of Gooch in 1754 it elected the tory James Burrough (Winstanley, 1922: 156). But Emmanuel and Caius were exceptions which proved the more general rule. By the 1730s Cambridge as a whole had largely abandoned the political and religious principles which had been instilled in it after the Restoration and had assumed, at least in general outline, the whig complexion by which it was later commonly recognised. Though Oxford had produced fewer nonjurors it remained more faithful than Cambridge to the ideals of Church and State associated with the tory party – a divergence which owes much to the activities of the largely Cambridge-educated bishops who came to office after 1688 and to the work of their protégés within the university.

Though contemporaries – and particularly the more anti-clerical whigs – thought the growth of university patronage helped to explain why some dons could afford to remain obstinately opposed to the ministry (Best, 1964: 102) there is little evidence that the difference in political outlook can be explained by differences in their reserves of internal patronage. Early eighteenth-century Cambridge had some 250 livings (117 of which were worth more than one hundred pounds per annum) (CUL, Mm.1.48: 454) while Oxford had about 290 (148 being worth more than one hundred pounds) (Langford in SM: 116) which, when one allows for the fact that Oxford with 535 dons had about 130 more fellows, placed Cambridge on a slightly better (and more independent) footing. Nor within Cambridge were colleges with a higher proportion of livings to fellows any more independent in their politics than their less well-endowed counterparts: of the four colleges which had more livings than fellows (CUL, MS Mm.1.48: 454–5) three – Clare, Christ's and Trinity – were firmly whig while the fourth (Caius) was politically divided. Thus the creation of whig Cambridge can be better explained by the role of external patrons than by the nature and extent of the prizes which the university itself could offer.

The anti-clerical wing of the whig party, however, did not view the growth of the universities' patronage in such a detached spirit. In the agitation which preceded the Mortmain Act of 1736 there were those who argued that the increase in the number of college livings represented a dangerous increase in clerical power and 'would render the clergy independent on the laity' (HMC, Egmont diary, in Egmont MSS, II: 256). Faced by such a threat the universities mounted a counter-attack – even Somerset was roused from his retirement to enter the fray on Cambridge's behalf with a letter to Hardwicke on 2 April 1736 decrying 'the very pernicious' effects of the bill on the universities (BL, Add. 35585: 325). Such lobbying persuaded court whigs like Walpole, Thomas Townshend and Henry Pelham to defend the universities from the more drastic assaults of their whig colleagues; none the less, reported Lord Egmont, there was 'scarce one who spoke for the Universities but declared that they ought not to be suffered to go on in purchasing more livings' (HMC, Egmont diary, II: 255). Ultimately, the universities were exempted from the full rigours of the Mortmain Act since the colleges were allowed to continue to purchase advowsons up to a maximum of half as many livings as there were fellows; a motion to allow the colleges to exchange small livings for larger ones was defeated (*GM*, 1736: 718). Such a compromise, it was hoped, would 'secure them [the clergy] in that good disposition towards the Government which they have of late made appear' (HMC, Egmont diary, II: 255). Cambridge made good use of this provision, expanding the number of livings in the gift of the colleges from about 250 in the early part of the century to about 300 by 1796 (*Cambridge University calendar*, 1796).

The Mortmain Act was one of a number of bills which threatened the fragile alliance between Walpole and the Church (or, at least, the dominant voices within the episcopate): Lord Hervey noted that in 1736 'all the considerable debates that passed this year in Parliament were upon Church matters' (Snapp, 1973: 90). Most contentious of all was the Quakers' Tithe Bill (Kendrick, 1968; S. Taylor, 1985) which prompted Bishop Smalbrook of Lichfield to remark to the earl of Egmont, a former pupil, that he did 'not understand the policy of Sir Robert Walpole in abandoning the clergy to their enemies, when the Church is the best support of the Crown and the country clergy never better disposed to the Government'. So indignant were the clergy, Smalbrook added, that Edmund Gibson, bishop of London, Walpole's chief advisor, along with other bishops was prepared to break with Walpole and possibly even rejoin the tories (HMC, Egmont diary, II: 266–7).

Gibson did indeed break with Walpole and later wrote angrily that as a result of the actions of the ministry the work of reconciling the clergy with the whigs 'grew heavy, and lost ground, not through any neglect or change of conduct on the part of the Bishops, but by difficulty they found to satisfy the clergy, that the Whigs meant no harm to them and the Church' (N. Sykes, 1926: 409). But it is an indication of how effectively Walpole and Gibson had laboured in the past that there were no episcopal defections to the tories and that the great bulk of the episcopate obediently continued to support the ministry. Within Cambridge, too, whig dominance was based on too firm a foundation to be shaken by the squalls of 1736; Cambridge's vice-chancellor (John Wilcox of Clare) was, as might be expected, vehement in his opposition to the Mortmain Act (W. R. Ward, 1958: 157–8) but the universities had cause to be thankful that they fared much better than other ecclesiastical foundations.

Perhaps the main effect of the anti-clerical measures of 1736 on Cambridge was to prompt Newcastle to assume full control of ecclesiastical affairs now that Gibson was a spent force. Newcastle had, of course, been involved in church patronage since his appointment as secretary of state for the southern department in 1724 but after 1736 he became in effect the 'ecclesiastical minister', his power being further strengthened by two other developments in the same year: the death of Queen Caroline, who had hitherto taken an active interest in matters ecclesiastical, and the appointment of his friend, Lord Hardwicke, as lord chancellor, an office which controlled most of the crown benefices (Barnes, 1934: 165). Newcastle's increasing involvement in the affairs of the Church after 1736 may well explain why, in 1737, he became a candidate for the post of high steward of the university on the death of Arthur Annesley, fifth earl of Anglesey, the former tory MP. Newcastle was duly elected with no serious opposition (Browning, 1975: 80). Traditionally, the high steward had played only a minor role in university affairs but since Somerset, the chancellor, had been largely a political nonentity since 1716 Newcastle became the natural focus for university intrigue and place-hunting – especially since the duke had made ecclesiastical affairs his special concern. Thus at the election of 1741 we find Newcastle canvassing the vice-chancellor and the heads of St John's, Peterhouse, Clare, Trinity and Christ's to ensure the re-election of Finch and Townshend following reports that 'there is likely to be an Opposition to Mr. Finch' (BL, Add. 32696: 365). Both MPs were duly returned even though Finch was such a lack-lustre representative that one of Newcastle's Cambridge clients suggested that he should be replaced by someone 'who could be more in Parliament, and was at the same time most firmly attach'd to those Principles, which your Grace has so constantly, and so gloriously pursued' (*ibid.*: 387). Newcastle's relations with Cambridge, then, reflected in miniature his policies towards the Church more generally, with New-castle exhibiting the same appetite for influencing the Lilliputian affairs of the university as he displayed in his ministerial machinations. In both Church and university Newcastle's basic rule was (as he explained to Hoadly in 1760 in a letter where he warmly praised that prelate's 'Noble Defence of Our Constitution') that he would 'recommend None, whom I did not think most sincerely well affected to His Majesty, and His Government, and, to the Principles upon which It is founded' (BL, Add. 32906: 388).

Newcastle's activities as high steward and, from 1748, chancellor served to strengthen and consolidate the whig ascendancy within the university but they cannot be said to have opened a new chapter in its political and religious affairs. The battle for supremacy within the university had been largely won by the whigs before Newcastle's advent, though his political skills helped to ensure that the university remained firmly within the whig camp. Frequently, however, Newcastle's influence within the university had to be used not for the straightforward task of favouring whig as against tory but for the more delicate operation of choosing between two whigs. Newcastle's copious papers provide ample scope for following the twists and turns of college politics but the predominantly whig character of the university was too well established to be threatened by the outcome of such donnish disputes (which have already been urbanely recounted by Winstanley (1922)).

Newcastle's election to the chancellorship in 1748 after Somerset's death was a natural progression from his appointment as high steward and indicated his continuing and absorbing interest in ecclesiastical affairs. Manœuvres for the post began some months before Somerset died in December 1748 with Newcastle being challenged for the post by George II's estranged son, Frederick, the prince of Wales. Though in the previous year Frederick had made an alliance with the tories as part of a campaign to undermine his father's administration (B. W. Hill, 1985: 38; McKelvey, 1973: 13), within Cambridge he was anxious to present himself as a friend to disaffected whigs – an indication of the weakness of the tory interest within Cambridge even before Newcastle became chancellor. Thus Thomas Chapman, the master of Magdalene, reported in April 1747 that Frederick 'was desirous of receiving this favour [the Chancellorship] from the hands of the Whigs, & that from them he had reason to expect it, from their particular attachment to his Person & Family'. Frederick's strategy was based, too, not so much on an appeal to deeply held beliefs about the role of Crown or Altar but rather on the hope that disaffected dons would respond to his promise that 'he would bestow the most signal marks of his Favour upon such as should be instrumental in conferring it [the Chancellorship] upon him' (BL, Add. 32710: 408).

However, even disaffected whigs found it difficult to ignore the King's evident and increasing displeasure at his son's candidature for the position, which may have been further fuelled by Newcastle's determination to have Frederick eliminated from the contest (Browning, 1975: 171). In May 1747 the vice-chancellor was summoned before the Privy Council and presented by the lord chancellor with a royal decree stating that the King hopes 'that they [the university] will not choose any of the Royal Family [as Chancellor], without his Majesty's Approbation' (BL, Add. 5852: p. 114). The message was further driven home soon after when, in July, the vice-chancellor received a letter from the duke of Bedford informing him that 'the King had left Orders . . . to signify to the Vice Chancellor that his Majesty would very highly disapprove the Election of the Prince of Wales to be Chancellor of the University' (*ibid.*: 116). Faced by such a clear royal veto few Cambridge whigs dared support Frederick and his followers came chiefly from the relatively small band of tories. In August Dupplin could reassure Newcastle's close ally, Lord Hardwicke, that 'The Whigs who revolt are very few' and that most of Frederick's support was coming from the tories (though even they were divided), particularly 'the fribbling Master of Emanuel and his party' (BL, Add. 35657: 5). When Somerset finally died on 2 December Frederick realised that his cause was hopeless and withdrew from the contest (BL, Add. 5852: pp. 117–18). He then turned his attention to Oxford which offered more fertile ground for factional politics (Colley, 1982: 258).

Though Newcastle's election as chancellor was assured after the King had vetoed the election of his son – particularly as the duke stood at the virtual invitation of the vice-chancellor (BL, Add. 32716: 201) – Newcastle, as was his wont, left nothing to chance. In ensuring his election he squandered much of his valuable store of patronage (Hartshorne, 1905: 218; BL, Add. 5833: p. 225b) and created divisions within Cambridge between those who benefited from his largesse and those who were turned empty away. In the event he was elected unanimously though there were some signs of protest since (as the master of Magdalene remarked) the entire fellowship of 'pure Emanuel' abstained, together with 'the three or four tories they still have at Peterhouse, all of the same stamp at King's, one or two of Trinity & Pembroke, several of Caius, and Dr. Rutherforth & some few of St. John's' (BL, Add. 32717: 446). Newcastle's triumph was further heightened by the unanimous election in July 1749 of Hard-wicke as high steward, this time, as Dupplin assured Newcastle, 'without the least objection, or murmur' (BL, Add. 32718: 273).

Abortive though it was, Frederick's attempt to gain the chancellorship did illustrate that there was a small core of opponents of Newcastle within the university consisting of the few remaining tories together with those whigs who felt themselves slighted by Newcastle or who looked to rival patrons for advancement. Though too small and disunited to be significant, this nucleus of opposition could be quickly swelled if Newcastle appeared to be intruding excessively into the university's internal affairs (Winstanley, 1922: 198–9). Soon after becoming chancellor Newcastle was given an object lesson in the need to tread warily when dealing with issues related to the university's autonomy by the proposed reforms of 1750. These seemingly innocuous proposals which Newcastle, along with Archbishop Herring and Bishop Sherlock of London, helped to formulate in conjunction with the heads were all concerned with rather mundane points of discipline though some of them did weaken the privileged status of fellow-commoners and noblemen (C. H. Cooper, 1842–1908, IV: 278–80).

Those most actively involved in their formulation and defence in the subsequent pamphlet war were the heads of colleges most closely identi-fied with Newcastle: Keene of Peterhouse (the vice-chancellor), Gooch of Caius, Newcome of St John's, George of King's and Chapman of Magdalene, together with Samuel Squire (a fellow of St John's and the duke's chaplain) – all of whom were later to reap the reward of high ecclesiastical office thanks to Newcastle's intervention. The opponents of reform portrayed these men as Newcastle's creatures who were conniving with him in weakening the university's autonomy (BL, Add. 5821: p. 81; Wordsworth, 1874: 617–33) – a view which indicates the hostility which these seemingly unremarkable proposals aroused. The extent and vigour of this reaction can be largely explained by the fact that they came soon after another attempt, in 1749, to instigate a parliamentary visitation of the universities.

The chief target of this proposed visitation was Oxford where under-graduate demonstrations at the end of 1748, which appeared to be condoned by the university authorities, cast doubt on its loyalty despite its official rejoicing after the defeat of the Pretender in 1745. Cambridge's conduct, by contrast, had been exemplary: it had organised a loyal association for the defence of the King and the vice-chancellor, Rooke of Christ's – a client of Newcastle and one of his chief supporters when the duke stood both for the high stewardship and for the chancellorship (N. Sykes, 1926: 107) – used the opportunity to advertise his Hanoverian loyalties by presenting a royal address which praised 'the admirable conduct and heroick bravery' (Peile, 1913: 205) of 'Butcher Cumberland'. Cambridge, then, had been exempted from the proposed visitation at Newcastle's insistence, the duke arguing that his university's 'Behaviour is as meritorious, as the other is justly to be censured' (BL, Add. 32718: 31), an outbreak of drunken undergraduate jacobitism before his installation as chancellor being tactfully overlooked.

None the less, there was always the risk that Cambridge might suffer from guilt by association with its sister university if such a visitation did come to pass. As the vice-chancellor of Oxford was reported to have caustically remarked of Cambridge in October 1749, when it had 'unnaturally triumphed in our Misfortunes', it, too, 'would be consumed (were we to perish) in . . . *iusdemque Flammis*' (BL, Add. 32719: 210). In the event the proposed visitation of 1749 proved as abortive as that of 1719 but it reawakened in some Cambridge dons their long-standing fears that the anti-clerical voices within the whig party might once more determine ministerial policy. Against this background it becomes more obvious why Newcastle's modest proposals excited such controversy: if viewed with sufficient paranoia his reforms could be seen as the beginnings of an assault on the university's independence. Ultimately, the regulations were passed in a modified form though there was further controversy about their enforcement which eventually largely subsided in 1752 (Winstanley, 1922: 199–222).

Though Cambridge was predominantly whig this did not necessarily translate into a majority endorsement for Newcastle's actions, as the fate of the 1750 reforms indicates. Despite Newcastle's control over the Crown's ecclesiastical patronage he had to move circumspectly within Cambridge to obtain his ends – as indeed he had to do within the Church at large (Hirschberg, 1980: 137–8). Dons who were not given their share of the fruits of office could become recalcitrant: Newcastle experienced the humiliation of being snubbed by his own college of Clare because Goddard, its master, was embittered at not receiving any preferment from the duke (Winstanley, 1922: 298–303). The university as a whole could also become unco-operative if it was felt that the chancellor was meddling overmuch in its affairs: though prepared to permit two of Newcastle's clients a second term as vice-chancellor, contrary to precedent, in 1750 and 1753 the heads of colleges drew the line at permitting this to happen a third time in 1755, despite pressure from the chancellor (ibid.: 172–4). When, in 1764, Newcastle once again attempted to intervene in the succession to the vice-chancellorship his loyal client, Caryl of Jesus, warned him that such a break with custom 'would in all probability lose us several of our own friends' among the heads (BL, Add. 32963: 6).

While the university as a whole might occasionally take such a stand there were few heads of colleges who were individually prepared to defy Newcastle, particularly since he devoted most of his political energies within the university to ensuring that his protégés were elected as masters – no doubt in the well-founded belief that this was the best means to influence the mass of dons. However, the chancellor frequently worked through intermediaries, an approach which made his involvement in the internal affairs of particular colleges less apparent and thus probably more acceptable. Though Newcastle treated Archbishop Herring with undisguised contempt and so offended him on a point of protocol that the archbishop, though a Cambridge man, declined to attend the installation of Newcastle as chancellor (Hartshorne, 1905: 218, 50), Herring none the less recommended to his old college of Corpus in 1750 that they elect as master John Green, a client of the duke and of his friend, Lord Hardwicke (ibid.: 237). Green was duly elected as master despite murmurings within the college about the consequences of surrendering their freedom of election and of electing someone who had no associations with the college (Nichols, 1817–58, VI: 794). Having made Corpus a centre of Newcastle's influence within the university he was duly rewarded with the see of Lincoln and replaced by Barnardiston, another of Newcastle's clients in 1764: Green's predecessor as master of Corpus, Edmund Castle, had also been a Newcastle protégé who was elected at Herring's recommendation (BL, Add. 32942: 329v).

When Edmund Keene, whose vigorous defence of the reforms of 1750 had 'justly endeared him to his great patron [Newcastle]' (GM, 1781: 343), resigned as master of Peterhouse in 1754 after becoming bishop of Chester he was able to ensure that he was replaced by another client of Newcastle, Edmund Law (Dyer, 1824, II: 237), despite the fact that Law, like Green, had no links with the college to which he was elected master (Winstanley, 1922: 238). After the mastership of Jesus became vacant in 1752 (a position which was in the gift of the bishop of Ely) Newcastle persuaded the bishop, Thomas Gooch, to give the post to Philip Yonge, one of Newcastle's most active Cambridge agents (BL, Add. 5828: p. 129b). Yonge, in turn, was succeeded in 1758 by Lynford Caryl who, after his appointment by Bishop Mawson, thanked Newcastle 'for your kind and effectual recommendation of me to his Lordship' (Winstanley, 1922: 236). But even such indirect methods had their limits. When the mastership of Magdalene was vacant in 1760, for example, Newcastle failed to gain the post for his nominee since it was in the gift of Lady Portsmouth who angered Newcastle and his Cambridge clients by appointing an Oxford man, George Sandby, to the post (BL, Add. 32907: 184, 209, 351).

If the prize were big enough and the interests of his clients sufficiently involved Newcastle could also play a part in elections to chairs and, in particular, to the Regius professorship of divinity, the university's pre-eminent chair. Within a few weeks of his election as chancellor Newcastle had been involved in the delicate task of deciding which of the three candidates for this post – Green, Rooke and Yonge, all Newcastle clients – should receive his support. After much consultation the chancellor decided to persuade Yonge and then Rooke to withdraw to allow Green to be elected unopposed, Green having a particularly strong claim because of his long association with Hardwicke (BL, Add. 32717: 463–547). After Green vacated the chair in 1756 Newcastle was active in ensuring the election of Thomas Rutherforth, after he assured the chancellor that despite his earlier support for Prince Frederick in his bid for the chancellorship the duke could now be confident of 'my sincere attachment to His Majesty's person and government, and of a steady regard for your Grace and for the interest of your friends' (Winstanley, 1922: 190). In general, however, Newcastle was content to allow appointments to chairs to be decided without his intervention – no doubt because he thought it wiser to save his ammunition for the more important battles. When a successor to Colson as Lucasian professor was being sought at the end of 1759, for example, Newcastle played a part in seeing that the academic merits of the candidates were properly assessed but otherwise allowed the electors a free hand (BL, Add. 32900: 216, 229, 395–6, 500).

The success of Newcastle's methods in building up a strong following within Cambridge was to be put to a demanding test after 1762 when he was forced to resign the prime ministership after what he considered was a series of humiliations from Lord Bute. Though some dons deserted their former patron when he was no longer a source of preferment Newcastle's ascendancy within Cambridge survived surprisingly well – far better in fact than the duke's control over his episcopal and parliamentary clients. Soon after Newcastle lost the seals of office in July 1762 the university orator was dispatched to convey to the duke the university's 'gratefull and steady attachment to your Grace, at all times and on all occasions' (BL, Add. 32939: 256). To Newcastle, still smarting from his political disgrace, this address was, of all the university's letters to him, the one which had done him greatest honour; in his reply he also reasserted his belief that 'Nothing could be of more Service to the Maintenance of our Happy Constitution in Church and State' than the strong links between the university and the House of Hanover (*ibid.*: 357). In the following year, however, one of Newcastle's opponents, Goddard of Clare, served as vice-chancellor and sought to embarrass the duke by asking him to present to the King a loyal address from the university in praise of the Peace of Paris – a treaty which Newcastle had publicly opposed. Newcastle's Cambridge allies amended the address to make it appear less obviously partisan though, at Pitt's urging, Newcastle none the less declined to present it (CUL, Add. 4251: 544, 565, 1011).

In 1764 Newcastle faced the most public and hard-fought test of his standing within the university: the election for the high stewardship following the death of Newcastle's ally, the earl of Hardwicke, in which Newcastle threw every ounce of his influence behind Hardwicke's son who was opposed by the dissolute earl of Sandwich (who enjoyed the support of the Court). It was an election that split the university asunder so that, as the master of Jesus remarked to Newcastle on 8 November 1764, 'Nobody has now any character in this place, but that of Sandwichian or Anti-Sandwichian' (BL, Add. 32963: 312v). Newcastle fought this campaign with particular vigour now that he could no longer exercise his talents on matters of greater political moment; as one of the duke's long-suffering Cambridge clients remarked to the young Hardwicke: 'He loves a bustle & thinks also his friends love it as well. He hates to be unemploy'd, and takes all the care he can, that none of his acquaintance shall want Employment' (BL, Add. 35657: 157). For some in Cambridge the contest was a chance to settle old scores with a chancellor who had hitherto overlooked their claims to preferment: the unwaveringly tory Roger Long, of whom Cole wrote that he 'got nothing of Course with a Whig Administration for too Long a Run' (BL, Add. 5841: p. 35), responded to the duke's request for his vote for Hardwicke with the blunt admission that 'all the great persons now in his Majesties service are zealous' for Sandwich which 'weighs with me, as a member of the University which cannot expect to flourish without the favour of the court' (BL, Add. 32953: 186). Despite the compelling force of Long's arguments for supporting Sandwich enough of the university remained loyal to its patron for Hardwicke to be narrowly elected – an indication that his donnish followers were not actuated solely by self-interest.

As Long had less than subtly intimated, Newcastle's ability to reward his Cambridge clients was greatly weakened after 1762, apart from when he briefly returned to office as lord privy seal between July 1765 and August 1766. Newcastle's return to the political wilderness in 1766 was once again marked by a loyal address from the university from which the duke drew solace (BL, Add. 32977: 13). But even after this final fall from office Newcastle still attempted to gain what patronage he could for his clients by reminding his episcopal allies of past debts. As he bitterly remarked, 'Even fathers-in-God sometimes forget their maker' (*DNB*,

Thomas Pelham-Holles), but there were some bishops who were prepared to throw some of the small change of clerical preferment in Newcastle's direction. Thus in 1767, a year before his death, he thanked Bishop Trevor of Durham for conferring a prebend on Edmund Law since such an action 'must be the most agreeable favour conferred on a chancellor of the university who has at present no other way of rewarding men of merit than by the goodness of his friends' (N. Sykes, 1934: 180).

But in his heyday, before the accession of George III, Newcastle's activities within Cambridge – apart from furnishing the duke with a further opportunity of exercising his considerable talents and industry as a patronage-monger – provided both universities and the Church more generally with an object lesson in the benefits that could be obtained through supporting the whig ministry. Thus one Oxford poet enviously greeted Newcastle's election as chancellor with the lines:

> See Granta's Senate by Inducements led,
> Elects wise Newcastle for their Head:
> All, or in Church and State, they now may claim,
> Lawn, Furs, Posts, Pensions await the happy Cam.
>   (in Ward, 1958: 176–7)

Some of Newcastle's Cambridge clients also served his purposes on the larger political stage by providing the court whigs with valuable ideological support. Samuel Squire, a fellow of St John's who acted as Newcastle's chaplain and Cambridge agent from 1748 until his elevation to the see of St David in 1761, argued, literally, for a whig interpretation of British history in two works, *An enquiry into the foundation of the English constitution; or, an historical essay upon the Anglo Saxon government* (1745) (which was dedicated to Newcastle) and *An historical essay upon the ballance of civil power in England, from its first conquest by the Anglo-Saxons to the time of the revolution* (1748). In the former book Squire argued in a Lockean vein that civil society was based on an original contract and that in Anglo-Saxon society full citizenship was contingent on the ownership of property. Squire rejected the view of his Cambridge predecessor, Robert Brady, that the power of the monarchy after 1066 was based on conquest and argued for a basic continuity before and after the Norman invasion (Browning, 1982: 119–44). Consistent with this Squire maintained that England's present political system corresponded to an ancient constitution which stretched back to the Anglo-Saxon period when one could 'trace the outlines of that rational liberty, which is the strong basis upon which our present excellent constitution stands raised and supported'. Squire maintained therefore that 'Our present constitution cannot, so truly, be said to have been changed or altered, as improved and matured by time. Where then', he asked in a whiggish vein, 'is that divine, hereditary, and indefeasible right of princes?' (1753 ed.: 5).

This defence of the present political order also underlay his *Historical essay* (1748). The Glorious Revolution, he argued, had not broken the continuity of the Ancient Constitution but rather conformed to 'the undoubted customs of their [Englishmen's] first ancestors in Germany'. Political order had traditionally depended on a balance 'between the three several Orders which constitute the sovereign Authority' (p. iv): the Monarch, Lords and Commons. No doubt with an eye to the difficulties that his patron faced in mustering a parliamentary majority, Squire argued that Britain's 'excellent Establishment' was 'as much endangered, when the House of Commons has too great, as when it has too little a share in the Government' (p. vii) and attacked the view that the monarchy had excessive influence in elections. Predictably, he asserted 'that under the present Administration supported by a Whig Parliament, every Thing will be done for the common Good' and warned against the dangers to the constitution from tories and republicans (p. xxv).

In his sermon preached before the House of Lords in 1762 on the anniversary of the execution of Charles I, Squire attempted to undertake the delicate task of reconciling whiggish conceptions of government with Anglican veneration for the Martyred King. He used the occasion to criticise those 'ambitious and worldly minded time-servers' who had used this day 'to recommend themselves to the favour of the Sovereign by magnifying his prerogative, and almost deifying his title and person' (1762: 9–10). Overall Squire adopted a rather apologetic tone in his attitude to the cult of the Royal Martyr, asserting that the day should still be formally remembered even though it 'has been, sometimes perverted to bad principles' (p. 10). This polemic against high church views of the monarchy also underlay the moral he drew from the events of 30 January 1649: that Charles's fate should serve as a warning for kings against 'those who flatter them with boundless prerogative and arbitrary power' (p. 12). Like Squire, Green, another of Newcastle's Cambridge confidants, used the same feast day to combat clerical conceptions of the monarchy which could weaken the Church's attachment to the whigs. In the following year Green also argued before the Lords that Charles's downfall was partly due to some of the clergy who had 'preached up the divine right of kings in so exalted a strain, as led their hearers to think, that it could scarcely be subject to any limitations of law, or controuled in the exercise of its powers by any appointments of men' (J. Green, 1763: 10).

Squire's historical arguments in support of the whig view of the constitution were echoed by Thomas Hayter who, though he took his first degree from Oxford, moved to Emmanuel for his MA (1727) and DD

(1744) and was an influential figure within the university. Hayter was a less dependable client of Newcastle than Squire since, although he owed his elevation to the see of Norwich in 1749 to the duke, he subsequently deserted his patron for the earl of Bute (Hartshorne, 1905: 359). However, it was while still one of Newcastle's protégés that Hayter wrote his *Essay on the liberty of the press* (1754) in which he argued that the English constitution was based on an 'original Compact'; he maintained, too, that the principle of freedom of speech (and, by extension, freedom of the press) was part of an ancient constitution which preceded the Magna Carta. To Hayter the only true defenders of such constitutional traditions were the whigs and he deplored the claim that 'Party Distinctions are . . . abolished' (p. 46). He also criticised the growth of faction and disunity within the ranks of the whigs – prompted, perhaps, by the difficulties that Newcastle faced in establishing his administration after the death of Henry Pelham in 1754.

Of less national importance but none the less of significance within the clerical estate were the university addresses of Newcastle's clients which helped to strengthen the hold of whig principles within the university and among Cambridge's alumni. In his commencement sermon of 1749 (delivered in Newcastle's presence) John Green took up the familiar theme that it was the Hanoverian regime which ensured 'the just liberties' of the nation and ensured the survival of 'pure and reformed religion' (1749: 14, 16). The zeal of George Rooke (master of Christ's, 1745–54), to assert his loyalty to the whig cause and his abhorrence of a divine right view of monarchy was so great that in a sermon on the anniversary of the execution of Charles I he (or so the tory Cole claimed) 'vindicated the Rebellion, . . . [and] openly approved of the Murder of King Charles' (BL, Add. 5821: p. 80).

Such public affirmations of whig principles on the part of prominent Cambridge churchmen are a further instance of the way in which New-castle's long ascendancy within Cambridge (which, in effect, dated from his election as high steward in 1737 until his death as chancellor in 1768) served to consolidate Cambridge's attachment to the whig cause – although Newcastle had the advantage of building on political founda-tions which had already been securely laid before he became high steward. The earlier work of winning over Cambridge from its high church allegiance and its reverence for divine right monarchy, which had been so strongly inculcated within the university in the period from the Restora-tion to the Glorious Revolution, was, however, chiefly the work of those members of the Nottingham circle who were raised to the episcopate after 1688. It was they and their protégés within the university who helped to persuade the majority of their colleagues of the necessity of abandoning their nostalgia for the Stuarts and for Sancroft's dream of a truly national Church which (as South had put it in 1661) 'glories in nothing more than that she is the truest friend of kings and kingly government' (Bennett, 1975: 5). The pedestrian realities of a foreign, Lutheran dynasty, enmeshed in the intrigues of ministerial faction, might appear mundane in comparison with such past ambitions but that, most Cambridge dons were finally persuaded, was where the future lay.

5

The clash of creeds

The gradual weaning of Cambridge from an allegiance to conceptions of
Crown and Altar which were the foundations of tory thinking was
paralleled by a retreat from a view of Christianity which made it difficult
for the clerical estate to accept the submissive role which the Hanoverian
regime was to require of it. Basic to these theological disputes, which were
intertwined with the political debates which divided Cambridge and the
Church more generally in the decades after the Glorious Revolution, was
the issue of how far Christianity could be equated with the exercise of
human reason unaided by the truths of the Revelation. Though no one in
the Anglican fold denied that Christianity relied to some degree on
Revelation there were those among the latitudinarians who appeared to
suggest that natural religion differed little from Christianity; Tillotson, for
example, had argued that 'As for the *revealed religion*, the only design of
that is, to revive and improve the natural notions which we have of God,
and all our reasonings about divine revelation are necessarily gathered by
our natural notions of religion . . .' (Sullivan, 1982: 63). More succinctly he
expressed the same view in his remark: 'Excepting a very few particulars
they (natural law and Christianity) enjoin the very same things' (McAdoo,
1965: 175). Moreover, when the latitudinarians conceded that recourse to
Revelation was necessary they tended to argue that doctrinal matters could
be resolved by the reading of Scripture without much need to invoke
expert clerical guidance.

Such a position called into question the role of the clergy and of the
Church more generally. If Christianity could be understood by the light of
human reason or through a largely untutored reading of the Bible, what
need was there for a clerical estate which claimed a particular expertise in
the interpretation of Christianity and the exclusive right to perform
religious rituals? There were even those within the gates of the Established
Church, like Hoadly and his disciples, who did indeed draw the conclusion that since Christian truths were largely self-evident there was there-

fore little need for a Church: such an institution might serve useful
administrative and social functions which were allocated to it by the State
but it had no right to claim the role of an arbiter of doctrines – as
Bolingbroke put it, Hoadly maintained that 'A bishop is nothing but a
layman with a crook in his hand' (Stephen, 1962, II: 135). These views
were greatly at variance with the conception of the role of the Church that
had been inculcated into a generation of Cambridge undergraduates by
Sancroft and his high church colleagues after the Restoration. Reacting
against what they perceived as the religious anarchy of the Interregnum
they had looked to the re-established Church of England to provide
acceptable doctrinal boundaries and a sacramental system which could act
as a focus for the nation's religious life. In such a Church the clergy were
naturally of critical importance as teachers and priests and the divine
mission of the Church was underlined by an emphasis on the apostolic
succession of the episcopacy, a view largely foreign to pre-Laudian
Anglicanism. The Oxford high churchman, Robert South, summed up
this position by arguing that if the clergy were once again given due
respect 'men would be less confident of their own understandings, and
more apt to pay reverence and submission to the understandings of those,
who are both more conversant in these matters than they can pretend to
be, and whom the same wisdom of God has thought fit to appoint over
them as their guides' (Sullivan, 1982: 81).

The ultimate extension of the high churchmen's emphasis on the
apostolic succession was the position adopted by the nonjurors that the
Church could (as Francis Turner, the ejected bishop of Ely, put it) be 'kept
up in a Remnant' (BL, Add. 29546: 106v) by consecrating new bishops
even though it was opposed to the post-revolutionary State. Appropriately, the nonjurors always appeared in public in full clerical attire – a
means of symbolically affirming their belief in the importance of a separate
clerical estate. Those raised on such principles – including the great bulk of
Anglican clergy who did not follow the nonjurors into the wilderness –
naturally regarded with considerable suspicion latitudinarian divines who
argued for a theology and an ecclesiology which had the effect of reducing
the clergy to something approaching servants of the State entrusted with
the maintenance of public morals. As early as 1691 the nonjuror George
Hickes remarked that it is 'the modern Latitude, which hath brought all
things to confusion, and will in time bring the church to ruine' (Stewart,
1978: 201), while in 1718 a clerical pamphleteer argued that the church
canon prohibiting 'plot[ting] any thing against the Doctrine of the Church
. . . seems to have been made by a Spirit of Prophecy against the
Latitudinarians' (Anon., 1718: 45). Thus in theology, as in politics, post-
1688 Cambridge was characterised by acrimonious debate – debate which

was focused on two main issues: firstly, how far a knowledge of Christianity could be arrived at by the use of human reason without recourse to Revelation, and secondly, the related issue of whether the Church and the clergy could claim a special role as custodians of Christian doctrine and tradition.

The chief target for those opposed to the view that Christianity could largely be derived from the exercise of human reason was Samuel Clarke who came to be regarded as the Cambridge latitudinarians' theological spokesman. The tenor of Clarke's theology was evident in his choice of disputation topics in 1709 for his Cambridge doctorate of divinity, namely 'No Article of the Christian Faith delivered in the Holy Scriptures, is Disagreeable to Right Reason' and 'Without the Liberty of Humane Actions there can be no Religion' (Hoadly, 1738, I: vi). To Clarke the central truths of Christianity were evident to anyone willing to examine the evidence impartially in the same way that a natural philosopher could appeal to the accuracy of his data. Thus, in the preface to *A demonstration of the being and attributes of God* (Boyle lectures, 1704), Clarke stated plainly his desire to follow a method as near as possible to that of mathematics and hence he adopted a deductive structure, each demonstration having its own propositions and proofs (Ferguson, 1976: 24). Elsewhere, in a sermon revealingly entitled 'The Character of Oppressive Power in Religion', Clarke made even more apparent his desire to minimise as much as possible those elements of Christianity which could not be reconciled with reason. 'What matters it in point of *Truth*', he asked, 'to have rejected the *unintelligible Doctrines of Rome*; if men still continue fond of *unintelligible Notions*?' (S. Clarke, 1742, I: 635).

Moreover, for Clarke the primary end of Christianity was to confirm adherence to moral laws which could largely be arrived at through rational analysis. Every Christian doctrine, argued Clarke, 'has a natural tendency and a direct and powerful influence, to reform men's lives and correct their manners. This is the great end and ultimate design of all true religion' (Cragg, 1964: 59). These moral commands, Clarke argued in his Boyle lectures of 1705 (entitled *A discourse concerning the unchangeable obligations of natural religion . . .*), were apparent to any man of good will since the moral laws were as evident as the laws of nature. Moral perversion, he contended, is as much an absurdity as 'for a man to pretend to alter the Proportions of Numbers' (Selby-Biggs, 1897, II: 15).

Consistent with his views that the basic goal of Christianity was to promote adherence to the natural moral order Clarke regarded religious duties as 'but subordinate to the Practice of moral Virtues' since 'the former can be considered only as Means to the latter' (S. Clarke, 1742, I: 708). Accordingly, he viewed the Christian sacraments as being an aid to moral behaviour rather than as an end in themselves (Ferguson, 1976: 175). In such a scheme of theology there was, then, little emphasis on Revelation as separate and distinct from natural knowledge. Moreover, the logic of his position called into question the whole justification for a separate clerical estate as custodians and interpreters of the Word since, if the moral principles which it was the basic goal of Christianity to instil were evident to any man of good will, the need for an ecclesiastical establishment was weakened – a conclusion that Clarke's admirer, Hoadly, later did not hesitate to draw. By implication, then, Clarke was providing a theological basis for that expansion of the State's power at the expense of that of the Church which had been one of the features of the post-revolutionary order that many churchmen most bitterly opposed.

The major difficulty in Clarke's theological scheme was to accommodate the doctrine of the Trinity since, although natural reason could, in Clarke's view, be used to prove the existence of God, Christian tradition held that only Revelation could provide an understanding of the nature of God. Clarke was closely questioned on his Trinitarian beliefs by Henry James, the Regius professor of divinity, at Clarke's celebrated defence of his Cambridge DD theses; though Clarke acquitted himself honourably some of the Cambridge heads still doubted his orthodoxy and Clarke had to swear to abide by the Thirty-Nine Articles (Redwood, 1976: 168). Clarke later attempted to answer such criticisms by a detailed analysis of Scripture itself in his *Scripture doctrine of the Trinity* (1712), but this work only served to confirm many of his fellow clergy's doubts about Clarke's orthodoxy, resulting in his censure by the Lower House of Convocation in 1714. However, this confrontation served to demonstrate that Clarke had the support of influential episcopal patrons thus highlighting the divisions within the post-revolutionary Church. Clarke had been appointed Boyle lecturer by Tenison in 1704 and the first volume of Clarke's *Paraphrases on Scripture* was dedicated to the archbishop whom he praised for defending true religion which was endangered 'not only from the bold Pretenders to Atheism and Deism, but even from the many Controversies about smaller Matters, raised and uncharitably managed among Christians, while little regard is had to, the great Duties and most essential Parts of Religion' (Hoadly, 1738, III, Dedication). It was Tenison who was active in seeking a compromise when Clarke's works were before Convocation and in withholding the bishops' support for the Lower House's censure of him. Bishop Gilbert Burnet also used his influence to help protect Clarke, much to the indignation of the Lower House of Convocation (T. E. S. Clarke and Foxcroft, 1907: 467). Another defender of Clarke in his hour of need was Samuel Bradford, a former protégé of Tillotson who later became master of Corpus (1716–24) and bishop of Carlisle

(1718–23) and Rochester (1723–31). Bradford assured Clarke that he regarded the *Scripture doctrine* as intended to arrive at 'the best method of bringing Christians to as perfect an agreement as might be' (CUL, Add. 7113: 5). Clarke also had the support of two other future bishops – Benjamin Hoadly and Francis Hare – the latter of whom was prompted by Clarke's experiences to publish a satirical pamphlet entitled *The difficulties and discouragements which attend the study of the Scriptures in the way of private judgement* (1714) which Convocation duly censured.

Within Cambridge Clarke attracted several disciples who defended his work and popularised his theology. His most fervent disciple was John Jackson who, after reading the *Scripture doctrine*, declared to Clarke that he regarded Arianism as being scripturally sound and viewed the received view of the Trinity as verging on the ancient heresy of Nestorianism (CUL, Add. 7113: 11). After Clarke promised Convocation not to write anything more on the subject of the Trinity, Jackson became his virtual theological amanuensis (Whiston, 1753: 267) and when Jackson's heterodox views on the Trinity resulted in his being denied an MA at Cambridge in 1718 it was therefore a slight both to himself and to Clarke. After Clarke's death in 1729 Jackson succeeded him as master of Wigston's Hospital in Leicester, a position which did not require any doctrinal test.

Another warm defender of Clarke was Arthur Sykes (MA Corpus, 1708) whose *Modest plea for the baptismal scripture-notion of the Trinity* (1719) was both a defence of Clarke's orthodoxy and a plea for greater latitude of interpretation of the Thirty-Nine Articles. Such views naturally attracted the hostility of the Cambridge high churchmen: when Sykes took his Cambridge DD in 1726, wrote one of his admirers, 'he stood, like the sturdy oak to receive and return back the fiery darts of the orthodox' (Disney, 1785: 155). In his main theological work, *The principles and connexion of natural and revealed religion* (1740), Sykes spelt out the theological position on which much of Clarke's position had been based – that 'He that destroys Natural Religion, necessarily must subvert the *Christian Religion*, which stands upon That as its Foundation' (p. 3). Sykes did allow that there was a place for Revelation though, like Clarke, he saw it as providing further '*Motives* and *Reasons* for the practice of what is right; more and different from, what natural Reason without this help can suggest' (p. 244). In a passage which indicates the theological basis of the latitudinarians' interest in natural philosophy Sykes argued that 'The greater Discoveries and Improvements we make in the true Principles of Philosophy, the more we are enabled to establish and confirm those Principles [of natural religion]' (p. 3). It was this approach to theology which had earlier prompted that arch-high churchman, Henry Sacheverell, to attack those who seek 'to explain the *Credenda* of our *Faith* in *New-fangl'd Terms of Modern Philosophy*' (Stewart, 1978: 214). Appropriately, Sykes was closely associated with Newton: he served with Sir Isaac (and Clarke) as one of the directors of the King Street Chapel in London and he defended Newton's chronological works against the strictures of Warburton. It was Sykes, too, who was chosen by Catherine Conduitt, Newton's niece, to act as Newton's literary executor for his theological papers though Sykes died before doing more than compiling 'a digest' of his religious and chronological papers (Whiteside, 1967–81, I: xxii n.27).

A rather more equivocal sympathiser with Clarke's theological views was Richard Bentley. Bentley shared with Clarke the belief that Christianity was best defended by the application of reason: 'We look upon right reason as the native lamp of the soul', proclaimed Bentley in his Cambridge Commencement Sermon of 1696 in language reminiscent of the Cambridge Platonists, 'placed and kindled there by our Creator . . . so that the Christian religion is so far from declining or fearing the strictest trials of reason, that it every where appeals to it . . . Whatsoever, therefore is inconsistent with natural reason, can never be justly imposed as an article of faith' (Dyce, 1836–8, III: 222–3). Like Clarke, too, Bentley's orthodoxy on the issue of the Trinity was suspect: Bentley had called into question the genuineness of one of the same Trinitarian proof-texts which Newton had also challenged (Ferguson, 1976: 154–5) and there were rumours that Bentley was a member of a circle of Arians which included Newton, Whiston and Clarke (Westfall, 1980: 650).

In a letter to Clarke in 1716 Bentley remarked on the hostility that he had attracted within Cambridge both as a result of his defence of the Hanoverian regime and of his proposed edition of the Greek New Testament which, it was claimed, would endanger the Church. Such attacks had, however, only served to strengthen Bentley's always well-developed fighting spirit and he urged Clarke to join him in countering the influence within Cambridge both of 'Jacobite principles' and 'Hicksian doctrines' – a reference to the work of the nonjuror George Hickes (Wordsworth, 1842, II: 527–8). As his remarks to Clarke indicate, Bentley – like Hoadly – was a resolute foe of the nonjurors, regarding their arguments for the independence of the Church from state control as subversive of the post-revolutionary order. In 1716, in his capacity as archdeacon of Ely, Bentley delivered a visitation sermon to the clergy of the diocese of Ely in answer to a claim by Hickes that the conforming clergy were schismatic – on the contrary, argued Bentley, the nonjurors had no right to appoint bishops without the authority of the presently constituted political order and were therefore themselves schismatic (Dyce, 1836–8, III: 281–5). Hearne commented of Bentley's sermon that 'it shows Dr. Bentley to be (as he certainly is) a rascal, and an enemy to the

King [i.e. the Old Pretender] and all the King's friends' (Monk, 1830–3, 1: 428).

But though Bentley was associated with men like Samuel Clarke he was careful not to stray too far outside the accepted bounds of Anglican orthodoxy. Bentley was a university careerist and one of his goals (which he successfully attained) was to become Regius professor of divinity; consequently, it would have been imprudent for him to appear too theologically *avant-garde*. Significantly, in his inaugural lecture as Regius professor he endeavoured to put to rest fears that his scriptural scholarship inclined him to heresy (BL, Add. 22560: 51). In July 1718, the year after Bentley became Regius professor, Brook Rand of Corpus wrote to his former colleague, Samuel Kerrick (nephew of Charles Kidman, one of Tenison's protégés at Corpus), and commented of Bentley, with not unmerited cynicism:

I find by the news you sent me that the spirit of Orthodoxy reigns still in Cambridge, and that the men of the Church of England are still very brisk in defence of it. It takes Bentley to be the best heterodox bull-dog you have in your university only not of a good breed, and upon the accounts I am afraid this enmity to the Church of England men will last no longer than he finds it in his interests. (Corpus Christi College, Cambridge, Hartshorne MSS, XI: 46)

While Bentley was inclined to keep his theological doubts to himself, William Whiston, another prominent member of Clarke's Cambridge circle, shouted his dissent from orthodox doctrine from the rooftops – with the result that he was expelled from the university in 1710 for propagating Arianism (Duffy, 1976). During this trial Bentley distanced himself from Whiston's heretical opinions but vainly endeavoured to prevent Whiston being expelled from the university; furthermore, Bentley delayed the appointment of a successor to Whiston in the hope that he might recant and take up his post as Lucasian professor once again (Monk, 1830–3, II: 290–1). Like Bentley other Cambridge latitudinarian divines were loath to see Whiston tried for heresy but were also careful not to identify themselves too closely with his doctrines. When Clarke was asked at his DD disputation by Dr James, the Regius professor of divinity, to comment on Whiston's work on the Trinity, Clarke replied guardedly 'that he would not condemn the man, but would condemn the doctrine' (BL, Add. 22560: 42). Later, when Whiston founded his Society for the Study of Primitive Christianity, Clarke, Hare and Hoadly were among those 'particularly invited' to attend, an offer they declined (Nichols, 1812–15, I: 500). While men like Bentley, Clarke and Hoadly sympathised with Whiston and perhaps even tacitly shared his beliefs, they did not wish to cause a full-scale confrontation with their high church colleagues of the sort that Whiston's headstrong behaviour provoked.

Indeed, in some ways Whiston was more, not less, orthodox than some of his latitudinarian associates. To him true doctrine was a matter of enormous importance and his attempt to restore what he regarded as the true teachings of the early Church was a means towards the biblical 'restitution of all things' which would accompany the new millennium. For a man like Clarke, on the other hand, the niceties of doctrine did not carry the same chiliastic overtones; consequently, he was more prepared to compromise his beliefs for the peace of the Church which, in Whiston's eyes, made Clarke a traitor to the cause of primitive Christianity – particularly as Whiston's espousal of Arianism had been partly influenced by Clarke (Whiston, 1730: 12–13). It is an index of the difference between the two men that while Clarke's Boyle lectures took as their subject the basics of natural religion Whiston chose as his topic *The accomplishment of scriptural prophecies* (1707). Despite Whiston's fate Joseph Wasse of Queens' was prompted by his study of Clarke to publish a largely Arian work entitled *Reformed devotions* (1719) while other Cambridge dons like John Balguy and John Laurence continued to defend Clarke's Trinitarian views.

But if Cambridge produced many of Clarke's allies it was also the home of many of his opponents. Dr John Edwards of St John's, who was one of Locke's most vehement critics, criticised Clarke both for his scriptural exegesis and for his conceptions of space and time which, Edwards argued, limited the omnipotence of God. Moreover, in Edwards's view, Clarke's influence could be discerned in the general scholium to the second edition of the *Principia* where, wrote Edwards, in 1714, 'the learned knight seems to me to lay open his heart and mind, and tell the world what cause he espouses of this day, viz. the very same which Dr. Clarke and Mr. Whiston have publicly asserted' (Ferguson, 1976: 215). (Interestingly enough, Jackson soon afterwards commented approvingly to Clarke that Newton's general scholium was 'exactly agreeable to your *Scripture doctrine*' (CUL, Add. 7113: 18).) A colleague of Edwards, Thomas Bennet (MA St John's, 1694), a determined opponent of the dissenters, also published a critique of Clarke's Trinitarian views in a pamphlet published in 1718. While Clarke was under scrutiny by Convocation Edward Potter of Emmanuel published a work entitled *A vindication of our blessed saviour's divinity; chiefly against Dr. Clarke* in which he urged Convocation to show 'a just indignation against a heresy that undermines our most holy faith' (Ferguson, 1976: 79). This same cry of 'the Church in Danger' lay behind a pamphlet by Edward Wells of Oxford which criticised Clarke for his defence 'of those latitudinarian, alias comprehension, alias moderation principles' which were causing 'the almost total decay of true Christianity both as to belief and practice' (*ibid.*: 68).

Clarke's most formidable and persistent opponent was Daniel Water-land of Magdalene who, like his friend Bishop Edmund Gibson, saw the Church's future as being linked to the whigs but opposed the latitudinarian theology associated with many of the divines who had supported the Hanoverian succession: hence the remark of the antiquary, Cole, that 'his Church notions did not exactly square to the fashionable opinions' (BL, Add. 5831: p. 172). Indeed Waterland would have shared Gibson's view that the 'men of latitude' were 'semi-infidels who . . . [had made] Christianity little more than a system of morality' (N. Sykes, 1926: 264). One of the main sources of this canker was, in Waterland's opinion, the works of Clarke which had disseminated Arianism, which was 'the dupe to *Deism*, as *Deism* again is to *Atheism* or *Popery*' (Van Mildert, 1823, IV: 230). Waterland also attacked Clarke's view that religious duties were entirely subordinate to those prescribed by natural law. Sykes's defence of Clarke on this point led Waterland to comment thus to Bishop Gibson in 1731:

In a word it was *Supernatural* Religion (and not natural) both as to duties and sanctions, which Christ came to restore, and to advance to perfection: natural religion is a good thing: but many have honoured it too much, for the Prejudice of Supernatural: which has brought deism among us, as I conceive, and has done a great deal of mischief. (Lambeth Palace Library, MS 1741: 73)

– a passage which sums up the theological divide between Waterland and latitudinarians like Sykes and Clarke.

If Clarke and his followers were the centre around which debates about the relative significance of reason and Revelation swirled it was Clarke's friend and editor, Hoadly, who was the focus for the disputes about the closely related issue of the nature of Church government. Like Clarke, Hoadly argued that the best defence of Christianity was to emphasise its fundamental consonance with human reason, even if some points of Revelation which were clearly set out in Scripture did transcend human capabilities. Never one to shrink from debate Hoadly was not afraid to draw out the implications of such a view in a way that (as Stephen put it) made him 'the best-hated clergyman of the century amongst his own order' (Stephen, 1962, II: 129); as J. C. D. Clark writes, 'It was not Lockeian contractarianism but Hoadlian latitudinarianism which pro-voked the most bitter domestic ideological conflict of the century' (1985: 302). If Christianity was based on reason and Scripture, Hoadly argued, there was no necessity for a Church capable of defining doctrine: the Church therefore became in Hoadly's view an essentially administrative institution which was totally under the control of the State. Hoadly was largely prompted to develop such views by his debates with the nonjurors who justified their refusal to acquiesce in the Revolutionary Settlement by arguing that the true Church to which they remained faithful was independent of the State – thus Hoadly's *Preservative against the principles and practices of the nonjurors* (1716) was a defence of a thoroughgoing Erastian church order. This position was linked by Hoadly with a defence of 'rational Christianity' since it was part of his argument that if religion were divorced from reason the way would be left open for a revival of the sacerdotal claims of the nonjurors with their divisive consequences for both Church and State. This same hostility to what he regarded as sacerdotal pretensions can be seen in his *Plain account of the nature and end of the sacrament* (1735) in which he argued that the Eucharist had no special symbolic significance and that the function of the minister was simply to remind the congregation of Christ's noble work.

The year after the publication of the *Preservative* Hoadly's views on the nature of the Church were further developed in his sermon, 'The nature of the Kingdom or Church of Christ', in which he maintained that the Church was an entirely human institution which should be organised by the State since Christ had 'left behind Him no visible, human authority . . . no judges over the consciences or religion of His people' (N. Sykes, 1928: 143) – a work which set off the pamphlet war which became known as the Bangorian controversy (since Hoadly had been rewarded by the whigs with the bishopric of Bangor in 1715). Appropriately, among the pamphlets stirred up by Hoadly's famous sermon was one by the nonjuring Bishop Brett (LL B Corpus, 1689), the contents of which are succinctly summarised by its title: *The independency of the church upon the state . . .* (1717). Nor was hostility to Hoadly's ecclesiology restricted to the nonjurors: in the same year as Brett's pamphlet appeared the high church-dominated Lower House of Convocation moved that Hoadly's sermon was designed 'To subvert all government and discipline in the church of Christ' (Disney, 1785: 57). Even among those of Hoadly's episcopal brethren who were staunch supporters of the Hanoverian succession there was considerable disquiet at the extent to which he had undercut any claims to ecclesiastical power or independence. Indeed, Hoadly's *Preservative* may not only have been directed at the nonjurors but also at Hanoverian churchmen like Bishop Gibson who were seeking to revive some of the Church's disciplinary powers (Every, 1956: 161).

Though Hoadly's views on the nature of the Church and Christianity attracted considerable opposition even from those of a similar political persuasion such views (like those of Clarke) took firm root at Cambridge. Hoadly had been educated at Catharine Hall while that college was under the rule of Dr John Leng, a Boyle lecturer (1717–18) and a staunch whig, who was rewarded with the bishopric of Norwich in 1723. However,

Hoadly's support within Cambridge came chiefly from Corpus, Tenison's college, where men like Thomas Herne, Arthur Sykes and Thomas Pyle rose to his defence during the Bangorian controversy (Sykes and Pyle later being rewarded by Hoadly with positions as prebendaries). But, like Clarke's, Hoadly's views also provoked fierce opposition within Cambridge – hardly surprising since Hoadly had made his opposition to the high churchmen within the university apparent in a work of 1715 which described Oxford and Cambridge as being more concerned to produce a '*Furious Zealot*' than a '*Hard Student*' (J. Hoadly, 1773, I: 544). Hoadly's most persistent critic was Andrew Snape (master of Eton, 1711–19; provost of King's, 1719–42) who was described by that inveterate tory, William Cole, as a man whose principles were those 'of a true Son of the Church of England; [which] in his time [were] rather going out of fashion' (BL, Add. 5817: p. 116). The first of Snape's many *Letters to the bishop of Bangor* (1711) was particularly popular and passed through seventeen editions, though it cost Snape his position as a royal chaplain since George I warmly approved of Hoadly's views. Another of Hoadly's Cambridge critics – the tory Thomas Sherlock – was a contemporary of Hoadly's from Catharine Hall who was elected to the mastership of that college in 1714. Sherlock took so active a role in opposing Hoadly's views that in 1717 he was chosen by the Lower House of Convocation as chairman of the committee appointed to examine Hoadly's contentious sermon – an appointment that resulted in Sherlock's temporary disgrace at court. The most fundamental challenge to Hoadly's principles appropriately came from a nonjuror: William Law, an ejected fellow of Emmanuel. Law attacked the whole drift of Hoadly's style of divinity which, Law implied, led to deism: thus Law set out to rebut Hoadly's demystification of such Christian fundamentals as prayer and the Eucharist, and on the crucial issue of ecclesiastical authority Law argued that all 'sacerdotal Power is derived from the Holy Ghost' (Walker, 1973: 22–7) rather than, as Hoadly contended, being in the gift of the State. Attacks of this kind were later to prompt John Balguy (BA St John's, 1706) (who was appointed a prebendary of Salisbury thanks to Hoadly) to defend his patron by arguing that 'whoever maintains the Reality and Dignity of Revelation, at the Expense either of Natural Religion, or Morality, highly injures and weakens all Three' (J. Hoadly, 1773, I: xxxv).

After his death in 1761 Hoadly was described as being

so happy as to live long enough to reap the full (earthly) reward of his Labours; to see his Christian and moderate opinions prevail over the Kingdom, in Church and State . . . to see the general Temper of the Clergy entirely changed, the Bishops preferring few or none of intolerant Principles, and the Clergy claiming no inherent Authority, but what is the natural Result of their own good Behaviour as Individuals, in the Discharge of their Duty. (J. Hoadly, 1773, I: xii–xiii)

Though such a eulogy both overestimates Hoadly's influence within the Church at large (J. C. D. Clark, 1985: 138) and underestimates the continuing strength of tory churchmanship (Colley, 1982: 153–6) it none the less does capture something of the theological milieu within Hoadly's own *alma mater* of Cambridge. Though some Cambridge dons might draw back from the full rigours of Hoadly's views on church government, the theology and ecclesiology of Hoadly and Clarke found fertile soil in Cambridge – particularly as the high church opposition gradually withered beneath the rising sun of whig ecclesiastical patronage.

Within Cambridge what teaching there was in divinity – and there was less and less formal instruction as the university's curriculum became ever more dominated by the mathematical sciences – largely consisted of variations on the themes which had been enunciated by Clarke (and, before him, by latitudinarian preachers like Wilkins and Tillotson). Given the basic propositions of latitudinarian theology – that Christianity could be reconciled with reason and natural religion, that the chief end of Christianity was the ethical improvement of mankind, and that in a few areas where Revelation supplemented natural religion doctrinal issues could be settled by reading the Bible – there was little room for theological development or originality. Thus Cambridge theologians continued to restate such views with less and less opposition or debate – as the character of theological instruction in St John's, once the high church college *par excellence*, illustrates.

There a succession of tutors provided lectures on the foundations of religion and morality which emphasised the need to defend Christianity and its ethical system by demonstrating that it had secure foundations in reason and natural law. James Tunstall, a famous St John's 'pupil-monger' who was a fellow and tutor from 1729 to 1747, delivered a set of *Lectures on natural and revealed religion* . . . (published posthumously in 1765) which repeated the familiar refrain that 'Christian revelation must be entertained upon the certain and uncontested principles of natural religion' (p. 1). In an oblique reference to the controversy over subscription to the Thirty-Nine Articles Tunstall revealed his dislike of doctrinal debate by arguing that the Church should not prescribe 'any thing as necessary to the salvation which is not contained in the holy scriptures' (p. 12). Tunstall was followed as a tutor at St John's by Thomas Balguy (the son of John Balguy, the defender of Clarke and Hoadly), father and son sharing both a similar theological outlook and the patronage of Bishop Hoadly. As tutor Thomas Balguy lectured from 1741 to 1758 on moral philosophy and Christian evidences (Scott, 1903: 451), the tenor of his teaching being evident in his manuscript lectures on *A system of morality* (first delivered in

1753) (St John's College, Cambridge, MS 545) which treat ethical problems in a largely secular way by reference to natural law and to Locke's political writings; he also espoused an early form of utilitarianism arguing that 'Pleasure is to be rejected, when productive of greater pain, and pain to be chosen when productive of greater pleasure.' In his *Discourses and charges* (published posthumously in 1820) Thomas Balguy adopts a view of the Church similar to that of his patron, Hoadly: thus he attacks the idea of apostolic succession and argues that ecclesiastical government should be based on principles of social utility and should be under the control of the State. Like Hoadly, too, he viewed the Eucharist as simply a memorial service (Hunt, 1870–3, III: 363–4).

Balguy's colleague, Thomas Rutherforth (who served as a principal tutor from 1740 to 1751), also delivered lectures on moral philosophy which were published in 1754 as his *Institutes of natural law*. Like Balguy's *System of morality* they treat ethical and political questions with little reference to Christianity; as the title suggests, Rutherforth was chiefly concerned with natural law and, as he acknowledged, the work was largely based on Grotius, though in his section on political philosophy he also appears to draw on Montesquieu's concept of the division of the powers – an indication of Rutherforth's wide-ranging reading. In an earlier work, *An essay on the nature and obligations of virtue* (1744) – in which Rutherforth praised the ethical writings of John Balguy – he did make rather more play of the Christian basis of moral behaviour by arguing for a kind of Christian hedonism. 'Every man's happiness is the ultimate end which reason teaches him to pursue' (chapter 8), he asserted, and Christianity promised not only 'temporal happiness' but 'happiness in a life to come, upon easier conditions than the law of Moses had promised it' (chapter 13). Such a position naturally led to the Christian utilitarianism of Paley who drew heavily on Rutherforth's work (Le Mahieu, 1976: 124). The fact that Rutherforth was also a doughty defender of Christianity against infidels such as Hume, a strong opponent of the anti-subscription movement and, as Regius professor of divinity from 1756 to 1771 (as Cole puts it) 'the great and unrivalled ornament of the Divinity Scholes' (Winstanley, 1935: 360), only serves to emphasise how pervasive and uncontroversial the style of theology which largely derived from Clarke had become.

While the well-worn arguments of Cambridge latitudinarianism left little room for originality in theological matters the continual emphasis on the overriding importance of ethics rather than doctrine (which was such an important part of the tradition) was a spur to new approaches to moral theory – as the works of Thomas Balguy and Rutherforth, with their intimations of utilitarianism, indicate. One of the most original of Cambridge moral philosophers of this period, John Gay, is also one of the most obscure. We know only that he was a fellow and tutor of Sidney Sussex from 1724 to 1732 and thereafter held a living in Bedfordshire where he died in 1745 leaving a wife and five children in poverty (CUL, Add. 2615: 112). Though he was thought by his contemporaries to be 'eminent as a metaphysician and biblical critic' (Dyer, 1824, II: 106) he published only one work (and that anonymously): the *Dissertation concerning the fundamental principles of virtue and morality* (which originally appeared as a preface to Edmund Law's edition of Archbishop King's *Essay on the origin of evil* in 1731). In this brief work Gay presented what Burtt calls 'the first clear statement of the combination of associationism in psychology and utilitarianism in morals which was to exercise a controlling influence on the development of the next century and a half of English thought' (1939: 767). Gay was greatly influenced by Locke (whose *Essay* had become a staple part of the Cambridge curriculum) as his argument that the moral sense is not 'innate or implanted in us . . . [but] acquired from our own observation or the imitation of others' (*ibid*.: 785) suggests. The chief means by which such a moral sense was developed, argued Gay, was through the association of certain actions with pleasure since 'that which he [everyman] apprehends to be apt to produce pleasure, he calls *good*' (p. 777): happiness, then, 'is the general end of all actions' (p. 779).

This whole line of argument was to be developed by Hartley who acknowledged in the preface of his seminal work, *Observations on man* (1749), that it was Gay who suggested to him 'the Possibility of deducing all our intellectual Pleasures and Pains from Association'. Hartley became aware of Gay's theory even before it appeared in print – thanks, no doubt, to the connections he had built up at Cambridge while at Jesus from 1722 to 1730. While there he also appears to have been influenced by latitudinarian theology: his reservations about the Thirty-Nine Articles and the practice of subscription help account for his decision to undertake postgraduate studies in medicine rather than divinity and in Part Two of his *Observations on man* he argued that 'It seems intirely useless to all good Purposes . . . to form any Creeds, Articles, or Systems of Faith, and to require an Assent to these in Words or Writing' since 'Men are to be influenced, even in respect of the principal Doctrines of God's Providence, a future State, and the Truth of the Scriptures, by rational Methods only, not by Compulsion' (1749: 351). Among Hartley's closest friends at Cambridge was his colleague at Jesus, John Jortin, who, though he was thought by some of his contemporaries to be a virtual Socinian (*GM*, 1773: 388), was a protégé of Archbishop Herring. In his influential *Remarks on ecclesiastical history* (1751–4) (based on his Boyle lectures for 1749) Jortin, like Hoadly, attacked the view that any particular form of church government was divinely sanctioned and appealed for a spirit of religious moderation in keeping with the works of those whom the eighteenth-century latitudinarians regarded as their forbears: Erasmus, Episcopius, Grotius, Hales, Chillingworth, Taylor, Tillotson and Locke (1846 ed., II: 420).

Another close friend of Jortin was Edmund Law who was also well known to Gay and Hartley (with whom he carried on a lengthy correspondence on the *Observations on man* (GM, 1787: 745)). Edmund Law was the most influential Cambridge theologian of the mid-eighteenth century, the most important of his many works being the *Considerations on the state of the world, with regard to the theory of religion* (1745). In a largely unhistorically minded age, this book put forward the original thesis that mankind's understanding of Christianity was, like all other branches of knowledge, advancing with the passage of time. Law's firm belief in the idea of progress (Crane, 1934) is evident in the goal he set himself in his advertisement of 'showing that Arts and Sciences, Natural and Revealed Religion, have upon the whole been progressive from the creation of the world to the present time'. By religion Law meant 'the way of promoting our most perfect happiness' in this world and the next (1820 ed.: 256) – a form of religiously based utilitarianism that Law shared with a number of Cambridge latitudinarians, most notably his disciple and biographer, William Paley whose ethical system, Stephen wrote, was like that of Bentham with the addition of sanctions in the next world (1962, II: 106). Nor, like Tillotson and Clarke before him, did Law view the ethical commands of the Gospel as differing fundamentally from those discoverable by reason: 'The Morality of the Gospel', he wrote in his *Reflections on the life and character of Christ* (1776), '[is] not beyond what might be discoverable by reason; nor possibly could be' because morality is based on experience (p. 61). Here we see Law's profound debt to Locke whose works he later edited; Locke's epistemology also underlies his progressive view of history and religion since, as human experience is cumulative, time will bring with it greater understanding (Stephen, 1962, I: 344). Such a position naturally implied a reluctance to accept one particular set of doctrines as valid for all time; appropriately, then, Law (who became bishop of Carlisle in 1768) was the only one of the bishops to approve of abolishing clerical subscription to the Thirty-Nine Articles in 1772.

As evidence for the progress of mankind the whiggish Law cited the benefits of the eighteenth-century English constitution which enabled his compatriots to 'enjoy the blessing of *liberty* in that perfection which has been unknown to former ages' and he urged his readers to prevent any sedition against such a government (1820 ed.: 297–8). A similar line of argument (no doubt drawn from Law) was developed by John Ross (fellow of St John's, 1744–70; bishop of Exeter, 1778–92) in a *Commencement sermon* delivered in 1756. Ross (who became an FRS in 1758) justified a preoccupation with the study of nature since 'an improvement in science naturally produces a spirit of liberty' as well as of 'virtue and religion' (pp. 7, 10). To Ross it followed that a scientifically inclined university such as Cambridge should also be a defender of the whig constitution 'under which we enjoy all the blessings, that liberty can produce' (p. 14).

Within Cambridge there was sufficient suspicion of Law as a crypto-Socinian and a propagator of the ancient heresy that the soul slept between death and the final resurrection for there to be some objection to his receiving a doctorate of divinity in 1749, but he none the less received the degree with the approval of Herring, the archbishop of Canterbury (Nichols, 1812–15, II: 70). Nor were such objections strong enough to prevent his appointment to a number of prominent university positions – master of Peterhouse, 1756–87 (a post he retained after becoming bishop of Carlisle in 1768), principal librarian, 1760–9, and Knightsbridge professor of moral theology, 1764–9. He used such positions to win others over to his basic conviction that (as Paley wrote of him) Christianity needed 'to recover the simplicity of the gospel from beneath that load of unauthorized additions, which . . . [had been] heaped upon it' (M. L. Clarke, 1974: 14). To this end he provided those of his students who intended to take orders with instruction 'in the original sense, and design' of both the New and the Old Testament in their original languages (*GM*, 1787: 745) as a means of returning to the foundations of Christianity which, in his view, were 'very plain and practical; level to all capacities, and calculated for the common good of mankind' (E. Law, 1774: 2). It is not surprising, then, that among his disciples were future Unitarians such as Jebb, Disney and Wakefield together with prominent (and controversial) late eighteenth-century Cambridge theologians such as William Paley, Richard Watson and John Hey.

Among Law's Cambridge contemporaries one of his closest friends was Francis Blackburne, who graduated from Catharine Hall but left the college in 1728 (the year after Law became a fellow of Christ's) after having been denied a fellowship. According to his son, Blackburne's study of Locke and Hoadly encouraged a 'strong attachment to the principles of ecclesiastical and civil liberty' which made him 'obnoxious' to the fellows of Catharine Hall who were mostly 'high royalists on the principle of hereditary right' (Blackburne, 1804, I: iv). Though Blackburne left Cambridge for a living in Yorkshire he and Law remained closely associated – so much so that after Law's elevation to the episcopate he was to be described in a set of verses entitled 'Cambridge triumphant', as being

With Blackburne leagued, in many a motley page
Immortal war with Mother Church to wage.
(in Abbey, 1887, II: 247)

Law, wrote Blackburne's son, was 'the only person who knew of *The Confessional* [Blackburne's major work] for some years, and indeed actually suggested the title of it while the work was yet in embryo' (Blackburne, 1804, I: lxxxviii). It was the publication of this work in 1766 which brought the long-simmering issue of subscription to the Thirty-Nine Articles into the heat and glare of public controversy.

The eighteenth-century debate over subscription had begun with Samuel Clarke who maintained in the introduction to his *Scripture doctrine of the Trinity* (1712) that the Articles permitted considerable latitude of interpretation since a person could subscribe to them 'whenever he can in any sense at all reconcile them with Scripture' (Ferguson, 1976: 179). This view was attacked by Waterland who was concerned that it opened the doors of the Church of England to those, like Clarke, whom he suspected of Arianism. However, disciples of Clarke like Sykes continued to argue for what Disney called 'the latitudinarian scheme' – the view that by subscribing 'we think those general propositions agreeable to the work of God, without regarding the sense either of the compilers or imposers of the articles' (Disney, 1785: 118). Given the close agreement between Clarke and Hoadly on most theological matters it is not surprising that the latter maintained a similar position, arguing that 'the Articles were never so much as confined to any one particular determinate sense' (Abbey, 1887, I: 222). The logical outcome of Hoadly's views on church government was to argue for the abolition of such doctrinal tests altogether: if, as he contended, the Church was merely a human institution it was not entitled to demand compliance with statements of belief other than those clearly stated in Scripture. However, Hoadly drew back from such a position and insisted that clergy under him subscribe to the Articles; thus he denied Clarke's lieutenant, John Jackson, a prebend's position because he would not conform to this requirement (Nicols, 1812–15, II: 524). Jackson's case against subscription (which he set out in his *Grounds of civil and ecclesiastical government . . .*, 1718) was, however, largely an extension of the principles enunciated by Hoadly in his famous sermon on Church government of the previous year. Like Hoadly, Jackson rejected the notion that the Church had any special powers other than those which derived from 'the Principles of Natural Reason improv'd by Revelation' (p. 5); in Jackson's view it followed, then, that the Church had no 'Power or *Right* to impose upon any Person, any Doctrine . . . which is not *clearly* and expressly contain'd and *declared to be necessary* in the Gospel' (p. 38) – in short, 'The Articles of Christian Faith ought to be as comprehensive as the

Gospel' (p. 52). Suiting his actions to his words Jackson declined any further preferment which required subscription – a decision which Blackburne also took after 1750.

The most obvious explanation for Hoadly's reluctance to pursue the logic of his own position with the same unflinching zeal as Jackson is that it would have brought his steady rise up the episcopal ladder to a sudden halt. But Hoadly was probably moved by more than an understandable desire to avoid ecclesiastical disgrace: latitudinarians like Hoadly, Clarke or Sykes might argue for a remarkable degree of freedom of interpretation in theological matters but became more cautious when the institutional foundations of the Established Church were at stake. The Articles formed part of the constitution of the Church and hence their wholesale reform or abolition might set in train other changes which could revive and intensify the very civil and ecclesiastical divisions which they sought to avoid. It was, then, probably more than simple expediency which prompted most clergy with latitudinarian views to regard subscription as a public acknowledgement of their adherence to the Church of England as by law established, even though the Articles themselves had largely been drained of theological meaning. Such an outward conformity was generally all that was required in an age that was less and less given to prying into men's souls and the subscription issue largely faded from public view – apart from the occasional protest from high churchmen like John White (a former fellow of St John's) who, in 1746, vigorously defended the need for subscription in a pamphlet which decried the 'modern, latitudinarian, fashionable way of thinking' (p. 56) whereby conformity to the doctrines of the Church of England was a matter of individual choice.

However, this lull in the subscription debate was broken by the publication of Francis Blackburne's long-gestating *Confessional, or a full and free enquiry into the right, utility and success of establishing confessions of faith and doctrine in Protestant churches* in 1766 – Blackburne's rejection of the prevailing justification for subscription having been partly prompted by a university sermon in defence of subscription delivered by William Powell of St John's in 1758. Powell stated, with provocative candour, the view of subscription which had been largely accepted in latitudinarian circles since Clarke and Hoadly: that subscription to the Articles meant basically that those making this declaration 'acknowledge themselves members of the Church of *England*' and that the more scrupulous could console themselves with the reflection that 'we may understand them [the articles] in any of those senses which the general words comprehend' (p. 15). Powell added that if the Articles were changed this 'would give occasion to perpetual changes; and every change to fresh disputes' (p. 16) – a view with which Hoadly probably would have agreed.

In a pamphlet of 1758 Blackburne rejected such defences as mere sophistry but this was only a foretaste of the full-scale attack on the practice of subscription in the *Confessional* (1766) in which he set out to counter the arguments of those (like Powell) who 'went into the church at the same door which Dr. Clarke had opened for them' (Blackburne, 1804, v: 355) – though it was Clarke's arguments (together with those of Law) which had originally persuaded Blackburne to subscribe. Like Chillingworth before him Blackburne asserted that the Bible alone was the religion of Protestants and that therefore the Church had no right to demand compliance with anything other than the text of Scripture. Moreover, the Church could not compel its members to subscribe since 'The church hath no legislative authority' – a phrase he quoted from Clarke while citing the authority of Hoadly (and St Paul) who, he argued, had proved this assertion 'beyond the possibility of an answer' (Blackburne, 1804, v: 338–9). His debt to Hoadly's ecclesiology is evident, too, in his claim 'that an *immediate visible* appointment of governors or superintendants *under* Christ . . . was never vouchsafed to any churches' (*ibid.*: 42). It followed, then, that 'protestant churches ought not to employ human powers to establish religion upon civil and political principles, nor ought conscientious christians to receive their religion so established' (*ibid.*: 339). None the less, like Hoadly, Blackburne was prepared to allow the State to regulate the institutional forms of Christianity: 'Our legislative powers', he wrote, 'have a right to establish human forms of religion, so far at least as to require conformity of profession' (*ibid.*: 374). Blackburne also remained a minister of the Church of England; though he refused to take any further office which required a declaration of conformity to the Thirty-Nine Articles he took the view (as he put it to Lindsey in 1757) that having subscribed 'in *ignorance* and *unbelief* . . . I wrong or deceive no body by holding my Benefice by that Title, provided I bear my Testimony . . . that I do not hold my self any longer bound by those terms' (DWL, MS 12.52: 36).

Both Hoadly and Blackburne agreed that religion played such an important part in ensuring social stability that it was appropriate that the Church should be firmly under the control of the State. Indeed, it was part of the argument of the *Confessional* (the subtitle of which included the word 'utility') that even considerations based on social utility demanded the abolition of subscription – an indication of the growing strength of utilitarianism within the Cambridge latitudinarian tradition. 'The use of religion to society', argued Blackburne, is '. . . that men, having in their hearts the fear of God, and of his judgements, may be restrained from evil, and encouraged to be virtuous, in such instances as are beyond the reach of human laws. Points of doctrine, therefore, established for the public good of society, must have this use of religion for their object.' But the practice of subscription to the articles does not serve this purpose since it can lead to an individual making a profession of outward belief in a doctrine that he inwardly rejects and which therefore 'has no hold of him' with the result that 'society has no more benefit from his profession, than if such points of doctrine had not been established' (Blackburne, 1804, v: 363). While Blackburne admired the principles of both Hoadly and Clarke he decried their practice since their justification of the practice of subscription had denied the Church the opportunity for reform: 'What might not the firmness of an Hales and a Chillingworth formerly', he lamented, 'or more lately of a Clarke or an Hoadly, have obtained for us by this time?' (*ibid.*: 333). Blackburne himself was determined to institute such a reform and the *Confessional* was intended to act as a rallying-call for those of like mind; the result of this agitation was the drawing up of the Feathers Tavern Petition requesting parliament to abolish the requirement that Anglican clergy should subscribe to the Thirty-Nine Articles – a proposal that was resoundingly rejected by the House of Commons in 1772.

While those involved in the subscription debate clearly saw themselves as reformers rather than underminers of Christianity there were – even within a citadel of the clerical estate such as Cambridge – occasional examples of outright infidelity together with an undercurrent of religious belief which hovered uncertainly between Christianity and deism. Such developments were not altogether surprising in an institution where there was frequent emphasis on the need to reduce clerical pretensions and on the apologetical importance of the conformity between natural and revealed religion; predictably, there were a few who took such principles to their logical extreme and began to advocate the abolition of the Established Church and the propagation of a religion based entirely on reason or even the rejection of religion altogether. How widespread such views were within Cambridge it is difficult to know since there was an obvious incentive not to state publicly opinions which could lead to disgrace and expulsion; none the less, there are sufficient examples of Cambridge free-thinkers who were exposed to the public gaze to suggest that there may well have been considerably more who remained in welcome obscurity.

As early as 1713 Hearne claimed that a former member of Cambridge was 'very great with Collins, and others of that Atheistical Gang' as well as being an admirer of Giordano Bruno (Hearne, 1885–1921, IV: 172). Hearne is often a doubtful authority (especially in relation to his political and religious opponents) though the suggestion that there were some deistic fellow-travellers associated with early eighteenth-century Cambridge is not altogether far-fetched. The deist, John Toland, was on sufficiently close terms with Barnham Goode (who resigned his fellow-ship at King's in 1700) to send him in 1720 a long account of Toland's *Pantheisticon*, in the course of which Collins is described as your 'quondam fellow collegian' (BL, Add. 4295: 40; Jacob, 1981: 172), a reference to Collins's education at King's where possibly he came to know Goode and introduced him into deistic circles.

The clearest example of a free-thinking fifth-columnist within the gates of Anglican Cambridge is provided by the case of Tinkler Ducket, a fellow of Caius, who, in 1739, was tried before the university court on the charge of atheism. Ducket was a disciple of Samuel Strutt, author of *A philosophical enquiry into the physical spring of human actions and the immediate cause of thinking* (1732) which constructed a system of thoroughgoing philosophical materialism on Newtonian and Lockean premises. Ducket's adherence to such principles was, unfortunately for him, plainly set out in a letter to his colleague, Stephen Gibbs, which, by accident, fell into the hands of the university authorities. In this letter Ducket describes himself as having arrived at 'the ne plus ultra' of atheism and waxes lyrical on his debt to 'the most adorable and omniscient Father Strutt, his Brother, Whitehead, Windle & c' (BL, Add. 5822: pp. 90b–91), phrases which suggest that Ducket regarded himself as a member of a surreptitious society of atheists to which he was attempting to recruit Gibbs. At his trial Ducket attempted to defend himself by arguing 'that Reason was the sovereign Guide of all Mankind; that Freedom of Thought, and private Judgement were the Right of every one' (*ibid.*: 92) – sentiments for which he claimed the authority of Locke and Bishop Burnet. Ducket also adopted the less controversial defence that he was now once more a Christian and no longer held the principles expounded by Strutt. This sudden conversion, however, availed him nothing for he was duly expelled from the university.

Nor was Cambridge alone in discovering such free-thinking 'moles' in its midst. In 1729 there was great consternation at Oxford when it was learnt that Stevens, a fellow of Trinity College, Oxford was a secret deist and that he 'made it his business to propogate deism, but through Bangorianism, that it is sufficient at first to bring them to Bangorianism', a reference to the works of Hoadly, bishop of Bangor 1715–21 (W. R. Ward, 1958: 146). Though the significance of Hoadly's work may have been embellished by a hostile witness, such a case only served to confirm high church suspicions that latitudinarian theology led naturally to deism – Swift, for example, had claimed that 'Tillotson is the person whom all English free thinkers own as their head . . . This great prelate assures us, that all the duties of the Christian religion with respect to God are no other but what natural light prompts men to except the two sacraments and praying to God in the name and mediation of Christ' (N. Sykes, 1955: 300). The Stevens case was soon followed by an Oxford sermon in which the preacher attacked 'the raging insolence of Arians and Atheists, of Libertines and Latitudinarians, of Socinians and Deists' (W. R. Ward, 1958: 147).

Both Ducket and Stevens were discovered accidentally and it is possible that there were other dons who shared their principles but not their misfortune in being publicly exposed. There was, however, one Cambridge fellow who paraded his heterodoxy for all to see. William Woolston of Sidney Sussex came to deism not through contact with the work of figures like Collins or Toland as was fashionable among some of the ultra-whigs but rather through his study of the Church Fathers and, in particular, Origen. Such works helped shape his conviction that all of Scripture should be interpreted allegorically (Whiston, 1753: 198) and that the biblical miracles should be regarded as symbolic of spiritual mysteries rather than as accurate historical accounts. This view, first put forward in his *Old apology for Christianity* (1705), grew more strident until in his *Fifth discourse on the miracles of our Saviour* Woolston argued that 'all Opposition and Contradiction to spiritual and allegorical Interpretations of the Scripture, is the Sin of *Blasphemy* against the Holy Ghost' (1729 ed.: 68). Earlier, in his *Third discourse* Woolston had contended that attempts to argue for the reasonableness of Christianity were ludicrous, for 'Christianity, as it is understood' is 'the most unreasonable and absurd Story, that ever was told' (1729 ed.: 66). To drive home his point he proceeded to parody the biblical account with examples which Voltaire was later to rephrase, using his rapier wit rather than Woolston's crude blunderbuss (Torrey, 1930: 59). Though Woolston's belief in a vague allegorical version of Christianity set him apart from the other deists he shared with them a vehement anti-clericalism – hence his assertion in his *Fifth discourse* that 'the Spirit and Power of *Jesus* will soon enter the Church, and expel Hireling Priests, who make Merchandise of the Gospel' (1729 ed.: 69).

Cambridge was much slower to act in the case of Woolston than of Whiston who was promptly expelled in 1710 on the less grave charge of Arianism. Woolston's break with orthodoxy was not unambiguously obvious until the publication of his two *Letters to Thomas Bennet* (a fellow of St John's who criticised Woolston's work) in 1720 and 1721. By this time the Hanoverians were on the throne and the whigs who had a number of scores to settle with the Church were in power; thus when Woolston was deprived of his fellowship in 1721 Sidney Sussex chose to act on the grounds of his nonresidency rather than his heresy. Woolston's work must have had the effect of exacerbating theological tensions within Cambridge since his vitriolic attacks on the high churchmen – whom he characterised as crypto-jacobites – were accompanied by appeals to a number of highly placed latitudinarians, no doubt to their considerable embarrassment. Thus his *Fourth discourse on the miracles of our Saviour* was dedicated to Francis Hare, then bishop of St Asaph, whom he credited with the conversion to deism of Collins, Hare's former pupil at King's. In his preface, too, Woolston argued that both he and bishops like Hare and Hoadly shared the common goal of wishing 'to set Mankind at perfect Liberty, and to lay open the dirty Fences of the Church, call'd Subscriptions, which are not only the Stain of a good Conscience, but the *Discouragements*, your Lordship [Hare] hints at, in the Study of the Scriptures' (1729 ed.: vii).

Moreover, the extravagance of Woolston's attacks on the clergy and Christian orthodoxy was an embarrassment to those advocating greater religious tolerance. Whiston at first attempted to help Woolston whom he saw as a fellow victim of ecclesiastical intolerance, but eventually he came to regard Woolston as a blasphemer with whom he could no longer associate (Anon., 1733: 18–19). However, Clarke continued to attempt to gain Woolston's liberty even after he had been imprisoned for blasphemy. Clarke, wrote Woolston's biographer, declared that he did not act for Woolston 'as an Approver of his Doctrines, but as an Advocate for that Liberty which he had through his life defended. He looked on Mr. Woolston as one under persecution for Religion, which he thought inconsistent with the Liberties of England, and with the Doctrines of Christianity' (*ibid.*: 18). That he was prepared to defend a man like Woolston shows the extent to which Clarke's conception of permissible theological debate differed from that of many of his clerical colleagues and must have served to heighten further the suspicion with which some in Cambridge regarded his influence and that of his disciples within the university.

While all shades of Anglican opinion could agree that the beliefs of Ducket and Woolston quite clearly fell outside the bounds of Christianity, there were individuals within Cambridge whose work served to draw attention to how ill-defined was the boundary between enlightened Christianity and free-thinking. In the same year that Ducket was tried for atheism another young Cambridge fellow, William Weston of St John's, was summoned before the deputy vice-chancellor and charged with preaching a sermon which was a 'zealous apology for Atheism' (Weston, 1739: x). The sermon which occasioned this accusation was entitled *Some kinds of superstitition worse than atheism*, in which Weston argued that an atheist was less of a danger to society than a religious zealot since 'however irrational the Atheist may have been in the Disbelief of the first and most necessary Principle, viz the Being of a God yet he is not hereby deprived of the use of his Faculties and Power of Reason' (p. 40). In defending himself against the charge of being an advocate of atheism Weston appealed to the right of 'Liberty of Thinking and Speaking' which 'has been the Occasion of adding a Lustre and Beauty to the Face of Christianity, which it wanted in the times of greater Ignorance and Credulity' (p. vii). This defence of his views as an expression of 'rational Christianity' was evidently successful since Weston retained his fellowship until 1767 and was awarded a bachelor of divinity degree in 1742.

A far more testing case for those wishing to draw a clear line between Chrisianity and free-thinking was the work of Conyers Middleton of whom Gibbon wrote that he 'rose to the highest pitch of scepticism, in any wise consistent with religion' (Cragg, 1964: 32–3). Middleton, who spent most of his life in Cambridge where he was a fellow of St John's (1706–19), principal librarian (1721–50) and Woodwardian professor (1731–4), was a close friend of latitudinarian divines like Sykes and Blackburne. His sympathy for the defenders of 'rational Christianity' is evident, too, in his remarks to Lord Hervey on Hoadly's *Plain account of the nature and end of the sacrament* (1735): Middleton defended Hoadly's 'design of reconciling Reason with Religion' and dismissed accusations that he was lessening Christian piety by arguing 'that he seeks only to destroy a superstitious doctrine, by establishing a rational one in its place' (BL, Add. 32458: 185). One of Middleton's correspondents, John Bretts, attributed him with a similar aim, commenting in 1740 that 'Christianity in my comprehension is a shrine big with Good Designs . . . and for that reason I wish to see it settled up on a rational footing: I think it is now in good hands, if it can be done you will do it' (BL, Add. 32457: 173).[1] On the other hand, Middleton also had links with whiggish free-thinkers like Gordon and Trenchard (Hudson, 1975: 219) and, according to that assiduous collector of ecclesiastical gossip, Thomas Pyle, Middleton had confessed his infidelity to an unnamed friend (Hartshorne, 1905: 313). In a letter to Lord Hervey of 1733 Middleton claimed that 'it is my Misfortune to have had so early a Taste of Pagan Sense, as to make me very squeamish in my Christian studies' (BL, Add. 5846: 22) and among the manuscripts which Middleton left at his death was one on 'the inutility and inefficacy of Prayer' which the deist, Bolingbroke, had recommended publishing but which his friend and executor, Heberden (who himself held latitudinarian theological views) was said to have regarded as so heterodox that he

---

[1] I owe this reference to Dr Paul Turnbull.

bought it from Middleton's widow and burnt it (Nichols, 1812–15, v: 423).

Middleton's published work – like his choice of friends – was also finely balanced between thoroughgoing latitudinarianism and disbelief. His *Letter to Dr. Waterland . . .* (1731), which was prompted by Waterland's critique of Tindal's deistic *Christianity as old as creation*, criticised both the orthodox and the deists for treating Scripture without regard to the historical circumstances of its composition. His *History of the life of M. Tullius Cicero* (1741) enthusiastically praised Cicero's system of natural religion but then added in a footnote that revelation had 'made known to babes' what had been hidden from the wise (Hudson, 1975: 226). His *Free enquiry into the miraculous powers which are supposed to have existed in the Christian Church through several successive ages* (1748) was thought by Hume to have 'eclipsed' his own *Essay on miracles* which appeared in the same year (Stephen, 1962, I: 222). However, Middleton confined his sceptical treatment of miracles to the period after the New Testament thus imply- ing that the scriptural miracles were a class apart, and perhaps he was sincere in his stated aim: not to question all miracles but rather to deny the claims of papists and enthusiasts that Providence continued to intervene on their behalf – claims which undermined any form of rational Christianity (Campbell, 1986: 48).

Within Cambridge the work which attracted most controversy was his *Letter to Dr. Waterland* (1731) in which Middleton set out to show that Waterland's attempt to refute the deists by arguing for the literal inspira- tion of Scripture was both misconceived and fruitless. Most eighteenth- century divines were not, however, ready for Middleton's anticipation of the Higher Criticism and his arguments prompted Waterland's ally, Zachary Pearce (fellow of Trinity, 1716–20; bishop of Rochester, 1756– 74), to accuse him of being a crypto-atheist, while Dr Williams, the university orator, declared that Middleton's books should be burnt and he himself banished from the university unless he recanted. Middleton commented to Lord Harley on 25 January 1732 that this uproar had made him determined 'to make as reputable a retreat as I can into the quarters of Orthodoxy' (BL, MS Loan 29/167). But Middleton found it harder to make a dignified exit from the controversy than he had anticipated: he found, for example, that Lord Harley became increasingly distant as his *Letter* came under further attack (BL, Add 32457: 84). By 1733 he was appealing to the commonwealthman and whig Arthur Onslow, the speaker of the House of Commons (Robbins, 1959: 280), for his support. Onslow duly responded with an affirmation of Middleton's right to free enquiry: '[I]t seems to me', Onslow wrote, 'the farthest thing in the world from what ought at least to be the design of a seminary of Learning, that any animosity should arise *there* against any man's sentiments in the search of knowledge' (BL, Add. 32457: 85v) – a view of the role of the university which was sharply at odds with that of Waterland and Middleton's other clerical opponents, who conceived of Cambridge as being first and foremost an arm of the Established Church. Two years later Middleton wrote to Onslow on behalf 'of those of my order, who are animated by sentiments of reason and liberty, whose number seems to be increasing at this place [Cambridge]' to thank him as 'their chief protector among the laity' from 'the progress of those counsils, which by carrying ecclesiastical power & principles to an unreasonable height, may prove the most dangerous in the end even to our civil liberties' (*ibid.*: 94).

As this letter indicates, Middleton, within a few years of the controversy set off by his *Letter to Dr. Waterland*, found that he was not as isolated in Cambridge as he had first thought. By 1737 he could tell Lord Hervey that 'the malice of my enemies was not able to keep up that clamour even in the University, of all places the most clamorous' – indeed, he added, 'that instead of giving scandal, I am more frequented & respected by the best of all professions than any other man in it' and that among his visitors were many of the heads including Bishop Gooch, master of Caius, who 'affects to treat me with particular familiarity' (BL, Add. 32458: 11). Though Middleton's *Free enquiry* (1748) stirred up the usual flurry of pamphlets it provoked little opposition in Cambridge. On the contrary, Middleton could remark to Bishop Gooch that following the publication of this work 'the generality of all parties [within the university] frankly declare themselves on my side' (BL, Add. 32457: 175).

Plainly by this time Cambridge had learnt to accommodate a very wide spectrum of religious opinion provided that at least the external forms of Christianity were preserved. Only the most overt attack on Christianity of a Ducket or the 'blasphemous libel' of William Waller of Trinity in 1752 (Howell, 1816–26, xxii: 723) was likely to lead to expulsion. By the mid-eighteenth century, then, the din of theological battle – so marked a feature of Cambridge, as of the Church more generally, in the period between the Glorious Revolution and the accession of George II in 1727 – was largely stilled. However, in a university which saw its primary task as the education of a new generation of clergy the main catalyst for intellectual innovation naturally tended to be religious change or debate. Hence the broad measure of religious harmony which characterised mid-eighteenth-century Cambridge also brought with it an atmosphere of complacency and a reluctance to venture beyond a by now well-established curriculum based largely on Newton, Locke and Samuel Clarke. Without the stimulus of debate – which in eighteenth-century Cambridge largely meant theological argument – this new intellectual order hardened into a new orthodoxy which was almost as settled and complacent as the scholastic curriculum it had replaced. In the late eighteenth century, however, Cambridge's theological complacency was once more to be shaken by renewed controversy about the nature of Christianity and of the relationship between Church and State – polemics which provided some of the impetus for the reforms which reshaped the university in the mid-nineteenth century.

6

Newtonian natural
philosophy established

It was in the period following the Glorious Revolution that Newton's work gradually became an integral part of the Cambridge curriculum, giving the university a reputation for pre-eminence in the mathematical sciences which its previous history had done little to justify. In a university where every activity was overshadowed by the political and religious conflicts outlined above the rise to prominence of Newtonian natural philosophy also came to be intertwined with the wider debate within the university and the country at large about the nature of the post-revolutionary settlement in Church and State. It was no coincidence, then, that the chief advocates of Newton's work within Cambridge were also among the most vocal apologists for the post-revolutionary order.

At first the publication of the *Principia* in 1687 changed little within the university. The work brought Newton some fame within Cambridge but did little to further an interest in the mathematical sciences – the *Principia* being regarded by Newton's Cambridge contemporaries as something to admire from afar rather than as a new intellectual frontier open to all. De la Pryme, an undergraduate at St John's, noted in his diary in 1692 that 'There is one Mr. Newton (whom I have very oft seen), fellow of Trinity College, that is mightily famous for his learning, being a most excellent mathematician, philosopher, divine etc'; De la Pryme commented that the *Principia* 'has got him a mighty name' but added that Newton's chief admirers were Scots, and he says nothing of any public acclaim for Newton within Cambridge (De la Pryme, 1870: 23). More pointed was the anecdote reported by Martin Folkes (a Clare graduate and president of the Royal Society from 1741 to 1753): 'After Sir Isaac printed his *Principia*, as he passed by the students at Cambridge said there goes the man who has writt a book that neither he nor any one else understands' (King's College, Cambridge, Keynes MS 130). Plainly, if Newtonian natural philosophy were to be taught to undergraduates it would have to be through the medium of simplified textbooks rather than by prescribing the *Principia* itself which few in Europe, let alone Cambridge, could master.

But Newton himself did not aspire to the task of producing such pedagogical aids – indeed, he was reported by Derham 'to have made the *Principia* abstruse to avoid being baited by the little smatterers in mathematics' (*ibid.*). Moreover, after his election as an MP in 1689 Newton became increasingly concerned with gaining a place in London and virtually left Cambridge in 1696 when he was made warden of the Mint (though he did not resign his fellowship and professorship until 1701). In consequence, he appears to have lost interest in his duties as Lucasian professor of mathematics; thus there is no record of any new lectures being deposited in the university library (as the statutes of the Lucasian professorship required) after 1687 (Edleston, 1850: xci–xcviii). Whiston reports attending Newton's lectures while an undergraduate at Clare between 1686 and 1690 but confessed that he 'had understood them not at all that time'. Evidently, Newton's lectures did little to alter the existing curriculum in natural philosophy since Whiston enviously contrasted his own Cambridge contemporaries with David Gregory's[1] students at Edinburgh who had been encouraged 'to keep Acts, as we call them, upon several Branches of the Newtonian Philosophy: while we at Cambridge, poor Wretches, were ignominiously studying the fictitious Hypotheses of the Cartesian' (1753: 36). As Lucasian professor Newton was the one man in the university employed specifically to teach the mathematical sciences; in the absence of any strong encouragement on his part to popularise his own work the curriculum in natural philosophy continued to be dominated by the Cartesianism that had spread throughout the university through the influence of Henry More.

Throughout the 1690s, then, there appears to have been little determined effort to promote the study of Newtonian natural philosophy among Cambridge undergraduates – though the example of Samuel Clarke indicates that one or two exceptional tutors may have introduced some outstanding pupils to the *Principia*. In 1694 Clarke, then an undergraduate at Caius, defended in the public schools a question drawn from the *Principia* at the instigation, suggests Ball (1889: 75), of Richard Laughton who became a tutor at Clare in 1694. A more probable explanation is that Clarke was introduced to Newton's work by his own tutor, Sir John Ellis (master of Caius from 1703 to 1716), who was a close friend of Newton (More, 1934: 247) and co-operated with him in recording astronomical observations (Turnbull *et al.*, 1959–77, II: 347 n. 6). Ellis,

---

[1] Eagles (1977) points out that Whiston was probably confusing David with his brother, James Gregory, whose Edinburgh disputation topics of the 1690s are still extant in Clare College library and include a summary of the *Principia* (Edleston, 1850: viii).

described by Whiston as 'that eminent and careful Tutor' (1730: 5), had previously taught Henry Wharton (MA Caius, 1687) who appears to have been the only Cambridge undergraduate to examine Newton's mathematical manuscripts (Whiteside, 1967–81, VI: xvi). Ellis was later to serve with Newton and Flamsteed as an adviser on the statutes for the new Plumian professorship of astronomy and experimental philosophy and was active in having Roger Cotes appointed to that post (Edleston, 1850: lxxiv).

Ellis may also have played a part in encouraging Clarke to include some references to Newton's *Principia* in Clarke's Latin translation of Rohault's *Traité de physique* (a standard textbook of Cartesian natural philosophy), a project undertaken by Clarke at Ellis's suggestion, though Whiston claimed that it was he who persuaded Clarke to include some reference to Newton in his translation of Rohault (Whiston, 1730: 5–6). 'Clarke's Rohault', as Hoskin (1961) has shown, grew progressively more Newtonian in character with each of its three successive editions though in the first edition of 1697 there was little of Newton apart from an account of his work on optics and his views on the nature of comets (*ibid.*: 357). In the second (1702) edition Clarke strengthened the Newtonian content considerably and by the third and final edition of 1710 Clarke's Newtonian notes and Rohault's Cartesian text were in open conflict. 'By this means', wrote Hoadly in his introduction to Clarke's works, 'the True Philosophy has without any Noise prevailed: and to this Day, His translation of Rohault is, generally speaking, the Standing Text for Lectures; and his Notes, the first Direction to Those who are willing to receive the Reality and Truth of Things in the place of Invention and Romance [i.e., Cartesianism]' (Hoadly, 1738, I: ii). But in his first edition of Rohault Clarke did not set out to remedy the lack of a simplified textbook of Newtonian natural philosophy, a lacuna to which Whiston had drawn attention but did not himself attempt to rectify until Newton had left Cambridge permanently.

It is an index of the lack of interest in Newton's work within Cambridge during the 1690s that Whiston himself was prompted to study the *Principia* after his election as a fellow of Clare in 1691 not because of any contact with its author but through reading a paper by David Gregory (Whiston, 1753: 32). Whiston then attempted to master the *Principia* 'with immense pains but no Assistance', not meeting the author until 1694 though both men were resident in Cambridge. Whiston's enthusiasm for 'Sir Isaac Newton's wonderful discoveries' (*ibid.*) was such that he set out to revise Thomas Burnet's *Sacred theory of the earth* in the light of Newton's work – in particular, using the *Principia*'s explanation of the behaviour of comets as a means of making intelligible the history of the earth. In his *New theory of the earth* (1696) Whiston also set out to demonstrate the apologetical significance of Newton's work and, in particular, his theory of gravity – a continuing theme in the work of Whiston and Newton's other Cambridge popularisers (Metzger, 1938). 'Mechanical philosophy, which relies chiefly on the Power of Gravity', argued Whiston, 'is, if rightly understood, so far from leading to Atheism, that it solely depends on, supposes and demonstrates the Being and Providence of God; and its Study by consequence is the most serviceable to Religion of all other' (1708 ed.: 7).

Whiston showed a draft of the *New theory* to Bentley and to Newton himself who suggested a number of changes (*ibid.*: 8–9). According to Whiston, Newton 'well approved of it' (1753: 38) when the *New theory* was published in 1696 with Newton as its dedicatee. Whiston must have made a fairly favourable impression on Newton since he appointed him as his deputy when he resigned his chair in 1701; two years later Whiston was appointed as Newton's successor. As Lucasian professor Whiston actively set about providing students with a simplified account of the *Principia* both in his lectures and in the textbooks based on those lectures: ironically, then, it was only after Newton's departure from the university that Cambridge undergraduates were provided with a comprehensible introduction to Newtonian natural philosophy. Clearly, then, Newton's presence in Cambridge was not enough in itself to stimulate an interest in his work. Since natural philosophy was a secondary concern of the university it took more than the acclaim of Newton's scientific contemporaries to persuade Cambridge to adopt the findings of her Lucasian professor; in a university principally concerned with the training of clergy it was religious and ecclesiastical change which served as the chief catalyst for intellectual advance. The response to Newton's work was therefore coloured by the changes wrought in the Church and the university by the Glorious Revolution.

The relative neglect of Newton's own work at Cambridge while Newton himself remained there is underlined by the fact that it was at Edinburgh and, subsequently, Oxford rather than at Newton's own university that students were first introduced to the *Principia*. This was largely the work of a small group of early Scottish disciples of Newton, of whom the most notable were David Gregory (professor of mathematics, Edinburgh, 1683–91; Savilian professor of astronomy, Oxford, 1691–1708) and the physician, Archibald Pitcairne (professor of medicine, Leiden, 1692–3). These men were active in disseminating Newton's work not only in their native Edinburgh but also in Oxford and Leiden. A less prominent member of this group was Gregory's student, John Craige, who, in 1685, moved to Cambridge to consult Newton on a number of mathematical problems (Cohen, 1971: 204) – the beginning of a lifelong association between the two men. On his return to Scotland in 1685 Craige, as he himself put it, 'became very friendly with Mr. Pitcairne, the celebrated physician; and with Mr. D. Gregory, to whom I signified that Mr. Newton had a series of such a kind for quadratures, which each of them admitted to be unknown to them'. (Turnbull *et al.*, 1959–77, III: 9). Craige's experience of the richness of Newton's mathematical and scientific manuscripts – together with Gregory's familiarity, through the correspondence of his uncle, James (professor of mathematics, St Andrews, 1668–74; inaugural professor, Edinburgh, 1674–5), of the extent of Newton's scientific activities – prompted further visits from Newton's Scottish admirers. On his way to Leiden in 1692 Pitcairne stopped at Cambridge and was given by Newton a copy of his unpublished 'De natura acidorum' which Pitcairne in turn passed on to David Gregory along with a few annotations of his own (Thackray, 1970: 25–6; Guerrini, 1985: 250; Guerrini, 1987). Gregory himself paid an extended visit to Cambridge in May 1694 in order to consult Newton and to study his scientific papers, the two men having previously met in London in 1691, the year in which Gregory had been appointed Savilian professor of astronomy at Oxford (partly thanks to Newton's recommendation). Indeed, Gregory was far more closely associated with Newton's scientific work than anybody in Cambridge before Cotes began work on the second edition of the *Principia* in 1709.

At Oxford Gregory's astronomical lectures (which, in 1702, were published under the title *Astronomiae physicae et geometricae elementa*) provided an introduction to portions of the *Principia* (especially those concerned with astronomy). A more comprehensive introduction to Newtonian natural philosophy was provided by Gregory's former student from Edinburgh, John Keill, who followed Gregory to Oxford in 1691 and there (as Desaguliers put it) was the 'first who publickly taught *Natural Philosophy* by *Experiments* in a mathematical manner' (Strong, 1957: 53). His lectures were printed in 1701 under the title *Introductio ad veram physicam*, the first popular exposition of Newtonian natural philosophy. Soon afterwards, in 1704, John Freind gave some popular lectures in chemistry at the Ashmolean Museum (probably at Gregory's instigation) which attempted to explain chemical phenomena in Newtonian terms; the lectures were subsequently published in 1709 with a dedication to Newton.

Gregory and perhaps, too, the high church John Keill were refugees from the anti-episcopal purge that followed the Glorious Revolution in Scotland. Freind was so closely associated with the leader of the high church cause, Francis Atterbury, that he was briefly imprisoned following

Atterbury's abortive jacobite plot of 1722 – though he was sufficiently pro-Hanoverian subsequently to become a member of Queen Caroline's household. It was possible, then, as Guerrini (1986) has recently emphasised, to be both a Newtonian and a tory, though it does not follow that the association between Newton's work and whig/latitudinarian allegiances did not play an important part in establishing that veneration for Newton which was to be a hallmark of the English Enlightenment. It is true that scientific assumptions were not of central importance in defining one's politico-religious position in the highly polarised post-revolutionary era and that therefore there was no fundamental contradiction in being both a tory and a Newtonian. None the less, the high church/tory view of society and learning offered a number of obstacles to the whole-hearted endorsement of Newtonian natural philosophy: firstly, it gave considerable emphasis to ecclesiastical tradition and, with it, to a form of education which accorded recent developments in natural philosophy a relatively minor place; secondly, it tended to adopt a guarded, and, at times, even suspicious view of change, whether social or intellectual; and lastly, it was inclined to emphasise the gulf between Revelation and human reason (Olson, 1983). By contrast, the whigs and latitudinarians were more inclined to welcome change and to emphasise the importance of natural rather than revealed theology and, as a consequence, stressed the need to demonstrate the workings of Providence through the application of reason and the study of the natural world – characteristics which provided a more fertile soil for the cultivation of Newton's work. Furthermore, the latitudinarians' tendency to emphasise the text of Scripture as forming, along with reason, the best guide to a comprehensive form of Protestantism was well suited to Newton's own religious beliefs and, as Force (1985) has suggested, helps account for Newton's sympathy for the attempt on the part of a number of his low church popularisers (and, in particular, William Whiston) to defend Christianity by arguing for the literal fulfilment of the biblical prophecies as well as by recourse to a Newtonian version of the argument from design. Such considerations help to explain why Newton's work eventually took much firmer root at Cambridge than at Oxford, despite the latter's earlier interest in the *Principia*. Though individual high churchmen, such as Freind, may have been interested in Newton's work, Oxford as a whole, with its growing sense of alienation from the Revolutionary Settlement in Church and State, provided a less congenial environment for the changes in theological, philosophical and educational beliefs and practices which were to be associated with the diffusion of Newtonianism in its English guise than was to prove the case at Cambridge, where the whigs and latitudinarians were to make much greater inroads.

Moreover, even among Newton's early Scottish disciples, on whom
Guerrini's useful study (1986) is based, there is evidence in the case of
Craige and, to a lesser extent, David Gregory, that their careers owed
something to the patronage of their compatriot, the latitudinarian Bishop
Burnet. Burnet entrusted the education of his son, William, to Craige
who, Burnet noted with satisfaction, 'carried him a great way into
Mathematicks and Philosophy' – subjects in which Burnet himself had
previously taken an interest (Foxcroft, 1902: 512, 461). Thanks to Burnet,
too, who, to the indignation of many English clergy, was made bishop of
Salisbury in the year following the Glorious Revolution, Craige was
appointed to a number of English clerical posts and, after Burnet's death,
he benefited from the patronage of Burnet's theological ally, Benjamin
Hoadly (Mayo, 1922: 260). David Gregory, like Craige, his former pupil,
also was assisted by Burnet, for it was through the bishop's influence that
Gregory obtained the post of mathematical tutor to William, duke of
Gloucester, in 1699 (though the young prince died before Gregory took up
office) (Turnbull *et al.*, 1959–77, IV: 295).

Craige and Gregory, then, were both members of Burnet's circle and
through him Craige, and probably also Gregory, came to know other
Anglican clergy who shared Burnet's latitudinarian views. One such
protégé of Burnet was William Wotton who, after his graduation from
Catharine Hall in 1680, had been invited by Burnet to London and
introduced to Bishop William Lloyd of St Asaph in whose household
Wotton lived for a time (BL, Add. 4224: 153). After returning to
Cambridge, where he was elected a fellow of St John's in 1683, Wotton
was appointed chaplain to Daniel Finch, second earl of Nottingham, in
1691; later, in 1705, Burnet made Wotton a prebendary at Salisbury. Since
both Wotton and Craige had Burnet as their patron it was natural that the
two men became acquainted and that it was to Craige that Wotton turned
when his friend, Bentley, needed scientific guidance in studying the
Principia. Craige's reply to Wotton's enquiry about the necessary preliminary reading for studying the *Principia* is the only letter between the two
men which survives, though the tone of the letter indicates that they were
well acquainted; Craige addressed his letter to his 'most reall friend and
humble servant' and concluded by expressing his willingness to serve
Wotton 'for whose sake there is nothing that I will refuse to do that lies
within the compass of my power' (Brewster, 1855, I: 469). With an excess
of enthusiasm Craige's reply to Wotton recommended that Bentley read a
veritable mathematical library before beginning the *Principia* and Bentley,
in search of more realistic advice, was probably induced to apply directly
to Newton himself for scientific counsel. Thus in about July 1691 Bentley
received from Newton a far more manageable list of preliminary reading

(Turnbull *et al.*, 1959–77, III: 155–6) – a note which acted as a prelude to the famous correspondence between Bentley and Newton in late 1692 on the issues raised in Bentley's Boyle lectures which used parts of the *Principia* to shore up the argument from design.

Though Craige's letter may have been of little use to Bentley, its very length illustrates Craige's enthusiasm for promoting the study of Newton's work. It is quite possible, too, that, through previous discussion with Wotton, Craige knew that Bentley planned to use the *Principia* for apologetical ends, a project with which Craige would have had considerable sympathy. Indeed, Craige later wrote a work entitled *Theologiae Christianae principia* (1699) – which was dedicated to Burnet – an attempt to use a Newtonian mathematical format to calculate the reliability of the evidence of the Gospels (Craig, 1964: 1). The fact that it was Craige to whom Bentley and Wotton first applied when seeking advice about studying the *Principia* indicates that at the time neither Bentley nor Wotton was on intimate terms with Newton nor were they familiar with his work. Surprisingly, then, it was partly through John Craige that Wotton and perhaps Bentley were introduced to Newton's work though both men had been at Cambridge while Newton was writing the *Principia* and giving regular lectures. Even after the popular reception of Bentley's Boyle lectures there was little sign that Newton's work attracted much interest within Cambridge – a situation which was to change markedly after Bentley's return to Cambridge as master of Trinity in 1700, when the university's curriculum in natural philosophy gained a new dynamism. Thus the mathematical tradition which was to prove Cambridge's finest intellectual flower owed little to Newton's own cultivation; indeed, in its earliest stages it was in some ways a transplant from Edinburgh and Oxford by way of London, a process facilitated by the connections built up by Bishop Burnet after 1688.

On his appointment as master of Trinity in 1700 (largely thanks to Tenison), Bentley left a position in London as keeper of the Royal Libraries which provided him with abundant intellectual stimulation, to take up a post as master of a college which, in his (no doubt jaundiced) view, was 'filled (for the most part) with ignorant drunken lewd Fellows and Scholars' (Wordsworth, 1842 II: 448–9). Inspired both by a desire to strengthen his own authority within the university and by a zeal for academic reform Bentley set out to revive Trinity's reputation for good learning by making it the scientific centre of the university, an ambition which probably owed much to the success of his Boyle lectures with their popularisation of sections of the *Principia* and to his continuing contact with Newton himself (*ibid.*, I: 152). With an imperious disdain for the fellows' objections Bentley used Trinity's facilities to attract to the college those at Cambridge interested in scientific research and teaching – thus Whiston (though a fellow of Clare) was provided with rooms to conduct his teaching and experiments and Vigani, who had been appointed Cambridge's foundation professor of chemistry in 1703 (an honorary position), was provided with a laboratory (at the cost of the fellows losing their bowling-green).

Unlike Whiston and Vigani, Bentley's most illustrious scientific protégé – Roger Cotes – was a Trinity man from the time he was admitted to the university in 1699, the year before Bentley became master of the college. Even while an undergraduate Cotes received 'signal marks of favor' from Bentley who evidently approved of Cotes's devotion to 'Mistress Mathesis' (Edleston, 1850: 192). One year after Cotes's election to the Trinity fellowship in 1705 Bentley used his considerable influence within the university to gain for Cotes the position of foundation Plumian professor of astronomy and experimental philosophy which was established, along with an observatory, under the terms of the will of Thomas Plume (MA Christ's, 1649; BD, 1661), vicar of East Greenwich from 1658 to 1704 where he had come to know John Flamsteed, who stimulated his interest in astronomy (Rowbottom, 1968: 50). Bentley appears to have dominated the negotiations concerning the Plumian professorship from the beginning (Gowing, 1983: 9–14). Even before Plume's bequest he had planned to establish an observatory in the Trinity gatehouse (Price, 1952: 2) and, against the wishes of Flamsteed who thought Trinity gatehouse 'not fit for it [an observatory]' (Gowing, 1983: 14), Bentley ensured that the Plumian bequest went to Trinity. Bentley also insisted that Cotes be appointed as the foundation Plumian professor in 1706 despite Flamsteed's proposal that his assistant, John Witty, be given the post. All of which led Flamsteed to complain to Newton that Bentley 'has determined [the appointment of the Plumian professorship] without ever so much as letting me know that hee was about such a business and I fear directly contrary to the Archdeacon's designe wherewith I am apt to thinke none of the Trustees in Cambridge were so well acquainted as I am' (Turnbull *et al.*, 1959–77, IV: 473–4).

It was Cotes, too, whom Bentley chose in 1709 to act as editor of the second edition of the *Principia*. Bentley himself had begun the project (and even printed up a draft sheet in 1708) but had not continued – perhaps because Newton understandably mistrusted his mathematical competence (Cohen, 1971: 216–23). Though Bentley had had to forgo the honour of being the editor of the second edition, Cotes in his preface none the less gave his patron full credit for initiating the work and for demonstrating that 'Newton's distinguished work will be the safest protection against the attacks of atheists' (Newton, 1974 ed.: xxxiii). Nor did Bentley altogether abandon the privilege of an editor since he changed those lines of Halley's prefatory 'Ode to Newton' which he felt implied that the world had always existed (Albury, 1978: 39–40).

Cotes's preface to the second edition of the *Principia* was one of the most influential documents in popularising Newton's work both in England and on the Continent (Brunet, 1931: 66). His meticulous revisions of Newton's demonstrations and proofs also did much to improve their accuracy and clarity: of 494 pages in the first edition, 297 are in some way altered in the second (Ball, 1893: 74). As Newton noted in his own short preface to the second edition (which makes no mention of Cotes) the new work incorporated such major revisions as an enlarged section on 'the determination of forces, by which bodies may be made to revolve in given orbits' (Book I), fuller treatment of the theory of the resistance of fluids, drawing on new experimental data (Book II), and, most importantly, in Book III 'the lunar theory and the precession of the equinoxes were more fully deduced from their principles; and the theory of the comets was confirmed by more examples of the calculation of their orbits, done also with greater accuracy'.

However, Newton made no public acknowledgement of Cotes's assistance and, after the publication of the second edition of the *Principia*, sent Cotes a letter bluntly listing several minor errors, which taxed the patience of even long-suffering Cotes (Turnbull *et al.*, 1959–77, VI: 48–9). None the less, Cotes continued to correspond with Newton after the publication of the second edition in 1713 in order to keep him informed of the work done at the Plumian observatory; thus after the eclipse of 22 April 1715 Cotes sent Newton a long and detailed letter since he felt it his 'Duty to send You what Observations I could make of the late Eclipse' (*ibid.*, VI: 218). Newton evidently approved of the work done at the Plumian observatory since he donated a clock worth some fifty pounds to be used for astronomical calculations (*ibid.*: 223; Gowing, 1983: 87). Cotes also sent his observations of the eclipse of 1715 to Halley who had them published in the *Philosophical Transactions* (XXIX: 253). Cotes's only other astronomical paper was a description of the meteor of 6 March 1716 which had been sent to his friend, Robert Danny (a former fellow of Corpus), and which Danny published in the *Philosophical Transactions* (XXXI: 66) after Cotes's death. However, Cotes also recalculated Flamsteed's and Cassini's solar and planetary tables and, before his untimely death, had planned to reconstruct the tables of the moon's motion in conformity with Newtonian principles (*DSB*, Cotes).

As well as his work in astronomy Cotes gave 'a course in philosophical experiments' which provided students with practical demonstrations of the work of Torricelli, Pascal, Boyle and Hooke. These lectures, wrote Robert Smith in the preface to his edition of Cotes's *Hydrostatical and pneumatical lectures* (1738), were 'performed before large assemblies at the Observatory in Trinity College Cambridge; first by the Author in conjunction with Mr. Whiston . . . [and] then by the Author alone, and after his decease by my self'. After Whiston was expelled from the university in 1710 (despite Cotes's attempt to persuade him to recant (Edleston, 1850: 201)) the former Lucasian professor proceeded to offer a similar course of experiments in London with the assistance of Hauksbee (Whiston, 1753: 118). Despite his expulsion Whiston remained on friendly terms with Cotes who sent him both scientific and personal news from Cambridge (Edleston, 1850: 225–7). During 1707 and 1708 Cotes was also assisted in performing his course of experiments by Stephen Gray who had been invited to Cambridge by Cotes to aid him in establishing the new observatory. While at Trinity, Gray sent Sloane, then secretary of the Royal Society, a series of letters recounting his electrical experiments (Chipman, 1954). However, Gray found his employers at Trinity 'mercenary' and he also resented Cotes's plans to recalculate the astronomical tables of his friend, Flamsteed; consequently he left Cambridge permanently in 1708 (*DSB*, Gray).

During his lifetime Cotes published only one work in his own right: the *Logometria*, a mathematical treatise which was dedicated to Halley and published in the *Philosophical Transactions* for 1713 (XXIX: 5). After his death, however, Cotes's literary executor – his cousin, Robert Smith – published his papers under the title *Harmonia mensuarum, sive analysis et synthesis per rationum et angulorum mensuras promotae . . .* (Cambridge, 1722), a work which included some of Cotes's mathematical lectures. In 1738 Smith also published Cotes's lectures on hydrostatics and pneumatics. From the time that Smith came up to Trinity in 1708 he had been encouraged by Cotes to take an interest in mathematics and natural philosophy – indeed, Cotes had made Smith one of his assistants at the Plumian observatory. After Smith's election as a fellow in 1715 Cotes had recommended him to Whiston as 'capable of instructing his Pupils in some parts of Knowledge which You and I esteem, and which very few Tutors in the University do at all pretend to' (Edleston, 1850: 227). Like Cotes, Smith was a protégé of Bentley (whom he succeeded as master of Trinity in 1742); in a letter to Lord Trevor Cotes commented that if the choice of a tutor for Trevor's son was left to Bentley he would appoint Smith who could instruct his pupils in 'the Mathematicks and the new Philosophy' (*ibid.*: 228). Smith himself warmly praised Bentley as a patron of science in his preface to Cotes's *Harmonia mensuarum*, describing the great classicist as 'a second founder' of Trinity (Monk, 1830–3, II: 168). Like his patron,

Smith stood in high regard with the House of Hanover, being made master of mechanics to George II as well as holding the post of mathematical praeceptor to William, duke of Cumberland.

Smith's first scientific work, *A compleat system of opticks* (1732), included a tribute to Cotes – one section of the work (Book II, chapter 5) being based, in Smith's words, on a 'noble and beautiful theorem' developed by his cousin. This book, which Voltaire praised in a letter to Smith (Edleston, 1850: 236–7), set out to demonstrate the coherence of Newton's total *œuvre* by attempting to link together the queries of Newton's *Opticks* and the laws of motion of the *Principia* through a treatment of light based on thoroughgoing corpuscular principles; all optical phenomena, Smith argued, could be explained through the attraction and repulsion of particles of light and particles of matter (Steffens, 1977: 27–8; Cantor, 1983: 34–9). 'It is not too much to say', writes Guerlac (1977: 221), 'that this Master of Trinity was, if not the real author of the corpuscular theory of light, at least its most influential advocate.' Smith's other scientific work – the *Harmonics, or the philosophy of musical sounds* (1749) – was less influential than his *Opticks* but, like its predecessor, became a standard text at Cambridge. Throughout his fifty-two years as Plumian professor and twenty-six as master of Trinity, Smith was active both within Trinity and within the university as a whole in promoting the study of Newtonian natural philosophy and mathematics, a cause which he continued to support even after his death in 1768 since he left £1,750 to found the Smith prizes for the two junior BAs who had made the greatest progress in mathematics and natural philosophy and a similar amount to augment the Plumian professorship (BL, Add. 32988: 150).

A mutual friend of Cotes and Smith was James Jurin who was elected a fellow of Trinity in 1706 and served as secretary of the Royal Society from 1721 to 1727. When editing Cotes's *Hydrostatical and pneumatical lectures* Smith included an appendix on capillary tubes by Jurin whom he described in his preface as Cotes's 'particular friend, as well as my own'; similarly, Smith added to his *Opticks* Jurin's essay 'On Distinct and Indistinct Vision'. Like Cotes and Smith, Jurin was a protégé of Bentley who gained for him a post at Christ's Hospital (School) in 1708, having recommended Jurin to the school's governors as 'a youth of very great hopes' (*DNB*, Jurin). At Bentley's suggestion Jurin revised Bernard Varenius's *Geographia generalis*, previously edited by Newton in 1681. In the manner of Clarke's edition of Rohault, Jurin's edition of Varenius (which was dedicated to Bentley and published at the university) added Newtonian notes to a largely Cartesian original. Jurin later acted as a defender of Newton's religious orthodoxy against the criticisms made by Bishop Berkeley in his *Analyst*. Under the pseudonym 'Philalethes Cantabrigiensis', Jurin published two pamphlets in this controversy: *Geometry no friend to infidelity; or A defence of Sir Isaac Newton and the British mathematicians* . . . (1734) and *The minute mathematician* . . . (1735). In this latter work he displayed his suspicion of high church claims by asserting that 'If the Clergy obtain more power, I [as a layman] shall have less liberty' (p. 9).

Brook Taylor who, like Jurin, served as secretary of the Royal Society (from 1714 to 1718), was also associated with Cotes and Smith, though he himself was a St John's graduate (taking his LL B in 1709 and his LL D in 1714). Taylor greatly admired Cotes's abilities as a mathematician: having vainly offered to assist Smith in editing Cotes's posthumous papers (Edleston, 1850: 231–4), Taylor used his influence with Smith's friend, William Jones, to hasten the publication of Cotes's work (Turnbull *et al.*, 1959–77, VII: 40), a project in which Newton also expressed some interest (*ibid.*: 28). Taylor's undergraduate commonplace book (St John's College, Cambridge, MS U. 19), though chiefly concerned with law, also includes notes on mathematical and astronomical problems (fols. 119–34) which probably derive from Cotes's Plumian lectures. Cotes and Taylor are chiefly remembered for their work in pure mathematics but both also displayed an interest in experimental science: Taylor's first paper in the *Philosophical Transactions* was entitled 'An account of the ascent of water between two glass planes' (XXVII: 538) and a subsequent paper, published jointly with Hauksbee, had as its title 'An experiment in order to discover the law of magnetic attraction' (XXIX: 294). Taylor's interest in such subjects was no doubt stimulated by his friendship with Stephen Gray (RS, MS 82: 19) whom he would have come to know while Gray was assisting Cotes in his 'course of philosophical experiments at Cambridge' in 1708–9. Like Smith, Taylor was also interested in the science of harmonics: among his manuscripts at St John's is a paper 'On Musick' which was intended to be part of a joint work by Taylor, Newton and the composer Pepusch (*DSB*, Taylor).

Though Bentley was not himself anything more than a scientific layman he had the ability to recognise scientific talent and the political skills necessary to gain advancement for his protégés: as the careers of Cotes, Smith, Vigani, Jurin and (to a lesser extent) Whiston illustrate, it was chiefly Bentley who obtained recognition for Newton's early popularisers at Cambridge. His eagerness to aid the study of Newton's work within the university presumably derived from the success of his Boyle lectures (which utilised some aspects of Newtonian natural philosophy), a success which made Bentley confident that Newton's work provided both a bulwark against atheism and the foundation for a form of natural theology which would undermine the sacerdotal pretensions of his high church opponents. As Bentley intended, Trinity acted as a catalyst for the cultivation of scientific activity within the university as a whole: in 1712 Bentley could claim (with characteristic hyperbole) that other colleges 'began to be apprehensive that (if things went on a little further) all the Quality would come to us; . . . that we were grown an University within ourselves, having within our own walls better instruments, and lectures for Astronomy, Experimental Philosophy, Chymistry, and etc, than Leyden, Utrecht, or any University could shew'. Through Trinity's example, Bentley continued, 'the whole youth of the University took a new spring of industry, Oriental learning was cultivated, Mathematicks was brought to that height, that the questions disputed in the Schools were quite of another set than were ever heard there before' (Wordsworth, 1842, II: 448–9).

Bentley had cause to be proud of Trinity's scientific achievements, but it was not the only college which played a role in the early popularisation of Newton's work within the university. A number of Newton's early Cambridge disciples also came from Clare, a college which, after 1714, shared with Trinity a reputation for whiggery – so much so that at the festivities at Cambridge in May 1716 to celebrate the King's birthday 'the scholars of Clare Hall were miserably insulted for their loyalty to the Government, together with those of Trinity College' (Wordsworth, 1874: 48). Within the acrimonious world of early eighteenth-century politics such common sympathies naturally created close personal bonds between the fellows of the two colleges: thus both Richard Laughton and William Grigg (Clare's master from 1713 to 1726) aided Bentley in his disputes within the university while Bentley remained an ally of Whiston during his prosecution for heresy (Monk, 1830–3, II: 12–13; I: 290). Such associations further strengthened the intellectual links between the two colleges, a notable feature of which was their common interest in the work of Newton.

At Clare the men most active in promoting the study of Newton's work – Whiston, Richard Laughton and Charles Morgan – were all clients of Bishop Moore and shared his whig sympathies. Though Moore's most illustrious protégé, Samuel Clarke, was a graduate of Caius he, too, had close links with Newton's disciples at Clare. Thus in the preface to the third (and most Newtonian) edition of his revision of Rohault's textbook of natural philosophy – a work that he had undertaken partly at the instigation of Whiston – Clarke acknowledged 'that there are a great many things owing to the learned and industrious Dr. Laughton and the Reverend Mr. Morgan'. Like his friends at Clare, Clarke was also well acquainted with both Bentley and Cotes at Trinity – the latter of whom turned to Clarke for advice when revising the famous preface to the second edition of the *Principia* (Turnbull *et al.*, 1959–77, v: 412–13).

One example of the links between Clare and Trinity was the long professional association between Whiston and Cotes: the two men jointly taught a course in experimental philosophy at Trinity and remained intimate friends after Whiston's expulsion from the university. As Lucasian professor Whiston introduced his students to Newton's work, an activity which gained for him the favour of Bentley who provided Whiston with rooms for teaching in Trinity. In 1707 the university press, which had been recently revived by Bentley, published Whiston's *Praelectiones astronomiae Cantabrigiae in scholis publicis habitae . . .* and in 1710 his *Praelectiones physico-mathematicae Cantabrigiae in scholis publicis habitae quibus philosophia illustrissimi Newtoni mathematica traditur; et facilius demonstratur*, these two works being the first expositions of Newtonian natural philosophy produced at Cambridge. Whiston's two textbooks (particularly the *Praelectiones physico-mathematicae . . .*) consisted largely of a paraphrase of the *Principia* though Whiston also drew on Newton's *Opticks* (1704) and his unpublished Lucasian lectures, as well as the work of other recent natural philosophers, notably Huygens and Halley (Cohen in Whiston, 1972 ed.). As one would expect, Whiston's tone is quite evangelical in his enthusiasm for Newton's natural philosophy which, whenever possible, he contrasts with 'the gross errors of Descartes'. Whiston also obtained Newton's reluctant permission to publish the manuscript of his Lucasian lectures on algebra under the title *Arithmetica universalis* (1707), though Newton later threatened 'to buy up the Coppyes' (Hiscock, 1937: 36). Even after his expulsion from Cambridge in 1710 and after he fell out with Newton himself, Whiston continued to be active in popularising Newton's work which he saw as a prelude to the biblical 'restitution of all things' (Whiston, 1753: 34); and when Pemberton neglected to include the scholia of the *Principia* in his *View of Sir Isaac Newton's philosophy* (1728) Whiston himself published an English translation with his own commentary. The tribute accorded to Whiston in the *Gentleman's Magazine* for July–August 1752 was well merited: 'In that [Lucasian] professorship, he continued till 1721, during which time he so clearly explained the Newtonian philosophy in his mathematical and astronomical lectures, which he then published, as to introduce into the University a noble system, which till then was understood by few, and these deep geometricians' (Farrell, 1973: i.41).

Whiston's 'bosom-friend', Richard Laughton, complemented Whiston's activities as Lucasian professor by promoting disputations within the public schools of the university based on Newtonian principles while serving as proctor in 1709–10. Sir William Browne, president of the

Royal College of Physicians in 1765, records that while an undergraduate at Peterhouse in 1711 he was persuaded by Laughton to choose mathematical questions for his disputation topics in return for a promise that he would be given the honour of being made a senior optime (Nichols, 1812–15, III: 322). To encourage such questions, Browne remarks, Laughton drew up 'a sheet of questions for the use of the Soph schools, on the Mathematical Newtonian Philosophy' (*ibid.*: 322). Earlier, in 1709, Laughton had delivered a speech in the schools praising Newton's allegiance to the Revolutionary Settlement and dwelling on his involvement in the struggle against James II's attempt to obtain a Cambridge MA for the Benedictine monk, Alban Francis. Appropriately for a client of Thomas Parker, the would-be university reformer, Laughton also suggested that the study of Newtonian natural philosophy could help the universities gain greater public acceptance and acclaim, particularly since a knowledge of experimental philosophy might help in the training of military engineers who could help defeat England's foes abroad (CUL, MS Oo.6.111: 6–8). Laughton's enthusiasm for Newton's work is also evident in his unpublished papers. These include a copy of Newton's *Lectiones opticae* (Clare College, Cambridge, Fellows' Library, MS P.5.16) and a copy of the *Principia* with annotations by Laughton (Clare, Fellows' Library, MS G.6.14). He also left an unpublished tract entitled *The principles of natural religion establish'd* (Clare, Fellows' Library, MS G.3.21) which argued that the basic tenets of Christianity were evident by the light of nature – thus providing a theological justification for the study of natural philosophy. Another of his theological manuscripts, *Exposition of the articles of our church* (*ibid.*), makes his latitudinarian sympathies even more evident since he advocated a simplification of doctrine, arguing that the present formularies were a departure 'from the primitive Simplicity of the first ages of Christianity'. Significantly, Laughton avoided the customary subscription to the Thirty-Nine Articles for his doctorate (Dyer, 1824, II: 249).

In 1726 the undistinguished William Grigg was succeeded as master by Laughton's friend, Charles Morgan. Morgan was described by one of his Clare colleagues as being 'much admired for the elegancy of his Pen, and his great compass in the Mathematics and Natural Philosophy' (Wardale, 1899: 154); his contributions to Clarke's third edition of Rohault's textbook (which was dedicated to Bishop Moore, the patron of Clarke and Morgan) were so substantial that they were later published separately under the title *Dissertations on the mechanical powers, elastic bodies, falling bodies, the cycloid, the parabaloid, the rain bow* (1770). As well as assisting Samuel Clarke, Morgan was also on close terms with Samuel's brother, John (BA Caius, 1703). In 1721 John Clarke wrote to Morgan to ask his

opinion of Clarke's *Enquiry into the cause and origin of evil* (1720), concluding the letter by sending his 'humble Service to Dr. Laughton, Mr. Folkes,
if with you and all friends' (Clare College, Cambridge, Fellows' Library,
College Letterbook: 92). John Clarke's *Enquiry* was based on a set of Boyle
lectures which resembled those of his brother in using Newtonian natural
philosophy for apologetical ends, since John Clarke includes a lengthy
discussion of the theological implications of the concept of gravity (1972
ed.: 176). John Clarke also sought Morgan's assistance when producing an
English translation of Clarke's edition of Rohault in 1723 – a work which
includes some contributions by Morgan in addition to those he made to
the Latin third edition. In 1730 John Clarke produced his own simplified
account of the *Principia* with a work entitled *A demonstration of some of the
principal sections of Sir Isaac Newton's 'Principles of natural philosophy'* – a text
which consists largely of a paraphrase and, at times, even a direct
translation of parts of the *Principia* (Cohen in John Clarke, 1972 ed.).
Another, more distinguished, correspondent of Morgan was Cotes who
discussed both mathematical and philosophical matters with him (Clare
College, Cambridge, Fellows' Library, College Letterbook: 90b, 91);
Cotes also sent Morgan a number of his unpublished scientific papers and
presented him – along with Whiston, Francis Hare (the latitudinarian
theologian and future bishop), Clarke and Bishop Moore – with a copy of
the second edition of the *Principia* (Trinity College, Cambridge, MS
R.2.42: 156). After Cotes's death in 1716 Morgan received copies of many
of Cotes's manuscripts from Robert Smith (Clare, Fellows' Library, MSS
N1.2.9, G.3.14, Kk.5.14) and Smith also sent Morgan copies of some of
Newton's manuscripts including *De motu corporum liber* and *De natura
acidorum* (ibid., Kk.5.14).

A mutual friend of both Smith and Morgan was Martin Folkes (MA
Clare, 1717), a former student of Laughton and president of the Royal
Society from 1741 to 1753, who contributed some material to Smith's
Opticks. Through Folkes Morgan kept in touch with the London scientific
world: Folkes sent him details of recent experiments at the Royal Society
as well as news of the activities of Newton and of Morgan's former
colleague, Whiston (Clare, Fellows' Library, College Letterbook: 88b,
89b). Folkes gave Morgan a number of recent scientific works which
Morgan bequeathed, along with the rest of his well-stocked library, to
Clare; in addition to his books Morgan left to the college 'an eight foot
telescope, two telescopes with four glasses, a quadrant, Culpepper's set of
portable microscopes, a celestial globe, a quadrant' (Clare, Fellows'
Library, Morgan's Library Catalogue).

Whiston, Laughton, Morgan and Folkes all helped to make Clare a
centre for the study of Newtonian natural philosophy. The comprehen-

sive scientific education available to undergraduates in the college is indicated by Robert Greene's *Encyclopaedia, or method of instructing pupils* (1707). Greene, a tutor at Clare, had religiously based reservations about Newtonian natural philosophy but he none the less introduced his students to Newton's work along with that of many of Newton's scientific contemporaries. That Clare continued to offer the kind of wide scientific education recommended by Greene is evident in the five volumes of notes (Trinity College, Cambridge, MSS R.1.54–8) made by Edward King while an undergraduate at Clare from 1754 to 1757. King studied closely Cotes's lectures on experimental philosophy and contrasted them with other works in the field such as *A system of natural philosophy . . .* (1748) by Thomas Rutherforth, a tutor at St John's. Among the other texts used by King were Simon's *Conic sections,* MacLaurin's *Account of Sir Isaac Newton's philosophy* and Desaguliers's *Course of experimental philosophy,* along with frequent references to the *Philosophical Transactions* – a range of texts which indicates the success of Whiston, Richard Laughton and Morgan in establishing the study of Newton (and the physical sciences more generally) as an integral part of the undergraduate curriculum offered by their college.

Along with Trinity and Clare, Corpus was also a college where there was considerable interest in the implications of Newton's work. Again, the intellectual links between these three colleges were strengthened by the fact that Corpus – the *alma mater* of Archbishop Tenison – like Trinity and Clare, was known for its warm support for the House of Hanover. The bulk of the fellows of both Trinity and Clare, for example, voted for Matthias Mawson (master of Corpus, 1724–44) in the hotly contested election for vice-chancellor in 1729 (Lunn, 1883: 20–1). Richard Laughton's achievements as a tutor at Clare were also greatly admired at Corpus: in 1716, Thomas Green, a former master of Corpus and a future bishop of Ely, recommended to John Denne, a young tutor at Corpus, that he 'set Mr. Laughton, of Clare hall, as a pattern before you for the management of your pupils. You see what an universal credit he has gained thereby' (Nichols, 1817–58, VI: 788).

Our chief guide to the undergraduate curriculum of early eighteenth-century Corpus is the diary of William Stukeley, who came up to Corpus in 1704 and took an MB in 1708. Stukeley's tutor was Thomas Fawcett (fellow of Corpus, 1700–17) but he was taught jointly by Fawcett and Robert Danny who was elected to a Corpus fellowship in 1708 and later became a chaplain of Cambridge's chancellor. Danny was also a friend of Cotes who addressed to him his last scientific paper – an account of the meteor of 6 March 1716 – which was conveyed to the Royal Society by

James Jurin of Trinity (Edleston, 1850: 229). Danny, who was described
by Stukeley as 'a person of admirable learning, wit, and good conversation, a great Mathematician, divine, and universal Scholar' (Lukis, 1882–
7, 1: 134), taught Stukeley 'Arithmetic, Algebra, Geometry, Philosophy,
Astronomy, Trigonometry' using such texts as 'Tacquet's Geometry by
Whiston', 'Rohault's Physics by Clark', 'Clarks 2 Volumes of Sermons at
Boyles Lectures' and 'Varenius Geography by Sr. Isaac Newton' as well as
'all Newtons and Boyles works'. Danny also provided Stukeley and his
fellow-students at Corpus with 'mathematical and philosophical instruments, such as air pumps, telescopes, microscopes, & c.' (ibid.: 21, 143).

Fawcett, who taught Stukeley metaphysics, classics and divinity, was
evidently also sympathetic to Stukeley's scientific interests since he provided him with 'a Room in the College to dissect in, and practise Chymical
Experiments . . . the wall [of which] was generally hung round with Guts,
stomachs, bladders, preparations of parts and drawings' (ibid.: 33).
Among the works prescribed by Fawcett were 'Wilkins Natural Religion'
and 'Lock of human understanding' (ibid.: 21), the latter reflecting the
influence of Fawcett's and Danny's former tutor, Charles Kidman, who
served as a chaplain to Tenison and was reputed to be the first tutor to
introduce his pupils to Locke's work (Disney, 1785: 3). Stukeley also came
to know Kidman, providing him 'with a plentiful hand' with some home-
made medicines (Lukis, 1882–7, 1: 39). Having completed his basic
grounding in natural philosophy Stukeley sought for new scientific
worlds to conquer, attracting the attention of two other fellows of his
college, John Waller and Stephen Hales. Waller (fellow of Corpus, 1695–
1717) was Vigani's successor as professor of chemistry; though he
published nothing he evidently did not altogether neglect his duties as a
teacher since Stukeley records seeing 'many Philosophical Experiments in
Pneumatic Hydrostatic Engines and instruments performed at that time
by Mr. Waller' (ibid.: 21).

Stukeley's friendship with Waller's far more illustrious colleague,
Stephen Hales, grew out of Stukeley's increasing interest in natural
history. The eighteenth-century naturalist, Peter Collinson, wrote in his
obituary of Hales that Stukeley and Hales used 'to ramble over Gogmagog
Hills and the bogs of Cherry-Hunt-Moor to gather simples, with Ray's
Catalogus Plantarum circa Cantabrigiam Nascentium in his pocket' (GM,
1764: 273). The two men also shared a common interest in anatomy,
'frequently dissecting frogs, and other animals in their herbalizing walks'.
When Stukeley 'attended the chymical lectures that were then read by the
publick professor Signor Vigani' Hales accompanied him and both 'went
also to see the chymical operations which he [Vigani] performed in a room
in Trinity College, which had been the laboratory of Sir Isaac Newton' (ibid.:

274). Prompted, no doubt, by Vigani's lectures Stukeley and Hales 'applied themselves also to chymistry, and repeated many of Mr. *Boyle's* experiments' (*ibid.*). Though Hales and Stukeley were drawn together by their common interest in natural history both remained enthusiastic students of Newton and the physical sciences. 'Hales', wrote Collinson, 'was equally assiduous and successful in the study of Astronomy, for having acquired a perfect knowledge of the *Newtonian* system he contrived a machine to demonstrate it'; at Hales's request Stukeley drew up a diagram of this orrery and kept a copy of it throughout his life (*ibid.*). In his diary Stukeley noted, too, that he was introduced by Hales to 'the doctrine of Optics and Telescopes and Microscopes, and some Chymical Experiments' (Lukis, 1882–7, I: 21).

At Corpus Stukeley also came to know Stephen Gray whose nephew, John Gray (MB, 1711), was, like Stukeley, a pupil of Fawcett and a Corpus medical student. To amuse both Stukeley and his nephew, Stephen Gray (then working as an assistant to Cotes) 'showed us many times his electrical operations with a long glass tube. He had a particular knack of exciting this property by friction with his hand, and was the father, at least first propagator, of electricity' (*ibid.*, II: 378). Stukeley had considerable respect for Stephen Gray, describing him as an 'ingenious Man, well versed in Philosophy, Astronomy, Optics, Mechanics & c.' (*ibid.*, I: 41). Hales may well have shared Stukeley's interest in Gray's electrical experiments – certainly he later referred to the 'curious Experiments, made by that skilful and indefatigable Experimenter Mr. Stephen Gray', in his *Statical essays* (1733: 59); Hales also published a paper entitled 'An Account of some electrical experiments' in the *Philosophical Transactions* (XLV: 409).

While still a student Stukeley was also in contact with James Keill (Lukis, 1882–7, I: 42) who shared the enthusiasm of his brother, John, for Newtonian natural philosophy and set out to explain the workings of the 'animal oeconomy' in terms of attraction, using quantitative techniques (T. M. Brown, 1974: 185). James Keill first lectured at Oxford where one student described him as having 'a considerable knowledge of the Mathematics which help'd him very much in discovering the Reason of the Site of the Parts and chiefly, in explaining Muscular Motion';[2] he then moved to Cambridge where his lectures were received 'with great applause' (Valadez and O'Malley, 1971: 319). He settled at Northampton in 1703 but retained his links with Cambridge; in 1705 he received an honorary MD and, as Stukeley's diary indicates, he continued to offer some instruction to interested undergraduates. Hales probably also met James Keill; in any case he was a careful student of Keill's work, sharing his

---

[2] Corpus Christi College, Cambridge, Hartshorne MSS, Wallis to Postlethwayt, 1698.

ambition of explaining the physiology of plants and animals on mechanical principles. Indeed, Hales's two major works, *Vegetable staticks* (1727) and *Statical essays* (1733), may be regarded as the culmination of the British iatromechanical tradition of which James Keill and other medical disciples of Newton, like Pitcairne and Richard Mead, were representatives. Hales's work is also an indication of the way in which Cambridge's seventeenth-century bias towards the biomedical sciences could be fused with the more recent interest in Newton's work. In the *Vegetable staticks* (to which Newton contributed an *imprimatur* as president of the Royal Society) Hales affirmed his belief that 'the most likely way therefore, to get any insight into the nature of those parts of the creation, which come within our observation, must in all reason be to number, weigh and measure' – a procedure, he added, the worth of which had been proved by Newton, 'the great Philosopher of our Age' (1961 ed.: xxxi). Underlying all his work were the basic principles he learnt from Newton: that matter is composed of particles and that attraction is, as Hales put it, a 'universal principle which is so operative in all the very different works of nature' (Cohen, 1956: 124).

Hales was a fellow of Corpus from 1703 to 1719, but only visited Cambridge occasionally after being made perpetual curate of Teddington in 1709. However, as Stukeley's diary indicates, many of Hales's scientific interests were shaped while he was still at Cambridge and, at times, Hales himself refers to experiments performed while at the university. In the introduction to his *Statical essays* (1733), for example, Hales wrote that, 'I endeavoured about twenty-five years since, by proper experiments, to find what was the real force of the blood in the crural arteries of dogs' – which confirms that he had begun his experimental work while both he and Stukeley were still at the university (Clark-Kennedy, 1929: 27). A pamphlet by Richard Davies, addressed to Hales, also refers to 'your private Elaboratory in Bennet [Corpus] College; where you plan'd those statical Enquiries which have opened a new road into Nature' (1759: 44). Again, in the *Vegetable staticks*, Hales noted that he had first performed an experiment designed by Boyle 'about 20 years since . . . in the elaboratory in Trinity College Cambridge' (1961 ed.: 112) – no doubt that of Vigani whom both Hales and Stukeley came to know. It is probable, too, that Hales was also influenced by some of Cotes's experiments in hydrostatics and pneumatics (R. E. Schofield, 1970: 34).

Even after both men had left the university Stukeley continued to take an interest in Hales's work: it was Stukeley who put Hales's name forward for election as an FRS in 1718 (Guerlac, 1977: 172) and later persuaded him to read to the Royal Society 'his static experiments about vegetation, which he printed afterwards' (Lukis, 1882–7, 1: 133). Stukeley and Hales also continued to share a firm belief that the findings of natural philosophy could be used for the service of religion. Stukeley had been urged by his friend, Archbishop Wake, to join the ministry since in 'the prevailing infidelity of the present wicked age' Christianity needed to be defended 'by those who are in all respects as eminent in natural knowledge, and philosophical enquiries, as they [who oppose Christianity] can pretend to be' (Piggott, 1950: 116) – a mission to which Stukeley responded with enthusiasm. Hales also frequently dwelt on the apologetical significance of the study of both Newtonian natural philosophy and natural history. Thus in a sermon delivered to the Royal College of Physicians in 1751 Hales affirmed that 'Not only the Grandeur of this our solar System, and the other heavenly Bodies, declare the Glory of God, but also the exceeding Minuteness of microscopical Animals, and of their component Parts, shew forth the Skill and Power of the Creator' (Allan and Schofield, 1980: 28). In his sermons, too, Hales, in low church fashion, emphasised the accord between Christianity and the testimony of nature and generally eschewed doctrinal matters (Clark-Kennedy, 1929: 45).

The limited interest which Hales's work in applying Newtonian principles to biological phenomena received within Cambridge is an indication of the extent to which the mathematical sciences were increasingly supplanting the more traditional preoccupation with the medical sciences – a trend reflected in the sharp decline in medical enrolments after 1730 (Rook, 1971: 57). However, within the shrinking medical faculty his work did receive some attention, his chief exponent being John Mickleburgh (professor of chemistry, 1718–56) who had been elected a fellow of Corpus in 1714 and who continued to correspond with Hales about his chemical and physiological experiments after he resigned his fellowship (Trinity College, Cambridge, MS R.2.42: 181–7). Chemistry, in the words of Richard Davies (1759: 40), was one of 'the Arts subservient to Medicine'; Mickleburgh's close associations with the medical faculty are evident in the fact that the Senate appointed him as professor of chemistry since he 'hath been recommended to us by the King's Professor of Physick' (Coleby, 1952b: 166); moreover, he supplemented his income (for the professorship of chemistry was an honorary post) by practising as a pharmacist.

Mickleburgh was an avowedly Newtonian chemist: at the beginning of his lectures he refers his audience to Newton's *Opticks* (Query 91) for an exposition of the principles of attraction between small bodies; he also highly praised the work of John Freind whom he described as 'the first who applied Isaac Newton's Philosophy to Chymistry' (Gonville and Caius College, Cambridge, MS 619/342: 'Day Two'). None the less, Mickleburgh felt it necessary to add to Freind's system of explanation a further postulate, namely 'that in the smaller particles of bodies there is a vis repellens' (*ibid.*: 'Day 4'), a concept which, as R. E. Schofield (1970: 47–8) suggests, he may well have derived from Hales's *Vegetable staticks*. Elsewhere Mickleburgh refers to the 'accurate experiments made by the ingenious Rev. Mr. Hales' (Caius, MS 619/342: 'Day 7') and cites 'our great philosopher Newton and after him the learned Dr. Hales' to refute the claims of Boerhaave, Stahl and others that 'fire is a particular distinct kind of body' (*ibid.*: 2nd ser. 'Day 2'). However, if his lecture attendance lists are any guide, after 1741 Mickleburgh followed the example of many of his professorial colleagues and ceased to lecture. With his departure from active teaching 'the direct influence of Hales and Newton on Cambridge chemistry ceased' (Coleby, 1952b: 174) since Mickleburgh's successor, John Hadley of Queens' (who was appointed to the post after Mickleburgh's death in 1756), based his lectures on the work of Continental chemists (Coleby, 1952c) though he includes a passing reference to Hales's experiments with air (Trinity College, Cambridge, MS R. 1. 50–1: 15). Hadley's lectures are largely a record of experiments with little regard to chemical theory apart from a brief discussion of phlogiston – on the distinctively Newtonian issue of attractive forces he is silent.

The examples of Trinity, Clare and Corpus indicate the extent to which the advocacy of Newtonian natural philosophy was associated with members of the university who had broken with the high church principles that had been instilled in the university before the Glorious Revolution. However, while the association between Newtonian natural philosophy and low church theology which had been forged by Bentley and his followers helped Newton's work reach a larger public than it might otherwise have done, it also had the effect of drawing Newton's name into the often vitriolic clash between high and low churchmen which was so marked a feature of early eighteenth-century England. The nonjuror George Hickes, who crossed swords with such notable Cambridge latitudinarians as Bentley and Clarke, commented to Roger North in 1713 that, 'It is their Newtonian philosophy which hath Made Not onely so many Arians but Theists, and that Not onely among the laity but I fear among our devines' (Stewart, 1981: 65), while Hickes's nonjuring colleague, Hearne, declared bluntly that Newton's works were likely to become 'waste-paper' (Hearne, 1966: 409). Hutchinsonianism, which attempted to replace Newtonian natural philosophy by one based on Mosaic principles, has been described as 'a High Church response to this association between low church principles and Newtonian science' (Wilde, 1980: 7). As late as 1756 an Oxford sermon in defence of the Hutchinsonians could prompt an impassioned reply by Ralph Heathcote (MA Jesus, 1748; Boyle lecturer, 1763–5) whose low church inclinations are evident in his criticism of those 'who are continually depressing Reason, the better as they assume to advance Revelation, and who labor with all their might to destroy Natural Religion, as the best and only means of supporting Revealed' (1756: 1).

To the nonjurors and to many of their sympathisers who reluctantly swore allegiance to the new regime, the Glorious Revolution was a bitter demonstration that the ways of Providence were indeed unfathomable: that an anointed son of a martyred king should be cast out of his kingdom and his loyal followers be compelled to eat the bread of adversity seemed ample proof of their belief that God's ways did not conform with human reasonings. Partly as a result of these experiences the high churchmen tended to emphasise the gulf between human wisdom and the inscrutable decrees of God, frequently returning to the refrain of the Book of Ecclesiastes – 'vanity of vanity, all is vanity and vexation of the spirit' – as a comment on 'the pride of reason' of their contemporaries, a spirit which they saw as particularly rife among some of Newton's more enthusiastic publicists both within Cambridge and in the country at large.

The inadequacy of human reason is a recurring theme in the works of a number of the fellows of St John's who were not altogether reconciled to the Revolutionary Settlement. Thus the *Reflections on learning* (1709) of the nonjuring Thomas Baker (a work which went through seven editions) set out to illustrate how prone to error are human faculties in contrast to the certainty offered by Revelation – a task, writes Baker, which is necessary in 'an Age, in which it [Learning] seems to be too much magnified; and where Men are fond of Learning almost to the loss of Religion' (1727 ed.: iii). Thomas Baker was politically and religiously more irenical than many of his nonjuring brethren (Korsten, 1985: 492–3) – something which is reflected in his temperate, though none the less critical, remarks on recent intellectual developments. With some nostalgia Baker looks back to the time when natural philosophy was based principally on the works of Aristotle 'under whom we had more Peace, and possibly almost as much Truth as we have had since' (p. 4). Indeed, he argues that the changes in natural philosophy indicate forcibly how limited and uncertain is human reason. He points to the inadequacies of Cartesianism (p. 95) and refers obliquely to Newton as one who 'after the nicest Enquiry, seems to resolve all into *Attraction*', concluding that since the problems of natural philosophy will never be resolved we should 'be content to resolve all into the Power or Providence of God' (p. 99). After completing his survey of contemporary learning Baker plainly states the moral of his book: that the inadequacy of human knowledge 'brings the Mind to a Sense of its own Weakness, and makes it more readily, and with a greater Willingness, submit to Revelation' (p. 275).

Baker's reservations about the capabilities of human reason were shared by his lifelong friend and colleague, the poet Matthew Prior, who remained a lay fellow of St John's (though rarely resident) until his death in 1721. Though not a nonjuror, Prior feared for the position of the Church in the post-revolutionary order – hence he was attracted to the tory party and became a protégé of Harley. Like Baker's *Reflections*, the purpose of Prior's poems *Exodus* (1688) and *Solomon or the vanity of the world* (written 1708, published 1718) was to demonstrate the limitations of human knowledge and, consequently, the need to acknowledge the overriding importance of Revelation. In *Exodus* he portrays man as acting 'with dangerous curiosity', attempting to explain the phenomena of nature by hypotheses which become the 'jargon of the schools'; the inadequacies of such explanations, contends Prior, demonstrate the need for faith with which we can see what 'all the volumes of philosophy, with all their comments, never could invent' (W. P. Jones, 1961: 100). Prior's *Solomon* explores these same sentiments at greater length. Like Baker, Prior surveys the different categories of human knowledge with the aim of exhibiting their limitations; thus he bids the reader

> Remember, that the curs'd Desire to know,
> Off-spring of ADAM, was thy Source of Woe.
> (in Spears, 1948: 495)

Even less sympathetic to learning than Baker or Prior was Richard Marsh, a junior fellow of St John's, who in 1699 delivered a sermon entitled *The vanity and danger of modern theories*. Like Baker, he argued that the 'new philosophy' had discredited itself since each new theory was being overturned by another and he implied that Newtonianism would soon give way to some new fad: 'We have seen a Des-Cartes run down, whose Reputation is absorb'd by the more prevailing Power of new Theories: though if we take a view of them, we shall find they have not had the Happiness of giving any greater Satisfaction' (p. 5). Marsh was particularly scathing of attempts (like that of Thomas Burnet) 'to give a Rational Account of the Mosaical Creation' – such works he viewed as a form of deism since in them 'rather than Mechanism must be broke [*sic*], the Sacred Text must be rack'd into Confession of it' (p. 10). For Marsh, as for Baker and Prior, true knowledge is to be aware of the 'Bounds and Extent' of human learning (p. 3), especially in an age when 'Men are turning Levellers in Religion, as they were of old in Government; and nothing now pass for an Article of their Faith, but what is of the same Height within their Reason' (p. 8). Attempts to demonstrate the reasonableness of Christianity in the manner of the latitudinarians Marsh views as having been responsible for the growth of infidelity; nor, he argues, should religion be too ready to embrace new systems of natural philosophy for 'we are not to alter the sense of Scripture, as often as New

Reasons are found out in Nature, if we would not be thought to bring down Scripture to the same Uncertainty' (p. 23).

The most thoroughgoing attack on Newton's work from within Cambridge came from Robert Greene who, interestingly enough, was a fellow of Clare, a college which had done much to popularise the *Principia*. In his massive *Principles of the philosophy of the expansive and contractive forces* (981 folio pages, 1727), Greene expressed his intention of substituting for the mechanical philosophy (which he regarded as 'the Product of Popish Countries') 'a Philosophy which is truly English, a Cantabrigian and a Clarensian one . . . [which] I shall venture to call the Greenian' (Preface). Greene's fulsome dedication to Harley of his *Principles of natural philosophy* . . . (1712) indicates where his political sympathies lay, for he praised the tory leader as one 'Rais'd by the Providence of Almighty God for the Support and Patronage of our most Holy Faith, against the Insults of the Several Atheists, Deists, Socinians, and I may now say, Arrians [Whiston and Clarke?] of our Age'. Such enthusiastic support for the tories in 1712 suggests that Greene was involved in the political wranglings which were to divide Clare in the mastership election of 1713. The chief candidate of the whig party was Richard Laughton, one of the most ardent advocates of Newton's work within the university; in opposing the Newtonian natural philosophy, then, Greene may also have seen himself as striking a blow against the whig faction within the college. By 1727, however, Greene was prudent enough to dedicate his *Expansive and contractive forces* to Newcastle (a former student), though in his preface he was at great pains to reassure his readers that he had sworn allegiance to the Revolutionary Settlement despite rumours to the contrary.

Greene's adherence to the tory cause was of a piece with his theological principles which he set out in an uncompromising form in his first book, the *Demonstration of the truth and divinity of the Christian religion* (1711). In this work he argues against the latitudinarians (whom he describes as the 'Patrons of Reason') that Scripture was not intended simply to convey 'good wholesome Institutions only, for our Conduct and Acting, for our Worship of the Deity, and paying that Natural Homage which is due to Him': the biblical doctrines, he insists, are '*above* the highest stretch of our Faculties to find out' (pp. 139–40). Indeed, it is the thesis of this work that the most telling proof of the truth of Christianity was a defence of Scripture as an accurate historical record on which were based doctrines which could transcend the limits of human reason.

Throughout his work Greene emphasised this cleavage between human and revealed knowledge: in the preface to his next book, *The principles of natural philosophy* (1712), he commented caustically on 'those Divines in our present Age, who are too fond of what they call Rational, who put too great a stress upon their Reasonings from Nature, when so little of it is understood by us'. Greene's chief targets in this book were Hobbes, Spinoza and Locke whom he accused of seeking to introduce 'a Licentiousness of thought, under the Modern Terms of Free-Thinking', a charge from which he exempted Newton and Halley. None the less, Greene expounds at length on the inadequacies of the 'Corpuscular System, or the Philosophy of Homogeneous Matter' (e.g. Book I, chapter 9) which he sees as a revival of Epicureanism – an argument which inevitably brought him into conflict with Newton's view that 'God in the beginning formed matter in solid, massy, hard, impenetrable, movable particles' (Thayer, 1974: 175). Newton's disciples had no doubt that Greene's work was intended as an attack on the master: Cotes reported to Newton in 1711 that Greene was publishing a book 'wherein I am informed he undertakes to overthrow the Principles of Your Philosophy' (Turnbull *et al.*, 1959–77, v: 166). In his *magnum opus* of 1727, *The principles of the philosophy of the expansive and contractive forces*, Greene was more open in his opposition to Newton's work and, with characteristic lack of modesty, suggested that Newton had altered both the *Principia* and the *Opticks* as a result of Greene's comments in his *Principles of natural philosophy* (Thackray, 1970: 128). While respectful of Newton himself, Greene described his system of natural philosophy as 'much the same [as Cartesianism] as to the Principles of a Similar and Homogeneous Matter' (Preface), a theory of matter which Greene viewed as undermining Christian belief. Greene also specifically attacked such Newtonian concepts as absolute space and time (pp. 41–7) and action through a vacuum (p. 17), arguing that such ideas implied limitations to the power of God.

As an alternative to both the Cartesian and Newtonian natural philosophies Greene expounded his own theory of 'heterogeneous matter': like his opponent, Descartes, he argued that action at a distance implies a *plenum*, though, unlike Descartes, Greene viewed matter not as passive but as an active force, being 'nothing else but Action' (p. 409; R. E. Schofield, 1970: 119). Matter, Greene held, 'is distinguished into the Expansive and Contractive Forces, which, and the Different Combinations of them, are the occasion of those Diversities of Matter we Feel and See to Exist in Like and Equal Portions of Space' (p. 409; Heimann and McGuire, 1971: 259). Thus Greene resolved matter into an array of different forces, which ultimately derive from God – though he is far from consistent in applying these principles. Appropriately, the work ends with a dialogue entitled 'A Just Ridicule of Similar Matter' between two protagonists, 'Philomuthos, or a Lover of Romance' (a corpuscularian) and 'Philalethes, or a Lover of Truth' who, predictably, is Greene's mouthpiece.

Throughout the work Greene made clear his underlying theological objections to the corpuscular philosophy. In his preface he described his *Contractive and expansive forces* as forming with his *Principles of natural philosophy* 'my second Demonstration of Christian Religion [a reference to his work of 1711] by shewing the Fallacies of those Reasonings in a Philosophy, which seems to Oppose it, or to have very little Regard for it'. As in his previous works Greene was also at pains to counter the growing vogue for natural theology, devoting a whole chapter (Book VI, chapter 1) to the topic 'Concerning the Little Importance of Natural Religion after the Revelation of the Christian' in which he was particularly concerned to refute the views of Samuel Clarke (p. 768), Newton's chief theological spokesman. For all their extravagance Greene's works do represent one of the most thoroughgoing critiques of the growing alliance between New-tonian natural philosophy and the latitudinarian theologians. Greene may have been an eccentric but he was not an obscurantist: unlike most high churchmen he had studied contemporary natural philosophers in some detail and attempted to criticise such authors not only on theological grounds but also through a detailed examination of their own subject. In Newton's work, argued Greene, the natural order appeared to be con-trolled by essentially random forces: hence Greene's determination to develop a more teleological system of explanation of natural phenomena which, in Greene's view, posed less of a challenge to revealed religion than the mechanical philosophy.

John Edwards, a former fellow of St John's, wrote of Greene's *Principles of natural philosophy* that it 'disdain[ed] all Plainness and Perspicuity' (Edwards, 1714: 87). None the less, Edwards shared with Greene the same theologically based suspicions of Newton's work; in the same book in which he made this unflattering remark on Greene's style – *New discoveries of the uncertainty, deficiency, and corruptions of human knowledge and learning* (1714) – Edwards also criticised Newton, arguing that his concept of attraction was a principle of 'such universality as to threaten the direct dependence of nature on God' (p. 75). As the title of his work indicates, Edwards was concerned to demonstrate the limits of human knowledge and, consequently, the need for reliance on Revelation. Like Greene he criticised those theologians who, because of their studies in natural philosophy, attempted 'to new model our Religion, to mend the Gospel, and present us as it were with a New Christianity' (p. ii). Though Edwards, who devoted a number of pamphlets to attacking the theologi-cal views of Clarke and Whiston, had much in common with Greene and the St John's high churchmen he differed from them in his firm adherence to Calvinist principles – something which had cost him his fellowship at St John's (Stromberg, 1954: 111), though he continued to live in Cambridge and took his DD there in 1699. However, from their different theological perspectives Greene and Edwards both agreed that the growing vogue for natural theology, which had become associated with Newtonian natural philosophy, imperilled the revealed doctrines of Christianity.

A more sympathetic reader of Greene's work was the diarist and poet John Byrom, who records that in 1729 he had 'much talk with Dr. Green . . . about his philosophy of contractive and expansive forces' during which Greene explained to Byrom 'that all matter was active not passive' (Parkinson, 1854, I, pt. 2: 397–8). Byrom (BA Trinity, 1712) was greatly interested in natural philosophy and was an active member of the Royal Society. However, he wished to combine his studies in natural philosophy with a more spiritually vital form of religion than the 'nominal Christianity' (Talon, 1950: 105) which he felt characterised his con-temporaries – hence his interest in Greene's work and that of the Hutchin-sonians (Kuhn, 1974: 402) before he finally became a devoted follower of the nonjuring mystic, William Law. Byrom and Law both shared con-siderable reservations about the Revolutionary Settlement. Byrom had scruples about taking the Abjuration Oath in 1714 and throughout his life was a cautious supporter of the jacobite cause (Talon, 1950: 19–20). Law was suspended from his degrees in 1713 for publicly casting aspersions on those who had forsaken their oath of loyalty to James and in 1717 was ejected from his fellowship at Emmanuel as a nonjuror.

Law and his disciple, Byrom, were prepared to countenance the linking of human philosophy (including the work of Newton) with Christianity – provided it was done in a manner which gave more scope to the supernatural character of Christian belief than the writings of their latitudinarian opponents. Thus, like the Hutchinsonians, Law argued that natural philosophy could provide an insight into Christian belief since fire, light and air were 'but the Trinity itself in its most outward, lowest, kind of existence or manifestation' (Kuhn, 1974: 408). Law also took the view that Newton's *Principia* was rooted in mystical religion since 'the true and infallible ground' of Newton's three laws of motion 'was to be found in the Teutonic Theosopher [Jacob Boehme] in his three, first properties of Eternal Nature' (Hobhouse, 1948: 399). Furthermore, in Law's thought Newton's principle of attraction is transformed into a universal, vitalistic principle, which manifests the ever-present hand of the Creator: to Law attraction 'gives essence and substance to all that is matter and the properties of matter, it holds every element in its created state' (Wormhoudt, 1949: 418).

Law's claim that Newton was influenced by Boehme prompted an enquiry for further details from Dr George Cheyne. After early adherence to the iatromechanical school of medicine Cheyne had come to use

Newton's work (and, in particular, his concept of attraction) as the basis for a theological system in which the physical world was seen as an emanation of the Deity (Bowles, 1974). He had also become increasingly suspicious of the vogue for natural theology to which he himself had earlier contributed; by the 1730s he was denouncing the influence of 'spurious Freethinkers, active Latitudinarians, and Apostolic Infidels' (Jacob, 1981: 97). Cheyne's interest in the alleged links between Boehme and Newton was understandable since Byrom (who corresponded with Cheyne on religious matters (Talon, 1950: 207)) tells us that it was he who first introduced Law to the works of Boehme (*ibid.*: 221). In answer to Cheyne Law replied that 'When Sir Isaac died, there were found among his papers large abstracts out of J. Behmen's works written in his own hand' (Hobhouse, 1948: 400). In fact, there is no evidence for Law's claim which appears to have been based on an unreliable second-hand report of Newton's amanuensis, Humphrey Newton (*ibid.*: 412); Law's insistence on the point, however, indicates the importance he placed on demonstrating the conformity between Newtonian natural philosophy and his own form of mystical Christianity. It also indicates the vastly different view which Law took of the religious implications of Newton's work (and of natural philosophy generally) as compared to that of Law's latitudinarian contemporaries.

The work of Greene, Byrom and Law, along with that of the Hutchinsonians, demonstrates the suspicion which existed in high church circles towards the 'holy alliance' that had been formed between Newtonian natural philosophy and latitudinarian theology. One should be cautious, then, of regarding Newtonian natural philosophy as so totally identified with the Church as a whole as to drive the Church's critics to adopt alternative natural philosophies: Jacob, however, writes of Toland adopting the thought of Bruno in order 'to devise a philosophy of nature that he could effectively posit against the church's Newtonianism' (Jacob, 1976: 228). If, indeed, Toland was concerned to construct an alternative to Newton's natural philosophy out of his hatred for the clerical establishment there was the ironic consequence that he shared his opposition to the Newtonian form of the mechanical philosophy with those members of the Church who were not fully reconciled to the Revolutionary Settlement nor to the strain of theology promulgated by some of the Revolution's apologists which, in its emphasis on natural religion, left little place for a sacerdotal class.

High church suspicion of Newton's work was heightened by the fact that it also suffered from guilt by association with the thought of Locke whose philosophical writings – and still more his religious works – were viewed with considerable alarm by many of the custodians of orthodoxy: more so, indeed, than those of Newton whose published work impinged less directly on the volatile religious and political issues of the day. In the 'Epistle to the reader' of the *Essay concerning human understanding* Locke had praised the abilities of the 'incomparable Mr. Newton' and at a number of points in this work referred to Newton's 'never enough to be admired Book' (1975 ed.: 530, 599). Locke, of course, had also been a loyal friend to Newton since they met when Newton came to London as an MP in 1689, suffering Newton's paranoid outburst of 1693 with dignity and forbearance (Turnbull *et al.*, 1959–77, III: 280). Furthermore, both men shared similar reservations about the doctrine of the Trinity, Locke describing Newton to Peter King as 'a very valuable man, not only for his wonderful skill in mathematics, but in divinity, too . . .' (*ibid.*: 79 n. 1).

This association between Newton and Locke was further strengthened in the eyes of the Cambridge high churchmen by the fact that many of Newton's followers within the university were also active in disseminating the views of Locke. In 1696 Molyneux, the Anglo-Irish philosopher, remarked to Locke that, though Locke's view that 'the idea of God is not innate' had earlier led to charges of infidelity, 'yet now we find Mr. Bentley very large upon it, in his sermons at Mr. Boyle's lectures . . . And Mr. Whiston, in his new theory of the earth' (in Locke, 1708: 162–3). At around the same time Cambridge undergraduates began to defend questions drawn from Locke's philosophy (*ibid.*: 156–7), perhaps as a result of the initiative of Tenison's protégé, Charles Kidman, who encouraged his students to read both Locke's *Essay* and *Two treatises* (Disney, 1785: 13). Whiston was particularly zealous in defending Locke's work. In his *New theory of the earth* he described Locke as 'the best of metaphysicians' (1708 ed.: 182) and in a pamphlet of 1713 he set out to defend Locke against the charge of being a deist (Yolton, 1956: 180–1). Whiston's colleague, Richard Laughton, was also an admirer of Locke for it was to him that Lady Masham sent her famous letter of 1704 describing Locke's last hours (Fox-Bourne, 1876, II: 556).

Many of Newton's latitudinarian followers were naturally attracted to Locke's own undogmatic religious views, as presented in *The reasonableness of Christianity*, as well as to his advocacy of religious toleration in his *Letters concerning toleration*. Moreover, Locke's dismissal of innate ideas and his emphasis on the role of experience and reason acted as a solvent of many of the traditional concepts of monarchical and ecclesiastical government to which the latitudinarians themselves were opposed.[3] For similar

---

[3] However, not all latitudinarians were followers of Locke. One of Locke's chief critics was Stillingfleet who, though a friend of Locke, became concerned at the implications of his work when he saw how it was used by the deist Toland and by the Socinians (Sullivan, 1982: 76–80; Popkin, 1971).

reasons, however, many of the high churchmen within Cambridge viewed the growing interest in Locke within the university with some disquiet. Robert Jenkin, a former nonjuror who became master of St John's in 1711, described Locke's work as having 'offered violence to Scripture and every thing else that opposes it' (1709: 122); earlier, in his *magnum opus, The reasonableness and certainty of the Christian religion* (1700)[4] – one of the aims of which was 'To convince men . . . of the Narrowness and Weakness of Humane Reason' (II: 3) – Jenkin had expressed his suspicion of those (like Locke and the latitudinarians) who 'would endeavour to present us with a Religion without all Mystery' – an approach, he argued, which led to Socinianism (I: xi). Also from St John's were Matthew Prior, who satirised Locke's ideas in his 'Dialogue between Mr. John Locke and Monsieur de Montaigne' (Spears, 1948: 503), and the Calvinist John Edwards, Locke's most determined opponent from Cambridge, the author of *Socinian unmask'd . . .* (1696), one of the most vitriolic of the attacks on Locke's *Reasonableness*. The most detailed Cambridge critique of Locke's *Essay* was *Antiscepticism, or notes upon each chapter of Locke's Essay . . .* (1702) by Henry Lee, who was made a fellow of Emmanuel by royal mandate in 1667. In his 'epistle dedicatory' to Sir Nathan Wright, the tory keeper of the great seal (who was described as being 'ever a warm stickler' for the Church (N. Sykes, 1935: 439)), Lee criticised what he considered to be the present reaction against established authorities, both political and intellectual: 'Our Philosophy, our Policy, our Religion', he commented critically, 'must be all new or none at all.' Lee regarded Locke's work as being a prime example of this intellectual restlessness, being appropriate 'to the inquisitive Genius of this Age'. Lee was particularly critical of Locke's refusal to derive knowledge from general principles – something, he argued, which caused scepticism since 'there can be no *certain* Knowledge of the Truth of any *general* Proposition whatever; because our Senses can reach but to *particulars*, and Reflexion no farther' (p. 67; Yolton, 1956: 73). Such scepticism undermined not only 'Philosophical and Theological Speculations but also the general receiv'd Maximes of Natural and Reveal'd Religion' (dedication).

Though Locke had supporters like Laughton and Whiston at Clare this college also produced a number of his critics, reflecting the politically and intellectually divided character of the college in the period after the Glorious Revolution. Four years after the appearance of the *Essay* Locke was criticised in a pamphlet entitled *A discourse concerning the nature of man* . . . by James Lowde, a former fellow of Clare. Lowde argued that Locke's attack on innate ideas made custom the arbiter of behaviour, thereby

---

[4] The 1700 edition is the second edition of Volume I (first published in 1697) though the first edition of Volume II.

undermining public morality – a charge which provoked Locke into adding a section to his preface to the fourth edition of the *Essay* in which he set out to refute Lowde by arguing that the purpose of the *Essay* was not the 'laying down [of] moral Rules, but [rather] shewing the original and nature of moral *Ideas*' (Locke, 1975 ed.: 354). Lowde's colleague, Robert Greene, took an even more hostile view of Locke's work, claiming in the *Expansive and contractive forces* (1727) that the 'Philosophy of ideas' aimed to 'propose itself as Judge in all Matters of Reason' (p. 600). Predictably, Greene's distrust of Locke was theologically based, Greene regarding him as 'willing to prefer the Reasonings of a Natural Religion and the Refined Heathenism of Socrates or Plato, to the Evidence of Revelation, and the Precepts of a Messiah' (p. 718).

Nevertheless, it is an indication of the declining importance of the high churchmen within Cambridge that such opposition did little to prevent the steady assimilation of both Lockean philosophy and Newtonian natural philosophy into the undergraduate curriculum. At Oxford, by contrast, the heads officially banned the study of Locke's *Essay* in 1703 and although, in practice, undergraduates were exposed to this work (Yolton in SM: 586–7) it never enjoyed the same status it came to assume at Cambridge. By the late eighteenth century Bishop Edmund Law, the master of Peterhouse and the author of an edition of Locke's works, could remark on the way in which Newtonian mathematics 'together with Mr. Locke's *Essay* [and] Dr. Clarke's works went hand in hand through our public schools and lectures' (Fuller, 1840: 214). Ironically, one index of this gradual absorption of Newtonianism into the normal round of undergraduate studies was the declining importance of the Lucasian professor's lectures, since the courses they once offered came to be superseded by the instruction given by college tutors. This reflects the increasing importance of the college tutors who, by the eighteenth century, had largely taken over the responsibility for teaching undergrad-uates (Winstanley, 1935: 270–6) despite the emphasis laid on the role of the professors in the Statutes. As professorial teaching came more and more to be regarded as an adjunct to the instruction offered by the tutors the status and level of activity of the Cambridge professoriate declined accordingly. However, professorial instruction remained important in those subjects which fell outside the accepted range of tutorial instruction since they were thought to be at the periphery of the curriculum and therefore of interest to only a small number of students – a category which included most scientific subjects, at least for a time.

The lack of scientific expertise on the part of college tutors therefore helps explain the foundation of professorships in a range of scientific subjects in the late seventeenth and eighteenth centuries (Frank, 1973: 239). Most such chairs were founded from bequests left by donors who wished to broaden the scope of the university's curriculum; such was the case with the Lucasian professorship of mathematics (first appointment 1663), the Plumian professorship of astronomy and experimental philosophy (1708), Woodwardian professorship of geology (1731), Lowndean professorship of astronomy and geometry (1750), and Jacksonian professorship of natural experimental philosophy (1783). The university itself, however, founded the chairs of chemistry (1703), anatomy (1707) and botany (1724) on its own initiative – though these were originally only honorary posts, the professors drawing their income from student fees.

Though the foundation of a new professorship generally indicated that the subject was not considered part of the normal instruction offered by the college tutors the new subject was likely to become part of the college curriculum if it proved popular; tutors were wary of allowing professors to gain too great a following since this might diminish the pre-eminence of college teaching. When opposing Jebb's proposed reforms of the late eighteenth century, William Powell, master of St John's, acknowledged that many students 'have of late years attended the Professors of Anatomy, Botany and Chemistry' but asserted that 'by far the most useful institution of this sort is the constant daily lectures of the tutors in the separate colleges' (1774: 5). In 1792 Heberden made a similar point by arguing that 'The Tutor's lectures, in each particular College, are certainly preferable to the original mode of instruction by public professors, who read lectures for the benefit of those, and those only, who chose and could afford to attend them.' Rather less tactfully the same author also commented that the decline of professorships into sinecures 'is overbalanced by the opportunity it gives to several industrious men of emerging from the state of indolent uselessness, to which College fellowships are unavoidably subject' (1792: 46).

Consequently, the teaching of mathematics and Newtonian natural philosophy which, in its early stages, was largely the responsibility of the professors became more and more the province of the tutors as it became an integral part of the university curriculum. By 1803 the *University calendar* could make the claim that 'there are so many excellent lectures in mathematics delivered in the private colleges by their respective Tutors, that public lectures in that science are now become less necessary' (Winstanley, 1935: 132). However, since tutors were expected to teach the whole university curriculum, few could reach the standard of expertise that could be expected (though not always obtained) from a professor who was responsible for teaching but one subject; as John Brown (BA St John's, 1735) put it in his *Estimate of the times* (1750): 'The great lines of knowledge are broken, and the fragments retailed at all adventures by every member of a college who chooseth to erect himself into a professor of every science' (Abbey, 1887, I: 327). The tutorship system, then, was less likely than the professorial to introduce students to problems at the cutting-edge of the discipline which might serve as the basis for future research and scientific advance; the increasing importance of tutorial instruction in eighteenth-century Oxford and Cambridge may therefore help to account for the dearth of original scientific work in the English universities during this period. The disadvantages of tutorial, as against professorial, instruction were particularly evident in the case of medicine which required specialist training and a centrally organised course structure; thus Rook (1971: 6) suggests that a possible explanation for the decline of the eighteenth-century Cambridge medical school lies in the growing pre-eminence of tutorial instruction.

At the beginning of the eighteenth century Whiston as Lucasian professor and Cotes as Plumian professor had done much to popularise Newtonian natural philosophy in the public schools of the university and this work was continued by their successors, the blind Nicholas Saunderson (Lucasian professor, 1711–39) and Robert Smith (Plumian professor, 1716–60). Saunderson, who had gained both his honorary MA and professorship partly through Newton's influence (Davies, 1740: vii), saw his role as Lucasian professor as requiring him to expound Newton's work rather than to develop its findings through original research; his only published works were the *Elements of algebra* (1740) and his *Method of fluxions* (1756) which were little more than textbooks. However, as a teacher, Saunderson exerted considerable influence, his biographer, Richard Davies, claiming that thanks to his lectures

those wonderful *Phaenomena* of Nature, whose Solution was before attained with Difficulty by the best Mathematicians, became the *Theses* which the Youth of three or four Years standing defended in their Disputations for their first Degree in Arts. We every Year heard the Theory of the Tydes, the *Phaenomena* of the Rainbow, the Motions of the whole Planetary System as upheld by Gravity, very well defended by such as had profited by his Lectures. (1740: v–vi)

The manuscripts of Saunderson's Lucasian lectures still exist (CUL, Add. 589) and include expositions of hydrostatics, optics, mechanics, astronomy and the tides – all of course based on Newtonian principles. Saunderson also refers to recent experimental work done by members of the Royal Society like Jurin and Hauksbee and, as in the works of many of Newton's early disciples, Saunderson's lectures include attacks on Cartesian natural philosophy.

After establishing a lofty standard for the Lucasian professorship with the appointment of Barrow and Newton as its first two incumbents, the university appointed two creditable, if less eminent, successors in Whiston and Saunderson. However, with the appointment of John Colson in 1739 as Saunderson's successor (on the recommendation of Robert Smith) the reputation of the Lucasian professorship declined markedly. The antiquary Cole described Colson (who died in 1760) as 'a plain honest Man, of great Industry, [and] Assiduity' but added that 'the University was much disappointed in their Expectations of a Professor that was to give credit to it by Lectures' (BL, Add. 5866: p. 200). None the less, Colson, too, was a disciple of Newton, albeit of a lowly stature, for he published Newton's tract on fluxions (in an English translation) together with a commentary in 1736 (Whiteside, 1967–81, VIII: xxiii).[5] Colson also aided the dissemination of useful textbooks based on Newton's scientific and mathematical works: in 1746 he published Saunderson's *Elements of algebra* and soon afterwards translated from the Latin Peter van Musschenbroek's *Elements of natural philosophy* (first English ed., 1744) a work 'chiefly intended for the Use of Students in Universities'; he also edited the second edition of Brook Taylor's *New principles of linear perspective* (1749).

Quite apart from Colson's personal inadequacies as a teacher there was less cause for undergraduates to attend his lectures than those of his predecessors since Newtonian natural philosophy and mathematics had become part of the instruction offered by their college tutors. To judge by the *Quaestiones philosophiae* (1735) of Thomas Johnson (a fellow of Magdalene) – a guide to students preparing disputation topics – by the 1730s students were commonly called on to defend topics drawn from the *Principia* and were expected to display a familiarity with other scientific works relevant to the topic chosen. Johnson's proposed reading for those defending the proposition, 'Whether the cause of gravity may be explained by mechanical principles', includes works by Descartes, Rohault, Hooke, Le Clerc, Huygens and Bernoulli; those opposing the question were recommended to read Newton's *Principia* and *Opticks* along with works by Pemberton, Samuel Clarke, 'sGravesande, Musschenbroek, Keill and Cheyne (p. 15). Students were expected to master a similar range of reading to answer such questions as 'Whether Newton's three laws of nature are true' (p. 62) or 'Whether light is a body' (p. 99). Johnson also set such topical questions as 'Whether electrical phenomena can be explained by mechanical principles', recommending Newton's *Opticks* along with works by Desaguliers, Keill, Hauksbee and Stephen Gray (p. 46). Though the range of reading recommended by Johnson may have been well beyond the average run of students, his proposed disputation topics show that by the 1730s the study of Newtonian natural

---

[5] John Colson was probably also the 'Ivan Kolson' who introduced one of Peter the Great's entourage to Newton's natural philosophy in 1698 (Gjertsen, 1986: 125).

philosophy – once the preserve of a few exceptional students – was now considered an integral part of the undergraduate curriculum. Johnson's colleague, Daniel Waterland, the master of Magdalene from 1713 to 1740, had published in 1730 a pamphlet entitled *Advice to a young student . . .* which was popular enough to be reprinted five times and which was probably a more reliable guide to what was expected of the average undergraduate than Johnson's work. None the less, in the section on natural philosophy Waterland listed such Newtonian popularisers as David Gregory, John Keill, William Whiston and Samuel Clarke together with Newton's *Opticks* (the *Principia*, understandably, is left for post-graduate study).

The extent to which Newtonian natural philosophy had become part of the staple round of undergraduate studies by the 1730s is also reflected in the growing number of Newtonian-based textbooks and manuscript sets of lectures on natural philosophy by college tutors. In 1735 John Rowning (another fellow of Magdalene) published at the university press the avowedly Newtonian *A compendious system of natural philosophy*, a work which was reprinted several times up to 1772. It is divided into two parts: Part One being devoted to the properties of matter and the laws of motion, and Part Two to hydrostatics and pneumatics. The manuscript 'Course of mechanical lectures' for 1737 (St John's College, Cambridge, MS O.85) of Henry Wrigley (fellow of St John's, 1722–45) is a more elementary introduction to Newtonian mechanics, though it adds a section on his optics and includes more anti-Cartesian polemic. A suspiciously similar set of lectures (CUL, Add. 5047; Christ's College, Cambridge, MS 26) was probably also delivered around this period by Gervase Holmes of Emmanuel; he appears to have been followed by his colleague, Henry Hubbard, who gave a series of lectures on Newtonian optics, mechanics and astronomy (Emmanuel College, Cambridge, MSS 193–5). This demand for systematic introductions to Newtonian natural philosophy suitable for undergraduates continued into the 1740s, prompting the publication of William Powell's *Heads of lectures in experimental philosophy* (1746) – a work based on a set of lectures at St John's (St John's College, Cambridge, MS O.84) – and the more influential *System of natural philosophy* (1748) by his colleague, Thomas Rutherforth. Smith's *Optics* (1738) and *Harmonics* (1749), which were also frequently used as text-books, also belong to this period.

By the mid-eighteenth century, then, Newton's work had been duly systematised and codified by a number of Cambridge tutors and had become an integral part of the undergraduate curriculum. Having achieved this transformation, however, Cambridge receded as a centre of scientific activity. Newtonian natural philosophy became the new orthodoxy and, once it was established within the curriculum, there was little incentive to break new scientific ground. Cambridge had been associated with many of Newton's disciples – notably Bentley, Whiston, Clarke and Jurin – but as these disappeared from the scene there was little in the way of a new generation to take their place. Those interested in science within the university after Newton's death in 1727 devoted most of their energies to simplifying and systematising Newtonian natural philosophy for pedagogical ends – an activity that provided little incentive to pursue original research (Cantor, 1983: 51). Even the production of such texts declined markedly: only two new textbooks of natural philosophy were published at Cambridge between 1750 and 1780 as compared with eleven in the period 1720 to 1750 (*ibid.*). This drop may be partly explained by the fact that there was less demand for new textbooks after the first wave of such works had established themselves in the university but this in itself is an indication that there was little interest in revising the curriculum in the light of more recent research. Largely as a result of fundamental economic and social changes, scientific advance after the mid-eighteenth century became more closely associated with new centres like the Scottish universities and the expanding provincial cities where there was less commitment to established modes of scientific explanation than in London and the English universities (*ibid.*: 51–2).

Within the limits of the rather narrowly defined Newtonian heritage to which the university had devoted itself there were, however, some signs of scientific activity in mid-eighteenth-century Cambridge. Interest in astronomy was firmly entrenched. Though, as Plumian professor, Smith did not carry on the astronomical work of Cotes, the Trinity observatory was used by Charles Mason, a fellow of Trinity and Woodwardian professor of geology, 1734–62, who in 1737 published a paper in the *Philosophical Transactions* on a solar eclipse (XL: 197). Roger Long, master of Pembroke from 1733 to 1770, published in 1742 the first volume of an astronomical textbook (presumably based on the lectures which he had been giving at the college (Long, 1742, II: 730)) which he completed in 1764 after having been made foundation Lowndean professor of astronomy in 1750; his astronomical lectures were enriched by the use of a planetarium which he erected at Pembroke (Long, 1742, II: 730; I: x). Long's astronomical observations were greatly assisted by Richard Dunthorne whom Long made butler of the college; in this unlikely role he published a series of astronomical papers in the *Philosophical Transactions* between 1747 and 1762 (XLIV: 412, XLVI: 162, XLVII: 281 and LII: 105).

Other scattered examples further illustrate the wide interest in astronomy in mid-eighteenth-century Cambridge: in 1747 Ralph Heathcote of

Jesus published a Latin history of astronomy; John Martyn (professor of botany, 1730–61) published two astronomical papers in the *Philosophical Transactions* (XLI: 840; XLVI: 345); and Samuel Hardy of Emmanuel published a *Theory of the moon . . .* (1752) and a *Treatise on dioptric telescopes* – both with a view to determining longitude at sea. By 1764 the Trinity observatory had a competitor: John Smith, master of Caius, 1764–95, erected a transit telescope over the Caius ante-chapel (C. Brooke, 1985: 176). In the following year Dunthorne sponsored the building of a new observatory over the Shrewsbury gate at St John's, using it to prepare his *New tables of the moon* and to observe the transit of Venus in 1769. It was also used by William Ludlam, a fellow of St John's, who published several astronomical works, among them his *Astronomical observations made in St. John's College, Cambridge, 1767 and 1768 with an account of several astronomical instruments* (1769) (Stratton, 1949: 2). This interest in astronomy within the university helps to explain the subsequent careers of Cambridge graduates like Nevil Maskelyne (fellow of Trinity, 1757) who served as astronomer royal from 1765 to 1811 with William Hirst (BA Peterhouse, 1751) as his assistant.

Though, as will be shown below, by the mid-eighteenth century mathematics had come to dominate the undergraduate curriculum, Cambridge produced relatively little original mathematical work. What work there was was shaped by the Newtonian algebraic heritage. Thus in 1758 there appeared the *Dissertation on the use of the negative sign in algebra* of Francis Maseres (fellow of Clare, 1755–9) and in the same year Israel Lyons's *A treatise on fluxions*. Though not formally attached to the university, Lyons carried on both his botanical and mathematical researches within Cambridge and owed much to the encouragement of Robert Smith (to whom this work was dedicated); his links with Cambridge are evident, too, in the fact that he consciously built on Cotes's earlier work on fluxions (Lyons, 1758: vii).[6] The most influential mathematical work produced at Cambridge in this period was Edward Waring's *Miscellanea analytica de aequationibus algebraicis et curvarum proprietatibus* (1760–2). An early version of this work gained for its author the post of Lucasian professor at Colson's death in 1760, in which capacity his examinations for the Smith prizes 'were considered the most severe test of mathematical skill in Europe' (*DNB*, Waring); he did little, however, to revive the pedagogical importance of the Lucasian chair since, as Dr Parr

---

[6] The extent of Lyons's mathematical interests is evident in the collection of his mathematical papers preserved in the Maskelyne MSS at the Royal Greenwich Observatory, Herstmonceux (RGO 4: 236–59). These include manuscripts on mechanics, logarithms, planetary motion, capillary forces and analyses of the *Principia* and of Cotes's work, together with the original MS of the *Treatise on fluxions*.

put it, his 'profound researches' were not 'adapted to any form of communication by lectures' (Parr, 1801: 121). His researches did, however, result in a number of further publications, notably the *Meditationes algebraicae* (1770) and the *Meditationes analyticae* (1776).

More indirectly, Cambridge Newtonianism played a part in shaping the work of one of the most original minds of the century, David Hartley. While an undergraduate at Jesus from 1722 to 1726 he attended Saunderson's lectures and as a fellow of Jesus (1727–30) he came to know Robert Smith and Stephen Hales (in collaboration with the latter of whom he later discredited a supposed cure for 'the stone' (Langdon-Brown, 1946: 63–5)). Hartley's theory of vibrations, which underlay his associationist psychology, was prompted by Newtonian concepts of motion and the ether (Guerlac, 1977: 162). It may also have been influenced by Smith's work on musical vibrations (Kassler, 1979, II: 952). Hartley's work also indicates the close association between the study of Newton and Locke which was such a characteristic feature of eighteenth-century Cambridge. As Hartley himself wrote, his theory of vibrations was 'taken from some hints concerning the performance of sensation and motion which Sir Isaac Newton has given at the end of his *Principia*, and in the questions annexed to his *Optics*' while the concept of association derived from 'what Mr. Locke and other ingenious persons since his time, have delivered concerning the influence of *association* over our opinions and affections' (C. U. M. Smith, 1987: 124).

Though there is no record of Henry Cavendish's studies as an undergraduate at Peterhouse from 1749 to 1753 it is probable that he, too, laid the foundations for much of his subsequent work while at Cambridge. A basic theme of Cavendish's diverse (and largely unpublished) *œuvre* was to demonstrate that all natural phenomena could be explained in terms of particles and attractive and repulsive forces (McCormmach, 1969), a fundamental premise that clearly derives from Newton whose work Cavendish would have studied at the university. It was almost certainly at Cambridge, too, that Cavendish came to know John Michell, a fellow of Queens' (1749–64) and, from 1762 to 1764, Woodwardian professor of geology before he left Cambridge to take up a Yorkshire living (where he was in touch with Priestley). Though the surviving correspondence between Michell and Cavendish dates from the 1780s (McCormmach, 1968: 128) their scientific partnership indicates a longer acquaintance. Michell's wide-ranging scientific interests encompassed astronomy, geology, magnetism, electricity and optics, though a particular focus of his work was the role of attractive and repulsive forces – a preoccupation he shared with his friend, Cavendish, reflecting their common Newtonian allegiance (Hardin, 1966). Michell's concern with these issues was apparent in his first published work, *A treatise of artificial magnets* (published at Cambridge in 1750 while Cavendish was still there), in which Michell demonstrated that the inverse square law applied to magnetic as well as gravitational forces. The most obvious scientific debt which Cavendish owed Michell was the design of the apparatus for measuring gravitational attraction by means of a torsion-bar. Michell had constructed this device but did not live to use it; after his death in 1793 it passed to F. J. H. Wollaston (Jacksonian professor of natural experimental philosophy, 1792–1813) who, in turn, gave it to Cavendish (Geikie, 1918: 84–5). Michell's work was also closely studied by a number of his other Cambridge contemporaries: William Powell of St John's, for example, repeated Michell's experiments from the 1750s designed to prove the momentum (and hence projectile nature) of light by focusing sunlight on a suspended copper plate (Gjertsen, 1986: 135) – though Powell challenged Michell's conclusions (Cantor, 1983: 86–7). The preoccupation of both Michell and Cavendish with interparticulate forces set them apart from much of the rest of the scientific community in the latter part of the eighteenth century which increasingly devoted its attention to the role of the ether and of imponderable fluids (McCormmach, 1968: 150). This cleavage between Cavendish and Michell and their scientific contemporaries can partly be explained by their education in a university which remained preoccupied with the work of Newton and his early disciples and was therefore largely impervious to subsequent scientific developments (R. E. Schofield, 1970: 242).

Cambridge's devotion to Newton also helps to explain the decline of the biomedical tradition which had been a feature of the university in the seventeenth century – particularly as, after the 1740s, the biological sciences turned increasingly away from mechanistic explanations derived from Newton (T. M. Brown, 1974: 179). In any case the increasing importance of clinical studies requiring big city hospitals made Cambridge something of a medical backwater, a situation that changed little even after the foundation of Addenbrooke's Hospital in 1766, perhaps because the increasing dominance of the colleges inhibited the development of a hospital-based university medical school (Rook, 1971: 62). This decline in the importance of the medical school is evident in the falling numbers of those taking MBs – in the 1720s there were 67, in the 1730s 46, in the 1740s 35 and in the 1750s a mere 15 (Rook, 1969a: 110). Though Oxford experienced a similar decline its was not quite as precipitous (Webster in SM: 685) perhaps because at Oxford the medical sciences were less overshadowed by the mathematical than at Cambridge.

Christopher Greene and Russel Plumptre, the Regius professors of physick from 1700 to 1741 and from 1741 to 1793, both appear to have regarded their positions as sinecures though some teaching was provided by a few interested dons. John Addenbrooke of Catharine Hall gave lectures on *materia medica* from about 1705 until he left Cambridge in 1711 – a tradition continued by William Heberden of St John's from 1734 until 1748 (Rook, 1969a: 118). Heberden's pupil, Robert Glynn, kept the flickering flame of the Cambridge medical school alight after Heberden's departure though he, too, appears to have abandoned the struggle after 1752 (Rook, 1969b). Though the university founded a chair of anatomy in 1707 the only eighteenth-century incumbent who left a mark on the academic world was Charles Collignon (professor, 1753–85)[7] who published a series of works which used medicine as a vehicle for his moral reflections. Collignon's apologetical intent and his continuing allegiance to the iatromechanical tradition are both evident in the remark in his introductory textbook of anatomy that 'Upon the whole then it will appear, that Man's Body may be termed a Machine; such a one as is worthy of the divine Architect' (1763: 35). He also played an important role in the early history of Addenbrooke's Hospital (Rook, 1979). The chair of botany, founded in 1724, made scarcely more impact on the university. Robert Bradley, the first incumbent, delivered a course of lectures on *materia medica* in 1729 and, after giving another ill-attended series of lectures from 1733 to 1735 (Walters, 1981: 24, 34), he lapsed into silence, an example followed by his successor, John Martyn (professor, 1733–62), three years after he took up the position. By 1759 the Cambridge-trained physician, Richard Davies, could complain that 'The Arts subservient to Medicine have no appointments to encourage Teachers in them. Anatomy, Botany, Chemistry and Pharmacy have been but occasionally taught' (1759: 40).

By the time that Davies was writing, medicine lacked the institutional support and recognition that was increasingly being accorded to the mathematical sciences through the Cambridge mathematical tripos or (to give it its correct pre-1824 name) the Senate House examination. It is this institution which did most to preserve and nurture within the university the mathematical tradition which owed its origin to Newton's influence – a tradition which, in the nineteenth century, was again to act as a catalyst for scientific innovation and fresh discovery. I have traced the obscure evolution of the mathematical tripos elsewhere (Gascoigne, 1984a) but it is worth remarking on the extent to which the growth of the tripos was intertwined with the university's response to changes in the wider political climate. The initiative to make the Senate House examination more

---

[7] Though Collignon's successor, Sir Busick Harwood (professor, 1785–1814) did publish an anatomical tract on the olfactory organs in 1796.

rigorous and mathematical in character in the early eighteenth century owed much to the work of Cambridge latitudinarians like Bentley, Richard Laughton and Whiston at a time when they were under attack from their high church colleagues. They probably also played a part in the division of the traditional *ordo senioritatis* into a first and second tripos in 1711, reflecting different degrees of merit – a seed from which subsequent, more refined, systems of grading were to grow.

More critical still was the division of the successful candidates in the tripos of 1753 into wranglers and senior and junior optimes, which formalised the university's system of academic honours. This innovation took place when the university was still preoccupied with the issues raised by the proposed parliamentary visitation of 1749 and Newcastle's disciplinary reforms of 1750, events which forcefully reawakened fears that the university might be subject to government action. For those in Cambridge anxious to avoid such a confrontation one way of displaying the university's educational prowess, and hence of weakening the case for government intervention, was to draw attention to the increasingly competitive and demanding nature of the Senate House examination – a motive which may help to explain the use of the highly public system of classifying honours students after 1753. The increasing attention accorded to this examination also served to distinguish Cambridge from its politically more suspect sister university. Cambridge's scientific traditions, then, were influenced by the university's response to the external political situation as well as by the internal divisions which coloured intellectual life within the university – conflicts which largely derived from the challenge to deeply engrained notions of the role of Church and State which had been caused by the Glorious Revolution, illustrating, once again, the deep imprint that the events of 1688 left on the eighteenth century.

Part Three

The 'holy alliance'
questioned, 1769–1800

7

The eclipse of whig Cambridge

At the death of Newcastle in 1768 Cambridge could reflect on how successfully it had accommodated itself to the Hanoverian order. The disputes generated by the Glorious Revolution and the Hanoverian succession were now a distant memory and the old high church rallying-cry of 'The Church in Danger' was rarely heard in Cambridge common-rooms – except perhaps in that of the obstinately tory stronghold of Emmanuel. Both in its politics and its theology Cambridge had largely eschewed any claims which challenged the accepted order: the almost sacerdotal view of kingship with which the Stuarts had been associated had been effectively eliminated in a university which based its political philosophy on contract theorists such as Locke and Hoadly, while any pretensions to the independence of the clerical estate had been largely undercut by a theology which, with its emphasis on the role of individual interpretation of Scripture and unaided reason, left little room for clerical claims to a special status as custodians and interpreters of the Word.

But such comfortable conformity with the status quo was increasingly under threat after George III, the first English-born Hanoverian monarch, ascended the throne in 1760. The view of politics and theology which, together with the judicious use of patronage, had gradually reconciled Cambridge to the post-revolutionary order became less appropriate in the more troubled age which followed George III's accession. For much of the eighteenth century Cambridge dons had attempted to justify the prevailing order by countering the views of those critics of the Hanoverian order who looked back to a monarchy which was thought to be independent of the machinations of ministers and a church which could claim to embody the spiritual life of the nation as a whole; after 1760, however, the defenders of tradition once more became respectable as jacobitism lost its menace and the threats of Wilkites, American rebels and, most threatening of all, jacobins prompted a renewed defence of Church and King.

Cambridge, then, which for so much of the eighteenth century had prided itself on its reputation as the 'whig university' and had contrasted its allegiance to the House of Hanover with the more doubtful loyalty of Oxford, now found itself less clearly favoured; there was a hint of this as early as 1761 when George III gave a warmer response to Oxford's loyal address on his marriage than to that of Cambridge (Walpole, 1845, 1: 74). While Cambridge's chancellor, the duke of Grafton, was estranged from the Court for most of his long period of office (1768–1811) Oxford was praised by George III for its election of Lord North as chancellor in 1772, an action which the monarch regarded as 'a compliment to me' (W. R. Ward, 1958: 259n). Oxford's more vigorous support for the administration's American policy prompted rumours that the King was to visit Oxford 'without paying the same attention to Cambridge' – something, it was claimed, which 'will shock the prejudices of his most respectable subjects' (*ibid.*: 274). As Mitchell writes, 'The dissenting campaigns of the 1770s, linked with the rebellion in America, forced Oxford into an alliance with the government, which the outbreak of the French revolution made unshakeable' (in SM: 190).

Most Cambridge dons found little difficulty in adjusting to the new political realities; few found any great clash of principles in once more emphasising their loyalty to a king who regarded himself as a victim of political faction and a church which felt itself under threat from an increasingly assertive body of dissenters, particularly as the defence of the royal prerogative and Anglican privilege no longer smacked of disloyalty to the Revolutionary Settlement. Even the many dons who still regarded themselves as whigs were glad to distance themselves from the anti-clericalism and reforming zeal which continued to characterise some sections of the whig party. While slow to adopt the name 'tory' with its connotations of a lukewarm and even hostile attitude to the Hanoverian succession, a growing number of Cambridge dons began to feel uneasy about the use of the term 'whig' as it was increasingly annexed by the opponents of the King and his ministers (B. W. Hill, 1985: 233–4; Pocock, 1985b: 284). Like the anonymous correspondent to the *St. James Chronicle* of 1777 such ambivalent whigs would have claimed to be whigs 'once, at least till these rascally Patriots, by taking that name to themselves, had rendered it infamous . . . [and] Whiggism ran stark staring mad' (BL, Add. 5870: p. 107b). After the French Revolution demanded a more unambiguous statement of political loyalties such dons once more proclaimed themselves as tories.

The path from mid-eighteenth-century whiggery to the new toryism of the 1790s was, then, a relatively smooth one for dons who regarded both political creeds as a means of defending the established order against its opponents, be they jacobites or jacobins. The seeds of such a transformation are apparent in the writings of one of Newcastle's more influential Cambridge clients, Samuel Hallifax (fellow of Trinity Hall, 1760–75; bishop of Gloucester, 1781–9, and of St Asaph, 1789–90) as early as the 1760s. In 1768 Hallifax praised his recently deceased master, with high whiggish praise, as one who was 'a strenuous assertor of Liberty, civil and religious' (1768: 20), yet in the following year Hallifax was anxious to caution the House of Commons on the anniversary of Charles I's execution 'lest our love of liberty degenerate into licentiousness, and our private vices and party quarrels defeat His [Majesty's] endeavours, and counteract His designs for the public welfare'. He also warned against the actions of would-be reformers 'lest in our zeal for imaginary improvements we part with real blessings, and through an intemperate fondness of correcting parts, we risk the safety and preservation of the whole' (Hallifax, 1769: 13–14). Though both Hallifax's sermons could be accommodated within the whig fold, his suspicions of the reforming elements within the whig party were to become more and more pronounced among his clerical brethren, prompting many of them ultimately to look to a reconstituted tory party, rather than the whigs, as guardians of the Establishment in Church and State.

But the reforming impulses within Cambridge whiggery were not altogether extinguished by the slow rise of this new political tide. The work of Hoadly and his disciples like Jackson, with their enthusiastic assault on the apologists for divine right and clerical privilege, had established too deep a root in Cambridge not to continue to bear fruit even after such teachings seemed to challenge rather than protect the existing order. The principles which had brought Hoadly advancement were, in the changed circumstances of the late eighteenth century, more likely to lead to clerical obscurity – a transformation which helps to explain the increasing radicalism and bitterness which characterise some of the late eighteenth-century products of the Cambridge latitudinarian tradition. The latitudinarian emphasis on simplicity of doctrine and elimination of non-essentials in church government and ceremony had naturally inclined churchmen with such views to recognise the need for reform of many aspects of the Established Church, though such reforming impulses were often largely extinguished by advancement up the clerical ladder. In the late eighteenth century the near-exclusion of churchmen with latitudinarian views from the episcopate helps to explain why a theological tradition which had once produced some of the staunchest defenders of the established order should become increasingly associated with those demanding widespread ecclesiastical reform. Moreover, in a constitution such as that of eighteenth-century England where, as Burke put it, Church and State were 'one and the same thing, being different integral parts of the same whole' (E. N. Williams, 1960: 325) agitation for reform of the Church naturally led to an interest in political reform. Thus the Cambridge latitudinarian tradition which, in the troubled conditions that followed the Glorious Revolution, had helped to provide some of the theological foundations for the Church's accommodation with the State now, in the late eighteenth century, helped shape some of the critiques of the unreformed constitution.

Such developments lay ahead, however, when, in November 1768, Cambridge pondered on who should succeed Newcastle as its chancellor. Hardwicke, for whose election as high steward in 1764 Newcastle had laboured so long and hard, made some half-hearted attempts to become chancellor but withdrew after his chief supporters assured him that he did not have sufficient support within the university (BL, Add. 35628: 78). According to Cole, Hardwicke's proposal was 'looked upon to be so languid, cool, tepid and forbidding, just like himself, that it was deemed such a Chancellor would never be active enough to sollicit Preferment' (BL, Add. 5870: p. 106b). With Hardwicke eliminated, the field was then left to Augustus Fitzroy, third duke of Grafton (MA Peterhouse, 1753), who had begun preparations for gaining the chancellorship as early as January 1767 when the duke of Newcastle was intrigued to hear that he had re-entered his name on the Peterhouse books (BL, Add. 32979: 385, 405). When Grafton was duly elected unopposed as chancellor at the end of 1768 he was at the peak of his career: in 1766 he had been appointed first lord of the treasury and had acted as nominal head of the Chatham administration but, in 1768, when Chatham's mental illness prompted his resignation, Grafton was prime minister in fact as well as name. Unfortunately for Cambridge Grafton's star was thereafter in decline. In January 1770 he resigned as prime minister having been submerged under a sea of troubles both private and public; from 1771 to 1775 he served as lord privy seal under Lord North, an office he held briefly once again in 1782 during the Rockingham and Shelburne administrations, but thereafter he was a spent force politically. To compound Cambridge's misfortunes Grafton (like Somerset) was not only politically impotent for much of his career but he was also long-lived – not until 1811 did he finally die and thus enable the university to choose a politically more useful chancellor. After Grafton began to languish in opposition Cambridge's respect for a chancellor who lacked friends at Court steadily diminished; in 1778 a potential competitor for the headship of Corpus withdrew from the contest on the grounds that 'the being Head of an House, now the Duke of Grafton the Chancellor was in opposition to the Court & took no concern about the university, was no longer a step to Preferment' (BL, Add. 5877:

p. 82). After 1789, wrote Gunning, 'the duke was treated with great coolness by the University', a sentiment reciprocated by the chancellor who declined to attend any further university addresses (Gunning, 1855, I: 121).

However, after its long training by Newcastle in the need to respect a chancellor's political wishes, Cambridge was slow to disregard Grafton's demands. Soon after his election in March 1769, the university dutifully sent an address in defence of Grafton's administration against the attacks of the Wilkites – a grace which was opposed by only two dons, Tyson and Jebb (C. H. Cooper, 1842–1908, IV: 354), the latter being described by Professor Rutherforth as 'a professed and eager defender of Mr. Wilkes' (BL, Add. 35640: 362). Grafton himself clearly played a part in prompting the address since it was drafted by his client, John Hinchcliffe (master of Trinity, 1768–88) (*ibid.*), who, while vice-chancellor in 1768, had played a key role in ensuring Grafton's election as chancellor (BL, Add. 5811: p. 51b). In his installation speech the duke also spoke rather pointedly of the need for the university to set an example in 'bringing to their senses, those persons, who are deluded by factious men' (BL, Add. 35658:8).

In the period before 1782, when he finally quit public office, Grafton also had considerable influence over the university's choice of burgesses, though he could not match Newcastle's record of continually returning the same two MPs unopposed. Grafton's endorsement of William de Grey (attorney-general, 1766–71) was sufficient to ensure his election unopposed in 1770 (Namier and Brooke, 1964, I: 308). When de Grey resigned in 1771 to become chief justice of the common pleas Grafton nominated the unremarkable Richard Croftes – a choice which prompted considerable opposition within the university, particularly from Richard Watson of Trinity who chided the chancellor, informing him that 'you must not consider us as a *venal borough*' (Watson, 1817: 48). None the less, Croftes was duly elected and remained MP for the university until 1780 without having once spoken in the House. Ironically, Watson's spirited, if unsuccessful, opposition to Croftes made both Hinchcliffe (master of Watson's college) and his patron, Grafton, aware that Watson was 'an adversary worth regarding' – the master fearing 'for the peace of his Society' and the chancellor 'for the peace of the University' (W. Vincent, 1780: 6). Thanks to Grafton Watson became Regius professor of divinity in 1761 and remained a lifelong client of Grafton – predictably, he also dropped his opposition to Croftes. In 1779 Croftes was accompanied to parliament by James Mansfield, another Grafton protégé (BL, Add. 35628: 238), who was also returned in 1780 (though he came last in the 1784 poll).

In 1784 Grafton's son, George Fitzroy, earl of Euston, was elected and remained an MP until 1811, though his continued popularity probably owed more to his close alliance with William Pitt (who was returned with him at the 1784 election) than to his being the son of the chancellor. Indeed, by this time it was even a possible disadvantage to be closely connected with the increasingly unpopular chancellor: in 1784 William Ewin, a Cambridgeshire MP, remarked of Grafton that 'He has been no Chancellor to us . . . [and] the general disgust he has given as Chancellor will greatly hurt his son's interest' (Cook, 1935: 279). Prudently, Grafton took no part in his son's 1784 electioneering though he had been active on his behalf when he had contemplated standing for the university in 1780 (before withdrawing from the contest). Father and son later diverged in their politics, Grafton being an opponent of Pitt's war policy and Euston a vigorous champion of his fellow Cambridge burgess – a contrast which led the anti-war radical, Flower, to write in 1796 that 'Euston's guilt is aggravated when we consider the contrast which the conduct of his noble father . . . presents to his view' (ibid.: 282–3).

Though Grafton only held power briefly his ecclesiastical appointments helped to give prominence to a number of representatives of the Cambridge latitudinarian tradition in a period when they were unlikely to receive recognition from any other quarter (except perhaps from the equally politically short-lived Rockingham or Shelburne). Grafton's aversion to tests of orthodoxy was evident soon after he became chancellor since he declined the customary honorary doctorate rather than subscribe to the Articles. As he grew older he turned from his earlier preoccupation with horses and hounds and took a close interest in ecclesiastical reform; in 1782, for example, he contributed to Richard Watson's letter to the archbishop of Canterbury on the reform of the distribution of church revenues (Watson, 1817: 347), a pamphlet which alarmed Shelburne and was ignored by the primate. In 1789 Grafton published his *Hints submitted to the serious attention of the clergy, nobility, and gentry, by a layman* in which he argued for a reform of the liturgy and creeds of the Established Church since one should 'never allow our faith and worship to be bound down, without redress by the fallible decisions of men'; he also urged wider religious toleration in accordance with 'the principles of the Revolution' (pp. 37–8). By this time Grafton had become a member of the Essex Street Unitarian congregation and, as his personal notes of 1789–90 make apparent, had totally rejected the doctrine of the Trinity (Belsham, 1873: 213–16).

Though Grafton's heterodoxy was not made public until after he finally left public office, there were some indications of his future theological leanings while he was still a minister, since among his clerical clients were those who were known to favour ecclesiastical reform and had even (as in the case of Edmund Law) been accused of Socinianism. In the same year that he became chancellor Grafton advanced Law to the see of Carlisle, an appointment which prompted Cole to write of him that 'He is looked upon as a man of latitudinarian Principles, on which account many who had the Interest of the established Religion at Heart were not pleased with the Designation' (BL, Add. 5875: p. 12b). Law, on the other hand, regarded his elevation to the episcopate as 'proof that decent freedom of inquiry was not discouraged' (Paley, 1800: 13). Grafton's closest Cambridge confidant was John Hinchcliffe whom he had first met on his travels in Italy in 1761 where, as he put it in his *Autobiography*, 'my intimacy with Hinchcliffe, Bishop of Peterborough, began, and continued steadfastly till his death' (Anson, 1898: 18). Hinchcliffe owed both his position as master of Trinity and his elevation to the see of Peterborough in 1769 to Grafton, though his hopes of further advancement were dashed by the duke's political demise and (as Camden remarked to Grafton in 1788) the enmity of Pitt (SRO, MS 423/92). In the House of Lords Hinchcliffe sided with the opposition with his spirited defence of the American colonists, his only episcopal ally being Bishop Shipley (1769–88), another Grafton appointee. He further alienated himself from his episcopal brethren by supporting the Catholic Relief Act of 1778. In 1782 Hinchcliffe was joined on the episcopal bench by another ally, his former colleague, Richard Watson – a promotion that Watson owed to both Grafton and Shelburne.

A more obscure Cambridge protégé of Grafton was John Symonds who, as his obiturist put it in 1807, 'had long been in habits of intimacy with the duke of Grafton and his family' (*GM*, 1807: 281), friendship that probably dated back to Grafton's days at Peterhouse where Symonds had been a fellow. In 1771 he was appointed Regius professor of history – a post he owed to Grafton (Dyer, 1814, II: 29) – and in contrast to his predecessor, the poet, Thomas Gray (another Grafton appointment (BL, Egerton MS 2400: 182)), actually delivered lectures; in them he 'made a great point of reprobating Intolerance in Religion and in Civil Government, whatever form that Government might bear' (Scott, 1903: 569). Thus he praised early Rome for having established a monarchy 'with its bounds limited' since it thereby 'enjoyed the blessings of a free constitution'. Nearer to the present he briefly summarised the eighteenth-century whig interpretation of history by arguing that 'The Governments of Europe have most lost the liberties, [while] we preserve ours and our constitution has continued regularly improving . . . Ours is the only constitution which has civil and religious liberty for its main object' (CUL, Add. 5803: 9, 125–6). As well as sharing Grafton's political outlook Symonds also sympathised with his increasingly radical religious ideas. He closely consulted Grafton on the contents of *The expediency of revising the present edition of the gospels and acts of the apostles* (1789) (SRO, MS 423/

952) – a work which he dedicated to Grafton and which prompted a critical reply thought to be written by two bishops. Through Grafton Symonds kept in touch with Unitarians like Disney; by 1803 both men also shared a common hostility to the war with France, Symonds viewing Napoleon as a divine punishment for England's sins in maintaining an empire 'supported by every engine of fraud and oppression' (*ibid*.: MS 423/789).

   Grafton's influence, then, provided some encouragement for those in Cambridge who continued to hold the sort of political and religious views which Hoadly and his followers had promoted within the university. But Grafton's power was too transient and limited to do very much to help his protégés in the race for ecclesiastical preferment. Even while serving as lord privy seal in 1782 Grafton could not persuade Shelburne to promote Hinchcliffe to the see of Salisbury despite his ardent support for the bishop as one who had opposed North's American policy (Anson, 1898: 327). To placate Grafton after his defeat Shelburne appointed Watson to the see of Llandaff but, as Grafton angrily noted, Watson was to remain in this 'insignificant see, so little adequate to his eminent virtues and character . . . [and] much to the discredit of the Government of the country' (*ibid*.: 325). Indeed, Grafton's episcopal appointees – Hinchcliffe, Law, Watson and Shipley – all remained marooned in their lowly sees while many of their episcopal brethren were translated to more lucrative bishoprics.

The arrested careers of Grafton's episcopal clients were an indication of the growing gulf between those who continued to subscribe to the political and religious opinions which had been widely prevalent in Cambridge before 1760 and the increasingly more conservative character of the Church more generally. The event which did most to highlight this growing gulf between those, like Law and Watson, who looked back to Tillotson, Clarke and Hoadly as their theological mentors and the mood of the Church more generally was the Feathers Tavern Petition of 1772. This was an appeal to the House of Commons to remove the obligation for clergy to subscribe to the Thirty-Nine Articles, the petition being largely a result of Blackburne's widely influential *Confessional* and of the organisational abilities of his son-in-law, Lindsey. While the subscription issue had been a source of controversy as far back as 1712, when Clarke published his *Scripture doctrine of the Trinity*, many clergy with latitudinarian sympathies had continued to subscribe on the understanding that such an act was little more than a recognition of the authority of the Church of England as established. After Blackburne's attack on what he regarded as this casuistical defence the issue of subscription came to take on a new urgency, particularly as more and more of the Church's theologians were insisting on the need to take literally those articles concerned with the particularly contentious issue of the Trinity. As might have been expected, the petition was closely associated with Cambridge – so much so that Norman Sykes describes it as 'largely a Cambridge movement' (1934: 381). Within the university the main advocates of the petition were Jebb of Peterhouse, James Lambert (Regius professor of Greek, 1771–80 and fellow of St John's) and Robert Plumptre, the president of Queens', who signed the petition along with the entire resident fellowship of his college (DWL, MS 12.44: 1).[1] At Emmanuel, by contrast, it was said that the master would discipline those who signed the petition (BL, Add. 5882: p. 105).

The petition also had the support of Grafton who later wrote of the Feathers Tavern petitioners that their conduct 'was perfectly suitable to their station, and I shall ever lament that they were not successful in their application to Parliament' (Anson, 1898: 268). It also was defended by some of Grafton's Cambridge clients. Edmund Law, who was the only bishop to vote in support of the petition, published an (anonymous) pamphlet criticising the practice of subscription in which he argued, in a characteristically latitudinarian manner, that 'The Christian Religion, as originally constituted, was very plain and practical' and that an individual's religious beliefs 'must be a thing purely personal, transacted only between God and his own conscience'; he also argued that it was 'the duty of everyone . . . to contribute . . . to the improvement both of church and state by embracing all fair opportunities to further, and complete their reformation' (1774: 2, 5, 37). Watson also published an anonymous defence of the petition under the pseudonym of a 'Christian Whig' in which he argued that 'It would be just as reasonable to reduce our Universities' to the study of Aristotle's natural philosophy and the astronomy of Ptolemy 'as to continue the Obligation upon our clergy to conform to the Scriptural Systems of Cranmer and Ridley', though he was averse to change if it were 'likely to produce any Disorders in the Civil Constitution' (1772: 28–9, 33). When the issue of subscription for Cambridge graduates was raised Hinchcliffe was in favour of abolition of the practice for non-divinity degrees though, as Lindsey caustically noted, as he was 'not in it out of any true protestant principle but [through] pure worldly policy and in obedience to his political masters, it is hardly expected he will succeed' (DWL, MS 12.44: 7).

The main opponent of the petition within Cambridge was Samuel Hallifax who, in three university sermons delivered in 1772 (which

---

[1] McLachlan (1920: 43) gives Jesus as the college where the entire resident fellowship signed the Petition but this appears to be based on a misreading of the original of this letter. Norman Sykes (1934: 381) states (without a source specified) that it was Peterhouse – which I followed in Gascoigne (1986: 26) – but again this may be a mistake for Queens'.

Edmund Law opposed publishing (BL, Add. 35628: 137)), argued that the State had a duty to protect the doctrinal purity of the Established Church particularly since 'It is now no secret, that many of the truths of Revealed Religion . . . are considered by our new divines [the petitioners] as *Speculative Opinions*'; Hallifax then proceeded to defend the chief Christian doctrines (and, in particular, the Trinity) against the advocates of what he termed '*Rational* Christianity' (1772: [i], 28). Whereas for Hoadly the Church was merely a convenient administrative institution which should be supervised by the State, for Hallifax the Established Church had a duty to act as a guardian of Christian orthodoxy – a task in which it ought to receive the support of the State. Two years after these sermons Hallifax was made a royal chaplain and in 1781 he became bishop of Gloucester, promotions which indicate how far his emphasis on the importance of the Church and the need to reassert the importance of revealed, as against natural, religion were in accord with the dominant views of the age. Predictably the petition was also vehemently opposed by the tory Cole who regarded it as 'a Latitudinarian, Presbyterian & factious Scheme' citing the views of Professor Lambert who had said 'that he thought Christianity laid in a very little compass' in support of his argument that the petition would lead to 'Arianisme, Socinianism & Quakerism' (BL, Add. 5863: p. 170). Cole contrasted Cambridge's active involvement in the petition with Oxford's subsequent opposition to a similar proposal for relaxation of subscription, a move which was in his view 'the natural Consequence of the Roaring after Liberty, Toleration, Latitudinarianism of your Burnets, Hoadleys, Locks, Clarkes & other of the Sort for the last Century' (BL, Add. 5878: p. 213b). To Cole the petitioners were of a piece with 'their fellow-labourers in the same cause, the Wilkites, and his abettors' and shared with them the aim of 'ruin[ing] the constitution in Church and State' (Rutt, 1831, II: 140n).

The petitioners were to find that relatively few in either Church or State sympathised with their views. Despite the attention it attracted within Cambridge the petition received only about 250 signatures and it was overwhelmingly rejected by the House of Commons by 217 votes to 71 in 1772. The debate in the House largely avoided doctrinal matters but stressed the potentially unsettling effects on the constitution as a whole of change in the Church. Sir Roger Newdigate, MP for Oxford University and the most vigorous opponent of the petition, asserted that to abolish subscription was to challenge the constitution since 'Civil and religious establishments are so linked and incorporated together that, when the latter falls, the former cannot stand' (Howell, 1816–26, XVII: 255). Hans Stanley declared himself a friend of 'religious as well as civil liberty' but opposed 'the licentiousness of innovation, which the extreme leniency of our ecclesiastical discipline seems to have bred' (*ibid.*: 259). In support of the petitioners Lord Germain characterised some of the Thirty-Nine Articles as 'not warranted by scripture' nor 'reconcil[able] to common sense'; he argued, too, that Clarke, Hoadly, Locke and Newton would not have subscribed to them 'in the literal and grammatical sense' (*ibid.*: 265–6). But the view which prevailed was that of Lord North who argued that no aspect of the constitution should be 'lightly and wantonly altered' and abhorred the possibility of awakening once more 'the many-headed hydra, religious controversy' (*ibid.*: 272–3). Oxford rewarded North for his opposition to the petition (and his service to the King) with the post of chancellor together with an address in which Oxford was described – in what was possibly intended to be an implied comparison with Cambridge – as 'your orthodox University' and 'a lasting Bulwark of that genuine apostolical Church' (Mitchell in SM: 171).

The failure of the Feathers Tavern Petition brought home to its proponents the gulf that existed between their conception of Christianity and the role of the Church and that held by those who controlled the destiny of the Church. A number of the petitioners drew the conclusion that there was no further hope of changing the Established Church and followed the lead of Lindsey who, in 1774, resigned his living and established a Unitarian chapel at Essex Street in London. Lindsey was joined by other notable Cambridge Unitarians such as Jebb and Disney (both protégés of Law) and the Essex Street chapel became a meeting-place for both political and religious radicals including Benjamin Franklin and the duke of Grafton. The liturgy of the chapel was based on Clarke's proposed amendments to the Book of Common Prayer together with modifications suggested to Lindsey by 'his friends Dr. Jebb, Mr. Tyrwhitt, and a few other learned and liberal members of the University of Cambridge' (Belsham, 1812: 103). This secession from the Established Church was, however, vehemently opposed by Blackburne, the father-in-law of both Lindsey and Disney. Though Blackburne's work had prompted the Feathers Tavern Petition, he remained committed to working within the Church of England: in 1775 he told Lindsey that his secession (which had been followed by that of Jebb) 'has been the utter ruin of the Plan of the . . . Petitioners' (DWL, MS 12.52: 102). Blackburne was also opposed to the Unitarian beliefs of his two sons-in-law and commented in 1783 that 'If I believed as Messrs Lindsey and Disney say they believe, I should certainly think I had no right to profess myself a Christian' (DWL, MS 12.45: 111v).

As I have argued elsewhere (Gascoigne, 1986), the debates which had led to the Feathers Tavern Petition disposed both those petitioners who left the Established Church and those (like Wyvill and Blackburne) who remained within the Anglican fold to look more critically, not only at the need for reform within the Church, but also within the larger constitution of which the Church of England was an integral part. Thus the defenders of the petition were to be found among the founding members of the various societies that vainly attempted to reform the late eighteenth-century political order. Jebb, along with his close friend Major Cartwright – another opponent of subscription (Cartwright, 1826, 1: 165) – played a critical role in the establishment of the Society for Constitutional Information in 1780 in which he was joined by his former Cambridge pupils, Capel Lofft and John Baynes (E. C. Black, 1963: 179–80). Baynes shared both Jebb's political and religious outlook, being described by his obiturist as 'an Unitarian–Christian, and Protestant in political principles, the friend of the civil liberties of mankind; and the genuine constitution of his country' (GM, 1787: 743). Another of Jebb's former pupils who became involved in the campaign for parliamentary reform was Thomas Fyshe Palmer who left his Queens' fellowship for a post as a Unitarian minister in Scotland, whence he was transported to Australia in 1794 on a charge of sedition – a charge that also resulted in his expulsion from his Queens' fellowship in the same year (Twigg, 1987: 161). Jebb also taught Hamilton Rowan who was imprisoned in 1794 for his activities as secretary of the United Irishmen (Rutt, 1831, II: 220).

Perhaps the most important reformer produced by Cambridge was Christopher Wyvill (LL D Queens', 1764), founder of the Yorkshire Association in 1779 and the moving spirit behind the petitioning movement of the early 1780s – a cause in which he had the support of Blackburne (Wyvill, 1794–1806, III: 133–7). Wyvill's links with the Cambridge latitudinarian tradition (to which he would have been exposed while a student at Queens', whose president, Robert Plumptre, was a strong supporter of the Feathers Tavern Petition) are apparent in his invocation of Locke and Clarke in his attack in 1771 on some of the articles as 'the Scholastic Rubbish of the sixteenth century' (1771: 5). Later in life Wyvill, disillusioned with his lack of success in achieving political reform and out of sympathy with the more radical demands of the early nineteenth-century political reformers, turned back to the cause of religious reform where he saw himself as carrying on the work of such representatives of Cambridge latitudinarianism as Hoadly, Jortin, Blackburne and Law (Wyvill, 1794–1806, III (Appendix): 49). In 1806 he finally resigned his living as a protest against the continued imposition of the Articles and the lack of church reform more generally (GM, 1814, 1: 316).

As has been suggested, the large number of late eighteenth-century political and religious reformers produced by Cambridge can partly be explained by the continuing effects of the latitudinarian theological tradition with its tendency to seek a simplification of church doctrine and organisation – an attitude of mind which was also likely to encourage attempts to prune the tangled thickets of the unreformed constitution as a whole. One connecting link between the latitudinarian theologians of the early eighteenth century and the would-be reformers of the latter part of the century was the continuing influence of Hoadly and his works. It was Hoadly who had done so much to popularise the contractual view of government which underlay many of the proposals for late eighteenth-century political reform. In arguing for such a view of government Hoadly had invoked, in his *Origin and institution of civil government* . . . (1710), the authority not only of Locke but also of the more venerable and less controversial figure of Richard Hooker, satirising his opponents with the claim that they would make Hooker 'the *Father* of the *Whigs*, and Latitudinarians' (p. 135). Drawing on Hooker, Hoadly further argued that if one grants that government is contractual then 'after such *Compact*, and *Composition*, there must remain in the Governed Society a *Right* to defend, and preserve itself from Ruine' (p. 139) – hence the justification for the Glorious Revolution and (as Hoadly's many readers in the Thirteen Colonies were to argue) for the American Revolution (Bailyn, 1967: 37–8).

For those who held Hoadly's view that the Church was an essentially voluntary institution created for good order rather than the custody of doctrine there was a natural tendency to argue that government, too, had no particular sanctity and that, since it was the result of a voluntary pact, it should be reformed or, if necessary, overthrown if it failed to meet the needs of the governed. As Hoadly himself put it in 1708: 'The great end of government is the happiness of the governed society' (N. Sykes, 1928: 136). The close links between Hoadly's political theory and his ecclesiology were made more apparent by some of his early followers in the course of the debate over subscription. Thus Thomas Herne (BA Corpus, 1715), in his *Essay on imposing and subscribing articles of religion* (1719), criticised the practice of compulsory subscription on the grounds that 'CONSENT is the only FOUNDATION of *Ecclesiastical* as well as of *Civil* Government' (p. 8); similarly, John Jackson in his *Grounds of civil and ecclesiastical government* (1718) argued that just as there were no '*Civil* Powers . . . which are not deriv'd from the People; so it is no less an Error on the other hand, to believe that there were any *Spiritual* or *Religious* Powers, the *Exercise* of which may not be deriv'd from them also' (p. 20).

Hoadly's principles of both church and civil government continued to influence a number of prominent reformers in the late eighteenth century, particularly the Cambridge-educated. Richard Watson – who in 1780 drew up a petition from the county of Cambridgeshire urging the cause of parliamentary reform – acknowledged that his political views and his criticism of ecclesiastical practices such as subscription were 'in perfect coincidence with those of Bishop Hoadley; and I glory in this, notwithstanding the abuse that eminent prelate experienced in his own time, and notwithstanding he has been in our time sarcastically called, and what is worse, injuriously called by Bishop Horsley, a *republican bishop*' (Watson, 1817: 43). When Watson's university sermon, *The principles of the [Glorious] Revolution vindicated* (1776, in the course of which he defended the actions of the American colonists), caused considerable controversy he republished the sermon with a motto drawn from Hoadly: 'Men of Republican Principles – a sort of dangerous Men who have of late taken heart, and defended, the Revolution that saved us' (*ibid.*: 60).

While at Peterhouse, the future Unitarian John Disney was particularly drawn to the study of government as expounded by those 'who have placed its origin on a popular basis' (DWL, MS 28.165 (4): 9). Presumably among such authors was Hoadly; in any case Disney certainly knew Hoadly's theological works well, for, in 1773 (a year after the Feathers Tavern Petition), he published an abridgement of Hoadly's controversial *Plain account of the nature and end of the sacrament* (1735) together with a communion service 'as altered & revised by Clarke' (*ibid.*: 29). Writing in the fateful year of 1789 Disney's future successor as minister at the Essex Street chapel, Thomas Belsham, placed Hoadly (along with Locke and Price) in 'the long train of illustrious Writers . . . who have maintained . . . that the people are the fountain of all just power, and that oppression is a sufficient ground for resistance'. He also contrasted 'the conduct and sentiments' of high churchmen like Laud, Sacheverell and Horsley who, he alleged, had brought disgrace to the Church of England, with latitudinarians like Tillotson, Hoadly and Watson (Belsham, 1789, II: 502, 543). The Cambridge Unitarian and reformer George Dyer (BA Emmanuel, 1778) took a similar view, arguing that 'since the Revolution, the writings of the clergy have, many of them, caught a tone from Locke' – a spirit that he regarded as being particularly evident in the works of Gilbert Burnet and Hoadly (Dyer, 1818: 81–2). A more jaundiced observer, William Cole, agreed that the reforming zeal of Cambridge Unitarians like Jebb could be traced back to the work of 'Tillotson and a thousand other moderate and Latitudinarian Clergy' who had shaped 'the Principles in Fashion ever since the glorious Revolution'. In particular Cole deplored the influence of Hoadly who 'was made a Deity of' and the fact that 'Dr Clarke's Books' were used as a basis for university lectures; 'they may thank themselves', he added, 'if Arianism prevails, when they idolise the Promoter of his Doctrines' (BL, Add. 5873: pp. 48–9).

Not only did Cambridge-educated reformers like Jebb and Watson leave their mark on the larger national stage but they were also active within the microcosm of Cambridge in attempting to change that particular embodiment of the old regime. The clearest link between the debates within Cambridge and those that involved the political nation as a whole was the issue of subscription.[2] When the Feathers Tavern Petition was presented in February 1772 there were in fact discussions within the House of Commons as to whether the issue of subscription for university degrees should be confronted as well as the problem of clerical subscription with which the petition was immediately concerned. After the proposed relief for clerical subscribers was rejected the issue of university subscription still attracted considerable attention – the Commons being far more concerned at the laity being compelled to subscribe to doctrinal formularies than at the clergy having to fulfil such requirements. Indeed, Sir William Meredith made the practice of university subscription the subject of a specific bill though it lapsed after it was argued that the universities themselves should deal with the issue; but the solicitor-general added that if the universities did not act then parliament ought to take the initiative (Cobbett, 1806–20, XVII: 269, 294). This message was driven home to Cambridge by its two burgesses and the chancellor, who advised the university to reform its subscription requirements rather than risk parliamentary meddling in its internal affairs (DWL, MS 12.44: 3; BL, Add. 35628: 135).

In fact this very issue had been raised earlier in December 1771 by Robert Tyrwhitt, a friend of Law and Watson (*GM*, 1817: 286), who subsequently, in 1779, resigned his fellowship at Jesus because his study of Clarke had led to his becoming a convinced Unitarian. However, his proposal to abolish subscription for intending graduates was summarily rejected by the Caput (a sort of standing committee of the Senate) partly because of the vigorous opposition of Dr Hallifax (BL, Add. 35628: 127). A petition from a body of undergraduates for relief from subscription which followed soon afterwards had also been dismissed on the grounds that the university did not have the power to change the regulations. This argument for maintaining the status quo soon wilted in the face of possible parliamentary action – particularly after the attorney-general sent an opinion stating that not only could the university change the regulation but also that it should proceed to do so since it did not form part of its statutes but was based on a royal directive of 1616 (DWL, MS 12.44: 6). There followed a lively debate in which Plumptre of Queens', Law,

---

[2] For further detail on the Cambridge subscription debate and on the controversy about academic reform in the 1770s, see Winstanley, 1935: 297–334.

Hinchcliffe and Grafton and, most vehemently of all, Jebb supported the anti-subscriptionist cause. Their arguments later prompted a don who was opposed to relaxing the subscription requirements to attack 'the latitudinarians vehemently'; he also 'maintained that the liberty of private opinions rent the church of Christ, and made as many creeds as persons' – an assault which caused a minor riot among the undergraduates (Disney, 1787, I: 57).

Eventually, the predictable academic compromise was arrived at in June 1722, whereby the traditional subscription to the three articles – the supremacy of the Crown and a declaration that both the Book of Common Prayer and the Thirty-Nine Articles contained nothing contrary to the will of God – was removed and replaced by a declaration that the intending BA graduate was 'bona fide a member of the church of England as by law established' (C. H. Cooper, 1842–1908, IV: 363). This same provision was extended to bachelor's degrees in law, medicine and music, together with the doctorate of music in 1779 (ibid.: 390). The continued insistence on a test which still implied Anglican orthodoxy was a grievous disappointment to those, like Jebb, who had hoped for the total abolition of religious tests (at least for non-divinity degrees) and the new formula was still rejected by Blackburne's son when he came to graduate in 1773 (Blackburne, 1804, I: lx). None the less, it was an indication that Cambridge's reputation for latitudinarianism was still not altogether superseded – particularly as Oxford refused to enact a similar measure early in the following year (Mitchell in SM: 176–7). Shortly after Oxford's decision not to change its subscription practices Sir William Meredith attempted to bring in a bill to remove all doctrinal tests but it was defeated by 159 votes to 67 (C. H. Cooper, 1842–1908, IV: 367) – thus confirming that Oxford's assumption that parliament would not act was well founded. A further attempt to revive the issue of clerical subscription in the Commons in 1774 was largely defeated by Oxford's representatives, though it was also opposed by Richard Croftes, one of Cambridge's MPs (W. R. Ward, 1958: 271; McLachlan, 1920: 61).

It soon became evident, however, that the change in the form of subscription marked the limits of Cambridge's willingness to accept reform. Largely at the instigation of Jebb the controversy about subscription was followed by a long and ultimately fruitless debate over a number of proposals which were intended to improve the academic rigour of the university. The first major area of contention was the possible institution of annual examinations – such as existed, in the form of a well-entrenched system of quarterly examinations, together with an absence of subscription, at Jebb's original university of Trinity College, Dublin (McDowell and Webb, 1982: 90, 247). The second was the proposal to require both noblemen and fellow-commoners to sit for the same examinations as their less well-born counterparts. Jebb first raised such proposals with the vice-chancellor in November 1772 but no action was taken until July 1773 when Jebb moved in the Senate for the appointment of a syndicate to consider the desirability of annual examinations. The syndicate, which was composed of heads of colleges together with other senior members of the university, duly recommended against any change in the university's present system of holding only one examination at the end of an under-graduate's degree. Jebb, never one to take no for an answer, in February 1774 successfully moved in the Senate to establish another syndicate to examine the full range of undergraduate studies.

This time the syndicate included a number of dons more sympathetic to change, such as Plumptre, Lambert, Watson and Paley (who was closely associated with both Plumptre and Jebb (Meadley, 1810: 62, 99)), together with a smaller number of die-hard opponents such as Richard Farmer of Emmanuel (C. H. Cooper, 1842–1908, IV: 370). It recommended that noblemen and fellow-commoners (who were exempt from the Senate House examination) be examined annually – the system of examinations proposed including classics, algebra, geometry, natural philosophy, Locke's *Essay*, natural law and modern history; other undergraduates were also to be examined in their second year in classics and mathematics (*GM*, 1774: 161–2). These proposals were narrowly defeated in the Senate in April, both because of their alleged infringement of college autonomy and because of fears that such regulations would drive away from the university the gilded youth on which many a don pinned his hopes of future advancement. As Plumptre sagely commented to Lord Hardwicke, however, the chief objection was 'that disinclination to innovation and reformation that has been shewn by mankind in all ages' together with a prejudice against the chief advocates for change (BL, Add. 35628: 191v). The duke of Grafton made plain his support for the proposed changes by writing to the members of the syndicate to praise their plan, which if it 'had been carried into execution . . . would have given a pre-eminence to this University above all other places of Education'; he also expressed his hope 'that at some future period it would have a more favourable event' (BL, Add. 35628: 194). Predictably, among those who had voted for the proposal were clients of Grafton such as Watson, Law and Symonds together with prominent advocates of the Feathers Tavern Petition such as Plumptre and Tyrwhitt. On the other hand opponents of the petition such as Hallifax and Dr Richardson, the master of Emmanuel, also opposed the examination reforms (BL, Add. 5865: pp. 182–3).

Jebb – ever hopeful – took the proposals' narrow defeat and the chancellor's encouragement to mean that a compromise plan might

command a majority. Accordingly in October 1774 he modified the
original proposals by stipulating that the examinations be based on the
'settled lectures of the Tutors' (Disney, 1787, I: 76) in the hope that this
would lessen the opposition of those fearful of a threat to the colleges'
independence. Jebb's tactics very nearly worked: the new proposals were
embodied in twenty motions, the first of which was defeated by one vote
and the remainder rejected without a division. The defeat of these
proposed reforms owed much to the fact that they were associated with
the anti-subscription cause and even with the proponents of parliamentary
reform – an association considerably strengthened by the central role
played by Jebb. Thus Farmer of Emmanuel, whom the whig Samuel Parr
regarded as a 'Tory of high tone and temper. [And] Ardently devoted to
"the powers that be" . . . [who] constantly opposed every scheme, and
even every hint of reform, either in church or state, however reasonable or
moderate' (Field, 1828: 38), viewed these seemingly innocuous examination reforms as having the potential to 'shake the constitution both in
church and state' (Disney, 1787, III: 278). Cole, whose political and
religious views closely resembled Farmer's, wrote caustically of Jebb that
'this meddling Reformer seeing that his religious Project [the Feathers
Tavern Petition] failed, has now thought of reforming the University' and
added with a not inaccurate prophecy of Jebb's future activities, that 'if
that fails & miscarries, his reforming genius which cannot lie still will
prompt him' to other reforms (BL, Add. 5873: p. 68). Another staunch
defender of subscription who opposed Jebb's examination reforms was
William Powell, the master of St John's, whose hostility to Jebb was
further heightened by the fact that he regarded an expanded system of
university examinations as likely to subvert the system of annual collegiate
examinations which he had instituted at St John's – a practice later
emulated at other colleges. Thus in a pamphlet directed against the
proposed reforms Powell argued that annual university examinations
would result in 'the established and experienced Tutors' having to change
'their lectures every year according to the fancies of these Examiners'
(1774: 11–12).

Powell died at the beginning of 1775, thereby removing one of Jebb's
main opponents, but the chances of his achieving his reforms were steadily
diminishing as his theological heterodoxy became more apparent. Since
1770 he had been giving lectures on the Greek New Testament (DWL, MS
24.168–70) (with the encouragement of his early patron, Edmund Law
(Disney, 1787, I: 20)) which stirred up increasing controversy as their
Socinian character became more widely known (BL, Add. 5873: p. 48b).
Lambert, who had been actively involved with Jebb in supporting both
the Feathers Tavern Petition and the examination reforms, offered similar

lectures which, in 1775, led to the master of Trinity forbidding undergraduates to attend his classes (BL, Add. 5834: p. 276; Add. 5832: p. 88b). Finally, in September 1775 Jebb resigned his Anglican living and joined the Essex Street Unitarian congregation – an action which largely accounts for the failure of his last attempt to persuade the Senate to approve his reforms on 27 February 1776. Philip Yorke, then an undergraduate at Queens', summed up the prevailing view of Jebb when he wrote on 25 February that he 'is so obnoxious a person himself that every plan or proposal, however good in itself, provided it comes from him, is sure to be rejected' (Winstanley, 1935: 329). For Jebb this last failure to achieve academic reform was a clear illustration of the fact that the vice-chancellor (Richard Farmer) had 'behaved like a Tory' while Jebb saw himself as having 'testified [to] the principles of a protestant and whig' (Disney, 1787, 1: 116) – statements which underline the politically highly charged atmosphere in which the debates on academic reform had taken place.

The proposed reforms of the 1770s having failed, the issue of university reform was left dormant until the mid-nineteenth century when society more generally was more sympathetic to the idea of reform. Cambridge continued to live within the strait-jacket of the Elizabethan Statutes though these left more room for growth and development than their seemingly immutable character might suggest, as the growing importance of the Senate House examination – which had only the faintest foundation in the Statutes – attests. In a collegiate university it was not surprising that there was opposition to a system of annual examinations which would weaken the position of the colleges as against the central university. What is surprising, however, is that the university as a whole continued to permit the Senate House examination not only to survive but to grow and prosper so that it increasingly determined the character of undergraduate instruction. This apparent anomaly can partly be explained by the fact that the colleges could largely control the proceedings of the Senate House examination both through their choice of moderators and through the practice of permitting any MA to take part in the examination process – a right which was reaffirmed by Senate graces of 1779 and 1791 (Gascoigne, 1984a: 554–5). Not long after Jebb's proposals had finally been rejected, the Senate in 1779 formally agreed to extend the period of examination from three to four days and to increase the number of examiners from two to four (C. H. Cooper, 1842–1908, IV: 389–90). Less official, but none the less important in the development of the Cambridge examination system, was the adoption in 1791 of the practice of printing some examination questions and, in the following year, of allocating marks for the written responses to particular questions, thus making possible a closer comparison between candidates (Tanner, 1917: 352; Schneider, 1957: 35) – an innovation with a long history ahead of it. Late eighteenth-century Cambridge, then, was prepared to accept some measure of academic innovation so long as it was confined to further evolution of already well-established practices. It set its face, however, against proposals like those initiated by Jebb which involved a conscious new departure.

The polarisation of university opinion which was apparent in the debates about subscription and annual examinations in the 1770s reflected the more general political and religious divisions within the university in this period – an indication of how far the very large measure of political and religious consensus which had characterised mid-eighteenth-century Cambridge had been eroded. The defeat of the proposed reforms of the 1770s was also an indication that, although those sympathetic to change were still active and numerous within the university, they were, however, outnumbered by those suspicious of challenges to the existing order. One of the clearest litmus-tests of university opinion in this decade was the controversy generated by the university's loyal address to George III in 1775 in support of his American policy. As Cole wrote, with customary vitriol, during the American crisis, 'Faction was now in its Glory, & bestirred itself for its beloved Friends. The University of Cambridge had been long divided into Parties, on Occasion of the Articles of Religion, which had inflamed them; & now, an Opportunity offered of shewing their Principles' (BL, Add. 5842: p. 381). The initiative for this address came from Jebb's opponent, Richard Farmer, who, in 1775, had become both master of Emmanuel and vice-chancellor and whose links with the Court were sufficiently strong for him to have helped Dr Johnson gain a pension through the good offices of Lord Bute in 1762 (J. C. D. Clark, 1985: 188). In the eyes of Richard Watson, Farmer was 'the most determined of Tories' (Watson, 1817: 54) though Cole preferred to describe him as 'such a Whig as those who placed King William on the throne; and, of course, deemed a violent Tory by our present Republicans, of whom, to say the truth, he could hardly speak with temper' (Nichols, 1812–15, II: 642). The readiness of the opponents of the address to describe the supporters of the King's policy as 'tories' characterised the whole debate and illustrates the increasing polarisation of political opinion within the university. On the other hand, Cole's gloss on Farmer's political principles also illustrates the continued reluctance of the 'King's friends' to use the word 'tory' as a term of self-description. For those like the Rockingham whigs, however, who regarded themselves as the true upholders of the principles of a constitutional monarchy, men like Farmer were no longer entitled to the name 'whig' simply because they supported the Glorious Revolution. As Burke astringently put it in his *Thoughts on the causes of our present discontents* (1770): 'Few are the partisans of departed tyranny, and to be a whig on the business of a hundred years ago is very consistent with every advantage of present servility' (Guttridge, 1966: 42).

Farmer was prompted to propose such an address because Oxford had already produced a similar loyal effusion (BL, Add. 5841: p. 364) – another instance in the way in which Cambridge's once-close attachment to the House of Hanover was increasingly being overshadowed by its sister university which, after the American crisis, became closely identified with the administration's opposition to political as well as religious radicalism (Mitchell in SM: 178). The debate about whether Cambridge ought to endorse North's American policy was a matter of concern not merely within the university but also to the opposition Rockingham whigs whose chief agent within Cambridge was Richard Watson who, in 1771, had advertised his links with the opposition by dedicating his *Chemical lectures* to the marquis with the latter's enthusiastic assent (SCL, RI 1377). Hence when the address was under discussion Rockingham wrote to Watson urging him to ensure that 'the friends of Whig principles would bestir themselves to prevent what I really think will be a great disgrace to the University'. Rockingham added that 'I think the Whig University of Cambridge being called upon to play the second fiddle to the Tory University of Oxford, will even alarm that sort of pride, which is sometimes, not a useless guardian to virtue' (Watson, 1817: 55). By early November 1775 Rockingham had been joined in opposition by Watson's other patron, the duke of Grafton, who rather belatedly also used his influence within Cambridge to attempt to prevent the address (HMC, Round MSS: 308) – though its eventual passage only served to underline the chancellor's declining influence within the university. After the address had passed the Senate on 24 November Grafton told the vice-chancellor that if he had been consulted he would have advised against it since 'the loyalty of the University could not be doubted, as the Sentiments of the Nation were much divided on the subject' (BL, Add. 35628: 226). With rather bad grace he then refused not only to present the address to the King but also declined to provide the university bedel with the hospitality customary on such occasions (BL, Add. 5842: p. 381). None the less, Farmer duly delivered to George III the university's expression of 'warmest Loyalty & Affection for your Royal Person & Government' and abhorrence 'of the unnatural Rebellion into which many of our brethren in your Majesty's American colonies have been unhappily seduced' (C. H. Cooper, 1842–1908, IV: 380–1).

The address was passed by twenty-four votes in the non-regent house of the Senate and by a narrower margin of thirteen in the regent house; since the regent house was principally made up of MAs of less than five years' standing these figures indicate greater sympathy for the opposition among the younger members of the university. Among those opposing the address were some of the chief proponents of reform of subscription and of the university's examination system: Bishops Law and Hinchcliffe, Jebb, Symonds and Watson. Tyrwhitt, who had initiated the subscription debate within Cambridge, was so opposed to the measure that he refused to surrender to the vice-chancellor his key to the common-chest in which the university's seal was kept; Farmer did not, however, let this difficulty stand in his way and had the chest broken into (BL, Add. 35628: 228). With one exception the Peterhouse fellowship voted against the measure as did fourteen out of the twenty fellows of Trinity who voted, confirming Plumptre's comment to Hardwicke on 29 November that 'though there is a Party pretty constantly in opposition to the Bishop [Hinchcliffe], yet it is also pretty constantly in opposition to [the] Administration' (*ibid.*: 230v). Plumptre himself voted for the address, much to the outrage of his former allies in the subscription debate; as he remarked in the same letter to Hardwicke, 'Here I know there are [those] who abuse me as a deserter of the Whig-party. I hope I am still as good a Whig as those who take this liberty, but I have seen too much of Parties to follow any implicitly' (*ibid.*). The explanation for Plumptre's unexpected vote probably lies in the fact that, as Theophilus Lindsey wrote on 12 December, 'the late Tory address . . . was chiefly carried by the intrigues of Lord Sandwich, Lord Hardwicke [Plumptre's patron] & the Archbishop of Canterbury, combined'. Lindsey added that this trio had 'sent all the absentees they could to Cambridge, & prevented and intimidated all they could, that were whiggishly disposed from going to vote' (DWL, MS 12.57: 39). Such pressures – and, in particular, the fact that Cornwallis, the archbishop of Canterbury, was a former fellow of Christ's – may also explain why all save one of the fellowship of Christ's voted for the address, even though the college included men such as Paley who had earlier supported Jebb's proposals and Hugh Thomas, the master, who was known as a supporter of 'the warm Whigs and Americans' (Peile, 1900: 265). More predictable were the votes of the entire Emmanuel fellowship (led by Farmer) for the address (BL, Add. 5841: pp. 364–5; 5842: p. 381).

In a letter to Rockingham written the day after the address had been passed by the Senate Watson attributed what he regarded as this tory victory 'to the ministerial troops, which were poured in from the Admiralty, Treasury, &c. beyond expectation'. In a comment that does much to explain the changing political character of Cambridge Watson sagely observed that 'the clergy have a professional bias to support the powers that are, be they what they will'. He was at pains, however, to reassure Rockingham – whom he described as 'the head of the Whig interest in this kingdom' – of his own continued allegiance to the whigs and of his conviction that Rockingham's opponents merited the name 'tories': 'let the pensioners and place-men say what they will, *Whig* and *Tory* are as opposite to each other, as Mr. *Locke* and Sir *Robert Filmer*; as the soundest sense, and the profoundest nonsense' (Watson, 1817: 57).

Watson gave public expression to such sentiments in the following year in a university sermon entitled *The principles of the [Glorious] Revolution vindicated* (a work he dedicated to the duke of Grafton). The sermon was a whig manifesto forcefully reasserting a contractual view of government in the tradition of Locke and Hoadly and with it the right of the people to rebel 'when a civil Governor violates the Constitution of his country, or in other words, the compact made between himself and those who have condescended to be governed by him' (p. 5). Such a principle, in Watson's view, had 'of late become generally unfashionable, and exposed the Author of it to some little misrepresentation even in this place [Cambridge]' (pp. i–ii). Watson traced the origin of such principles back to the Glorious Revolution and, by implication, drew a comparison between the whig justification for 1688 and the right of the American colonists to rebel. Though he used hypothetical language Watson strongly implied that both in 1688 and in his own time there was a king willing to use 'degenerate Parliaments as the tools of a Tyrannic Government' (p. 11). Not surprisingly the sermon 'gave great offence to the Court' though, in Dunning's view, it contained 'just such treason as ought to be preached once a month at St. James' (Watson, 1817: 58–9). According to Philip Yorke, Watson's sermon was 'generally approved by the Junior part of the University but by several of the Graver People, it was thought rather too violent on the popular side of the Question' (BL, Add. 35377: 312–13). For Grafton's client, Symonds, however, Watson's sermon presented no such problems: Yorke reported that Symonds regarded Watson as 'having expounded the genuine whig doctrine, and fully answered his ideas of the principles of the Revolution' (*ibid.*: 316). In 1778 Symonds himself published his *Remarks upon an essay entitled, The history of the colonisation of the free states of antiquity, applied to the present contest between Great Britain and her American colonies* in which he used examples drawn from antiquity to criticise British policy towards America and, in particular, its taxation of the colonists.

Watson's sermon prompted a reply from William Stevens, an 'outspoken champion of all that was unWhiggish' (Gunn, 1983: 176), who found no difficulty in accepting Watson's description of those opposed to contractual principles of government as tories but argued that Watson had 'attacked the strongholds of Toryism, Reason and Revelation' in order to ensure that 'all government will then be from voluntary compact, and the supreme power in every State our sovereign lord the Mob' (Stevens, 1777: 3). Though Stevens published his pamphlet at Cambridge he was not a don, but this same nervousness about the democratic implications of Lockean principles of government could also be found within the university: it was evident, for example, in a commencement sermon entitled *The causes and consequences of evil speaking against government considered* . . . preached by John Gordon of Emmanuel, 'an avowed tory in religion and politics' (Meadley, 1810: 46). In this work Gordon rejected the view that men were naturally equal in the state of nature or, indeed, that any such state had ever existed (p. 8). He also attacked the view that 'power is derived from the People' – a particularly dangerous doctrine at a time when 'Clubs of the lowest artificiers have been formed to dispute and decide on the most abstruse questions in Religion and Government' (p. 12). On the other hand he also rejected 'the exploded doctrine of Government being founded in parental authority' (p. 10). His sermon probably typified the intellectual confusion of many in Cambridge who were increasingly concerned at the growing assertiveness of 'the lower orders' and who recoiled from the radical conclusions that self-proclaimed custodians of whiggery like Watson drew from the familiar contractual view of government, and yet were still too influenced by Cambridge's whig traditions to return to Filmerite views of government and society.

This clash of principles was resolved for some by the development of a political theory based on utility rather than the increasingly suspect contract theory (Ogden, 1940). Within Cambridge this move away from Lockean to utilitarian principles was evident in the *Observations on the nature of civil liberty and the principles of government* (1776) and *Happiness and rights* (1792) of Richard Hey (fellow of Sidney Sussex, 1768–78; Magdalene, 1782–96) and in the much more influential *Principles of moral and political philosophy* (1785) of William Paley (a work which was dedicated to Edmund Law). While Paley rejected any notion of a social contract and adopted in its place a system of political theory based on 'the will of God as collected from expediency' his work was still sufficiently influenced by the Lockean tradition to argue explicitly for a right of resistance. His sympathy with at least some measure of reform is apparent in the fact that one of his objections to the concept of a social contract was that it inhibited change since it implied that a citizen was obliged 'to abide by the form of government which he finds established, be it ever so absurd or inconvenient' (Paley, 1845: 104). Utilitarianism, then, could still be combined with Cambridge's whig traditions though, as Paley's opposition to any fundamental changes in Church or State illustrates, it could also be used in defence of the existing order – a role it increasingly performed in the 1790s in the wake of the French Revolution when Paley's work was used to counteract political claims based on the rights of man (T. P. Schofield, 1986: 606–7).

Cambridge's choice of MPs during the 1770s reflects the same divisions evident in the debate about the loyal address of 1775 and the controversy that followed Watson's 1776 sermon. The undistinguished Robert Croftes was elected in 1771 and 1774 but made little impact on the House of Commons where, after 1777, he followed the lead of his patron, the duke of Grafton, in voting with the opposition. However, in 1774 he was elected along with Charles Manners (MA Trinity, 1774) who had the support of the veteran Cambridge burgess, Thomas Townshend (BL, Add. 35628: 196), who, in 1774, finally declined to stand after having served since 1727. As befitted a former pupil of Watson, Manners was a committed member of the opposition and was particularly hostile to the government's American policy which he regarded as bound 'to terminate in nothing but blood . . . it shall, from me, meet the most constant, determined, and invariable opposition' (Namier and Brooke, 1964, III: 101). Predictably, he joined with Grafton in opposing the university's loyal address of 1775 (Cook, 1935: 269). When Manners became duke of Rutland in 1779 and left the Commons for the House of Lords the ensuing by-election became something of a trial of strength between the supporters of the administration and the opposition within the university. The government's candidate was Thomas Villiers, Lord Hyde, who had vainly sought Grafton's aid for the 1774 election (Bodl., MS Clarendon dep.c.347: 249–50; 431), and the opposition's the Foxite John Townshend of whom the bishop of Ely remarked to the earl of Hardwicke in June 1779 that 'the Opposition have exerted themselves for [him] with great warmth' (BL, Add. 35658: 45). In the event the election was won by a third candidate, James Mansfield, with the support of Grafton (Namier and Brooke, 1964, III: 109). Though not so clearly identified with the administration as Hyde, Mansfield, despite his past sympathies for Wilkes, voted with the government and in 1780 became solicitor-general. At the 1780 election he was supported (along with Hyde) by the administration (Bodl., MS Clarendon dep.c.347: 436) and was duly re-elected, while the hapless Hyde came third in the poll, with Croftes fourth and the young William Pitt fifth. But the continuing strength of opposition sentiment within the university was apparent in the success this time of John Townshend with the backing of Rockingham (SRO, 423/1009). In the Commons Townshend was a determined opponent of the American war which he regarded as being due to 'the total misconduct, ignorance, and mad obstinacy of his Majesty's ministers' (Namier and Brooke, 1964, III: 553).

A further indication of the strength of opposition sentiment both within the university and within the county of Cambridgeshire was the address from 'a very numerous and respectable Meeting of the Nobility, Gentry, Clergy and Freeholders' which in March 1780 was drawn up by Richard Watson with the support of Wilkes. This address formed part of the larger petitioning movement since it declared 'That they consider every system of public administration, carried on by means of parliamentary corruption, however sanctified by time, precedent, or authority, to be absolutely unjustifiable on every principle of good sense and sound policy' (C. H. Cooper, 1842–1905, IV: 394); a committee to support such 'measures as may conduce to restore the freedom of Parliament' was then formed under the chairmanship of the duke of Rutland (formerly Charles Manners, university burgess, 1774–9). In the previous month Watson had voiced similar sentiments in a university sermon in which he urged the need for the King's 'overgrown influence [to be] reduced by lawful and quiet means to its ancient size, and the several powers of the different branches of the legislature restored to their salutary poise and constitutional equilibrium'. He also attacked those who sought to drag the American colonists 'in chains to the foot of the throne' (1780: 18, 25).

In June 1782 Watson was again involved in drawing up an address from a meeting of representatives of the county of Cambridge, this time thanking George III for 'confiding your councils . . . to men of approved integrity, consummate ability, intelligent activity, undoubted loyalty, and firm attachment to the genuine constitution of their country' (C. H. Cooper, 1842–1908, IV: 405). In this address Watson was both testifying to his zeal for parliamentary reform and playing the part of a client of Rockingham, who had in fact approved this warm tribute to his own administration in advance (SCL, MS RI 2105). Thereafter, however, Watson's reforming ardour cooled. When, in December 1784, Wyvill requested Watson to use his influence in Cambridgeshire 'in favour of the General Question of Parliamentary Reformation', in the hope that this might encourage Pitt to do the same, Watson declined. With unaccustomed modesty he declared that his influence was 'too small to be mentioned' and that in any case his recent appointment as Bishop of Llandaff would not 'allow me, with decency, to exert it'. Moreover, Watson added, the national mood had changed now that there was no longer 'the calamity of the American war' which previously gave the reforming cause 'an energy which it could not have now' (Wyvill, 1794–1806, IV: 419–23).

As Watson's comments suggest, in Cambridge, as in the nation as a whole, the 1780s, and, in particular, the period after the fall of the Rockingham/Shelburne administration in February 1783, was associated with a retreat from the reforming energies which had been stimulated by the American war – a retreat which, in the 1790s, was to become a rout as a result of the reaction against the French Revolution. The excesses of the Gordon riots in 1780, the unaccustomed experience of military defeat and the increasingly radical demands of reformers like Cartwright and Jebb all combined to sap the strength of the movement for parliamentary reform. Moreover, Cambridge as a stronghold of the Established Church felt increasingly under threat from the more assertive stance taken by the dissenters which led to the attempts in 1787, 1789 and 1790 to repeal the Test and Corporation Acts (O'Gorman, 1982: 45). The increasing sensitivity of the university to attacks on the position of the Church of England was reflected in the summary dismissal in 1787 of yet another attempt to abolish the subscription requirement for intending BAs – a proposal that was moved by Dr Edwards of Jesus whom Lindsey described as being 'most liberal, & of a noble independent spirit, & one of the great supports of a good cause against the honours of the world in that University' (DWL, MS 12.57: 41). Though the defeat of such a measure was not new, such proposals had previously at least prompted long and heated discussions in the Senate; Edward's proposal was, however, vetoed by the Caput before ever reaching the Senate and no reason was given for its rejection (Dyer, 1796: 312–13).

The increasingly cautious attitude to reform both within the university and the country as a whole was typified by the rising star of the 1780s, William Pitt the younger, an early advocate of reforms but one prepared to bow to political realities when it was apparent that reform was not possible. A graduate of Pembroke (from which he took an honorary MA in 1776), Pitt had contested the university seat in 1780 as 'an Independent member of the University . . . not in favour of the present Administration' or, more succinctly as 'an Independent Whig' (HMC, Westmorland MSS: 26). Though he received the fewest votes of the five candidates for this election he did surprisingly well for such a young and still largely unknown candidate and attracted about 14% of votes cast. This rebuff did not discourage Pitt from standing again in 1784, the position of university burgess being in his view 'of all others most desireable, as being free from expense, perfectly independent, and I think in every respect extremely honourable' (Ehrman, 1969: 24). By 1784 Pitt was no longer a relatively obscure recent graduate but now could present himself to the university as first lord of the treasury. None the less, he avoided the appearance of complacency and actively canvassed for votes (*ibid*.: 150); so successful was he that not only did he come top of the poll with 359 votes but his close political associate the earl of Euston (son of the duke of Grafton), in whose campaign at Cambridge Pitt had assisted (BL, Add. 35626: 323), received 309, thus defeating both the Foxite John Townshend and James Mansfield (who had accepted office under the ill-fated North–Fox coalition in 1783). Pembroke was rock-solid in its support for its most famous son. Among his most devoted followers were his former tutor, Pretyman-Tomline, and William Mason, a former fellow, who had once held such extreme whig principles as to verge on republicanism but who had become a fervent admirer of Pitt to whom he addressed an ode in 1782. The only colleges where Pitt–Euston supporters were in a minority were King's (the college of Mansfield), St John's (Townshend's *alma mater*) and Jesus (which was known for its political and religious radicalism), where Townshend narrowly out-polled Pitt (Beverley, 1784). Pitt and Euston repeated their triumph in 1790 by an even more decisive margin, Pitt receiving 510 votes, Euston 483 and the third candidate Dundas 207.

So conclusive was his victory that the King expressed the hope that it would 'prevent the peace of the university being in future disturbed' (Thorne, 1986, II: 33). And, indeed, thereafter Pitt continued to be elected unopposed until his death in 1806 (Gunning, 1855, I: 171) and, as a further mark of the university's esteem, Pitt was elected high steward in 1790 – an appointment which prompted him to praise Cambridge for being 'conspicuous for its Loyalty and attachment to the Constitution' (BL, Add. 35658: 74v). Similarly, Pitt's ally, Euston, was returned until 1811 when he became the fourth duke of Grafton and entered the House of Lords. Like the long tenure of office of Finch and Townshend between 1727 and 1768, the ascendancy of Pitt and Euston as the university burgesses after a series of hotly contested elections was a sign that the university had once more arrived at a large measure of political consensus. While in the mid-eighteenth century the university's political quiescence reflected the defeat of toryism as an effective political force within Cambridge, the political calm that descended after Pitt and Euston's election in 1784 was the result of the university's growing fear of movements which threatened the traditional position of both Church and King – a fear that was greatly accentuated by the French Revolution. In such troubled times Pitt's remark in 1790 that he 'considered the Church of England, as by law established, to be so essential a part of the Constitution that whatever endangered it, would necessarily affect the security of the whole' (Norman, 1976: 19) reassured Cambridge's clerics that the ship of state was in secure hands.

The university's close association with Pitt illustrates once again the difficulty of clearly defining the university's political stance after 1784. As Pitt's description of himself as 'an Independent Whig' at the university election of 1780 suggests, he always saw himself as a whig. Indeed, O'Gorman writes, 'So long as Pitt the Younger lived, a new Tory party could not be born' (O'Gorman, 1982: 51). On the other hand, Pitt's reluctance to ally himself too closely with any party is also evident in his determination to present himself in 1780 as 'an Independent member of the University'. Throughout his career this same spirit of independence from party loyalties was to be apparent, Pitt's governments being shaped by the needs of the King's good government rather than any sense of party solidarity. It is significant, too, that he rarely used the term 'whig' and when he did so it was in the minimalist sense of one who supported the Glorious Revolution (Evans, 1985: 11).

To some in Cambridge, however, the political position of Pitt and his supporters represented so drastic a break with whig traditions that it no longer merited the name 'whig'. Such was the view of Benjamin Flower, the editor of the radical *Cambridge Intelligencer*, who wrote of William Frend's expulsion from the university in 1793 that it 'has entailed indelible disgrace on the once famous *whig* university, the principles of which were thoroughly corrupted under the administration of its most unworthy member – WILLIAM PITT' (Robinson, 1807, 1: cix). In more restrained language Watson took a similar view, writing in 1787 that 'the reign of George the Third was the triumph of Toryism. The Whigs had power for a moment, they quarreled amongst themselves, and thereby lost the King's confidence, lost the people's confidence, and lost their power for ever' (Watson, 1817: 194). In Watson's view true whiggery had been abandoned even before Pitt's elevation to the prime ministership; he regarded men such as Bishop Keene of Ely, who had previously gained office thanks to Newcastle, as guilty of 'apostasy from Whiggism' for co-operating so closely with administrations such as that of North that he was promoted from the see of Chester to Ely in 1771. Thus Keene had encouraged his son, Benjamin, to stand successfully as MP for the Cambridge borough in opposition to those whom Cole termed 'the violent Whigs' in favour of parliamentary reform and against the war with America in 1776 and 1780 (BL, Add. 5823: p. 181). Stung by the difference between Keene's ecclesiastical fortunes and his own, Watson wrote Keene a waspish letter in which he commented pointedly that 'My politics may hurt my interest, but they will not hurt my honour. They are the politics of *Locke*, of *Somers*, and of *Hooker*, and in the reign of George the Second they were the politics of this university' (Watson, 1817: 85–6).[3] By contrast Bishop Green of Lincoln, another of Newcastle's former Cam-

---

[3] Watson dated this letter 28 May 1786 but it must have been sent before Keene's death in 1781.

bridge protégés, remained so committed to 'true whig' principles of civil and religious liberty that he alone of all the bishops voted for a bill in favour of relief for Protestant dissenters in 1772 (an example later emulated by Watson). Green's action led George III to exclaim, 'Green, Green, he shall never be translated' (Wordsworth, 1874: 625) – and indeed Green died as bishop of Lincoln in 1779.

Watson at first greeted the French Revolution with enthusiasm. Thus, in October 1791, he had commented to the duke of Grafton that the Revolution was 'an example of a whole people . . . divesting themselves of the prejudices of birth and education in civil and religious concerns, and adopting the principles of philosophy and good sense', such principles, he argued are 'found in nature', 'notwithstanding all the ridicule which apostate Whigs have attempted to throw on the rights of man'. Watson had added, too, that 'In England we want not a fundamental revolution, but certainly want a reform both in the civil and ecclesiastical part of our constitution' (Watson, 1817: 256). Watson publicly decried the execution of Louis XVI but, as late as 1797, he was equivocal about the wisdom of the war since on 18 February he wrote to Pitt to warn of the growth of the 'Democratic sentiment' among the populace and suggested that the prime minister should deliberate on 'whether a continuance of the War may not elevate the popular turbulence to an irresistible height' (CUL, Add. 6958: 2076). But in the following year, after the breakdown of peace negotiations in September 1797, Watson gave Pitt's war policy his full public support with the publication of his highly influential *Address to the people of Great Britain* (1798) – a work that passed through fourteen editions. In the pamphlet he defended the war with France on the grounds that 'Under whatever circumstances the war was begun, it is now become just; since the enemy has refused to treat on equitable terms, for the restoration of peace' (p. 11). Watson also set out to arrest the spread of that 'Democratic sentiment' on which he had commented to Pitt; thus he argued in his *Address* that 'it is better to tolerate abuses, till they can be reformed by the counsels of the wisest and the best men in the kingdom, than to submit the removal of them to the frothy frequenters of ale-houses' (p. 32).

Some of Watson's former allies in the cause of political and religious reform regarded his support for Pitt with dismay. His pamphlet was vehemently attacked by the Cambridge Unitarians Gilbert Wakefield and George Dyer, and by Benjamin Flower, who described Watson in the *Cambridge Intelligencer* as the 'Right Reverend time server and apostate' (Murphy, 1977: 39). To someone such as Flower, who remained committed to sweeping political and religious reform, Watson's support for Pitt typified a more general political sea-change within Cambridge. In 1796 he had lamented in the *Cambridge Intelligencer* that the university had re-elected 'the man [Pitt] who had totally apostasised from the sentiments he professed when he was first elected . . . The University of Cambridge was once famed for its Whig principles . . . But alas, how is the gold become dim, the most fine gold changed' (Cook, 1935: 282–3).

Another vehement critic of Watson was William Burdon of Emmanuel, a close friend of Flower (Emmanuel College, Cambridge, MS 269: 230) and one of the few remaining critics of Pitt within the university; in 1795 he wrote of the prime minister that he regarded him as 'guilty of the greatest degree of moral turpitude' both because of his abandonment of reform and because of his war policy (*ibid.*: 200–1). In 1795, in a pamphlet published by Flower, Burdon attacked Watson as one 'among those base betrayers of their country, who, at the end of the year, 1792, surrendered the strength and credit [of the nation] into the hands of the minister, upon the mean pretence that the state was in danger' (Burdon, 1795: 22). He also castigated Watson for neglecting his duties as Regius professor of divinity and for appointing as his deputy the egregious Kipling who, in 1794, had borrowed a copy of a DD sermon by Charles Symmons and had then reported him to his ecclesiastical and lay patrons on the grounds that the sermon 'hinted some disapprobation of the conduct of ministers' (p. 5). None the less, Symmons gained a small living thanks to his long-standing patron, William Windham, Pitt's secretary for war from 1794 to 1801 – though thereafter his ecclesiastical advancement was blocked. Symmons's continuing adherence to Lockean conceptions of government is apparent in a letter to Windham of May 1797 in which he affirmed that he 'regard[ed] all legitimate power as emanating from the people; – as a trust delegated for the publick good, and liable on its' abuse to be resumed. To these principles age and reflection have only strengthened my attachment' (Murray, 1975: 104). Soon after the Symmons affair, in 1796, Burdon left Cambridge after refusing to take holy orders (*GM*, 1818, II: 87). Though he had opposed the French war in the 1790s he published in 1803 a pamphlet entitled *Unanimity recommended* in which he joined Watson in defending the war with France, though he was at pains to affirm that 'I have never swerved, in the minutest article from the great principles of political, civil and religious liberty . . . and I look upon the present [recently-renewed] contest as undertaken in their defence' (pp. 3–4).

Watson himself also defended his political consistency against his critics, arguing that he had betrayed no principles since those who criticised him held 'views of political and ecclesiastical reform [which] extended far beyond mine' (Watson, 1817: 303). Nor did Watson altogether abandon his interest in reform: he remained an opponent of the slave trade and in 1800 attempted to interest Pitt in a scheme for standardising the incomes of parish clergy and in proposals for reducing nonresidency (*ibid.*: 340–1; 350–4); by 1805 he was also one of the few episcopal supporters of Pitt's proposals for Catholic relief. But Watson's hopes of advancement at Pitt's hands were to be disappointed: in 1800 he invoked the support of Pitt's ally, Lord Euston, son of his old patron, in an attempt to gain the lowly see of Bangor but Pitt would not oblige (SRO, 423/763; 782), perhaps because he regarded Watson as still too sympathetic to the cause of reform. After Pitt's death Watson wrote bitterly that 'His treatment to me had been uniformly unkind, I might justly say ungrateful' (Watson, 1817: 429).

Though Watson was disappointed with Pitt, his support for his administration is an indication of Pitt's ascendancy within Cambridge (where Watson remained an absentee Regius professor of divinity until his death in 1816). If even someone with Watson's formerly close links with the opposition turned to Pitt rather than to his Foxite opponents during the French wars then Pitt clearly commanded the support of the great bulk of Cambridge dons – as his continued unopposed re-election by the university testified. There were, as always, a few isolated exceptions: when Pitt died in 1806 the whiggish Martin Davy, master of Caius, vetoed a proposal that the university commission a statue of the former prime minister (Gunning, 1855, II: 178). Few in Cambridge, however, shared Davy's hostility to Pitt; indeed, the sum of three thousand guineas was raised by private subscription and the statue was duly installed in the Senate House in 1812. By Pitt's death, then, the vast majority of Cambridge dons – including such self-proclaimed custodians of whiggery as Watson – were once again supporting the 'King's friends' in an administration which was soon to adopt once more the name 'tory'.

Of particular concern to Cambridge dons was the fact that Pitt's long tenure of the prime ministership brought with it a new ecclesiastical adviser, George Pretyman (who, after 1803, added the surname Tomline), his former tutor from Pembroke. Pretyman appears to have had some youthful sympathy with the opposition since in 1775 (two years after taking up his fellowship) he was the only member of Pembroke to vote against the loyal address in support of North's American policy (BL, Add. 5841: pp. 364–5). In 1784 he was still friendly with religious radicals like Gilbert Wakefield – something which was to cause him considerable embarrassment when he declined to act as a character witness for Wakefield at his trial in 1799 (Stephen, 1962, I: 374). However, Pretyman grew increasingly suspicious of the proponents of religious and political reform and may have played a part in weening Pitt from his early interest in reform. According to Theophilus Lindsey, Pitt was 'swayed entirely' by the arguments of Bishop Sherlock's *Vindication of the Corporation and Test Acts* (1718), an attack on Hoadly and a defence of the existing alliance of Church and State which had been republished in 1787 (possibly at

Pretyman's instigation) in response to renewed attempts to repeal the Test and Corporation Acts. The work was 'read over' to Pitt by Pretyman (J. C. D. Clark, 1985: 234) who, earlier that year, had been made bishop of Lincoln, thanks to his former pupil. Two years later Pretyman made his opposition to would-be reformers even more apparent in a speech in which he argued for the divine foundation of 'subordination of ranks, and the relation of magistrates and subjects' and attacked anyone who would undermine 'the particular form [of society] which is duly established and justly administered in the community of which he is a member' as a sinner 'against the ordinance of God'. By 1800 the bishop was warning his clergy that conspiracy theorists of the French Revolution like Barruel or Robison had proved the existence of 'a regularly digested plan for the extirpation of all belief in Christianity' (Soloway, 1969: 26, 37–8).

From his elevation to the see of Lincoln in 1787 until Pitt's death in 1806 it was Pretyman who largely pulled the strings on the ecclesiastical stage, though George III drew the line at having him appointed archbishop of Canterbury in 1805 despite Pitt's determination to gain the post for his old tutor. Among those in Cambridge who benefited from this new ecclesiastical regime was Richard Farmer, the chief instigator of the loyal address which Pretyman had opposed, who was made canon of St Paul's in 1788 and was offered (but declined) two bishoprics (Barker, 1828–9, I: 436). As Lord Clarendon had commented to Lord North in 1780, Farmer had 'shewn . . . more zeal for the government than any friend it has at that place [Cambridge]' (Bodl., MS Clarendon dep.c.347: 437). His belated recognition was, then, a potent indication to others in Cambridge of the favour with which opponents of reform in Church and State were now viewed. Another who benefited from the Pitt/Pretyman patronage was William Mansel who was appointed master of Trinity in 1798 as a reward for his opposition to the 'citizen duke' of Bedford (Carlyon, 1856, III: 51), a graduate of Trinity who had attached himself to the Foxite whigs. At a Cambridgeshire county meeting in 1797 which petitioned the King 'To dismiss the ministry from his councils for ever, as the most likely means of obtaining a speedy, honourable and permanent peace', Mansel had launched a 'vehement' tirade upon the duke of Bedford, whose name, he observed, was 'never to be found in those loyal & praiseworthy subscriptions which had done so much honour to the University & the County' (Gunning, 1855, II: 65–6). Mansel's loyalty to the established order was further rewarded in 1808 when he was made bishop of Bristol thanks to Pitt's successor, Spencer Perceval, a former pupil of Mansel at Trinity. Pretyman was also the patron of Isaac Milner, the declared foe of 'infidels and Jacobins', who in 1791 was (thanks to Pretyman (M. Milner, 1842: 71)) made dean of Carlisle, while remaining president of Queens'.

Pretyman's influence, then, helped to encourage the drift away from the reformist elements within Cambridge whiggery – a trend that was, of course, greatly intensified by the reaction against the French Revolution. As that unrepentant whig, Henry Gunning, wrote, after 1789 'the Whig party was very low in numbers and credit, both in the University and in the country at large. From this time', he continued, 'those who professed themselves Whigs for the sake of what they could get, saw immediately that their cause was unprofitable and hopeless; and in a very short time scarcely a Whig was to be found among the resident members of the University' (Gunning, 1855, I: 172). The gulf between the Cambridge of the 1770s and that of the 1790s is apparent in the contrast between the contentious passage of the loyal address of 1775 and the Senate's ready acceptance of a loyal address in 1792, following the proclamation against seditious publications, in which the university expressed its 'extreme satisfaction at the salutary measure now adopted by your Majesty, which we are persuaded is widely calculated to discourage & disappoint the wicked attempts of the enemies of our happy Constitution' (C. H. Cooper, 1842–1908, IV: 444). The address was enthusiastically received by George III who thanked the university and expressed his confidence that it would 'continue diligently to inculcate that love of Order and of well-regulated liberty, which must naturally prevail in every enlightened Society' (*ibid.*). In 1792, too, a Cambridge branch of the loyalist associations against 'Republicans and Levellers' was founded and Gunning reports that 'An attempt was made in the University and town to represent those who differed from Mr. Pitt as enemies of the constitution' (Gunning, 1855, I: 252).

This growing reaction was reflected in the political theory of the period, with further signs of movement away from the Lockean contractual assumptions about the nature of government with which Cambridge had so long been associated. Among those attracted to utilitarian rather than contractual political theory was Pitt himself who, according to Pretyman, 'reprobated [Locke's] notions on the origin of civil government, as unfounded and of dangerous tendency' (T. P. Schofield, 1986: 610). This same suspicion of the radical tendencies of Lockean thought was also voiced by Samuel Cooper (DD Magdalene, 1777) in his *First principles of civil and ecclesiastical government delineated . . .* (1791). In this work (which was prompted by Priestley's attack on Burke) Cooper criticised Locke's political writings and admonished Priestley for having become an 'open and declared *bigot* to the *infallibility* of LOCKE, and still more and more of a sceptic as to the *authority* of CHRIST, and his APOSTLES' (p. 32). Cooper resolutely rejected any view of government based on the 'NATURAL *equality* of mankind' (p. 43) and argued for an almost Hobbesian view of the state of nature in order to underline his argument that political rights did not derive from natural law but rather could be granted only by established authority (T. P. Schofield, 1986: 608). Daniel Peacock, who became a fellow of Trinity in 1792 (having been senior wrangler in the previous year), published in 1794 a defence of the existing political order against its would-be reformers. In this he also echoed Hobbes, rather than Locke, in taking as his premise that fear was the main incentive to form governments and that 'the primary object of political association is certainly the security of the several members of the community' (Peacock, 1794: 14). Peacock also sought to counter Wyvill's reform proposals by observing that 'the history of the French Revolution . . . affords an aweful lesson to the World on the consequences of introducing Democratic principles into an extensive empire' (p. 56).

Closely linked with such changes in political theory was an increasing emphasis on the importance of religious sanctions as a basis for political authority since the Revolution concentrated the minds of both clergy and laity on the extent to which civil and religious authority were intertwined. John Owen, a fellow of Corpus who, by his own admission, was at first 'of the number of those who admired with enthusiasm the Reformation of the French Monarchy, by the events of the first Revolution' (1794: v) was, by 1794, decrying it as a threat to 'the very existence of religion' (p. 2). By contrast, he praised the British constitution as one in which

the honour of Religion is of no small estimation in the scale of public policy. The celebration of its rites is by us maintained with a zeal and respect that proclaim its influence in the sphere of authority; all its sanctions are by us classed among the acknowledged records of undisputed veracity; and the observance of its institutions is connected with the first duties of civil obligation. (Pp. 27–8)

He also argued that, though he was sympathetic to some measure of political reform, such proposals should be deferred until the end of the present emergency (pp. 29–30).

By November 1795 the radical *Cambridge Intelligencer* could ask: 'Is there a spark of Freedom left in the breasts of the Inhabitants of this Town and County and of the members of an illustrious University? Illustrious not merely for its learning but for the honourable distinction it has acquired – that of the WHIG UNIVERSITY?' (F. Knight, 1971: 186). One response that might have been made to Flower's rhetorical question was to point to Cambridge's continued activity in the anti-slavery campaign – an area in which it was encouraged by Pitt and which indicates that both the prime minister and the university had not so completely abandoned their past interest in reform as radicals like Flower maintained. As Gunning wrote: 'In hostility to that traffic [of slavery], the town and country acted in unison most cordially. The University also, stimulated both by their own feelings, and the unrivalled eloquence of their Member, Mr. Pitt, zealously co-operated with them' (1855, II: 36–7). Hostility to the slave trade was sufficiently widespread within the university for the Senate to vote (both in January 1788 and March 1792) to send a petition to the House of Commons urging it to abolish the traffic in human beings (the latter grace including a vote of thanks to Wilberforce, Pitt, Fox, Granville Sharp and Clarkson for their work in the abolitionist cause). After this goal was finally achieved the Senate voted in 1826 to petition the Commons for the abolition of slavery itself (C. H. Cooper, 1842–1908, IV: 442–3, 550).

By the 1790s the anti-slave trade crusade had, of course, become closely associated with evangelicals like Wilberforce and his close friend, Isaac Milner (president of Queens', 1788–1820), who urged Wilberforce to devote all his energies to the cause even when, as in the 1790s, it appeared politically doomed (Bodl., MS Wilberforce c.3: 35). However, abolitionism was also still linked with those holding radical political and religious views: Milner, for example, was embarrassed by the political views of some of his fellow-abolitionists which the slave-owners had used as an excuse to brand 'with the name of Jacobin every friend of the abolition cause' (M. Milner, 1842: 76). The close association between the abolition campaign and the cause of political and religious radicalism had led the American John Adams to remark of the anti-slavery crusader Granville Sharp that he was 'as Zealously attached to Episcopacy & the Athanasian Creed as he is to civil and religious liberty – a mixture which in this Country is not common' (Bonwick, 1977: 7).

Within Cambridge the links between abolition of the slave trade and reform more generally were particularly strong since the most outspoken advocate of the abolitionist cause, Peter Peckard, was also conspicuous for his radical religious and political opinions. Though an Oxford graduate Peckard was appointed to the mastership of Magdalene in 1781 (a post that was in the gift of his friend Sir John Griffin, the owner of Audley End (BL, Add. 5878: p. 198b). Peckard had already achieved considerable notoriety for his defence of the 'Jew bill' in 1753, and (in 1757) for his advocacy of the view that the soul 'slept' between death and the resurrection – a proposition which Edmund Law had also maintained with the result that he was accused of heresy. In 1759 Peckard had returned to this controversy with a pamphlet in which he defended both Law and himself and argued (in the manner of Hoadly) that 'national Establishments of Religion . . . are all the Work of Men' (Peckard, 1759: 23). In his (anonymous) 1776 pamphlet defending the Feathers Tavern petitioners Peckard was more explicit in acknowledging his debt to Hoadly, 'the man to whose great abilities and noble efforts we are, for ought I know, indebted to all the Christian liberty both civil and religious that is left among us' (Peckard, 1776: 125). In the same work Peckard urged the need for reform in 'our ecclesiastical constitution' (p. 163) and, in particular, the practice of subscription. He praised Wyvill's work on this subject (p. 150) and also clearly sympathised with Jebb's anti-Trinitarian views since he asked why Jebb had not been refuted if his views were false (pp. 147–8).

Peckard's forthright style continued after his move to Cambridge. In his *Nature and extent of civil and religious liberty* – a university sermon preached on 5 November 1783 (the month before Pitt took office) – he decried the clergy's past adherence to the ideas of 'the Divine and Irresistible Power of Kings'. Such views had been refuted by Locke but were again being propagated, while Locke was 'declared to be pernicious to Society, and destructive of the Interest of his Country' (Peckard, 1783: 2, 3). Though conceding that the Scriptures 'teach proper submission to Governors' Peckard attacked the use of the Bible to justify despotism as 'a species of treason against our Establishment both in Church and State' (pp. 5–6). In this wide-ranging sermon Peckard also criticised the practice of subscription as 'an impediment only to those who are honest' (p. 20) and castigated the slave trade as a crime which would 'draw down upon us the heaviest judgment of Almighty God; who . . . gave to All equally a natural Right to Liberty' (p. 11). The latter was a theme to which he returned again and again – it was the subject of a pamphlet addressed to parliament entitled *Am I not a man? And a brother?* (1788) (in which he also supported relief for dissenters) and of a series of increasingly vehement university sermons delivered in 1788, 1790 and 1795 – in the last of which (delivered two years before his death) he also criticised the war with France.

When, in 1785, Peckard served as vice-chancellor he had the right to set the subject for the members' prize for a Latin essay. His question was 'Is it right to make slaves of others against their will?', the prize being won by Thomas Clarkson. Clarkson duly translated his essay and published it in 1786 as *An essay on the slavery and commerce of the human species . . .* – a work which helped win over Wilberforce to the abolitionist cause. Clarkson warmly praised Peckard's denunciation of slavery (1786: 254), a tribute he also paid in his later *History of the abolition of the slave-trade* (1808) in which he also explained how Peckard had prompted his lifelong interest in the abolitionist cause (1808: 203–5). Like Peckard, Clarkson combined his attack on the slave trade with an interest in political reform: he acted as the chairman of the committee of the London Corresponding Society which raised funds for the defence of Thomas Hardy and Horne Tooke in 1794 (F. Knight, 1971: 174).

Though Peckard had helped to launch the anti-slavery campaign within Cambridge his influence within the university, and even within his own college of Magdalene, appears to have diminished. Ironically, though

Peckard's own religious beliefs were liberal to the point of heterodoxy, he was appointed master of a college which was the university's first major centre of evangelicalism. At first Peckard appears to have accepted this situation with equanimity (Walsh, 1958: 504) but whether because of religious or more personal differences the gulf between himself and his colleagues at Magdalene steadily widened. By 1790 he was complaining bitterly of the internal bickering within the college which had made him resolve not to 'involve my private concerns with those of a body so at disunion in itself' (Corpus Christi College, Cambridge, Hartshorne MS xxi: 77). Peckard's career illustrates both the links between abolitionism and reform in Church and State and the way in which Cambridge in the 1780s and 1790s became less and less fertile ground for those (like Peckard) who derived their political and religious opinions from Locke and Hoadly. Cambridge's continued commitment to the anti-slavery cause is an indication that certain elements of the reforming creed of 'true whigs' such as Peckard could survive the icy blasts of the 1790s, though the continued respectability of the abolitionists owed much to the activities of evangelicals like Wilberforce and Milner who were known to be stalwart champions of the existing order in Church and State.

In the increasingly unfavourable conditions of the 1780s and, *a fortiori*, the 1790s the main preserve of reformist sentiment was Trinity which, by the late eighteenth century, was beginning to overtake St John's as the largest college. The political complexion of the college must have owed something to the influence of Grafton's protégés, Richard Watson (fellow from 1760; junior dean, 1769–71) and John Hinchcliffe (master, 1768–89). During their time at the college Trinity produced young Foxite radicals like Charles Manners (MA, 1774, the university burgess), Thomas Erskine (MA, 1778) and Charles Grey (1781–3, no degree). Hinchcliffe was, however, considered to have been neglectful of college business because of his political commitments. He also allowed fellows to be appointed without proper regard for the college's well-established system of fellowship examinations, with the result that in 1786 ten of the younger fellows presented him with a petition urging him to ensure that all candidates for fellowships were properly examined. Chief among the petitioners were John Baynes and Miles Popple, both of whom were active in the cause of reform, not only within the college but also within the nation at large. Until his death in 1787 (at the age of twenty-eight) Baynes acted as one of Jebb's lieutenants in the Society for Constitutional Information. Popple, who contributed to Edmund Law's 1777 edition of Locke's works an English translation of the *De toleratione*, was also the author of *Considerations on reform; with a specific plan for a new representation*

(1793) – a work he addressed to his former Trinity college acquaintance, Charles Grey – in which he attacked those (like Burke) who argued for a system of virtual representation as 'The foremost amongst the opposers of a parliamentary reform' (p. 8). Nor were Popple's activities confined to the written word: by 1795, when he was at Hull, he was actively involved in organising opposition to the war in conjunction with Wyvill and the Foxites (Cookson, 1982: 140).

Baynes's and Popple's reforming activities within Trinity were regarded with considerable hostility by Hinchcliffe who formally admonished the signatories of the petition (*GM*, 1787: 742). This in turn led to an appeal to the college visitor (the lord chancellor) who censured the petitioning fellows, though he agreed that the election of fellows without examination was 'a practice highly improper' (*ibid.*: 1017). He also recommended that Hinchcliffe's admonition be struck from the college records and that the matter be resolved by private agreement – both of which recommendations were followed. Though the lord chancellor's intervention provided Hinchcliffe with some face-saving measures, victory largely went to the petitioners and thereafter Trinity's fellowship elections followed rigorous examinations which became renowned throughout the university (Gunning, 1855, II: 100–1); by 1800 William Burdon could recommend to the archbishop of Tuam in Ireland that he choose a private tutor for his son from Trinity since that was the college where 'there are the most incentives to industry' since the fellows 'are all elected after a severe examination' (Emmanuel College, Cambridge, MS 269: 244).

As well as strengthening Trinity's meritocratic character – which was further encouraged by the fact that the college was the only one not to be hampered by statutes stipulating the geographical origin of fellows – the success of the petitioners also gave heart to the reforming elements within the college. It was probably no coincidence that soon after this affair, in 1789, Hinchcliffe resigned as master; he was replaced by Thomas Postlethwaite whom Pitt (presumably in collaboration with Pretyman) appointed at Farmer's suggestion. Given the political views of Farmer it is ironic that it was during Postlethwaite's mastership that (according to Isaac Milner in a letter to William Wilberforce in 1798) Trinity became a haven for 'heterodox and Jacobinical principles' (M. Milner, 1842: 161). It was also while Postlethwaite was head that Trinity emulated St John's by instituting a system of undergraduate examinations. It is doubtful, however, how much of a role Postlethwaite himself played in such developments: with the experience of his predecessor and, even more graphically, that of Bentley in mind he appears to have decided that the only way to live a quiet life was to be merely a titular head; as a contemporary put it, he 'soon discovered that, if he was alert, he and the Seniors should be at variance, according to antient usage' (Nichols, 1817–58, VI: 738). As a result (or, at least, so Milner claimed (M. Milner, 1842: 161)) the direction of the college fell into the hands of the bursar, James Lambert, and one of the main tutors, Thomas Jones. Both men were known for their reforming views: Lambert had been actively involved in disseminating both Jebb's anti-Trinitarian views and his plans for academic reform while Thomas Jones had been involved in the petition to Hinchcliffe in 1786 and, in the same year, while serving as moderator, had briefly reawakened one of the controversies associated with Jebb with a proposal that fellow-commoners be subject to the same academic requirements as other undergraduates (H. Marsh, 1808: 7). Jones was also known for his care both for his students' academic and personal well-being (Pryme, 1870: 38) and for the quality of his lectures in mathematics and natural philosophy which were 'interesting even to those, who otherwise had no relish for mathematical enquiries' (H. Marsh, 1808: 7).

It was Jones's and Lambert's influence within the college which helps to account for the election of fellows such as John Tweddell, a devoted pupil of Jones (Tweddell, 1816: 11*), who was elected in 1792 after giving a speech in Trinity Chapel in 1790 in which he urged the need for political reform if the heritage of the Glorious Revolution were to be retained; he also praised the French as 'a people rearing their trampled heads from under the heel of oppression'. 'Liberty', he continued, 'has begun her progress, and hope tells us, that she has only begun.' The spread of liberty will mean that 'No longer shall the slave, who now sickens under the pressure of english barbarity . . . [be] forcibly torn by the most outrageous devices of a legalized piracy.' In a final peroration Tweddell praised the political principles of Harrington, Sidney, Milton and Locke – the pantheon of 'the true whigs' – and attributed to their influence 'a new and hardy band of proselytes, who are warring with time, and gaining the mastery over custom' in contrast to those 'who think by tradition, and reason by authority' (*ibid.*: 101*, 109–11*). Tweddell remained a defender of the French Revolution even after the Terror since 'he indulged the hope that after the first excess, France might settle down into a free and constitutional government' (Gunning, 1855, II: 78) – not surprisingly, he and Farmer were to cross swords. John Losh, who graduated from Trinity in 1786, was of a similar mind to Tweddell and after the Revolution travelled to France to admire the outcome of the events of 1789 only to be saved from possible execution by Marat. In 1794 Losh and Tweddell, along with William Frend of Jesus and Godfrey Higgins, presented Priestley with a parting gift when he set sail for America (Rutt, 1831, II: 225) – an indication of their sympathy with Priestley's political and religious radicalism.

The other college which was also known for its political and religious radicalism in the late eighteenth century was Jesus. There anti-Trinitarian beliefs appear to have taken particularly firm root, probably because of the influence of Robert Tyrwhitt (BA, 1757) who initiated the anti-subscription debate within Cambridge. Although Tyrwhitt resigned his Jesus fellowship on account of his Unitarian beliefs in 1777 he continued to reside in the college until his death in 1817 and was active in associations such as the Unitarian Society for Promoting the Knowledge of the Scriptures. Jesus produced other prominent Unitarians such as Gilbert Wakefield (BA, 1776) and William Frend (BA, 1780), whose heterodoxy was combined with an active interest in political reform. It was probably Frend, along with Braithwaite and Tylden (who both refused livings rather than subscribe (Wakefield, 1792: 115–16)), whom Burdon had in mind when he commented to an Oxford correspondent in February 1787 that 'Socinianism . . . has gained some ground here, three of the fellows of Jesus College are avowedly of the persuasion and some others are thought to have a tendency towards it' (Emmanuel College, Cambridge, MS 269: 118). Another fellow of Jesus during this period was Thomas Edwards (who moved from Clare to take up a Jesus fellowship in 1787), the initiator of the 1787 proposal to abolish religious tests for degrees and author of *A discourse on the limits and importance of free enquiry in matters of religion* (1792). While an undergraduate at Jesus the young Samuel Taylor Coleridge (who matriculated in 1792) acquired an admiration for the radical political and religious opinions of Priestley, whom he praised in his *Religious musings* (1794) as 'patriot and saint and sage' (*DNB*, Coleridge). This attitude was probably due to the influence of Frend, whom Coleridge publicly applauded during his trial before the university in 1793, since Frend had been involved with Priestley in the translation of the Old Testament (Rutt, 1831, II: 76). Another young protégé of Frend, Felix Vaughan, travelled to France after taking his BA at Jesus. In July 1790 he sent back to Frend an enthusiastic account of the progress of the Revolution, writing 'that no nation upon earth was ever more powerfully united for destruction of despotism & the preservation of the public good' – though by December Vaughan was more cautious about recent developments, informing Frend 'that the *Republicans* are now in my opinion more to be feared than the *Aristocrats*' (CUL, Add. 7886: 263–4).

The common political and religious sympathies of a number of members of late eighteenth-century Jesus and Trinity naturally drew the two colleges together. Thus we find Jones of Trinity continuing to correspond with Frend on political and religious issues after his expulsion from the university in 1793 (CUL, Add. 7886: 119). Both Trinity and Jesus were jointly condemned by the conservative periodical *The Anti-Jacobin*, the former for its support for Frend and the latter for its 'jacobinical' tendencies since only three of its fellows took part in the prosecution of Frend (F. Knight, 1971: 191). The trial of Frend – the great *cause célèbre* of late eighteenth-century Cambridge – was, then, an event which brought before the public gaze the political undercurrents both within Jesus and Trinity and the university as a whole.

Frend was never one to hide his own opinions. In 1787 he had supported the attempt by his colleague, Thomas Edwards, to abolish the subscription requirements for graduates by publishing a pamphlet entitled *Considerations on the oaths required at the time of taking degrees*, a work in which he also advocated some of the other reforms for which Jebb had vainly striven: examination of fellow-commoners, annual examinations and a broadening of the mathematically dominated curriculum. The complete failure of Edwards's proposal to abolish subscription for degrees prompted Frend to proclaim publicly his Unitarianism in the provocatively entitled *Address to the members of the Church of England, and to Protestant Trinitarians in general, exhorting them to turn from the false worship of three persons to the worship of THE ONE TRUE GOD* (1788) – a pamphlet that was warmly praised by another Jesus Unitarian, Gilbert Wakefield, who also urged Frend to remain at the college (DWL, MS 12.45: 115; CUL, Add. 7887: 53). Frend also became a correspondent of Cambridge's most prominent Unitarian, Theophilus Lindsey, who discussed with him the work of other Cambridge Unitarians such as the duke of Grafton, Symonds and Disney.

   Frend's public advocacy of Unitarianism was overlooked by the university itself, though it did result in his being deprived of his tutorship at Jesus on 27 September 1788. None the less, Frend continued to propagate Unitarianism within Cambridge and by 1790 had established a Unitarian society there with about twenty to thirty members (CUL, MS 7886: 155, 162). He also continued to agitate for an abolition of subscription, broadening his attack into a critique of the whole principle of ecclesiastical establishments. In his open letter of 1789 to Henry Coulthurst, a fellow of Sidney and a prominent evangelical, Frend attacked Coulthurst for stopping Edwards's grace against subscription in the Caput and rehearsed the familiar arguments against subscription. He also went on to argue that 'the moment it [Christianity] was established as the law of the state, that moment did anti-Christ begin his sway, and genuine Christianity was lost in tricks of politicians' (Frend, 1789: 23). Frend's continued attacks on the doctrine and institution of the Established Church, which resulted in no other penalty apart from the loss of his college tutorship, illustrate the wide measure of freedom of discussion that still existed in Cambridge before the French Revolution – a situation that was to change after 1789.

Until the late 1780s Frend had taken little interest in political affairs but, with the coming of the French Revolution, his enthusiasm for reform in ecclesiastical and university matters also became apparent in the political sphere. His interest in the events in France was partly the result of his own visit to that country in 1789 and was further stimulated by Lindsey who greeted him on his return from Europe in November 1789 with the remark: 'the revolution in France is a wonderful work of providence in our days, and we trust it will prosper and go on, and be the speedy means of putting an end to Tyranny every where' (CUL, Add. 7886: 149). The French Civil Constitution of the Clergy of 12 July 1790, with its implied attack on clerical power and privilege, prompted Lindsey to congratulate Frend 'upon the most glorious and grandest and I hope happiest event in human things' (*ibid.*: 158). Lindsey also informed Frend of the progress of moves to reform parliament; thus on 13 April 1792 he commented in a letter that was sent to both Frend and Tyrwhitt at Jesus, as well as Lambert at Trinity, that Wyvill should 'cooperate with other efforts that are making to bring about a parliamentary reform' (*ibid.*: 168).

The outbreak of war between France and Britain in February 1793 and the consequent increase in taxes prompted Frend's pamphlet, *Peace and unity recommended to the associated bodies of republicans and anti-republicans*. Though the immediate stimulus to write this work was Frend's outrage at the burden of wartime taxation on the common people the pamphlet touched on a wide range of sensitive political and ecclesiastical issues at a time when all such discussion was overshadowed by the growing fear of the Revolution and its principles. Frend did comment on the excesses of the Revolution but he also made it apparent that he rejoiced at the overthrow of the old regime: in a passage that echoes Paine's famous remark about Burke's *Reflections* – that he 'pitied the plumage and forgot the dying bird' – Frend commented that 'he must be a weak or a wicked man, who lost in admiration of the beauties of a voluptuous and effeminate court, forgets the miseries of the poor subjects' (1793a: 1). He also included an appendix in which he argued that the execution of Louis XVI – to whom, revealingly, he refers as Louis Capet – should not cause any alarm in England since it, too, had deposed kings. As well as defending the basic principles of the Revolution Frend's pamphlet also served as a summary of some of the chief aspirations of the eighteenth-century reform movement: repeal of the Septennial and the Test and Corporation Acts, reform of the parliamentary boroughs and abolition of aristocratic privileges such as the game laws. What, however, made Frend's work particularly contentious within Cambridge was his attack on the Church of England, not only on specific points such as the need for the reform of the Church's liturgy, but through a critique of the very principle of an established church. Any such ecclesiastical establishment, he argued, should be 'considered only as a political institution' which gives dangerous power to the executive, 'For ten thousand men in black under the direction of an individual are a far more formidable body, than ten thousand times that number in arms, and more likely to produce the greatest injury to civil society' (pp. 26–7).

Though Frend had said similar things before, such criticism of the established order in Church and State was regarded in a far more hostile light after the Revolution. Frend's pamphlet resulted in a meeting of twenty-seven prominent members of the university who urged the vice-chancellor to discipline him. Prominent among Frend's opponents was Cambridge's growing band of evangelicals – 'that set of men', as Frend put it (1793b: [ix]), 'who, from pretensions to particular sanctity of manners and zeal for orthodoxy, have gained amongst us the appellation of saints'. The most active of these evangelicals was the vice-chancellor himself, the formidable Isaac Milner. Milner's determined opposition to 'Jacobins or infidels' had already been amply demonstrated within his own college of Queens' which (as Gunning wrote) he had transformed from being a college which 'under the Presidentship of Dr. Plumptre, had been distinguished for its attachment to Civil and Religious Liberty' to one which 'became afterwards as remarkable for its opposition to liberal opinions' (Gunning, 1855, I: 238).

Even before Milner became president of Queens' in 1788 he had played an increasingly important role in the election of fellows. In 1781 Reginald Bligh, a member of Queens' who had been rejected for a fellowship, published a pamphlet in which he accused the ageing Plumptre of being 'entirely at the disposal of this artful and designing man [Milner]' (Bligh, 1781: 11). Once he became president Milner could employ the powerful weapon of control over the appointment of college tutorships (a power which some in Queens' vainly contested). As Milner put it in a letter to Wilberforce in 1801,

At Queens', we happened unfortunately to have several clever Fellows, some time ago, who should have filled our offices of trust, as tutors, &c., but were disqualified on account of their principles. I was positively determined to have nothing to do with Jacobins or infidels, and custom has placed in my power the appointment of the tutors, provided they be Fellows of our own College. Our own being very unfit, we went out of college sorely against the wish of several; however, by determining to make no jobs of such things, but to take the very best men I could find, I carried the matter through, in no less than three instances: – Thomason, Barnes, Sowerby [all evangelicals]. (M. Milner, 1842: 243)

By such means, Gunning commented, Milner 'soon acquired that entire ascendancy over the Fellows, that, after a few years, no one thought of offering the slightest opposition to his will' (Gunning, 1855, I: 239).

Having brought Queens' under his control Milner extended his attentions to other colleges and, in particular, to Trinity Hall where his fellow-evangelical, Joseph Jowett, was tutor. At the Trinity Hall fellowship election of 1793 Milner was active in ensuring that the strongly whiggish Wrangham was rejected in favour of his evangelical opponent, John Vickers of Queens'. According to the hostile Gunning, Milner brought this about by giving Wrangham the reputation of being a jacobite. So great was Milner's influence in the affairs of Trinity Hall that the college became known 'as a Fief of Queens' ' (Gunning, 1855, II: 30).

Milner, then, needed little encouragement to bring Frend – the university's most conspicuous political and religious rebel – to trial. For Milner such a trial offered an opportunity to widen his offensive against 'Jacobin and infidel principles' from Queens' to the university as a whole. Milner and his fellow heads were, however, cast in the role of judges. The role of prosecutor was enthusiastically played by Kipling, Watson's deputy as Regius professor of divinity, who had joined with Coulthurst in opposing Edwards's proposal for the abolition of subscription in 1787 – something which Edwards had not forgotten or forgiven. Kipling's involvement in Frend's prosecution, wrote his obiturist, 'brought upon the deputy professor a shower of abuse from the zealots for innovation, at the head of whom was Dr. Edwards' (*GM*, 1822, I: 276). However, Kipling did not go without his reward for he was appointed dean of Peterborough in 1798. No doubt, it was partly Kipling's promotion which prompted Gunning to observe that the majority of those involved in prosecuting Frend 'were men, who, under the pretext of defending religion, were anxious to distinguish themselves as enemies of the French Revolution. To those who studied the signs of the times it was very evident that Whiggism would be an unprofitable profession, and that a good opportunity now presented itself for abandoning their principles' (*ibid.*, I: 277).

While such motives may well partly explain the prosecution of Frend, Gunning's staunch whiggism led him to underestimate the genuine fear and hostility that Frend's work occasioned at a time when many feared that the old regime in England would go the way of that of France. Farmer, who was sufficiently unambitious to decline two bishoprics, reflected such fears by remarking that Frend's pamphlet 'certainly would not have been noticed at any other time, but the damned iteration of appendix upon appendix to call up the mob is intolerable' (F. Knight, 1971: 164). Frend did make the telling point that his earlier, openly Unitarian, work had been ignored by the university authorities while his 1793 pamphlet with its political overtones was seized upon since such a trial was more likely to commend his prosecutors to the authorities (1795: 4–5). Again, while men such as Milner and Kipling were certainly ambitious for advancement, their lack of action in relation to Frend's earlier pamphlets and their emphasis on the political aspects of the case could be explained by the fact that the university's rarely used and highly contentious powers of banishment were only likely to command widespread support if the issue was one that was of concern to ministers of the crown as well as champions of orthodoxy such as themselves.

In his trial before the vice-chancellor's court Frend acknowledged that he had 'rejoiced at the success of the French Revolution' but argued that he had done so at a time when other prominent members of the university including the vice-chancellor's predecessor had expressed similar views. Moreover, he claimed that his political views, which had been characterised as those of the 'republicans and levellers', were the same as those of Bishop Watson for whom Kipling was acting as a deputy (Frend, 1793b: 90). Frend also denied the rumours (which Milner may have helped to spread) that he was part of a small group within Cambridge which was corresponding with the French National Convention (Beverley, 1793: 57) – a group which was supposed to include his old colleague and ally, Thomas Edwards (Gunning, 1855, 1: 284). During the trial Frend was supported by Jones and Lambert of Trinity and Tyrwhitt of Jesus (*ibid.*: 265); he also received a letter from Edward Evanson (MA Emmanuel, 1753) – who had also been prosecuted for his Unitarianism – in which Evanson warmly praised Frend and expressed his hostility to 'such contemptible time serving reptiles as the Vice-Chancellor and Dr. Kipling' (CUL, Add. 7886: 40). Another defender of Frend was Major Reynolds, a squire in the near-by town of Paxton, of whom Gunning wrote that he 'supported, almost single-handed, the cause of civil and religious liberty in his county [Huntingdonshire]' (1855, 1: 284). In Reynolds's view Frend's trial was part of a more general assault on 'All the Assertors of Civil & Religious Liberty' including Fox, Grey, Priestley and Frend himself (CUL, Add. 7886: 222).

Predictably, when the trial ended on 30 May 1793 Milner sentenced Frend to banishment from the university – a sentence which Milner urged the junior members of the university (some of whom had been noisily supporting Frend) to regard as an indication of Cambridge's determination not to 'suffer the sacred and venerable institutions of the Established Church to be derided and insulted . . . at a time when a profane and licentious spirit of infidelity and irreligion makes rapid advances, and threatens the destruction of our ecclesiastical fabric' (M. Milner, 1842: 97). Frend appealed to the Senate but it confirmed the vice-chancellor's verdict and an appeal to the King's Bench in the following year was equally fruitless. He was, however, permitted to retain his degrees and fellowship – something which appears to have come as a pleasant surprise to Frend, to judge by a letter of 1831 in which he wrote of his trial that 'in such a conflict and in such times the wonder is not that I did not lose every thing but that I did retain any thing' (F. Knight, 1971: 165). Frend was also compelled to leave Jesus, a resolution that was passed by the master and six fellows with four other fellows dissenting (*ibid.*: 134) – an indication of the ideological divisions that still existed in that college.

Having been banished from the university Frend moved to London where he became more actively involved with both Lindsey's Unitarian chapel and the cause of political reform. He joined the London Corresponding Society and became a lifelong friend of its founder, the radical shoemaker, Thomas Hardy; the continuing devotion to parliamentary reform of both men is apparent in a letter of Hardy to Frend of March 1831 which speaks of 'this wonderful change that is expected in this country, a *parliamentary reform*' and adds 'Had Major Cartwright & J. Horn Took and many more of our friends been alive how overjoyed would they have been to witness this Revolution' (Bodl., MS Autob.d.20: 85). After leaving Cambridge, Frend also became a critic of Pitt's increasingly repressive style of government, writing in 1795 'that under the pretext of a conspiracy by republicans, democrates, and levellers, a persecution has been excited against the friends of liberty by those who, with the word constitution in their mouths, are daily violating its first and best principles' (Frend, 1795: vii). Eventually, in 1806, Frend turned to a career as an actuary for the Rock Assurance Company – a post in which he could put to use the mathematical abilities which had originally gained for him a tutorship at Jesus.

After Frend's trial there were few indications of political or religious radicalism within Cambridge. Milner proudly wrote to Wilberforce in 1798: 'I don't believe Pitt was ever aware of how much consequence the expulsion of Frend was. It was the ruin of the Jacobinical party as *a University thing*, so that that party is almost entirely confined to Trinity College' (M. Milner, 1842: 162). Milner repeated similar claims to Lord Hardwicke in 1807 (in conjunction with a plea for the post of dean of York) writing that the

Government are not aware how much depended upon the successful management of that affair. There then flourished in this place a School of Jacobinism with Mr. Frend for its Leader which has never been able to hold up its head since his Banishment – It was crushed effectually; & at a most critical moment . . . Jacobinism is here scarcely heard of. Indeed, on all occasions, in public lectures, & in private conversation, I have exerted every nerve to crush that Monster. (BL, Add. 35658: 85–6)

Obviously, Milner's ecclesiastical ambitions do much to explain his high claims for his own role in cleansing the university of what he called

'Jacobinism'. In fact the decline of Cambridge radicalism can largely be explained by the ebbing fortunes of reform in the country as a whole after 1793 as Pitt's various repressive Acts began to take effect and as the growing threat from France heightened patriotic zeal. By 1798 Frend himself, along with other advocates of reform like Tooke and Burdett, passed a motion stating 'that this meeting will have nothing to do with politicks' (CUL, Add. 7887: 55). None the less, Milner's claims for the significance of the Frend trial are not completely far-fetched: with Frend's departure from the university we hear no more, for example, of his Cambridge Unitarian society which presumably served to promote political as well as religious radicalism. As Milner asserted in his letter to Hardwicke, the Frend case showed that the vice-chancellor's court which had been considered virtually defunct was capable of enforcing political and religious orthodoxy, and it took a brave don to risk Frend's fate by actively promoting the sort of views with which Frend was associated. The traditions of political and religious radicalism appear to have lasted longer at Trinity, the home of Frend's allies, Jones and Lambert (as Milner suggested in his letter to Wilberforce). But there, too, such views came under attack after Pitt and Pretyman appointed William Mansel master in 1798 'with a view to correct the disorders which had crept into the Society' (GM, 1820, I: 637). Significantly, Mansel had been actively involved in the prosecution of Frend (C. H. Cooper, 1842–1908, IV: 448) as well as having been a public opponent of political radicals like the duke of Bedford. It is probably significant that Lambert ceased to act as college bursar a year after Mansel's appointment as master. In any case by 1813 the college had been sufficiently purged of political and religious radicalism for Milner to praise 'the flourishing conditions to which Trinity College has been brought by the incessant attentions of its Right Rev. and Learned Master' (M. Milner, 1842: 169).

By the end of the eighteenth century, then, Cambridge had largely abandoned the reforming traditions in religion and politics which had been among the often unintended fruits of its whig loyalties. Thanks to the earl of Nottingham and his episcopal allies and, subsequently, the duke of Newcastle, most Cambridge dons had previously been persuaded that the best way of preserving the Church's privileges was by demonstrating clerical loyalty to the Revolutionary Settlement and the House of Hanover – a position which came to be equated with support for the whigs. But such a stance meant that at least some dons also imbibed an enthusiasm for the contractual views of government which (at least in retrospect) were used to justify the Glorious Revolution. While such political theories were generally used to defend the established order they also prompted some within Cambridge to argue that there were areas of both Church and State which needed reform to bring them into better conformity with the principles on which, it was claimed, the Glorious Revolution had been based.

Such reformist inclinations were strengthened by the closely related theological principles of the most conspicuous clerical defenders of the Hanoverian order who were particularly influential within Cambridge. The work of men such as Hoadly and Clarke encouraged their disciples to regard the Church as a human institution, the constitution and practices of which could be altered to accommodate the needs of the State and of social utility, and to argue that Christianity could be reduced to a few fundamental doctrines – thus rendering superfluous many of the Thirty-Nine Articles to which the Church of England continued to demand subscription. In a constitution such as that of eighteenth-century England where Church and State were inextricably intertwined, the view that one aspect of the established order – such as the creed or the liturgy of the Established Church – was open to change could have the effect of encouraging a more critical attitude to the constitution as a whole.

For much of the eighteenth century such unease about the character of the unreformed Church and State was counterbalanced by the need to combat the lingering threat of jacobitism and the less menacing, but more pervasive, clerical toryism with its nostalgia for a more paternalistic style of monarchy and a church that enjoyed more vigorous royal support. With the passing of jacobitism and the growing respectability of traditionally tory conceptions of Church and King after 1760, however, Cambridge whiggery was no longer so clearly a prop for the established order. For most in Cambridge their response to such changed circumstances was a gradual reshaping of their political and ecclesiastical views which would eventually take them into the camp of a revived tory party.

A minority of Cambridge dons, however, remained committed to the sort of principles that Thomas Rundle, the latitudinarian-inclined bishop of Derry (1735–43), had defined as those of a 'real Whig' in his posthumously published *Letters* (1789):

That government is an original compact between the governors and the governed, instituted for the good of the whole community; that in a limited monarchy, or more properly regal commonwealth, the majesty is in the people . . . that a parliamentary influence by places and pensions is inconsistent with the interest of the public . . . that as religion is of the utmost importance to every man, no person ought to suffer civil hardships for his religious persuasion, unless the tenets of his religion lead him to endeavour at the subversion of the establishment in church and state (*MR*, 1789, II: 505)

In the more troubled and critical period after 1760 such principles prompted some within Cambridge to advocate reform within both Church and State though, except for a fortunate few who were generally protégés of Grafton, such would-be reformers were unlikely to be placed in positions where they could influence the fortunes of the Church and some actually seceded from the Anglican fold.

By the end of the century, however, such representatives of Cambridge 'true whiggery' had become a rare species indeed, rendered almost extinct by the mounting challenges to the Established Church: the growing assertiveness of the dissenters in the 1780s, the menace of jacobinism and (after 1800) the agitation for Catholic Emancipation – developments which help to account for the increasingly tory complexion of the once whig university in the early nineteenth century. After the death of Pitt in 1806 Cambridge University elected in his place the whiggish Lord Henry Petty who had the support of Fox and the prince of Wales (Thorne, 1986, IV: 784) but he was defeated in the next year following a 'no popery' campaign. Another whig, John Smyth (university burgess, 1812–27), was elected in 1812 largely on account of the influence of his uncle, Lord Euston, who, in 1811, became the fourth duke of Grafton (ibid., V: 219). Apart from these two exceptions, however, the university did not elect another whig until 1829 when William Cavendish was chosen – probably because of his aristocratic connections and his academic prowess (he had been second wrangler). In 1831 both Cavendish and Viscount Palmerston (who had first been elected in 1811 as a tory) were defeated by candidates opposed to reform (Winstanley, 1940: 97n). Within early nineteenth-century Cambridge there were some notable Liberals such as Peacock, Sedgwick and Henslow but, as the last-mentioned remarked in his *Address to the reformers of the town of Cambridge* (1835), 'the professors of liberal principles are in a minority in the University' (p. 5). Cambridge's Liberals were indeed something of an embattled minority: in 1834 John Lamb, the whig master of Corpus, was excluded, on party grounds, from the normal succession to the vice-chancellorship while Thirlwall was excluded from his tutorship at Trinity and Dawes from his vice-mastership at Downing for publicly advocating university reform. Such incidents prompted Dr Allen, the whig bishop of Ely, to write to the prime minister, Lord Melbourne, in 1836 to warn him that Cambridge whiggery was in danger of being extinguished (Chadwick, 1970, I: 93). By the early decades of the nineteenth century, then, the majority of Cambridge dons had decided, like their late seventeenth- and early eighteenth-century counterparts, that in troubled and uncertain times the best defender of Church and Crown was the tory party.

8

The revival of revealed theology

For most of the eighteenth century the surest defence of the Revolutionary Settlement had been to emphasise its accord with reason or, at least, with a system of political philosophy such as that of Locke which was regarded as the outcome of a rational analysis of society. The Revolutionary Settlement, its defenders argued, entailed a rejection of such mystifications as the divine right of kings – views which still coloured the thinking of the chief opponents of the Hanoverian regime, the jacobites and their clerical allies, the nonjurors. Hanoverian apologists could point to the way in which jacobite sympathisers still looked for semi-magical confirmations of a monarch's legitimacy, such as touching for the King's Evil – a practice which the Hanoverian monarchs abandoned (J. C. D. Clark, 1985: 160–3). The Hanoverian regime also faced the opposite danger: that those who claimed to base their theories of government on rational principles might use such principles to mount a challenge to the status quo; but, before 1760, such critics were few, being kept in check by the need to ward off the still potent threat of jacobitism. After 1760, however, as jacobitism became only a memory, a growing number of the politically active began to argue that a truly rational system of politics entailed not a defence of the existing order but its reform or even, as in the case of Thomas Paine, its abolition. Such views were encouraged by the controversy sparked off by George III's use (or, as his opponents saw it, misuse) of his royal prerogative and were further stimulated by the increased scrutiny of the nature of the relationship between the government and the governed which accompanied the American Revolution. However, it was in the age of the French Revolution that the 'apostles of reason' came to assume a particularly menacing aspect when their opponents pointed out that the arguments of the *philosophes* and the revolutionaries, far from providing a defence of the British Constitution, were likely to sap its foundations.

While theological life had a momentum and rhythm of its own, the close entanglement of Church and State necessarily entailed that such political developments would help shape the nature of theological discourse. In the mid-eighteenth century, when the main threat to the existing order appeared to come from those who still looked back to the almost sacerdotal conception of monarchy associated with the Stuarts, it was natural that the dominant voices in the Established Church should emphasise the rational, unmystical aspects of Christianity – a theological climate which was conducive to the growth of the 'holy alliance', the association between Anglicanism and Newtonianism. However, by the late eighteenth century, when the main ideological enemies of Church and State were basing their attack not on tradition and sentiment but on an appeal to reason, it was not surprising that the Church's major spokesmen no longer placed such stress on a rationally constructed natural theology but rather turned more and more to those aspects of revealed religion which they regarded as transcending human reason.

Not that the mid-eighteenth-century Church had altogether neglected such features of Christianity: prominent prelates like Gibson or Berkeley had voiced suspicions of some of their clerical contemporaries' preoccupation with natural theology. None the less, along with primates such as the orthodox, high church John Potter (archbishop of Canterbury, 1737–47), the Church had been governed during this period by men such as Thomas Herring (archbishop of York, 1743–7; of Canterbury, 1747–57) and Matthew Hutton (archbishop of York, 1747–57; of Canterbury, 1757–8), whose writings and use of patronage indicate a remarkable degree of sympathy for the view that Christianity should be conceived primarily as a divine reconfirmation of a system of morality which could be largely arrived at by the independent use of reason. Such a view, after all, had been espoused by their predecessor at Canterbury, Archbishop Tillotson, whose sermons had left such a deep impression on the eighteenth-century Church. Tillotson regarded 'the great design of the Christian religion' as being 'to restore and reinforce the practice of the natural law, or, which is all one, of moral duties' (Sullivan, 1982: 65).

Herring, a true follower of Tillotson, was said 'carefully to have abstained from preaching upon the mysteries of religion; and to have confined himself to moral topics' (Ackerman, 1815, 1: 184). Like Tillotson – who, in his last letter, wrote of the Athanasian Creed that 'I wish we were well rid of it' (Reedy, 1985: 127) – Herring appears to have had no great liking for the emphatically Trinitarian Athanasian Creed; the case of a clergyman presented for not reading it after, as Herring put it, being 'grievously teased by folks who call themselves the "orthodox"' prompted the archbishop to exclaim, 'I abhor every tendency to the Trinity Controversy. The manner in which it is always managed is the disgrace and ruin of Christianity' (Rowden, 1916: 215). Herring also defended Hoadly's rationalistic account of the Eucharist and was sympathetic to

Clarke's Arian-inclined revision of the Book of Common Prayer – so much so that a reading of it, together with his reaction to the clamour over the Jewish Naturalisation Act of 1753, prompted him to observe to his latitudinarian protégé, John Jortin, 'into what times are we fallen, after so much light and so much appearance of moderation . . . What a thin covering of embers had kept down the fire of High-Church?' (Nichols, 1817–58, III: 465). Hutton, Herring's successor at Canterbury, was of a similar theological persuasion. He was an early patron of the anti-subscription campaigner, Blackburne, and was, according to him, well aware of his *avant-garde* views. Blackburne also claimed that he was not a 'stranger to the Archbishop's liberal notions on ecclesiastical affairs' (Rowden, 1916: 247).

It may well be that the reluctance of men such as Herring and Hutton to raise doctrinal matters sprang more from a fear of reviving the din of theological debate or from a belief that 'whereof we cannot speak it is best to be silent' than from heterodoxy, but, whatever their motives, such silence on the more transcendental aspects of Christianity had its consequences. In Cambridge, particularly, the *alma mater* of Tillotson, Herring and Hutton, the view that theological clarity (and charity) was best served by passing quickly over the more mystical aspects of Christianity provided fertile ground for the growth of a latitudinarian-inclined theology and even for the spread of Arianism and Socinianism. By 1765 an American clergyman was encouraging a young man at Eton to go to Oxford rather than Cambridge because of the 'cold Laodicean temper, and . . . low principles' of the latter (Caner, 1972: 123).

Though in the late eighteenth century the theological pendulum was once more swinging back to an emphasis on revealed rather than natural theology the latitudinarian tradition was too well established in Cambridge to be readily erased. The external circumstances of Church and State may have changed but the internal workings of a theological tradition which drew on such major Cambridge divines as Tillotson, Hoadly, Clarke and Edmund Law had a life of its own. Indeed, the Cambridge latitudinarian tradition produced a late flowering in the late eighteenth century in the work of three notable divines – Richard Watson, William Paley and John Hey – whose writings helped to keep alive that suspicion of doctrinal debate and emphasis on the large measure of conformity between Christianity and human reason which had been the hallmarks of latitudinarian theology. Ultimately, however, the strain of theology of which Watson, Paley and Hey were late, but able, representatives was largely to be supplanted by the work of divines who gave greater emphasis to matters of doctrine and to those areas of Christian belief which transcended human reason.

When Watson was appointed to the university's premier chair – the

Regius professorship of theology – in 1771 (a position he held until his death in 1816) he had spent little time on the systematic study of divinity. But to Watson this was almost an advantage since his chief goal was to simplify what he considered the unnecessarily complex and disputatious science of theology and reduce it to '*that* which the Father of the universe has written with the hand of what is called Nature . . . and . . . *that* which He hath declared to a peculiar people, by the mouth of his Son' (Watson, 1817: 377). These principles owed much to the example of his early mentor, Edmund Law, of whom Watson wrote: 'From my friendship with that excellent man, I derived much knowledge and liberality of sentiment in theology' (*ibid.*: 8). As Regius professor of divinity Watson resolved to reduce the study of theology 'into as narrow a compass as I could, for I determined to study nothing but my Bible, being much unconcerned about the opinions of councils, fathers, churches, bishops, and other men, as little inspired as myself'. Watson, then, was determined to instil in his students his own 'insuperable objection to every degree of dogmatical intolerance' and, to that end, would recognise in disputations no other authority than the New Testament – even articles of the Church were dismissed since they 'are not of divine authority' (*ibid.*: 39). Indeed, Watson went so far as to avoid any theological terms which he argued had no direct biblical warrant including terms like 'trinity', 'original sin' and 'sacrament'. '[L]et us not use unscriptural words', he wrote, 'to propagate unscriptural dogmas' (Wigmore-Beddoes, 1971: 22).

While Regius professor of divinity, Watson produced a six-volume collection of theological tracts which provocatively included works of dissenting theologians as well as classics of Anglican latitudinarian theology such as Samuel Clarke's Boyle lectures and the *Reasonableness of Christianity* by John Locke – the latter Watson regarded, as he remarked to the Unitarian Tyrwhitt, as the man who 'has done more for the enlargement of the human faculties, and for the establishment of pure Christianity, than any author I am acquainted with' (*ibid.*: 407). In the preface to this collection of tracts Watson again asserted, in the manner of Chillingworth or Blackburne, that the Bible alone is the basis of Protestant belief and he dismissed charges that he was 'an encourager of sceptical and latitudinarian principles' (Watson, 1971, i: xvi). Not surprisingly, however, Watson's approach to the teaching of theology was the subject of considerable controversy: in 1787 one don reported that he 'treated an argument brought in the school in Defence of our Saviour's Divinity, with a sneer' (Emmanuel College, Cambridge, MS 269: 118), while Watson himself acknowledged that his methods 'gained me no credit with the hierarchy' though 'it produced a liberal spirit in the University' (Watson, 1817: 39).

Among those who came under Watson's influence was William Paley, like Watson a protégé of Edmund Law and an admirer of Locke's *Reasonableness of Christianity* (Meadley, 1810: 80). Watson accepted from the young Paley a controversial disputation question which cast doubt on the eternity of hell's torments, though Watson obligingly allowed him to argue the opposite case when Hugh Thomas, the master of Paley's college (Christ's), took fright at such theological audacity (*ibid.*: 30–2). This incident was to epitomise Paley's more general approach to theological questions, since he combined a remarkable open-mindedness with a reluctance to disturb the peace of the Church. Thus, although during the Feathers Tavern subscription controversy Paley was 'personally attached to many of the reforming party, and avowedly favourable to their claims', he declined to sign the petition, declaring with characteristically self-deprecating humour that 'he could not afford to keep a conscience' (Lynam, 1825, 1: 15). None the less, Paley did publish a pamphlet defending his patron, Edmund Law, from the attacks that resulted from his criticisms of the practice of subscription. Paley himself made it apparent in this pamphlet, which was written 'in the boldest tone of latitudinarian enquiry' (*ibid.*: 16), that he favoured abolition of subscription and defended the right of those who felt some reservations about the Thirty-Nine Articles to remain within the Established Church – an issue on which he invoked the support of 'the excellent Hoadly'. Summarising his objections to both subscription and the continuing restraints on the dissenters, Paley argued 'That this experiment of leaving men at liberty, and points of doctrine at large, has been attended with the improvements of religious knowledge, where and whenever it has been tried' (Paley, 1845: 565). Paley returned to the issue of subscription in his *Principles of moral and political philosophy* (1785), a work based on the lectures he gave as a tutor at Christ's from 1768 to 1775 in conjunction with John Law, through whom he came to know his colleague's father, Bishop Edmund Law (to whom the *Principles* was dedicated). Paley devoted a complete chapter (Book II, chapter 22) to the subject of 'subscription to articles of religion' in which he again made it apparent that the Church would be best served by the abolition of the practice since, although they served 'some purposes of order and tranquillity', they were 'attended with serious inconveniences'. However, he argued that subscription did not require 'the actual belief of each and every individual proposition contained in them' since these formularies were intended to do no more than prevent those hostile to the Church of England like the papists, the anabaptists and puritans from gaining ecclesiastical office. Paley also expressed the hope that these 'articles of faith' might be transformed 'into articles of peace'. This was a section that Paley's critics were to point to as an example of his sophistry: the Cambridge Unitarian Wakefield, for example, referred to it as Paley's 'shuffling chapter' (Wakefield, 1804, I: 129).

Paley's highly qualified attitude to subscription was of a piece with his theology and ecclesiology more generally. Like Hoadly before him, he regarded the Church as entirely a human institution: 'A religious establishment', he wrote in his *Principles*, 'is no part of Christianity: it is only the means of inculcating it', consequently, 'the authority of a church establishment is founded in its utility' (Paley, 1845: 138–9). Subscription, then, could not be justified on the grounds that it was the Church's mission to protect doctrinal purity, though Paley was prepared to concede that the practice might be justified on utilitarian grounds as a means of preserving ecclesiastical order. This appeal to utility was, of course, characteristic of Paley's work as a whole. Ethical issues were resolved by an appeal to the principle of 'the greatest happiness of the greatest number' – though with the added sanction of reward or punishment in the next life. In common with the latitudinarian tradition Paley saw Christianity as primarily an ethical system: 'If I were to describe', he wrote in his *Evidences of Christianity* (1794), 'in a very few words, the scope of Christianity, as a *revelation*, I should say, that it was to influence the conduct of human life, by establishing the proof of a future state of reward and punishment' (*ibid*.: 366). The *Evidences* itself was a characteristically lucid distillation of much of eighteenth-century apologetics coolly assessing the objections to the historical claims of Christianity in the almost forensic manner of Thomas Sherlock dismissing the critics of the historicity of the Resurrection in *The tryal of the witnesses . . .* (1729). The *Evidences*, which was intended to meet the objections of the foes of Christianity rather than to discuss areas of doctrinal debate, was a largely uncontroversial and enormously popular work which finally achieved for Paley preferment apart from that dispensed by his patron, Law.

But, though he was among the most widely read divines of his age, Paley was denied a bishopric – an indication that his theological and political opinions were no longer altogether in accord with the dominant views in Church and State. According to one account Pitt's proposal to advance Paley to the episcopate was vetoed by George III with the words: 'What? Pigeon Paley?' or 'Not orthodox, not orthodox' (M. L. Clarke, 1974: 43). The regal reference to pigeons was an allusion to Paley's famous chapter on property in the *Principles* in which he compares the labour of ninety-nine pigeons for the weakest of their flock with the laws of property which compel large numbers of human beings to work for the benefit of an individual who 'oftentimes [is] the feeblest and worst of the whole set' (Paley, 1845: 23). Though Paley then proceeded to justify the laws of property on the grounds of utility, the striking passage aroused doubts about his political soundness which were further excited by his strenuous attack on the slave trade – a practice which, he wrote, called into question whether Britain was 'fit to be trusted' with its mighty empire (*ibid.*: 48). None the less, Paley rallied to the defence of the established order during the revolutionary period and produced in 1792 his *Reasons for contentment, addressed to the labouring part of the British public.*

Paley's hostility to the French Revolution and his general reluctance to advocate fundamental change in ecclesiastical or civil matters prompted some of his critics to portray him as a time-server: Benjamin Flower, for example, wrote in 1796 of Paley and Watson as 'apostatizing from many excellent sentiments they once professed, and floating down the stream of general corruption' (p. xiv), while Gilbert Wakefield, who admired Paley's works for their 'practical good sense', spoke of him as 'sophisticat-[ing] too frequently against his convictions, in vindication of his craft' (Wakefield, 1813: 167–8). Paley was vulnerable to such charges because he had attempted to marry together two largely incompatible partners: an intellectual tradition which sought to reduce the nature of government and society to first principles through the use of reason, and a political and religious system which was increasingly inclined to justify itself more in terms of tradition and sentiment than reason. Characteristically, Paley, after describing the unreformed electoral system as 'a flagrant incongruity in the constitution', proceeded to defend it on grounds of 'public utility' and opposed any reform except perhaps some reduction in the patronage of the Crown (Paley, 1845: 120). But, though Paley might justify the existing constitution on such grounds, his style of argument gave little comfort to those who wished to invoke the importance of tradition or a view of society or the State based on other than pragmatic considerations. Thus Paley contemptuously dismissed the growing revival of Filmerite ideas of monarchy with the comment that 'the divine right of kings is like the divine right of constables' – a remark that is said to have further alienated George III's regard from Paley (Barker, 1948: 252). None the less, Paley's works proved remarkably popular, particularly at Cambridge where the *Principles* became a set text within a year of its publication, thanks to Frend's ally, Thomas Jones of Trinity (Meadley, 1810: 145), and the *Evidences* continued to be prescribed until 1921 (Somervell, 1965: 19). Paley's popularity was more a tribute to his remarkable clarity of thought and crystalline prose than to the longevity of his views. His popularity was also an indication that at a time when the established order was re-equipping its intellectual armoury it was still prepared to press into service older weapons that belonged more to the needs of the earlier than the late eighteenth century – the latter being a period when Church and State were challenged not by an appeal to tradition but rather by reformers and revolutionaries who claimed the mandate of reason.

Even in his own lifetime Paley's works were criticised by a younger generation with a different conception of the role of Christianity. Thomas Gisborne, a young Cambridge evangelical, was prompted to publish a critique of Paley's *Principles* in the fateful year of 1789 because this work had become part of the standard undergraduate curriculum. Gisborne condemned Paley's emphasis on utility as the touchstone of morality both because it was 'incompatible with the precepts of Scripture' (p. 7) and because it invested any individual 'with an unlimited dispensing power, authorising him to take the government out of the hands of God' (p. 25). Gisborne's fellow-evangelical, Wilberforce, regarded this pamphlet as a conclusive refutation of Paley's ethical views (Le Mahieu, 1976: 157). Another of Paley's critics, Peter Roberts, focused his attack on the *Evidences* and in a pamphlet of 1796 he drew attention to the way in which Paley passed over Christ's 'attributes of Creator and Redeemer of man' (p. 60). The overall effect of Paley's work, he concluded, was to place so much emphasis on the secular character of morality that 'the first table of the decalogue' – those commandments concerned with man's duty to God – were allowed 'to fade from the memory' (p. 67).

By early Victorian times a number of influential Cambridge dons regarded Paley's work with outright hostility. In about 1837 William Whewell and Julius Hare publicly criticised the continued use of Paley's ethical system (Whewell, 1862: 277) – an attack repeated in Whewell's later *Lectures on the history of moral philosophy* (1862) where he wrote of Paley, and the Cambridge utilitarian tradition on which he drew, that: 'The bright and firm precepts of Christianity, like new pieces on an old garment, shone here and there the more conspicuously for the sordid, and flimsy ground on which they are placed' (p. 179). Like Gisborne before him, Adam Sedgwick in his *Discourse on the studies of the university* (1837) also attacked Paley's utilitarianism as a violation of Christianity and as an invitation to sophistry since morality would be based on 'the fluctuation of opinion' (p. 63). Sedgwick traced back the inadequacies in Paley's work to the dominance of Locke's *Essay* within the university, which had undermined any concept of an innate moral sense (p. 57). Hare, Whewell and Sedgwick were all prominent Cambridge intellectuals who were linked with the broad churchmen and their condemnation of Paley is, then, a striking indication of the gulf that separated eighteenth-century latitudinarianism from the theology of even broad church Victorians and underlines the extent of the change in religious outlook which took place in the era of the French Revolution.

Closely aligned with Paley's writings were those of his Cambridge contemporary, John Hey (fellow of Sidney Sussex from 1758 and from 1780 to 1795 foundation Norrisian professor of divinity). Like Paley, Hey was fundamentally an apologist for the existing order in Church and State but, again like Paley, he sometimes defended established practices and beliefs in a manner which also suggested their inadequacies. Thus Hey defended the subscription to the Articles but did so in a way that largely drained the requirement of any clear meaning. In his *Lectures in divinity* (1796) he argued, in a manner reminiscent of Edmund Law, that since the Articles were formulated to meet the needs of a particular historical situation they were subject to 'a tacit reformation' with the passage of time. The Articles should therefore be interpreted not simply in a grammatical sense but also with reference to their historical setting – consequently their literal meaning might no longer apply (1841 ed., I: 372–92). His theological lectures provided a systematic treatment of Christian doctrine but he avoided areas of controversy remarking that 'We do not know enough of the mysterious doctrines of religion to quarrel about them' (*ibid.*: 412); elsewhere, when discussing the Restoration period, he praised 'those eminent men who were called *Latitudinarian* Divines' for avoiding such doctrinal controversy' (*ibid.*, II: 159). Hey's delicate handling of the subscription issue prompted Dyer to describe him as being 'evidently for what has been called the Latitudinarian [position], that is, for taking them in any sense they will, under all circumstances, fairly admit' (1824, II: 109). Like Paley, and others influenced by the latitudinarian tradition, Hey viewed Christianity as a divine confirmation of a system of morality which was potentially discoverable by reason: 'the Christian religion', he wrote, 'seems to make good provision for the generality of the *people*, considered in contra-distinction to the learned or philosophical' (1841, I: 237). Though Hey was sufficiently admired within the university to be twice re-elected to the Norrisian chair his lectures do appear to have provoked some controversy since there were abortive moves to prevent their publication at the university press in 1796 (Corpus Christi College, Cambridge, Hartshorne MS XXVI: 202). Outside the university, too, there were those who viewed Hey's theological lectures with some suspicion; thus the *New annual register* voiced doubts about the orthodoxy of his work and its effect on morality (Murray, 1975: 94).

Like Paley's *Principles*, Hey's lectures on morality, which were delivered while he was a tutor at Sidney Sussex between 1760 and 1779, contained a number of hints of sympathy with reforming causes though their overall effect was to provide a defence of the existing order. Just as Hey argued in relation to subscription to the Articles that time brought about a 'tacit reformation' so, too, in the political sphere he saw a similar evolutionary process at work. Thus he described Charles I as having made the mistake of attempting to rule in the manner of Henry VII 'notwithstanding all the improvements which in the meantime had taken place in knowledge of the ends of Government, and in social manners'. In Hey's view the present French crown was making a similar mistake: 'I look', he wrote, 'upon the French monarch's keeping his subjects in subjection as he now does to be of the same kind with despotic tyranny' (Sidney Sussex College, Cambridge, MS 10.20.1. VII: 2897; 2915). The gradual development which, he argued, characterised religious and political institutions was also reflected in the law – an area where he saw the need for further improvement in his own society (*ibid.*, II: 625; VI: 2259).

Hey shared with Paley the utilitarian assumptions that had been popularised by earlier Cambridge moralists such as Gay and Rutherforth. He defined a virtuous action as one agreeable to God but then proceeded to argue that the will of God can be discerned by whether or not an action 'would promote the happiness of mankind' (*ibid.*, I: 131). He was sceptical of what he calls 'the imaginary Society among individuals in a State of Nature' (*ibid.*, II: 751) though he still appeared to retain some sympathy for Lockean views of government since he described both the Restoration and the Glorious Revolution in terms of a 'compact' between king and people (*ibid.*, III: 3001; VII: 2993). As befitted a utilitarian, he dismissed the concept of natural rights as implying nothing more than that a certain practice was likely to 'make men happier' (*ibid.*, III: 957). For Hey, as for Hoadly and Paley, the Church was essentially an institution concerned with the good order of society rather than a divinely sanctioned body; consequently, the authority of the Church to prescribe and enforce practices such as subscription should be kept to a minimum: 'the ends of religious society only require that such decency and regularity be maintained as is naturally productive of good sentiments; and therefore no member of a religious society need be absolutely compelled to observe its ordinances' (*ibid.*, IX: 2521). Predictably, Hey advocated both the abolition of subscription and the repeal of civil penalties for dissenters. Hey resembled Paley in another respect: he, too, was proposed for a bishopric but was denied it (*GM*, 1815, I: 371) – a decision which reflects the growing caution with which the views of Hey (and Paley) on the nature of Church and State were viewed by those whose task it was to defend the British old regime in an age of revolution.

Whatever doubts Watson, Paley and Hey may have voiced about particular features of the Church there was no doubt about their commitment to preserve the Establishment. But among those within late eighteenth-century Cambridge with intellectual and personal ties with these three divines were some who, by leaving the Established Church, exposed those of a latitudinarian disposition to guilt by association. It is striking how many of the Cambridge Unitarians were associated with Watson or with Edmund Law, the mentor of Watson, Paley and (at least, intellectually) Hey. Like Law, Watson remained on friendly terms with both Wakefield and Jebb even after they had made their Unitarian views public – indeed, Watson went so far as to write that 'I am desirous that my name should go down to posterity as the friend of Dr. John Jebb' (Watson, 1817: 62–3), while Paley's biographer wrote of Jebb that 'Mr. Paley shared largely in his esteem and confidence' (Meadley, 1810: 34). Appropriately, Watson and Paley were among the supporters of Jebb's proposed academic reforms (Lynam, 1825, 1: 17). Watson was also a friend and correspondent of Tyrwhitt, one of the first Cambridge Unitarians (Wakefield, 1804, 1: 489). Criticisms of the theological opinions of his patron, the duke of Grafton, prompted Watson to deny that Unitarians were other than true Christians (Watson, 1817: 47) – an opinion shared by Hey who took the view that the doctrine of the Trinity was so opaque to human reason that no clear line could be drawn between Socinianism and orthodoxy (Wigmore-Beddoes, 1971: 22–3). Such admissions that there was no clear theological divide between late eighteenth-century latitudinarian theology and anti-Trinitarianism help to explain why men such as Watson, Paley and Hey did not advance to an ecclesiastical eminence commensurate with their considerable abilities.

Though the Cambridge latitudinarian tradition was still ably represented in the late eighteenth century by divines such as Watson, Paley and Hey, other figures within the Church were focusing theological discussion on relatively neglected doctrinal issues which were eventually to overshadow and almost obliterate latitudinarian theology. The links that an increasingly embattled Anglican Church began to discern between latitudinarian divines like Law and Watson and Unitarian foes of the Establishment like Jebb and Wakefield were to hasten this eclipse of the latitudinarian tradition. George III was generally hostile to latitudinarian-inclined clergy (Every, 1956: 178) and after 1760 the Church turned a more sympathetic face to divines such as George Horne of Magdalen College, Oxford, a tireless defender of revealed, as against natural, theology in season and out of season. In 1756, for example, Horne had produced a pamphlet defending his fellow Hutchinsonians – the advocates of a biblically based cosmology as an alternative to that of Newton – against the charge that they 'den[ied] *the existence of moral duties, because we preach faith, the root from whence they spring*' (p. 8). Horne then went on to argue that natural religion was 'a religion without the *knowledge of God, or the hope of salvation*; which is deism' (p. 14). Around the same period he wrote of Tillotson – the most influential advocate of the view that Christianity consisted primarily of a set of moral duties which could largely be arrived at by the use of reason – that he 'makes Christianity good for nothing but to keep societies in order the better that there should be no Christ than that it should disturb societies' (Jacob, 1981: 98). Before the reign of George III such views were unlikely to secure preferment; as Horne bitterly remarked some time in the reign of George II, the Hutchinsonians were passed over by a group of bishops 'who are all entered into a league never to promote them'. For Horne this was 'a time when . . . the smoke of Arianism, Deism and Laodiceanism [a synonym for latitudinarianism] have darkened the sun and air' though the Hutchinsonians could pride themselves on the fact that 'they make no sect or schism – contradict none of the articles of faith but are fast & firm friends to the church of england in opposition to all jesuits whether popish or protestant' (CUL, Add. 8134/ B/1: 2). After 1760, however, Horne no longer languished in obscurity; he became a friend of both North and Liverpool and steadily rose up the ecclesiastical ladder, being made a royal chaplain in 1771, dean of Canterbury in 1781 and bishop of Norwich in 1790. Clearly, the ecclesiastical climate had changed.

Horne's belated advancement was symptomatic of a more general sympathy for an emphasis on revealed theology within the late eighteenth-century Church – a tendency which was strengthened and made more explicit by the debate which surrounded the Feathers Tavern Petition of 1772 and which was to be strengthened still further by the reaction to the French Revolution (Norman, 1976: 16). The subscription debate prompted a number of influential clergymen to spell out their reservations about the latitudinarian style of theology. Thomas Secker (archbishop of Canterbury, 1758–68), a determined opponent of Blackburne's *Confessional*, regretted that 'the distinguishing doctrines of the Gospel' had been 'neglected too much' while the Church had 'dwelt disproportionately on morality and natural religion' (Rowden, 1916: 299). Within Cambridge Samuel Hallifax, in his university sermons directed at the Feathers Tavern petitioners, abhorred the way in which the

doctrines of the Church of England, have been adulterated or explained away by divines, both within and without the Establishment; in order, as is pretended, to simplify the articles of faith into a consistent system of *Rational* Religion: indeed, so *very* Rational as to have almost nothing to do with Revelation, if by that word we understand any truths, not immediately deducible from the light of reason. (1772: 13)

Under the impact of the French Revolution such criticisms were to grow in intensity, as the work of the influential Samuel Horsley (LL B Trinity Hall, 1758; bishop of St David's, 1788–93; of Rochester, 1793–1802; and of St Asaph, 1802–6), a close friend of Hallifax (Horsley, 1813: 246), brings out. In 1791 he attacked the proposition 'That Moral Duties constitute the whole, or by far the better part of practical Christianity' (Norman, 1976: 39) and in 1796 spoke critically of 'Some of the philosophizing divines of later times, who, under the mask of zeal for religion, have done it more disservice than its open enemies' (Horsley, 1816, I: 240–1). Along with the style of theology which had characterised the latitudinarians, Horsley also attacked their ecclesiology and, in particular, the view of the Church which had been advanced by Hoadly, whom Horsley referred to as 'a republican Bishop' (Watson, 1817: 43). 'He who thinks of God's servants', wrote Horsley in 1790, 'as the meer servants of the State, is out of the Church, – severed from it by a kind of self excommunication' (Legg, 1914: 392). Consistent with such anti-Erastian views Horsley argued in the House of Lords in 1804 that the State could not defrock a clergyman since 'to extinguish the sacred character, is more than any act of the Legislature can effect' (Horsley, 1813: 424). Not surprisingly, Horsley rejected not only Hoadly's ecclesiology but also his contractual view of the State. In his famous 1793 sermon on the anniversary of the execution of Charles I, delivered shortly after the guillotining of Louis XVI, Horsley explicitly rejected both the concept of a state of nature and of a social contract since 'Mankind from the beginning never existed otherwise than in society and under government' (Horsley, 1816, III: 288). Though in the same sermon he also rejected a Filmerite view of divine-right monarchy (*ibid.*: 293), elsewhere Horsley appears to be advocating something very like the concept of passive obedience which Hoadly had laboured to overthrow: 'the peaceable submission of the subject', wrote Horsley, 'to the very worst of kings is one of the most peremptory precepts of Christianity' (*ibid.*, I: 141–2).

After 1789 an increasing number of churchmen echoed Horsley's *caveats* about the dangers of neglecting revealed religion. In 1792 Bishop Barrington of Durham warned his clergy that the doctrines of Christianity 'have been of LATE YEARS TOO MUCH NEGLECTED: as if doctrines of faith were subordinate parts of Christianity' (J. Overton, 1802: 40–1). When preaching before the bishop of Norwich in 1794 Charles Davy, a former fellow of Caius, warned against the influence of those who 'have distinguished themselves by philosophizing upon Christianity, by professing to clear and simplify and divest it of Mystery' (1794: 7–8). By 1800 an anonymous advocate for a view of the Church based on the apostolic succession was lamenting 'the fatal tendency of genuine principles of latitudinarianism' (Murray, 1975: 123).

While such reaffirmations of the importance of revealed religion issued from the heart of the Establishment these same preoccupations, in greatly intensified form, could be found in the writings of the evangelicals – representatives of a movement which, in the late eighteenth century, was still largely at the periphery of the Church but which, by the nineteenth century, was to assume an increasingly important role and even to begin to penetrate the hierarchy. Predictably, the writings of the evangelicals express that same sense of reaction against the effects of latitudinarian theology which can be found in the works of late eighteenth-century high churchmen. However, the evangelicals regarded such latitudinarian influences with particular hostility since the whole spirit of their movement involved a rejection of forms of religion which rested on the exercise of human reason rather than the confrontation of human inadequacy with Revealed Truth as expressed in the Bible. Thus Wilberforce made it his mission to eradicate 'the deadly leaven of Hoadly's latitudinarian views which had spread to an alarming extent among the clergy' (R. I. and S. Wilberforce, 1838, 1: 129). In his influential work, *A practical view of the prevailing religious system of professed Christians in the higher and middle classes in this country contrasted with real Christianity* (1797), Wilberforce decried the work of the late seventeenth-century divines:

> Towards the close of the last century, the divines of the Established Church ... professed to make it their chief object to inculcate the moral and practical precepts of Christianity, which they conceived to have been before too much neglected; but without ... pointing out how the practical precepts of Christianity grew out of her peculiar doctrines, and are inseparably connected with them. By this fatal error, the very genius and essential nature of Christianity imperceptibly underwent a change. (1958 ed.: 114–15)

Wilberforce's evangelical mentor, Isaac Milner, also decried the way in which many of his fellow-clergy had 'substituted, instead of Revelation, what they have called plain common sense; and the miserable fragments of our depraved faculty of reason, in the room of the influence of God's Holy Spirit' (I. Milner, 1820, 1: 108). His brother and fellow-evangelical, Joseph, in his critique of the works of Gibbon and Hume, attributed to Locke 'the fashion in introducing a pompous parade of *reasoning* into religion' (1781: 154). 'The reason of man', he added in a passage which helps explain the evangelicals' rather lukewarm attitude to human learning, 'in his present depraved state, is not only not friendly, but is most directly inimical to this Spirit of God' (p. 157). Joseph Milner held Cambridge, along with Locke, as being particularly responsible for the spread of rationalistic religion and he referred with disapproval to Gilbert Burnet's famous description of the Cambridge latitude-men – it was they, Milner wrote, who 'administered the poison, and posterity felt the malignant effect to this hour', so much so that 'the Church of England has drooped, as to every holy purpose, ever since this proud attempt of employing reason to correct the Gospel'. 'Philosophy and Christianity', he insisted, 'will not, cannot be united' (pp. 252–3). Erasmus Middleton (a young evangelical who, having been expelled from St Edmund Hall, Oxford, in 1763 as a 'methodist', enrolled briefly at King's) expressed similar views to Joseph Milner in his *Biographia evangelica* (1786). As a result of the excesses of the puritans in the mid-seventeenth century, he wrote, a new sect of theologians arose who 'were *Rationalists* more than humble Disciples of *Christ*, and, from the great laxness of their Principles, received the wild long Title of *Latitudinarians*' – a 'self taught sect' which 'urged the Powers of a corrupted, blinded and fallen *Reason*'. 'From this epoch', he continued, 'we may trace almost all our current Heterodoxies and Corruptions' – a situation for which Cambridge was particularly to blame since it was there that 'the prevalent Heterodoxy in the Establishment took its Rise' (1786, IV: 508–10).

Early in its history the evangelical movement had been closely associated with Oxford – the home of Wesley and Whitefield – but the expulsion of six students from St Edmund Hall in 1763 for 'methodism' made Cambridge appear a more attractive institution to those with evangelical connections. Thereafter Cambridge became more and more closely associated with the evangelical movement – ironically, since the evangelicals stood for a negation of almost all the features of the latitudinarian tradition which had hitherto largely prevailed within the university; it was as if, by an application of Newton's third law, the existing theological order had produced an equal and opposite reaction. There was, however, one area where the latitudinarians and the evangelicals – in so many other ways the theological mirror-image of each other – shared common ground: both tended to view forms of church government as being among 'the things indifferent' to the core of Christianity, though both were prepared to accept the hierarchical order of the Church of England to keep the ecclesiastical peace. This common characteristic of the two movements is encapsulated in the ambiguous use of the term 'low churchman' – a label that was, in the early eighteenth century, applied to the latitudinarians but by the nineteenth century was used as a synonym for an evangelical. (This ambiguity is, indeed, one reason why the term 'latitudinarian', rather than 'low churchman', is useful when describing developments in the late eighteenth-century Church even though it cannot be linked with a clearly defined theological programme or a tightly organised party.)

In consequence of the evangelicals' strongly individualistic style of piety it is difficult to point to institutional influences in the early formation of Cambridge evangelicalism. Like the spirit that blows where it will, the early Cambridge evangelicals appear to have turned to this form of Anglican belief as the result of random and highly personal experiences. The beliefs of William Grimshaw, who helped to establish the strong traditions of evangelicalism in Yorkshire, owed nothing to his time at Christ's from 1726 to 1731 nor, as far as we know, to any outside influences apart from his reading of seventeenth-century puritan divines. John Berridge, who was at Clare as an undergraduate and a fellow from 1734 to 1755, remained closer to the university than Grimshaw, both geographically and in terms of personal contact, but his only theological debt to the university appears to have been one of reaction; while a fellow at Clare, writes his evangelical biographer, he 'drank into the Socinian scheme to such a degree, as to lose all serious impressions, and discontinue private prayer for the space of ten years' (Whittingham, 1838: 5). When he preached at the university church in 1759 he 'gave great offence to the University' (Dyer, 1824, II: 122–3) and prompted a series of sermons from Samuel Hallifax on St Paul's doctrine of justification by faith (in which he explicitly attacked Berridge) and a critical pamphlet from John Green (the future bishop of Lincoln). Green was particularly wary of what he considered were the socially levelling implications of Berridge's preaching and warned that 'it may be and has often been dangerous to the publick peace, to raise in the vulgar too high notions of their favour and interest in heaven' (1760: 24).

Despite such opposition Berridge's preaching at Everton attracted some disciples from Cambridge: by 1768 Dyer noted 'some gentlemen of the University . . . were a good deal formed in Mr. Berridge's school' (1824, II: 122–3). Among the most notable of his Cambridge followers was Rowland Hill, a St John's undergraduate who formed a small society of about a dozen junior members who shared his evangelical beliefs – though Hill regarded the university in general as being 'in total darkness' (W. Jones, 1834: 18). After 1764 Hill regularly attended Berridge's services at Everton but this, together with his own preaching and religious teaching within the university and the town, exposed him to the displeasure of William Powell, the master of St John's, who thought Hill's behaviour smacked of contempt of authority and so refused him a testimonial when he took his BA in 1769. With the partial exception of Charles Simeon, Hill was, however, the only notable Cambridge evangelical who was influenced by Berridge. He appears eventually to have decided that Cambridge did not provide the right sort of recruits for his mission; by 1788 he was telling the prominent evangelical layman John Thornton that 'I am not very fond of College youths; they are apt to be lofty and lazy and delicate' (Whittingham, 1838: 461).

Henry Venn was more successful in cultivating followers within the university but, again, his evangelical beliefs appear to have owed little to his time at Cambridge as an undergraduate and fellow of Queens' from 1742 to 1757: as his son wrote, it was not until he left Cambridge 'that he became acquainted with any of those preachers who are usually known by the name of Evangelical' (H. Venn, n.d.: xii). When he moved in 1771 to

Yelling – a living about twelve miles from Cambridge – Venn set out to foster evangelical beliefs within the university; by the following year he could comment that 'There are some excellent young men at college, who come to me from the University' (J. Venn, 1834: 193). These links with the university were further strengthened while his son, John, was an undergraduate at Sidney Sussex from 1777 to 1781 – through him Venn senior came to know his most influential protégé, Charles Simeon, who later described Henry Venn as 'a father, an instructor, and a most bright example' (Carus, 1847: 23). Though Venn and, to a smaller extent, Berridge could provide some support for those within the university who shared their beliefs, Cambridge evangelicalism still remained a delicate plant – something which was underlined by the refusal of Trinity to take young John Venn in 1777 because of his father's evangelical convictions. John Venn also attributed his failure to obtain a fellowship at Sidney Sussex to prejudice against evangelicals and became so disenchanted with the university that he wrote of it: 'The very air of Cambridge seems infected by the breath of anti-Christ: everything serious dies in it' (V. H. H. Green, 1964: 238). If evangelicalism was to survive within the university it needed some form of institutional support – something that was first provided by Magdalene.

During the mastership of the Hon. Barton Wallop (1774–81), a fox-hunting absentee cleric, the management of Magdalene was in the hands of three fellows – Samuel Hey, the president (vice-master), William Farish, the mathematics tutor, and Henry Jowett, the classics tutor – who were 'patrons and promoters of that religion which bears the nearest affinity to that of the Reformation' (Sargent, 1833: 40). They, in turn, attracted to the college earnest young aspiring clergymen who wanted to train for the ministry in a more godly environment than prevailed in the normal run of colleges. In particular, Magdalene was the natural home for beneficiaries of the Elland Society, a body founded by Henry Venn and other evangelicals, to support would-be ordinands at the university. Though Wallop was replaced as master by the ultra-latitudinarian Peckard, Magdalene's reputation as a haven for evangelicals persisted: in 1786 it was remarked that the college was 'the general resort of young men seriously impressed with a sense of religion' (C. H. E. Smyth, 1940: 215). Peckard's successor as master, William Gretton (1797–1813) who protested against the college being turned into 'a nest of Methodists' (Balleine, 1951: 100), had the consolation of seeing Magdalene being replaced as the pre-eminent evangelical college by Queens', thanks to the vigorous efforts of Isaac Milner (Dyer, 1824, II (supplement): 23). Under Gretton's successor, the Hon. George Neville (1813–54) Magdalene's evangelical credentials declined still further to the point where the college differed little from any other (Walsh, 1958: 508) despite the continued use of 'Maudlin' as undergraduate slang for an evangelical.

It was with the election of Isaac Milner as president of Queens' in 1788 that Cambridge evangelicalism acquired a representative with the necessary political skills to entrench the movement in the university – just as it took the equally formidable (and controversial) Bentley to establish Newtonian natural philosophy in the undergraduate curriculum. Milner owed his evangelical faith to the influence of his brother, Joseph Milner (1744–97), who, while at Catharine Hall (from which he took a BA in 1766), had lost his evangelical faith after studying Locke, Samuel Clarke and other works of 'Cambridge metaphysics' (Walsh, 1959: 176), though he had subsequently recovered it in ample measure while serving as a schoolmaster at Hull. Henry Venn, who heard him preach there in 1771, described him as 'by much the ablest minister that I ever heard open his mouth for Christ' (J. Venn, 1834: 165). Joseph Milner was to do much to provide an historical basis for the evangelical movement through his *History of the Church of Christ* – a work shaped by Milner's reaction against 'profane philosophy' (*ibid.*: 178) – which was gradually published in five volumes (1794–7, 1803, 1809) with the assistance of Isaac. Having been converted by his brother, Isaac Milner was in turn to win over William Wilberforce to the evangelical faith when he accompanied him on a continental grand tour in 1784 – thereafter Milner was a lifelong correspondent and confidant of Wilberforce. As I have shown in chapter 7, Milner resolutely used his influence as president of Queens' to advance the careers of fellow-evangelicals both within Queens' and in other sympathetic colleges, notably Trinity Hall and Magdalene.

Along with Milner the other great (but very different) influence in consolidating Cambridge evangelicalism was Charles Simeon. While Milner represented the evangelical church militant Simeon worked more by persuasion and example, though in later life he used his considerable private means to establish the Simeon Trust, the object of which was to buy advowsons so that evangelical ministers could be appointed to influential livings at a time when many other patrons, both clerical and lay, were hostile to 'earnest Christians'. By Simeon's death in 1836 the Trust had twenty-one livings in its gift (Pollard and Hennell, 1959: 14). Simeon's own early religious history again displays the strongly individualistic character of evangelical belief: as an undergraduate at King's in 1779 he was won over to the evangelical cause as a result of private religious reading occasioned by the requirement that he take college communion. Once his new theological orientation had been established, however, he was encouraged in his beliefs by Berridge (who, in 1782, refers to a 'Mr. Simeon . . . [who] has just made his appearance in the Christian hemisphere' (Whittingham, 1838: 418)) and, more importantly, by Henry Venn. Venn was so impressed by his new protégé that in 1784 he declared to Lady Mary Fitzgerald: 'I have good news to send you from Cambridge – Mr. Simeon is made for great usefulness'; he added that 'There are nearly twenty promising young students' (J. Venn, 1834: 374). Simeon also received the support of Christopher Atkinson, tutor of Trinity Hall and vicar of St Edwards where he had been preaching the evangelical faith to a dwindling congregation; but when Simeon acted as his curate the church-wardens were dismayed to find large crowds in their previously quiet church. Like Venn, Atkinson may have helped to strengthen Simeon's attachment to the Established Church and his suspicion of 'irregularity' since Dyer notes that 'though a Methodist [an evangelical], Mr. Atkinson was a zealous churchman' (Dyer, 1824, II: 238).

In 1783 Simeon was appointed minister of Holy Trinity Church, Cambridge, through an old-fashioned act of patronage: the living was in the gift of the bishop of Ely and he in turn was a friend of Simeon's father. This was deeply resented by the parishioners who favoured John Hammond, the existing lecturer. Hammond was inclined towards Unitarian-ism and was to remain a lifelong friend of Frend (CUL, Add. 7886: 99–100) and it is possible that the clash between Hammond's and Simeon's supporters also had a theological dimension. In any case for about ten years Simeon's congregation had to stand in the aisles since the pews were kept locked by the churchwardens. They also had to contend with disruption caused by unruly undergraduates hostile to evangelicals – a state of affairs that ceased when Simeon insisted, with the vice-chancel-lor's support, on one offender reading a public apology. Eventually, however, Simeon won over his disgruntled parishioners and made Holy Trinity Church the chief focus of evangelical preaching within the university. As well as providing him with a prominent platform within Cambridge Simeon's position at Holy Trinity also gave him some limited patronage to encourage his evangelical disciples: some of his most influen-tial protégés – Thomason, Sowerby and Scholefield – acted for a time as his curates at Holy Trinity.

Simeon's preaching at Holy Trinity formed one part of his evangelical ministry within the university; another was his practice from 1792 of providing sermon classes and (after 1812) theological 'conversation parties' in his rooms at King's, occasions when young evangelicals could receive some informal training in their clerical duties when there was virtually none available in the university. These gatherings also provided some mutual solidarity in a university where 'sims' – as evangelicals came to be derisively known – were still regarded with some contempt. Simeon deliberately omitted prayers on these occasions to prevent any suspicion that he was holding an illegal conventicle (Moule, 1892: 229). It is a measure of the difference between the tactics of Milner and Simeon that the latter appears to have had only limited influence within his own college of King's where for much of his early career he was regarded with some hostility by his colleagues. At his early theological gatherings, he commented, 'I had none but Magdalene men' (A. W. Brown, 1863: 191). By 1790, however, he was popular enough to be elected vice-provost of his college and his influence throughout the university steadily advanced in the course of his long career – an indication not only of Simeon's charm but also of the growing respectability of evangelicalism within the Church more generally. By 1823 Simeon could remark that: 'The sun and moon are scarcely more different from each other than Cambridge is from what it was when I was first minister of Trinity Church; and the same change has taken place in the whole land' (Moule, 1892: 236). The extent of his influence by his death in 1836 prompted Thomas Macaulay to remark in a letter to one of his sisters in 1844 that 'As to Simeon, if you knew what his authority and influence were, and how they extended from Cambridge to the most remote corners of England, you would allow that his real sway over the Church was far greater than that of any Primate' (*ibid.*: 232).

Such a degree of influence was not, however, achieved without some opposition. Simeon's theology, with its emphasis on the natural degeneracy of man, was regarded by many in the university with dismay since it undermined that accord between man's natural reason and the doctrines of Christian Revelation which had been the theme of so many eighteenth-century sermons. One of his more influential critics was Edward Pearson (master of Sidney Sussex, 1808–11) who, Dyer wrote, was 'nearly of the same school with Dr. [John] Hey, but was more zealous against some of those feelings and doctrines, which we sometimes denominated Methodism' (Dyer, 1824, II: 111). In 1805 and 1810 Pearson published critiques of Simeon's sermons attacking his emphasis on 'the total corruption of human nature' (Carus, 1847: 209); he also objected to what he considered were Simeon's implied criticisms of the teaching of the Anglican clergy (Pearson, 1810: 13). A course of university sermons by William Sharpe of Trinity in 1817 also rejected Simeon's view of the total corruption of man as 'erroneous and pernicious' (1817: 4). High churchmen like Herbert Marsh (Lady Margaret professor of divinity, 1807–39) also objected to Simeon's emphasis on the Bible at the expense of the traditions of the Church. This was the basis of Marsh's objections to the founding, by a group of evangelical undergraduates associated with Simeon, of a branch of the British and Foreign Bible Society at Cambridge in 1811 since he feared that distribution of Bibles without the Book of Common Prayer might favour the spread of dissent. In a public letter to

Simeon, Marsh also objected to the tendency of such associations to promote a religious 'party spirit' (1813: 9) within the university. Some, indeed, feared that an undergraduate organisation of any sort was dangerous in the tense political climate of the Napoleonic Wars: as Simeon noted, there was a fear that if undergraduates 'were suffered to proceed in this way about the Bible, they would soon do the same about politics' (Moule, 1892: 125–6). None the less, the auxiliary branch was established with the support of such notables as the royal duke of Gloucester and Lord Francis Osborne, MP for the county (F. K. Brown, 1961: 295–311) – an indication of the growing strength of evangelicalism.

Simeon also had to face the opposition of Thomas Dampier who replaced Bishop Yorke, Simeon's early patron, as bishop of Ely in 1808. In 1811 Dampier wrote to the vice-chancellor requesting him to call a meeting of the heads in order to discuss the possible dangers posed by Simeon's teaching, a meeting at which Milner used his political skills to good effect in order to defend Simeon (Carus, 1847: 329–30). When Dampier died the following year the evangelicals must have found it difficult not to regard this as an act of Providence. A more formidable episcopal opponent of the evangelical movement was Pitt's ecclesiastical adviser, Bishop Pretyman-Tomline (as Pretyman became after 1803) of Lincoln, who (despite his patronage of Milner) was a declared foe of the evangelicals whose theology he attacked in his *Refutation of Calvinism* (1811). His influence, however, declined after the death of Pitt in 1806. Simeon's old sparring-partner, Herbert Marsh, after being appointed bishop of Peterborough in 1819, instituted a 'trap for Calvinists' – a set of eighty-seven questions designed to prevent evangelicals being ordained – but by this time the evangelicals were sufficiently influential for Marsh's action to result in a public outcry and a debate in the House of Lords.

Beneath such episcopal persecution of evangelicals lay the suspicion that these 'earnest Christians' were not true sons of the Establishment – a charge which the Cambridge evangelicals had been particularly concerned to refute. The influence of strong churchmen like Henry Venn, Milner and Simeon helped to strengthen their protégés' loyalty to the government and liturgy of the Established Church (Smyth, 1940: 311) at a time when the evangelicals' links with the Church of England were still somewhat fragile. Berridge, for example, had defied his bishop by continuing to preach outside his own parish and was tolerated only because of his friendship with the Pitt family (Ryle, 1978: 232–3). Berridge's impatience with church structures is apparent in his outburst to John Thornton in August 1774: 'Must Salvation give way to a fanciful decency, and sinners go flocking to hell through our dread of irregularity?' (Whittingham, 1838: 394). Rowland Hill's family regarded his irregular mode of preaching while an undergraduate with dismay and 'deeply regretted this signal mark of indifference to the establishment' (W. Jones, 1834: 19). His troubled relations with the Establishment continued after graduation and he was never ordained a priest; as a result Simeon declined Hill's request to preach when he returned to Cambridge many years later lest his appearance 'undo all that several resident clergymen had been for several years endeavouring to accomplish for the spiritual good of his Alma Mater' (Sangster, 1964: 16).

Henry Venn actively sought to counter Berridge's and Hill's impatience with the Establishment. It was his aim to inculcate in his Cambridge disciples 'much moderation, obedience to superiors, and no breaking out to be teachers, when they are mere novices' (J. Venn, 1834: 376). Venn was particularly anxious to discourage Simeon from following Berridge's example – hence Berridge's reference to Simeon as one whose 'feet are often put into the stocks by the Archdeacon of Yelling' (Loane, 1952: 108). Simeon himself later looked back on his early excursions into field preaching with some ruefulness and strongly discouraged his young followers from following his early example. He was, wrote his Cambridge disciple, A. W. Brown, 'resolutely and increasingly anxious that all men should love and venerate the Church of England, instead of watching and spying out her faults' (Moule, 1892: 107). Milner's praise for the Church of England was rather more qualified and was somewhat along the lines of 'And always keep a hold of nurse, for fear of finding something worse', but he was, none the less, insistent on the need to conform to the Establishment. 'She may have many faults', he wrote, '. . . but she must be proved to be Antichristian, before separation from her can be justified.' Furthermore, he continued, separation would result 'in the sacrifice of those sound principles by which mankind are kept in subjection to God and to one another, and by which alone social harmony and subordination can be maintained' (I. Milner, 1820, I: xiii–xiv).

As Milner's comments indicate it was particularly important for the evangelicals to avoid the suggestion of being disloyal or doubtful members of the Church of England in the age of the French Revolution, when any challenge to established institutions took on a political aspect (Murray, 1975: 272). Thus Thomas Kipling's attack on the spread of Calvinist ideas within the Church of England, which was published at the university press in 1802, included a warning to evangelicals that 'should our church be demolished, the downfall of the state . . . would not be far distant' (1802: 90). One manifestation of the Cambridge evangelicals' close identification with the Establishment, then, was their active role in countering the influence of those they considered foes of the constituted order in Church and State: they were, for example, among the most zealous opponents of Frend. Though less concerned with politics than Milner, Simeon's alarm at the progress of the French armies led him to promote prayers for the success of the British war effort. He also questioned the political reliability of the dissenters – an action which prompted the Baptist radical, Robert Hall, to reproach Simeon in the *Cambridge Intelligencer* of 8 August 1795: 'when I hear of your ascetic pretensions to political indifference', wrote Hall, 'I suspect a little disingenuity at the bottom . . . The fervour of religious zeal and ministerial attachment with you go hand in hand' (Flower, 1796: 81–2). This letter was reprinted by Flower together with a more general attack by him on the evangelicals' support for Pitt's administration – hence Simeon's subsequent comment about Flower to the bishop of Ely in 1809: 'Being the great organ of the Jacobins, he laboured to destroy the character of every supporter of order and government. His attacks on me were frequent, with my name in telegraphic characters' (Carus, 1847: 276).

Simeon's brush with Hall and Flower led in October 1797 to a fraternal letter from his fellow-evangelical, Henry Coulthurst of Sidney (whose opposition to Edwards's proposal to abolish subscription in 1787 had made him the subject of an open letter by Frend in 1789). Coulthurst reassured Simeon that 'You must expect for your loyalty to undergo the fiery ordeal of Jacobinical criticism' (Carus, 1847: 151). Coulthurst could speak with authority since in the previous year he had delivered a highly charged university sermon in which he praised Pitt's two Acts for extending the law of treason and restricting mass meetings, and attacked 'the uncouth Clamour for the Diminution of [monarchical] Influence and for parliamentary Reform' (1796: 11). Like Simeon, too, he questioned the loyalty of the dissenters, asserting that 'the principles of Non-conformity do ultimately produce Faction in the State, and Socinianism in the Church' (p. 20). The Cambridge evangelicals could clearly claim to have been among the most zealous defenders of Church and State in their time of greatest danger – which may well help to account for the growing acceptance of evangelicalism within both the university and the Church at large.

Through Milner's links with Wilberforce and Simeon's work with organisations such as the Church Missionary Society for Africa and the East and the British and Foreign Bible Society, Cambridge evangelicalism was closely associated with the wider evangelical movement. However, Cambridge evangelicalism had a character of its own: in particular the evangelical movement in Cambridge took on a rather more intellectual tone than it generally displayed elsewhere (V. H. H. Green, 1964: 222). (The rather lukewarm attitude with which evangelicals generally regarded learning was summed up by the earl of Shaftesbury with the remark that

'God cares little for man's intellect, he cares greatly for man's heart' (Bradley, 1976: 20).) Allied to the strong emphasis of Milner and Simeon on the need for the evangelicals to respect the government and practices of the Church was their stress on the importance of their young protégés conforming to the traditions of one of the major citadels of the Establishment: Cambridge University. In particular, they urged their followers to attend earnestly to the prescribed course of study even though it included little of direct theological relevance.

Some young evangelicals regarded the Cambridge curriculum as a distraction from the more urgent task of winning souls, but Milner, by his example as senior wrangler in 1774 (with the added distinction of being described by the examiners as 'incomparabilis'), FRS 1776, foundation Jacksonian professor of natural experimental philosophy (1783–92) and Lucasian professor of mathematics (1798–1820), helped to channel the energies of the evangelicals back into the established round of studies. Though Simeon had no particular interest in the mathematical sciences he reproved those of his young charges who neglected their university studies. Thomas Thomason, who served as Simeon's curate at Holy Trinity, had at first been reluctant to study mathematics rather than divinity but at Simeon's urging he applied himself to mathematics (Sargent, 1833: 54) and graduated in 1796 as fifth wrangler. He was eclipsed by Henry Martyn, Simeon's best-known disciple, who graduated in 1801 as senior wrangler and Smith's prizeman. Simeon's determination to prevent evangelical 'irregularity' both within the university and the Church at large is apparent in his refusal in 1816 to support the admission of a young evangelical to King's if he went 'about visiting the sick instead of attending to his academic studies' (Carus, 1847: 433). This emphasis on 'the need for all his young friends to pursue diligently the appropriate studies of the University' did much to put to rest suspicions about Simeon's influence within Cambridge (*ibid.*: 843). Quite apart from the urgings of Milner and Simeon there was a strongly practical incentive for the often ill-connected young evangelicals to apply themselves to their studies. If they neglected their studies they would be denied the positions within the university which were being increasingly determined by Cambridge's finely calibrated examination system (Gascoigne, 1984a: 561–5).

But while the Cambridge evangelicals often displayed both talent and determination in their mastery of the mathematical sciences which Cambridge prescribed for its examinations there was no real affinity between such studies and the theological foundations of the evangelical movement which contrasted human knowledge and natural religion unfavourably with revealed truth. Latitudinarian theology, by contrast, which accorded a much higher place to both human reason and natural religion was a more likely catalyst for an interest in natural philosophy. This difference between the evangelical and latitudinarian traditions can be seen as early as 1761 in a critique by John Green (master of Corpus, 1750–64) of the theology of George Whitefield. Green was concerned at 'some degrading expressions, which you [Whitefield] and your associates occasionally throw out about human reasoning, as well as learning' (1761: 11). 'The just conclusions of reason', he later continued, 'when employed in observing the constitution of nature, and our own situation in that system of rational beings with which we are connected, make up the substance of natural religion.' When the mind turned to revealed religion, he added, 'her way of judging is not changed nor her powers suspended, though the extent of her prospect be much enlarged' (pp. 14–15). Berridge – who was the subject of another of Green's pamphlets – would have confirmed Green's views on the evangelicals' hostility to the fruits of human reason with his remark in 1792 that 'I now lament the many years I spent at Cambridge in learning useless lumber – that wisdom of the world which is foolishness with God. I see nothing worth knowing but Jesus Christ, and him crucified' (Whittingham, 1838: 468). Though Cambridge evangelicals like Milner and Simeon were, of course, far less likely than Whitefield and his Methodist followers or Berridge to decry human reason, their strong emphasis on the depravity of man and the gulf between natural and revealed theology laid them open to criticisms similar to those that Green had levelled at Whitefield. In 1788 an early (anonymous) critic of Simeon accused him and his evangelical brethren of 'maintain[ing] that Christians will be most likely to succeed in the Pursuits of Truth, not by the Dictates of Reason, or by the Aids of Learning, but by laying their Minds open to the Direction and Influence of Divine Illumination' (Anon., 1788: 18).

Though the influence of Milner and Simeon did in fact ensure that Cambridge evangelicalism did not present a direct challenge to the university's scientific traditions the often rather dogged and dutiful attitude that young evangelicals adopted towards their studies was unlikely to encourage original enquiry. There were, moreover, some indications of an undercurrent of outright opposition by some evangelicals to the prescribed round of studies. Samuel Settle of Magdalene, for example, complained in 1796 that

I am tired of Cambridge studies, and I am persuaded I shall always consider my time spent in Mathematics, the least beneficial of any employed in the whole course of my life. Had I been engaged in searching the Scriptures, in composing sermons, and in reading the history of mankind, I should then have possessed some useful knowledge on going forth into the world. (Hervey, 1881: 46)

There are even hints in some of Simeon's *obiter dicta* that he regarded too much interest in natural philosophy as almost as reprehensible as too little. Thus he cautioned against what he considered were the overweening claims of the geologists and, although he invited his young followers to 'Investigate the works of creation; [since] it cannot do any harm', he also added the caveat: 'But beware of feeding upon science, lest your souls be starved' (A. W. Brown, 1863: 326).

The evangelicals, with their rejection of the natural theology which lay at the root of the 'holy alliance' between Newtonian natural philosophy and latitudinarian theology, posed a long-term threat to this accord between science and religion – even though the Cambridge evangelicals did not generally actively seek to reshape the university's intellectual preoccupations. Some indications of this same hostility to the association between science and natural theology can also be seen in the work of other churchmen of the period – illustrating once again that, although the evangelicals clashed with some of their fellow Anglican clergy on points of doctrine and church practice, they none the less formed part of a more general movement of ideas which served to re-emphasise the role of revealed religion. The most obvious example of the way in which suspicion of natural theology could also affect Anglican attitudes to natural philosophy was the interest in Hutchinsonianism on the part of George Horne and other Oxford high churchmen. In the late eighteenth century Horne continued to maintain 'that unbelief and blasphemy were gaining ground upon us, in virtue of some popular mistakes in Natural Philosophy, and threatened to banish all religion out of the world' (W. Jones, 1795: 31–2) and Hutchinson's biblically based alternative to Newtonian natural philosophy enjoyed something of a revival in the counter-revolutionary atmosphere of the 1790s (Thackray, 1970: 246).

Among Cambridge-educated high churchmen the upheavals of the late eighteenth century did less to undermine the long-entrenched belief in the 'holy alliance' between Newtonian natural philosophy and Anglicanism – though even in these circles there were some reservations about the claims of science. As befitted an FRS and a son of Edmund Law, George Law (a former fellow of Queens' and, after 1812, bishop of Chester and a strong opponent of ecclesiastical reform) adopted a more favourable attitude than Horne towards contemporary natural philosophy though, in his view, it was not without its dangers. In his university commencement sermon of 1804 Law conceded that 'the Book of Nature . . . is open to our search' though such enquiry could not illuminate the truths of Revelation. Indeed, the belief that science could discover all was an instance of that 'intellectual vanity' and 'overweening confidence in our own abilities' which 'when diverted into a different channel, has shaken the foundations of civil society, and still continues to agitate the political world' (1804: 30–1). The most scientifically inclined of the high churchmen was Samuel Horsley (LL B, Trinity Hall, 1758) who remained an enthusiastic supporter of Newton, defending his corpuscular theory of light in the *Philosophical Transactions* in 1770. He also published an edition of Newton's works between 1779 and 1785 with a preface stressing the links between Newton's science and his theology. Not surprisingly, however, he left Newton's heterodox theological manuscripts undisturbed though he was aware of their existence (Gjertsen, 1986: 262–3). But even Horsley regarded the religious implications of science with some caution. Though he remained confident that 'genuine revelation and sound philosophy are in perfect agreement with each other', he warned natural philosophers against 'build[ing] conjectures upon facts discovered, which they presently confound with the discoveries themselves'. He also expressed his reluctance about accepting 'without the conviction of the most cogent proof . . . any notion in philosophy . . . which should be evidently and in itself repugnant to an explicit assertion of any of the sacred writers' (Horsley, 1816, III: 180–1).

Such wariness about the claims of science, and of reason more generally, reflected both the increasing awareness of the atheistic tenor of French science and the growing disquiet about the relative neglect of revealed theology. This latter concern also helps to account for the mounting crescendo of voices urging the universities (and, in particular, Cambridge) to pay greater attention to theological education and the needs of intending clergymen. Archbishop Secker was sufficiently concerned about the problem to prompt Edward Bentham, Regius professor of divinity at Oxford, 1763–76, to offer theological lectures to all those intending to take orders and attendance at such lectures had become compulsory for ordinands by the early nineteenth century (Greaves in SM: 406–9). A similar concern to strengthen the teaching of revealed theology within Oxford was apparent in the inauguration in 1780 of the Bampton lectures (founded under the terms of the will of John Bampton who died in 1751) – one of the aims of which was to defend the orthodox doctrines of the Trinity and the Incarnation (*ibid.*: 419).

Intimations of unease at the way in which Cambridge was turning out clergymen who had learnt little apart from mathematics and natural philosophy can be seen as early as 1730 when Bishop Gibson corresponded with his friend, Daniel Waterland, the master of Magdalene – and, like Gibson, an opponent of latitudinarian theology – to ask whether the university might prescribe that all ordinands should spend their fourth year studying theology. Though Waterland was sympathetic he had to reply that 'There seems to be no way of changing the course of their studies for the first four years. It is fixed by custom and by the oath they take' (Lambeth Palace Library, MS 1741: 79). Cambridge's Elizabethan Statutes had envisaged that many of the clergy-to-be would proceed to a bachelor of divinity, but with the advancing age at matriculation and the increasingly demanding nature of the undergraduate degree a smaller and smaller percentage of students undertook postgraduate degrees: between 1660 and 1727, when something like 11,000 BA degrees were awarded, there were only 438 bachelors of divinity (Borlase, 1800). Despite such changes eighteenth-century Cambridge – and Oxford (Bennett in SM: 386) – continued to prescribe for its undergraduates the general and largely non-theological education which the statutes had envisaged would be merely a preparation for the higher faculties, of which divinity was by far the most important.

The inflexibility of the Statutes and the institutional inertia of the university meant that Cambridge was slow to remedy this neglect of theology, despite the growing number of critics who pointed out the incongruity of an Anglican university which did little to train its clerical graduates in divinity. As might be expected the evangelicals were particularly anxious to remedy what Joseph Milner called 'the neglect of true theological knowledge' at the universities (1781: 255). The fact that Simeon felt it necessary to provide sermon classes and theological 'conversation parties' for intending evangelical clergy was a more indirect criticism of the university's neglect of what was, by common consent, its primary function (Smyth, 1940: 100). To bring about any change, however, the evangelicals needed allies in the hierarchy – something which, in the late eighteenth century, they lacked, with the partial exception of Beilby Porteus (bishop of Chester, 1776–87; of London, 1787–1808) who, from a discreet distance, sympathised with many of the goals of the evangelical movement. In 1767, soon after leaving his post as tutor at Christ's, Porteus delivered a commencement sermon in which he remarked that, if the university had a defect, it was 'that revealed religion has not yet a proper rank assigned it here amongst the other initiatory sciences' (1767: 19). He also sagaciously observed that the neglect of theology could be largely traced back to the fact that it did not form part of the examination system and of the rewards that flowed from it: if the study of revealed religion were assigned 'a proper share of the usual honorary rewards', he argued, it would 'soon be pursued with the same ardour of mind and vigour of application' as other subjects (p. 21).

Porteus's sermon did bear some fruit since it prompted John Norris (Caius BA, 1761) to bequeath in 1777 an endowment for a new chair of divinity (Hodgson, 1811: 19). Though the first incumbent of the chair was John Hey, Norris himself appears to have been suspicious of the general drift of latitudinarian theology, commenting that 'freedom of Enquiry' had led to 'the Infidelity of the Age'; he was also a firm believer in the orthodox doctrine of the Trinity, a dogma which Hey had to swear not to call into question in his lectures (CUA, Guardbook 39.19: 1, 5). Norris also laid down that 'no pupil or auditor shall be admitted into the Lecture Room unless he be provided with the Old and New Testament, and with Pearson on the Creed' (Tanner, 1917: 92). Though Hey was far more diligent about his duties than most of his professorial colleagues the Norrisian chair did little to alter the prevailing state of Cambridge education since the lectures were only attended on a voluntary basis by the few students who wished to do something to prepare themselves for the ministry as well as undertaking the normal round of undergraduate studies. Not surprisingly Porteus, who had hoped that theology might become an integral part of the university's studies, looked on the Norrisian professorship with some disappointment (Knox, 1824, IV: 198). Another late eighteenth-century foundation with similar goals – the Hulsean Christian Advocate and Hulsean Christian Preacher (both founded in 1790 under the terms of the will of John Hulse, BA St John's, 1728, probably in response to Oxford's establishment of its Bampton lectures) – also did little to change the university's ways.

Though evangelical and high churchman might disagree about the type of theology which the university should teach both parties were agreed that it ought to pay more attention to revealed theology. Robert Ingram – the senior wrangler for 1784 and a former fellow and tutor of Queens' – criticised both the Calvinist theology and the doubtful political loyalties of the evangelicals in a pamphlet published in 1807 (in which he also invited accusations of popery by recommending the reintroduction of auricular confession). But in 1792 Ingram had also published another pamphlet the title of which aptly summarises its contents: *The necessity of introducing divinity into the regular course of academical studies considered* – a work in which he decried 'The general neglect in these seminaries [the universities] of almost every study, that has any immediate connection with revealed religion' (p. 19). In the same year another, more considerable, opponent of the evangelicals, Herbert Marsh, published at Cambridge his *Essay on the usefulness and necessity of theological learning, to those who are designed for holy orders . . .*, a work prompted by Marsh's embarrassment at not being able to answer his German colleagues' questions about the nature of clerical education in England.

Marsh's time in Germany from 1785 to 1792, when he studied under such eminent scriptural scholars as Johann Michaelis (1717–91), had also convinced him that the English clergy needed to be exposed to the linguistic and textual study of the Scriptures which the Germans had pioneered. As he put it in his 1792 pamphlet, 'The study of Divinity deserves to be scientifically treated as much as any branch of human knowledge' (p. 2). After another stay in Germany, where he translated Michaelis's *Introduction to the New Testament* into English together with his own speculations on the textual history of the New Testament, he was elected as Lady Margaret professor in 1807. His original approach to scriptural studies (at least so it was viewed by his English clerical colleagues) excited some criticism; Bishop Randolph of Oxford, for example, complained that Marsh and Michaelis had 'arrived at conclusions, which derogate from the character of the sacred books, and consequently are injurious to Christianity' (Baker, 1879, II: 763–4). However, he had the influential support of Bishop Pretyman-Tomline, though more on account of Marsh's forceful defence of Pitt's war policy than because of his abilities as a theologian (*ibid.*: 737). Marsh and Pretyman-Tomline also shared a common concern about the state of clerical education at the universities – a deficiency which in 1799 prompted Pretyman-Tomline to publish his *Elements of Christian theology*, a work intended principally for intending clergymen. As Lady Margaret professor Marsh revived the chair from its condition as a sinecure by delivering lectures in English rather than the traditional Latin; his lectures, which aimed both to introduce his students to the scientific study of Scripture and to protect them from the 'enthusiasm' of the evangelicals, were published by the university press in 1810. Despite Marsh's efforts, however, he was still commenting in 1822 on the poor state of theological learning of Cambridge graduates – a situation made worse by the fact that they were outshone by their counterparts from Oxford (H. Marsh, 1822: 6). More caustically Sir William Hamilton remarked in the *Edinburgh Review* of 1849 that 'Cambridge stands alone in turning out her clergy accomplished as actuaries or engineers it may be but unaccomplished as divines' (Sanderson, 1975: 71).

These continuing complaints about Cambridge's neglect of its clerical trainees were largely the result of the fact that the university's whole system of undergraduate education deliberately avoided any distinction between lay and clerical students. Moreover, Cambridge, with its predominantly mathematical curriculum, found it more difficult to graft onto its normal course of studies further theological instruction which was more naturally suited to the predominantly classical curriculum of Oxford. Given the integration of Church and State and the suspicion of the governing classes – particularly during the reigns of George I and George II – of any semblance of clerical independence it was considered one of the merits of the universities that they exposed future clergymen to the same course of studies as their lay counterparts. But the natural consequence of this uniform education was that it was extremely difficult to increase the emphasis on theology without requiring all students, lay and clerical, to change their studies. As Heberden commented in 1792, it might be true that Cambridge should pay more attention to basic religious instruction but the university should not insist on 'those studies which are more peculiarly adapted for the ministers of the Church' as 'part of the general plan of education' for to do so would be as pointless as obliging all students to undertake advanced study in law or medicine (1792: 38–9). For Heberden the obvious answer was for clergy to undertake post-graduate training but this involved both further expense and a degree of institutional flexibility which was lacking in the unreformed university. Eventually in 1842 a voluntary examination in theology was introduced which was taken in addition to the normal requirements for a degree but which became a virtual prerequisite for ordination (Heeney, 1976: 99); this was finally superseded in 1874 by a complete theological tripos.

In addition to the obvious institutional obstacles to change, Cambridge's slow response to the demands for a more professional training for the clergy was also partly due to the continuing reluctance to encourage the growth of clericalism by separating intending ministers from the laity. Such fears were indeed used by the advocates of further theological education within the university by concentrating the minds of their opponents on the likely alternative: specialist clerical seminaries. Thus Charles Perry, in a pamphlet which helped to establish the voluntary theological examination in 1842 (Winstanley, 1940: 169), urged the university to consider 'the danger of acquiring narrow and contracted views of human nature, and of the object and duties of the Ministerial office' (1841: 16) which clerical seminaries could pose. In 1854 a proposal to extend the system of seminaries prompted William Thompson (Regius professor of Greek, 1853–66) to defend the existing system of joint education of laity and clergy which rendered 'our clergy . . . more tolerant, our laity more religious' (Haig, 1980: 163). Underlying such suspicions of specialist seminaries was the fear that the clergy might come to view themselves as an order set apart from the larger society. Though such fears of clerical pretensions still existed in the nineteenth century, they had considerably abated when compared to the mid-eighteenth century when anti-clericalism was rife. After the equivocal attitude of many of the clergy to the Glorious Revolution and their even less enthusiastic response to the Hanoverian succession, England's governing classes frequently regarded the Church of England with exasperation and even suspicion. But such tensions between Church and State steadily diminished in the late eighteenth century as clerical nostalgia for the Stuarts faded. Moreover, as the Establishment generally came under attack in the age of the American and French Revolutions the governing classes came to regard the Church more positively as an integral part of a regime that was increasingly on the defensive. This change of attitude was reflected in the increasing role that the clergy began to play as JPs (Best, 1964: 70–1, 93–4) and the growing number of well-born bishops: during the reigns of George I and George II the percentage of bishops of genteel birth was 33 and 45 respectively, a figure that rose to 63% under George III (Ravitch, 1966: 120).

The greater social recognition and prestige of the clergy helps to explain the confidence with which many late eighteenth-century clerics asserted the importance and special mission of their estate. Horsley's vehement rejection of the Hoadlian view that the clergy were essentially servants of the State was echoed by William Jones of Nayland (a friend of Bishop Horne) who in his *Essay on the Church* (1787), argued that 'It is a very false suggestion that our civil government can alter the Church *at their pleasure*' (p. 77). Hoadly he regarded as 'a Socinian in principle' who had accepted a bishopric though he had 'banished all *Mitres* and *Lordships*, and *Spiritual Courts*, out of the Kingdom of Christ' (p. 129). As the ship of state was exposed to stormier waters in the period of the French Revolution the clergy more actively asserted their claims to a special eminence as custodians of religion, the better to defend and sanction both a political and religious order which was under attack. Thomas Rennell, a former fellow of King's and master of the Temple who was associated with the high church 'Hackney phalanx', by implication attacked Erastian views of the Church and the clergy by arguing in a Cambridge commencement sermon of 1798 that 'Religion was not instituted . . . for the purpose of *society* and *government*, but *society* and government for the purposes of *religion*' (1799: 15). Consistent with such a view he regarded 'A SOUND THEOLOGY' as 'the only sure and steady basis' of political principles and as a sure defence against 'the plausible delusions of fraternity and equality' (1799: 14, 18). The claims of the clergy were pressed with even greater vigour by Richard Ramsden of Trinity in a university sermon of 1800. The priest, he contended, was in some respects superior to the magistrate since the 'priest has the care of the more precious part of virtue; he teaches the mystery, which passeth knowledge, he regulates the heart and reins; whilst the other has the care only of the meaner and plainer part. . . . On this principle, the King should be anointed by the priest, before he mounts the throne' (1800: 13–14). If the state attempted to govern without such a divine sanction 'we might then expect to see the like to what has happened in a neighbouring kingdom' (p. 7). The *Anti-Jacobin* warmly applauded this growing self-confidence of the clergy: in 1799 it went so far as to criticise those latitudinarian-inclined clergy who tried to 'assimilate the clerical character as nearly as possible to that of the laity' (Murray, 1975: 90).

The clergy's greater sense of the importance and recognition of their own order was also related to the gradual drift away from an emphasis on natural theology towards a reassertion that what was distinctive about Christianity was its revealed doctrines which could not be arrived at by the use of human reason. If Christianity differed little from natural religion or could be largely mastered by an untutored reading of the Scriptures – as the latitudinarians had suggested – then there was little need for a clerical estate which could lay claim to particular functions and expertise and therefore to particular privileges. If, however, Christianity was viewed as being largely beyond the reach of human reason then the role of the Church and the clergy became more important since their traditions, liturgy and teaching were necessary to bridge the gap between human inadequacy and revealed truth. It is not surprising, then, that William Jones combined his attack on Hoadlian ecclesiology with the assertion that natural religion was 'but another name for Deism' (p. 77) or that Rennell in his 1798 Cambridge sermon commented on the falsity of 'the high prerogatives of human nature and human reason, which modern philosophy calls upon its disciples to assert' (1799: 12) and elsewhere attacked those of 'latitudinarian principles' (Murray, 1975: 12). It was possible, as some evangelicals demonstrated, to combine a strong emphasis on Revelation with a highly individualistic form of religion, but such an 'enthusiastic' style of belief lacked the institutional framework and stability which many from the educated classes were seeking in the troubled decades of the late eighteenth and early nineteenth centuries; thus most of the evangelicals made their peace with the Church and channelled their religious zeal into its established practices. As the Church and its clergy came to be seen more as custodians and teachers of revealed truth than guardians of a morality which could be largely derived from natural law then so, too, the demands for greater theological education of the clergy increased. To such demands Cambridge was particularly slow to respond – illustrating once again that the university had its own deeply entrenched traditions and practices which were only gradually reshaped to cope with the changing demands of the larger society.

9

Mathematics ascendant

The establishment of Newtonian natural philosophy as the foundation of undergraduate studies at Cambridge had owed much to the conviction of Newton's early clerical disciples that his system of natural philosophy was an invaluable ally to the cause of Christian apologetics. Cambridge, then, had been particularly important in fostering the 'holy alliance' between Anglicanism and Newtonianism which had been one of the characteristics of the Hanoverian Church and which had helped to diminish the accusation of clerical obscurantism which was so marked a feature of the French Enlightenment. As Cannon writes: 'how different the English Enlightenment was from the French. Sheltered under Newton's great name, science and religion had developed a firm alliance in England symbolized by that very British person, the scientific parson of the Anglican Church' (S. F. Cannon, 1978: 2).

Yet once Newtonian natural philosophy became securely established in the university's curriculum these apologetical motives were increasingly forgotten. As so often with institutions, a new impulse is gradually translated into established routines which only faintly bear the imprint of the intentions of the reformers. In Cambridge's case the Newtonian heritage was, by the late eighteenth century, increasingly narrowed to those aspects which could be most conveniently combined with the university's pedagogical processes which were increasingly shaped by the Senate House examination (after 1824 known as the mathematical tripos). Though this ever more rigorous examination was intended for the minority of students who took honours – between 1767 and 1799 there was a yearly average of 45 honours students out of 114 graduates – the Senate House examination set the tone for the university's studies generally. This was so much the case that those who wished to avoid the study of mathematics were virtually left to their own devices; as a students' guide of 1807 put it: 'If you neglect THE STUDY OF THE PLACE, there is little hope of your perseverance in *any* literary pursuit.

An Undergraduate at Cambridge is, in ninety-nine instances out of a hundred, a student for the senate-house, or no student at all' (Hyman, 1982: 24). The demands of the examination system with its emphasis on ranking students by means of fine discrimination between their academic performances naturally gave increasing weight to mathematical prowess since it lent itself so readily to a system of numerical grades; a subject like mathematics was also less likely to give rise to accusations of bias and lack of objectivity than more contentious subjects like moral philosophy. Moreover, when drawing up an order of merit it was more convenient for examiners to rank students by reference to their performance in a single subject rather than to have to take into account a range of subjects of varying difficulty. Such a system also had the not inconsiderable advantage of making fewer demands on the breadth of knowledge of the examiners.

The ever-mounting dominance of mathematics in the Cambridge curriculum was regarded with dismay by some within the university who felt, with some justification, that Cambridge was emphasising mathematics to the near-exclusion of other disciplines. Edmund Law looked back with considerable misgivings on the rise to prominence of mathematics within the university, describing how those opposed to

the dull, crabbed system of Aristotle's logic . . . called in the assistance of the Mathematics, little then imagining, that in a short time these same assistants, these comparatively meagre instruments, should, like Pharaoh's lean kine, eat up all that was good and well favoured in the sciences themselves; that they should usurp the place of those very sciences to which they were originally designed to be subservient, and for which station they were sufficiently qualified. (Fuller, 1840: 213–14)

Law's protégé, John Jebb, though himself an accomplished mathematician, wrote in 1777: 'Yet surely the study of the mathematics, and of nature's operations, should not intirely engross the youthful mind' (Disney, 1787, II: 270), but his efforts to widen the Cambridge curriculum to include more attention to subjects such as history and moral philosophy were in vain. The experience of Alexander Scott, an undergraduate at St John's in the early 1790s, was probably typical of many: 'the studies of Cambridge', wrote his biographer, 'were almost exclusively mathematical . . . [hence] He regretted to the last that he had not been sent to Oxford, where the classics were more read' (Anon., 1842: 13, 16). At Oxford mathematics, though unpopular with the undergraduates, appears to have been accorded increased emphasis in the latter half of the eighteenth century (Sutherland in SM: 481) though it never assumed anything like the dominance it enjoyed at Cambridge. Whether for this or other reasons, eighteenth-century Oxford's enrolments were substantially higher than those of Cambridge (J. A. Venn, 1908: 61–2).

Complaints about Cambridge's mathematical myopia continued into the nineteenth century. In 1818 the young Thomas Macaulay, an undergraduate at Trinity, exclaimed: 'I can scarcely bear to write on Mathematics or Mathematicians. Oh for Words to express my abomination of that science' (Fowler and Fowler, 1984: 185). A more considered critique was advanced by a pamphleteer of 1822 who wrote: 'A university is a society of students in *all and every* of the liberal arts and sciences. How then can that society deserve the name, which confines its studies almost entirely to one?' ('Eubulus', 1822: 12). But such complaints bore little fruit until the establishment of the classical tripos in 1824 and, up to 1851, even that was only open to those who had taken honours in mathematics. Meanwhile, the few non-mathematical components of the Senate House examination – chiefly based on Locke's *Essay* and Paley's *Principles of morals and political philosophy* – increasingly withered to vestigial forms; as Heberden wrote in 1792: 'the public honours of the University . . . are distributed merely according to mathematical merit, unless one evening dedicated to an examination in morality to which no attention is paid in ranking the candidates, may be called an exception' (Heberden, 1792: 32–3).

Not only were there complaints about the growing momentum of the mathematical juggernaut but there were also misgivings about the way in which the keen competition of the Senate House examination meant (as John Mainwaring of St John's complained in 1780) that 'in comparing the merits of the candidates . . . too much stress is laid on the abstruser parts of algebra and mathematics' (*MR*, 1780: 542), rather than testing mastery of the mathematical sciences in general. Thus Newton's work was studied less as a system of natural philosophy than as a source of problems for the mathematical duels which accompanied the examination. This tendency was sufficiently evident as early as 1774 for the vice-chancellor to comment that undergraduates had 'applied too much to the abstruser parts of mathematics, neglecting the study of natural philosophy, and even the elements of mathematics'. But his injunction that 'unless a person be found to have a competent knowledge of Euclid's Elements, and of the plainer parts of the four branches of natural philosophy [mechanics, hydrostatics, astronomy and optics], no attention will be paid to his other mathematical knowledge' (Disney, 1787, II: 351) appears to have had little effect: in 1827 the Senate was again demanding 'that the Candidates for Honours may not be induced to pursue the more abstruse and profound mathematics to the neglect of more elementary knowledge' (Bristed, 1852: 411). Thus Newtonian natural philosophy, which had originally been embraced by the university because of its perceived support for the argument from design, had, by the late eighteenth century, been more and more reduced to a demanding mathematical obstacle course for the university's annual climacteric, the Senate House examination. Newton's explanations of physical phenomena, which had originally prompted his Cambridge clerical disciples like Bentley, Clarke and Whiston to take up his work as a bulwark for established religion, were, ironically, over-shadowed by the demand for mathematical proficiency.

Moreover, the Senate House examination did little to foster mathemat-ical advance. Its demands meant that the energies of the more outstanding undergraduates and their examiners were devoted to the mastery of already well-established areas of mathematics. Since the lectures of college tutors were considered too elementary for those aspiring to high honours, future wranglers were generally taught by private coaches who had little time or inclination for research. Once the ordeal by tripos was thankfully past there was little institutional incentive to delve deeper into mathe-matics (with the partial exception of the Trinity fellowship examinations which also provided one of the few encouragements for classical learning (Wratislaw, 1850: 13)). By mathematics, too, Cambridge chiefly meant geometry which was seen as providing similar training in the virtues of close reasoning and deduction which the university had traditionally sought to cultivate through the study of logic – the foundation of academic studies from the Middle Ages. Indeed, the rapid rise to pre-eminence of geometry within the university's curriculum can perhaps be explained by the fact that it could be regarded as a legitimate substitute for logic which the Elizabethan Statutes – still the university's constitution – prescribed as an undergraduate's chief concern (Gascoigne, 1984a: 570–2). Thus Wil-liam Bennett, a tutor at Emmanuel in the 1770s and 1780s, could claim that 'Mathematics have been, in general, substituted for Practical Logic, because it furnishes more clear and certain Proofs and in this part of Public Education I consider our University having by far the superiority over Oxford' (Emmanuel College, Cambridge, MS 3.1.29: 197).

This emphasis on the pedagogical merits of geometry helps to explain why Cambridge did little to promote the study of algebra and hence why it added little to the existing store of mathematical knowledge at a time when the Continental analysts were making important advances. The author of a pamphlet of 1822 directed against the recent introduction of Continental analysis into the tripos summed up the traditional view when he praised mathematics (by which he meant geometry) for its tendency 'to produce habits of precision in other departments of knowledge, and to improve the power of deducing inferences correctly from given premises'; by contrast, he regarded the 'foreign analysis . . . as a system of intellectual discipline, very much inferior to the geometrical modes of demonstration' ('Academicus', 1822: 9–10). The alleged pedagogical superiority of geometry was also asserted by the *London Magazine* of 1826 which regarded the growing interest in new mathematical topics based on analysis 'as one more proof how strongly the tide of opinion at Cambridge sets in towards the belief that men are congregated in those Boethian flats for the promotion of science, rather than of education' (Enros, 1979: 246). The reluctance to adopt Continental (and, in particular, French) mathematics was further strengthened by English chauvinism and suspicion of French anti-clericalism: William Hales, for example, in the course of his attack on Continental mathematics described d'Alembert as 'a philosophizing infidel' and one 'of the original conspirators against Christianity' (Cajori, 1919: 268). Cambridge's geometrical obstinacy does much to explain why, as Robert Woodhouse (a fellow of Caius and the first advocate within the university of Continental analysis) put it in 1797, although Newton was regarded within England with the 'exultation of national pride, yet in France has been made the most just estimate of his merit, and the noblest monument has been erected to his memory' (Enros, 1979: 82).

English mathematical insularity and the lack of institutional incentives to proceed beyond an undergraduate mathematical competence help explain why late eighteenth-century Cambridge produced almost no original mathematical research apart from the work of Maseres and Waring[1] – neither of whom had much influence within the university even though Waring was Lucasian professor from 1760 to 1798. What activity there was in mathematics was largely devoted to producing textbooks, an indication of the strongly pedagogical character of Cambridge mathematics. The last two decades of the century saw the publication of works like *Rudiments of mathematics* by William Ludlam of St John's (1785; still in use in 1815), texts on conic sections by Samuel Vince of Sidney Sussex (1781) and by Thomas Newton of Jesus (1794), an introduction to fluxions by Vince (1795) and the *Elements of algebra* of James Wood (1795; sixteenth ed., 1861). Wood, the senior wrangler for 1782 and from 1815 to 1839 master of St John's, also produced two popular textbooks in mechanics and optics (two fields particularly amenable to mathematical treatment): *Principles of mechanics* (1796; seventh ed., 1824) and *Elements of optics* (1798; fifth ed., 1823). This wave of textbooks came after a long lull in the production of such works. In the period from 1720 to 1750 when Cambridge was integrating Newtonian natural philosophy into its curriculum eleven new texts had appeared; from 1750 to 1780, by contrast,

---

[1] On whom see chapter 6, pp. 180–1.

there were only two (Cantor, 1983: 51). The revival of textbook production in the 1780s and 1790s reflects the more demanding nature of the Senate House examination which, after 1779, was extended from three to four days. The increasing competitiveness of the examination was also reflected in the decision in 1792 to allocate marks for specific questions, a move that followed the introduction of printed papers in 1791. The dominance that mathematics had achieved within the university by the end of the century is illustrated by the fact that, while the texts of the period 1720 to 1750 were largely general surveys of natural philosophy, those of the 1780s and 1790s dealt with one specific branch of the mathematical sciences.

Given Cambridge's preoccupation with mathematical prowess it is not surprising that in the late eighteenth century there was little activity in the more experimental and observational aspects of the Newtonian heritage. Moreover, as the 1797 edition of the *Encyclopaedia Britannica* commented in its article on 'natural philosophy', the English universities paid little attention to two new branches of experimental natural philosophy, magnetism and electricity – something the article attributed to the fact that these fields 'are only subject to experiment, and not yet reduced to mathematical reasoning; which is the method of teaching philosophy in one of these celebrated seminaries [Cambridge]'. There was still some activity in astronomy but less than earlier in the century when Cotes and later Long had helped to popularise the science within the university. Long's successors as Lowndean professor of astronomy and geometry, John Smith (1771–95) and the aptly named William Lax (1795–1837), do not appear to have lectured though the latter did publish two astronomical papers in the *Philosophical Transactions* for 1799 (p. 74) and 1808 (p. 232) and a new set of nautical tables (1821). Cotes and Smith were followed in the Plumian chair by Anthony Shepherd (1760–96) who did little to promote astronomy except to publish a set of nautical tables in 1772 for the Commissioners of Longtitude. He was finally succeeded by Samuel Vince in 1796, by which time the Plumian observatory of Trinity had been demolished because it had fallen into such bad repair. Vince, a married man (and hence not a fellow) who had to earn a living from publishing and lecture-fees, appears to have been a conscientious if uninspired teacher: in 1790 he had published an introduction to astronomy based on a set of lectures he had given at Cambridge and in 1797 and 1808 there appeared his three-volume *Complete system of astronomy* which embodied his own astronomical observations. Despite the efforts of Vince, Cambridge's interest in astronomy remained rather tepid; though in 1790 the Senate proposed the erection of a new observatory to replace the defunct Plumian establishment, the new observatory was not actually built until 1824 (Stratton, 1949: 2).

Late eighteenth-century Cambridge did still provide some general lecture courses in natural philosophy which included experimental demonstrations but they appear to have done little to stimulate much in the way of original work. It is significant, too, that such lecture courses were not published as textbooks as had happened earlier in the century – an indication of the declining interest in natural philosophy as distinct from mathematics. The tradition of the Plumian professor providing a course of experimental natural philosophy, which had been established by Cotes and Smith, was carried on – at least for a time – by Smith's successor, Anthony Shepherd of Christ's (1760–96). In 1770 he published a syllabus of his *Course of lectures in experimental philosophy* with sections on mechanics, electricity, magnetism, astronomy, hydrostatics, pneumatics and optics. Daniel Bernoulli, who visited Shepherd in Cambridge in about 1771 and found him '*un savant très aimable*', reported that he had a collection of '*très beaux Instruments pour ces Courses de Physique expérimentale*' (BL, Add. 5880: p. 76b). Few students, however, benefited from these '*beaux Instruments*' since Shepherd only delivered his lectures every three years and after 1776 he ceased to lecture, appointing two deputies who, though they were reportedly 'more capable than Dr. Shepherd himself', were not reappointed (BL, Add. 35377: 151v, 356v). The dormant condition of the Plumian professorship after about 1776 allowed George Atwood, a tutor at Trinity, to attract a university-wide audience to his lectures on natural philosophy which, to judge from a printed syllabus of 1776, covered a similar range of subjects to those of Shepherd. Atwood's lectures 'were much attended and justly admired' (*GM*, 1807, II: 690); among his pupils was the young William Pitt who in 1784 appointed him to an influential post in the Treasury. Atwood was one of the few members of the university to undertake research into experimental physics and he developed an apparatus known as Atwood's machine for demonstrating and calculating the accelerative action of gravity (*DNB*, Atwood). His *Treatise on the rectilinear motion and rotation of bodies with a description of original experiments relative to the subject* (in which he first described this machine) was published at Cambridge in 1784, the year he departed for London. There his scientific researches continued, resulting in the award of the Royal Society's Copley medal for a paper on hydrostatics in 1796.

After Atwood's departure from the university in 1784 a course in experimental natural philosophy was provided by Isaac Milner who was appointed foundation Jacksonian professor of experimental philosophy in 1783. The terms of this new chair were wide: the founder, the Rev.

Richard Jackson, a former fellow of Trinity, specified that the incumbent be chosen for 'his knowledge in Natural Experimental Philosophy . . . and of Chymistry but he is allowed great latitude in the choice of the subjects of his lectures, provided they be of an experimental character' (Tanner, 1917: 93). Milner complied with this wide brief by giving, in alternate years, experimentally based lectures in chemistry and natural philosophy (M. Milner, 1842: 18). The course in natural philosophy, to judge from an undated printed syllabus, included sections on mechanics, hydrostatics, electricity, magnetism and light. According to Gunning (who was no friend of Milner) his lectures in natural philosophy were more notable for their entertainment than their instruction; his chemical lectures, by contrast, were well prepared (Gunning, 1855, I: 236–7). Milner's bias towards chemistry while Jacksonian professor was also reflected in his publications: before taking up the chair he had published in the *Philosophical Transactions* three papers on mathematical subjects (1788: 344, 380; 1779: 505, two of which were concerned with gravitational attraction), but his activities as Jacksonian professor did not lead to any further publications in the mathematical sciences. His one publication after taking up the post was a chemical paper in 1789.

Francis Wollaston, Milner's successor as Jacksonian professor (1792–1813), at first carried on the tradition of lecturing on both chemistry and natural philosophy but confined himself to chemistry after 1796 when the long-silent Anthony Shepherd died and was succeeded as Plumian professor by Samuel Vince. Vince revived both the astronomical and experimental traditions of the Plumian chair, providing a series of experimentally based lectures on 'mechanics, hydrostatics, optics, astronomy, magnetism and galvanism' (*Cambridge University calendar*, 1810: 29). In a thin field Vince was also the most active researcher of the late eighteenth-century Cambridge scientific professoriate producing, along with his astronomical publications, papers in the *Philosophical Transactions* on mathematics, mechanics and hydrostatics (1780: 546; 1782: 339; 1785: 165; 1786: 432; 1795: 24). In summary, then, during the late eighteenth century there was sufficient interest in experimental natural philosophy to provide the clientele for one lecturer, apart from the instruction given by college tutors who would generally have had little equipment or expertise; none of these tutors (apart from Atwood) appear to have published in the field. Such a limited degree of interest in the experimental aspects of natural philosophy indicates the selective and predominantly mathematical view Cambridge had taken of its Newtonian traditions. It is not surprising, then, that the university had such a meagre record of research in physics.

The only really notable scientific figure at Cambridge in the late eighteenth century was Thomas Young whose links with the university were rather slight. In order to qualify for membership of the Royal College of Physicians he resided at Emmanuel between 1797 and 1799 where, as a fellow-commoner, he was exempted from the normal academic discipline and was free to follow his own scientific interests (which were partly the result of his earlier medical studies at Edinburgh and Göttingen); after leaving Cambridge he took an MB from the university in 1803 and an MD in 1808. Young's scientific researches at Cambridge formed the basis of his paper 'Outlines of experiments and enquiries respecting sound and light', which was dated Emmanuel College, Cambridge, 8 July 1799 and published in the *Philosophical Transactions* in 1800 (p. 106); in it he first argued for the superiority of the wave theory of light (Steffens, 1977: 110–11). His work probably owed little to his Cambridge milieu except that his critical analysis of Robert Smith's *Harmonics or the philosophy of musical sounds* (1749) helped shape his own formulation of the principle of interference as applied to sound, a concept he later extended to his treatment of light (Steffens, 1977: 114–15) – a nice historical irony since it was Smith who had done much to establish the corpuscular theory of light. Young's optical theories made little impact within Cambridge both because of the university's fierce attachment to Newton's views and because English mathematics lacked the necessary expertise to put the wave theory on a mathematical foundation (Cantor, 1983: 148).

The general decline in interest in those aspects of Newton's work concerned with explaining the workings of nature helps to account for the way in which late eighteenth-century Cambridge dons were less inclined than their early eighteenth-century counterparts to invoke Newtonian natural philosophy in support of the design argument which, despite Hume's largely unnoticed objections, continued to remain one of the chief supports of institutional religion. There were still some traces of the apologetical arguments popularised by Newton's clerical disciples: Beilby Porteus in his commencement sermon of 1767 made some reference to the merits of the Cambridge curriculum in leading the student 'by the hand of science through all the useful and sublime discoveries of the Newtonian philosophy', an exercise which serves 'to carry him up to their [the heavenly bodies'] great Author, even the *Father of lights*' (p. 15), while Jebb, according to his former student, John Baynes, 'used in concluding Newton's "Principia", to insist on the Newtonian system, as the strongest, and, indeed, only rational demonstration of the existence of a deity' (Disney, 1787, 1: 15). Though college tutors may have made such passing references to the apologetical potential of Newton's work, Cambridge no longer produced the detailed Newtonian-based physico-theologies which had played an important part in popularising Newton's work at the end of the seventeenth century. This may have been partly because it was thought there was little to add to the already well-rehearsed arguments (Metzger, 1938: 200), though such an objection does not account for the continued popularity of works in support of the design argument based on natural history. Moreover, the progress made in physics and, in particular, celestial mechanics in the latter half of the century (chiefly by the French) meant that the apologetical arguments of Bentley, Clarke, Whiston and other clerical disciples of Newton needed considerable revision.

The one Cambridge figure at the end of the eighteenth century who appears to have appreciated this situation was Samuel Vince whose work is an exception to the general decline in the production of Newtonian-based physico-theologies. In his *Observations on the hypotheses which have been assumed to account for the cause of gravitation from mechanical principles* (Cambridge, 1806) Vince set out to counter the views 'of many of the most eminent Philosophers upon the Continent [who] have been endeavouring to account for all the operations of nature upon merely mechanical principles, with a view to exclude the Deity from any concern in the government of the system, and thereby to lay a foundation for the introduction of Atheism' (p. 4). Like Bentley, Clarke, Whiston and their ilk, Vince placed considerable emphasis on the phenomenon of gravity as an instance of the guiding hand of Providence at work in the universe; he was therefore at pains to demonstrate the inadequacy of mechanical explanations of gravity, notably those based on theories of the ether. But Vince's arguments on this point failed even to convince some of his fellow-believers: thus John Playfair, a Presbyterian minister and professor of natural philosophy at Edinburgh, rejected Vince's opinions and maintained that speculation about the physical causes of gravity was 'quite immaterial to the truths of natural religion' (Cantor, 1981: 143).

Vince's work not only indicated that the seemingly inexplicable nature of gravity no longer had the apologetical force it once had but also that another weapon of theological Newtonianism – the argument that the irregularities in the motion of the heavenly bodies required the intervention of an active Providence – had also been blunted. Vince conceded that 'the discoveries of modern Astronomers' have shown 'that the law of gravitation will correct the irregularities which the mutual attraction of all the bodies must necessarily produce'. He went on to argue, however, that this only strengthened the design argument since 'imperfection is always found in the operation of mechanical causes' and that therefore the perfectly regular motion of the heavens could only be explained by the directing hand of Providence (p. 26). But such an argument lacked the immediacy and specificity of arguments for design (like those suggested by Newton himself) based on such purportedly demonstrable phenomena as the erratic behaviour of the comets which necessitated a Deity who took an active role in the workings of the universe (Kubrin, 1967); once it was demonstrated that such supposed irregularities could be explained in terms of celestial mechanics the study of astronomy was no longer so clearly an ally of natural theology. Vince developed his arguments at greater length in his *Confutation of atheism from the laws and constitution of the heavenly bodies* (Cambridge, 1807) but, again, his views met with a lukewarm reception: the *Monthly Review* criticised him for not providing 'a stricter examination of the most formidable positions of scepticism' and for not 'engag[ing] at closer quarters with Mr. Hume' (1807, III: 164).

Though Vince's works had few readers, scientifically based natural theology was still enormously popular, as the great success of William Paley's *Natural theology* (1802) testified. But though a former Cambridge tutor and senior wrangler Paley devoted little of his book to the sciences on which Newton had left his imprint but turned instead to natural history and anatomy – an indication of the waning role of Newtonian natural philosophy as an ally for the argument from design. Indeed, Paley argued that astronomy was '*not* the best medium through which to prove the agency of an intelligent Creator' though, once the existence of God had been proved, astronomy 'shows, beyond all other sciences, the magnificence of his operations'. Always the astute teacher, Paley pointed to the lack of immediacy of astronomy in contrast to natural history and anatomy: while the composition of a plant or animal could be minutely examined all that one could see of the heavens was 'nothing, but bright points, luminous circles, or the phases of spheres'. The argument from design, he argued, was best demonstrated through an analysis of 'relation, aptitude, and correspondence of *parts*' to which astronomy was ill-suited. While Vince and earlier clerical Newtonians had regarded the inexplicable character of gravitational forces as a support for the design argument, Paley considered it a weakness: 'Their motions [that of the heavenly bodies]', he wrote, 'are carried on without any sensible intermediate apparatus; whereby we are cut off from one principal ground of argumentation, analogy' (1845: 517). Paley's preference for natural history rather than astronomy as a foundation for the argument from design was also shared by late eighteenth-century poets who, when discoursing on the role of Providence, 'changed from celestial systems to English flowers and birds' (W. P. Jones, 1966: 232).

This association between the design argument and natural history was not, of course, new: Ray and Derham (whose *Physico-theology*, the Boyle lectures for 1711–12, was cited by Paley) had employed similar arguments in the late seventeenth and early eighteenth centuries. Indeed, in the late seventeenth century Boyle had argued for the superiority of natural history over astronomy as a basis for natural theology: 'It seems probable to me', he wrote, 'that the situations of the celestial bodies do not afford, by far, so clear and cogent arguments of the wisdom and design of the author of the world, as do the bodies of animals and plants' (Open University, 1974: 20). Newton, on the other hand, had argued that the design argument could be better defended by showing 'that the most simple laws of nature are observed in the structure of a great part of the Universe' since 'Cosmical Qualities are as much easier as they are more Universall than particular ones, and the general contrivance simpler than that of animals, plants etc' (Guerlac and Jacob, 1969: 317).

Though works of natural theology based on natural history continued to be written after the publication of the *Principia*, the enormous public acclaim which was accorded Newton's work meant that design arguments based on this system were particularly popular for much of the eighteenth century. The image of a Creator who controlled the world through the orderly, law-abiding processes made manifest by Newton appealed to the Augustan age which prided itself on the orderliness of its political life. But the imaginative force of Newtonian-based natural theology declined in the late eighteenth century, perhaps because it had lost its novelty or, more speculatively, because the less confident and secure conditions of the late eighteenth century prompted a demand for the less remote and austere manifestation of the hand of Providence which it was thought natural history, rather than astronomy, could provide. Natural history was, after all, far more comprehensible to the scientific layman than celestial mechanics and could provide a far more immediate and obvious foundation for the argument from design in an age when traditional certainties were coming under attack.

This bias towards the biological sciences was evident as late as 1833–6 when the Bridgewater tracts – the last great monument to the tradition of English natural theology – were written. Of the eight Bridgewater authors only one, William Whewell of Trinity, used the astronomical and mathematical sciences as the basis for his work and he expressed such a degree of reservation about the apologetical uses of the mathematical sciences, in contrast to the experimental, that Charles Babbage was prompted to write a ninth, unofficial, Bridgewater tract to show that applied mathematics could serve as an ally for the argument from design (D. M. Knight, 1972: 57). Like Vince, Whewell had to reckon with the argument of Laplace that the workings of the universe could be explained by mechanical means without reference to Providence – a view which

Whewell sought to refute by arguing that, even if it were conceded that the principle of design could not be demonstrated from the present behaviour of the heavenly bodies, nevertheless 'a prior purpose and intelligence' must have controlled the processes which produced the universe as presently constituted (1862 ed.: 158). Whewell's defensive stance again indicates the way in which Newtonian-based natural theology, though by no means defunct, had lost much of its force and self-confidence; the main haven of the design argument by the late eighteenth and early nineteenth centuries lay in the observational sciences – natural history and, later, geology.[2] By persisting with its mathematically dominated curriculum Cambridge was, then, setting its face against those aspects of scientific enquiry which were most likely to assist in implanting in its students a belief in the argument from design. Plainly, Cambridge's continued adherence to its particular version of the Newtonian tradition could no longer be explained by the apologetical concerns which had first prompted Newton's clerical followers to promote his work within the university.

Cambridge's mathematical obstinacy also indicated its increasing estrangement from the larger English scientific community. At the end of the seventeenth century English scientists were mostly Oxbridge-educated and the focus of their activities was the Royal Society which, despite initial tensions, soon developed harmonious relations with the two universities at which, after all, most of its members had spent some time. By the late eighteenth century, however, Cambridge was less clearly within the orbit of the main centres of scientific activity (Porter, 1977: 95, 132–3): the proportion of active English scientists who had been educated at Oxford or Cambridge fell from two-thirds during the seventeenth century to one-fifth at the end of the eighteenth (Hans, 1951: 34) and the predominance of London and the Royal Society was being challenged by the Scots and by English provincial scientific societies, the activities of which reflected their members' greater preoccupation with the experimental and observational, as against the mathematical, sciences. Botany, zoology, chemistry and geology gained more and more followers since these were sciences better suited to the generally local and amateur activities of members of provincial scientific societies who looked to science to provide them with the cultural tone which the Enlightenment accorded to the study of nature (Porter, 1980) or who hoped that science could be used for utilitarian ends. Dissenting academies with their close links with provincial society were generally more responsive to such changes in scientific interests than the universities: it was no accident that

[2] For further discussion of this point see Gascoigne (1988).

England's two foremost late eighteenth-century chemists, Priestley and Dalton, were both teachers at dissenting academies. The growing scientific reputation of the dissenting academies exacerbated the long-standing antagonism between these institutions and the universities which was further heightened by the growing militancy of dissent in the late eighteenth century. Priestley stirred the troubled waters further in 1787 by writing to Pitt: 'While your universities resemble pools of stagnant water secured by dams and moulds, and offensive to the neighbourhood, ours are like rivers, which while taking their natural course, fertilize a whole country' (Kramnick, 1986: 13).

Not only was Cambridge increasingly remote from the scientific interests of much of the fast-growing provincial population of the late eighteenth century but the Royal Society, too, was turning more and more to the observational and experimental rather than the mathematical sciences. As the eighteenth century progressed the Society was increasingly dominated by gentlemen amateurs and came to reflect the interests of the landed classes. The growing fashionableness of agricultural improvement among the upper classes in the age of 'Farmer George' (George III) – whose wife, mother and chief adviser, Lord Bute, were all keen botanists (Allen, 1978: 43) – was reflected in the Royal Society's increasing preoccupation with natural history and, in particular, botany. The growing influence of the naturalists was made evident after the election of the botanist Joseph Banks, a confidant of George III, as president of the Royal Society in 1778, a post he held until his death in 1820. Soon after his election Banks was vainly challenged by a number of fellows who were chiefly mathematicians but these were outvoted by the gentlemen naturalists who were Banks's power-base (Miller, 1981: 288); thereafter Banks's dominance of the society was unchallenged. (By contrast, in 1719 the naturalist Walter Moyle had complained: 'I find there is no room in Gresham College [the Royal Society] for Natural History; Mathematics have engrossed all' (Raven, 1950: 477).) Along with the changes in the late eighteenth-century Royal Society, and the formation of the Linnaean Society in 1788, the enthusiasm for natural history was reflected in the increasing space devoted to such pursuits in the *Gentleman's Magazine*, the most popular journal of the age: in the early 1740s this publication devoted about 1.6% of its pages to natural history, a figure that had risen to 16.5% by the late 1750s (Baesel, 1974: 24).

Natural history, wrote Sir Leslie Stephen of the late eighteenth century, 'in the earlier part of the century had been regarded with good-humoured contempt as a pursuit of bugs, beetles, and mummies . . . Now it was beginning to be recognized that such pursuits might be a creditable investment of human energy' (1962, 1: 322). Nor was this change in the

scientific climate confined to England: d'Alembert's resignation from the
Encyclopédie prompted Diderot to exclaim to Voltaire: 'The reign of
mathematics is over. Tastes have changed. Natural history and letters are
now dominant. D'Alembert at his age will not throw himself into the
study of natural history' (Hankins, 1985: 169).

Cambridge's mathematically based curriculum was, then, increasingly
removed from the interests of both the larger scientific community and the
offspring of the landed classes who, by the late eighteenth century, were
attending the universities in growing numbers (Lucas, 1974: 259). But
though the prescribed course of studies made little allowance for those
who wished to stray from the mathematical path – particularly with the
virtual disappearance of any formal instruction in medicine – there are
some indications that what Jones (1937) calls 'the vogue of natural history'
in late eighteenth-century England did leave its mark on the university.
The study of natural history at Cambridge was greatly facilitated by the
foundation of the university botanical garden in 1763, largely thanks to a
donation from Dr Walker, the vice-master of Trinity, which was further
augmented in 1783 by a gift of two thousand pounds from Mr Betham, a
former fellow of King's (BL, Egerton MS 1970: 143). The opening of this
new garden was accompanied by a speech which presented a sort of
apologia for the study of botany. First and foremost the importance of
botany as an ally for the argument from design was stressed: that it 'has for
its Object the Wisdom & Goodness of God, which is no where more
manifest than in the vegetable Part of the Creation'. Botany was also
praised for its utility both in medicine and in 'many Branches of Manufacture & Commerce' (BL, Add. 5834: p. 27). However, such worthy ends
had been neglected at Cambridge since, as the speaker remarked, up to this
point the university had 'had Titular Professors of Botany' with 'nothing
worth mentioning left behind them' (ibid.). Walker hoped to remedy this
situation by establishing the garden, which he intended to be a centre of
botanical research since he made provision for a 'Reader on Plants, & a
Curator or Superintendant of the Works in the Garden' (ibid.: p. 28). The
first incumbent of this readership was Thomas Martyn who, after the
resignation of his father in 1762, also held the honorary post of university
professor of botany. After 1793 this post commanded an annual salary of
one hundred pounds (in addition to students' fees) thanks to a royal grant
(Gorham, 1830: 211) – an indication of the increasing official favour with
which the study of botany was viewed.

After his father's disappointing experience as professor of botany,
Thomas Martyn was doubtful about attempting to attract an audience to
lectures on an extracurricular subject but the foundation of the garden
prompted him to try: as he wrote in the dedication to Walker which

prefaced his syllabus of lectures for 1764, without this new foundation 'the Author would scarce have thought of attempting to restore the study of BOTANY, which was almost lost among us' (Martyn, 1764: iii). Martyn's lectures of 1764 were notable as the first set of lectures in England based on the classificatory system of Linnaeus (Gorham, 1830: 117) with whom Martyn's father had corresponded. Such scientific novelty, however, did little to attract an audience: by 1766 he reported rather dejectedly to his fellow-botanist, Dr Pulteney: 'I have almost ended my Course of Lectures for this year. My pupils are but few in numbers, & there are fewer still who give any attention to the science. I hope, however, by perseverance, to bring it more into repute among us' (*ibid.*: 132). Martyn did indeed persist and by 1782 he was attracting an audience of about thirty, but his hopes that of these 'one or two may not be found to follow it up, & make something of it hereafter' (BL, Egerton MS 1970: 80) do not appear to have been realised. By 1796 Martyn had abandoned his lectures altogether, his biographer commenting that 'there was so little zeal for the study in the University, that it was scarcely possible to form a Class!' (Gorham, 1830: 217). Martyn did for a time appoint a deputy (Winstanley, 1935: 166) but he, too, soon abandoned the attempt to teach botany in a university which reserved its rewards for mathematical pre-eminence.

But there was rather more activity in natural history at Cambridge than Martyn's disappointing experiences as lecturer might suggest. Firstly, though Martyn had little success in attracting an audience, he did promote the study of botany through his researches and writing. In 1763 he published his *Plantae Cantabrigienses* which employed the Linnaean system to classify the local flora; the book was used by the few students who accompanied him on his botanical expeditions (Walters, 1981: 38). Martyn's most popular work was his translation of Rousseau's *Letters on the elements of botany addressed to a lady* (1785) though his true *magnum opus* was a new four-volume edition of Miller's *Gardener's dictionary* (1807) on which he worked for twenty-two years.

In his *Plantae* Martyn referred to the botanical investigations of Israel Lyons who, though not a member of the university, had attracted the notice of Robert Smith, master of Trinity, because of his mathematical ability. In the same year as Martyn's work on the Cambridge flora appeared, Lyons published his *Fasciculus plantarum circa Cantabrigiam* which supplemented Ray's earlier listings. This was the fruit of botanical expeditions which dated back to 1755 and sufficiently established his reputation for the wealthy young scientific entrepreneur, Joseph Banks, to carry him off to Oxford in 1764 in order to provide some botanical instruction in a university which then paid even less attention to that science than Cambridge (Cameron, 1966: 299). (Though, with the appointment of John Sibthorp – one of those active in the foundation of the Linnaean Society – as professor of botany in 1784, 'Intellectual distinction returned to the [Oxford Botanical] Gardens' (Webster in SM: 721).) There were also other Cambridge residents who shared Martyn's botanical interests. Like Lyons (and Martyn) Thomas Green of Trinity (Woodwardian professor, 1778–88) was associated with Banks for whom he collected botanical specimens in the Cambridgeshire area in 1776.[3] Michael Tyson, a fellow of Corpus, who left a record of his 'Herbations chiefly in the Neighbourhood of Cambridge' in 1770 (SRO, MS 2785/1), passed on some of his findings to both Martyn and Lyons (BMNH, Banksian MS 105: 417). Another Cambridge botanist was Richard Relhan, a fellow of King's, who published a Cambridgeshire flora in 1785 with the assistance of Martyn (*ibid.*: 549, 557; Walters, 1981: 40). In 1787 Relhan printed a syllabus of botanical lectures – presumably while deputising for Martyn. Martyn also worked closely with Charles Miller, the first superintendent of the Cambridge botanical gardens. The two men remained in touch even after Miller resigned in 1770 to work in Asia and Martyn took over the superintendence of the gardens (which he described in a published catalogue of 1771). In 1773 Martyn sent him news of the botanical garden and Miller, in turn, forwarded him some Indian botanical samples (BMNH, Banksian MS 105: 405).

Another Cambridge don who shared the growing interest in botany was the poet Thomas Gray of Pembroke, who – wrote the Cambridge botanist, Tyson – regarded natural history as his 'favourite study' in the ten years before his death in 1771 (Mason, 1807, II: 203). Gray was at first interested in entomology: he collected botanical specimens, then exchanged them with Lyons and Miller for insects (W. P. Jones, 1937: 350). Gray did, however, become 'the disciple of the great Linnaeus' – something in which Martyn may have played a part – leaving among his papers a closely annotated copy of Linnaeus's work (Mason, 1807: II: 203). Along with Tyson, other keen botanists in Gray's circle were Sir John Cullum, a fellow of Catharine Hall, and George Ashby of St John's (W. P. Jones, 1966: 125–41). Gray's friend, former colleague and fellow-poet, Christopher Smart, shared both his interest in natural history and his distaste for the mathematical sciences – so much so that in his *Jubilate agno* (c. 1760) Smart wrote: 'For Newton nevertheless is more of error than of the truth' (D. J. Greene, 1953: 337).

Though the ever-hopeful Thomas Martyn wrote to his friend and fellow-naturalist, John Strange, in 1782 that 'the taste for Physics [non-

---

[3] Fitzwilliam Museum, Cambridge, Banks MSS, Green to Banks, 14 April 1776 (not folioed).

mathematical science] gains ground at Cambridge' – a situation he contrasted with their undergraduate experiences in the 1750s when 'we were looked upon as no better than cockle-shell pickers, butterfly hunters, and weed gatherers' (BL, Egerton MS 1970: 80) – nevertheless the interest in natural history within the university that was evident in the 1760s and 1770s appears to have declined thereafter.[4] By the end of the century Cambridge botany was virtually moribund; as Martyn's biographer, Gorham, put it: 'The language in which the illustrious Ray had expressed his feelings, on the neglect of Botany at Cambridge, in the middle of the seventeenth century, exactly describes the sentiments of Professor Martyn, on the same subject, at the beginning of the nineteenth century' (1830: 132). In the early nineteenth century the study of botany at Cambridge was revived by Darwin's mentor and early patron, John Henslow (professor of botany, 1827–61). One of the arguments he employed in urging Cambridge to pay more attention to his subject was that the university had a religious duty to foster such a powerful ally of the design argument. As he argued in a pamphlet urging the foundation of a new university botanical garden: it was 'well worth consideration, whether a University can safely cease from esteeming it a duty to encourage any department of sound learning which may assist in improving our general views of God's Providence' (Jenyns, 1862: 176) – comments which further underline Martyn's lack of success in establishing botany at Cambridge in the late eighteenth century.

Thus, although there was considerable informal interest in natural history within the university during the 1760s and 1770s, it was at the periphery of Cambridge intellectual life and left no lasting impression on the university; in contrast, the interests of Ray and his circle in the mid-seventeenth century had had a more lasting impact on late seventeenth-century Cambridge. The difference between the two periods can at least partly be explained by the fact that the medical faculty in the latter half of the seventeenth century was still of importance whereas, by the late eighteenth century, it was close to extinction. The medical faculty was the natural focus for sciences such as botany, zoology and chemistry and without its institutional support such activity as there was in these sciences was likely to be spasmodic and short-lived. The one faint contribution of the medical professoriate to the study of natural history in late eighteenth-century Cambridge was a series of lectures by Sir Busick Harwood (professor of anatomy, 1785–1814; foundation Downing professor of

---

[4] An exception to this general trend was the activities of a gardener who was employed under the terms of the bequest which established the Jacksonian chair and who left records of various experiments with vegetable crops (Trinity College, Cambridge, MS R.8.42: 15–24).

medicine, 1800–14) which interpreted anatomy sufficiently broadly to include material on 'the structure and animal oeconomy of quadrupeds, birds, fishes, and amphibia' (*Cambridge calendar*, 1810: 34); his researches in this area were published as a *System of comparative anatomy and physiology* (1796).

In contrast to Thomas Martyn's experiences, the lectures of Cambridge's professors of chemistry in the late eighteenth century appear to have been relatively popular despite the fact that chemistry, like botany, was a non-examinable subject. At Oxford, too, chemical lectures attracted sizeable audiences: in the 1750s nearly a third of freshmen paid the extra fee required to attend those given by James Bradley (Mitchell in SM: 6). Though, at Cambridge, there were still some tenuous links with the medical faculty – Isaac Pennington, the sinecurist professor of chemistry from 1773 to 1793, was, for example, a medical fellow of St John's and in 1793 resigned the chemical chair to become Regius professor of physick – nevertheless, chemistry's popularity appears to have owed little to its traditional connection with medicine. None of those who actually lectured in chemistry at Cambridge in this period were medically trained nor did they pay particular attention to medical topics in their lectures (in contrast to Vigani, the foundation professor of chemistry). Though we have no lists of those who attended these lectures, if the audience of Charles Daubeny (professor of chemistry at Oxford, 1822–54) is any guide, medical practitioners and students came a very poor fourth as a proportion of the audience after clergy, dons, and lawyers (Oldroyd and Hutchins, 1979: 234). Chemistry, as John Hadley (Cambridge's fourth professor of chemistry, 1756–64) remarked, was 'rising in its reputation, and becoming a very useful as well as entertaining branch of Natural Philosophy' (Trinity College, Cambridge, MS R.1.50: 2) and there appears to have been sufficient recognition within the university of the exciting developments occurring in that science to attract a fee-paying audience which would have consisted of fellows and town residents as well as undergraduates. Moreover, among those lecturing in chemistry in this period were some accomplished teachers – Isaac Milner, for example, was regarded as a 'first-rate showman' (Gilbert, 1952: 314) – which, together with the often dramatic nature of the chemical demonstrations themselves, may have helped to attract a larger audience than that of Thomas Martyn whose lectures were reportedly 'the dullest and heaviest things imaginable' (Jenyns, 1862: 38).

After Hadley left the university in 1760 to practice medicine the study of chemistry was dormant. When he finally died in 1764 the post was filled by Richard Watson who later cheerfully admitted he knew nothing of the subject at the time but was willing to remedy this since 'I was tired with mathematics and natural philosophy' (Watson, 1817: 29). With the help of a French laboratory assistant, he soon gained sufficient mastery of the chemical literature and of experimental technique to provide a series of lectures before 'a very full audience, consisting of persons of all ages and degrees' (*ibid.*: 29). As well as helping to re-establish the popularity of the subject within the university Watson also made another, characteristic, contribution to the standing of the chair: in 1766 he obtained through his patron, the marquis of Rockingham, an annual pension of one hundred pounds from the crown for the incumbent, who had hitherto relied only on student fees (*ibid.*: 32). Watson's lectures formed the basis of his five-volume *Chemical essays* (1781–7), the first three volumes of which sold two thousand copies within five years (1793 ed., IV: preface); among those whom the work helped to introduce to chemistry was the young John Dalton (Thackray, 1972: 64). These essays and his plan of chemical lectures (1771) were more concerned with descriptions and experiments than theory but, like the lectures of Hadley and Watson's successors, they indicate the decline in interest in the consciously Newtonian chemical speculations based on the attraction and repulsion of particles evident in the lectures of John Mickleburgh (professor of chemistry, 1718–56) and some of the work of Stephen Hales – a further indication of the way in which Cambridge's Newtonian heritage became more and more restricted to the purely mathematical sciences. Watson was particularly indebted to the Continental phlogiston theorists, notably Stahl. In the third volume of his *Chemical essays* which was published in 1782 (the year in which he became a bishop and largely abandoned chemistry), Watson referred approvingly to Lavoisier's experiments on the calcination of metals but he did not explore the implications of these findings for the phlogiston theory (Coleby, 1953: 105). He resigned the chair in 1771 after becoming Regius professor of divinity but continued his chemical experiments, publishing three of his five chemical papers in the *Philosophical Transactions* after that date – papers which reveal close reasoning and experimental ability but no great originality (*ibid.*: 108–13). Finally, Watson broke with his chemical interests which, despite their continuing appeal, he thought inappropriate for one with his episcopal duties, by the drastic expedient of burning his chemical manuscripts (Watson, 1793 ed., IV: preface).

Watson's success in obtaining a royal stipend for the professor of chemistry explains why, on his resignation, the chair was, for the first time, the subject of a contested election (with Paley being among the four unsuccessful candidates (BL, Add. 5834: p. 158)). After this drama, anti-climax followed since the successful candidate, Isaac Pennington, gave no lectures. He did appoint Isaac Milner as his deputy though probably not until 1782 – the year in which Queens' College gave Milner permission to build a chemical laboratory in the stable-yard.[5] Milner's chemical interests had probably been awakened by Watson who, in 1781, persuaded him to verify an experiment of Priestley's involving the reduction of lead (Coleby, 1954: 237). After becoming Jacksonian professor in 1783 Milner alternated his lectures on natural philosophy with a course in chemistry, being assisted by a German chemist named Hoffman (Gunning, 1855, 1: 237). Milner claimed that by about 1790, when he ceased to lecture, his chemical demonstrations attracted an audience of about two hundred (BL, Add. 35658: 85). He published only one chemical paper – on the production of what he called nitrous acid and nitrous air (*Philosophical Transactions*, 1789: 300), a subject on which he corresponded with Priestley – but his surviving lecture notes indicate that he handled the subject with greater theoretical sophistication than Watson, despite his reputation as a 'showman'. Indeed, he remarked in the course of his lectures that 'The Science of Chemistry consists only of a multitude of detached facts, unless they be well arranged according to some Theory' (Coleby, 1954: 253). He referred respectfully to a number of the queries in Newton's *Opticks* and was sympathetic to Newton's speculations about 'the existence of an ethereal medium' (CUL, MS Ee.5.35: 53v) but the real theoretical focus of his lectures was, appropriately, the contemporary debate between the pro- and anti-phlogistonists. Up until 1788 Milner attempted to avoid aligning himself too closely with either side though he continued to use the phlogistonists' terminology, but, in 1788, in his last extant lecture, he outlined Lavoisier's experiments on the calcination of metals and the formation of acids as a result of which he thought 'the antient hypothesis of Phlogiston seems overturned at one Stroke, and a new and simple theory substituted in its place' (Coleby, 1954: 256). No doubt it was with such lectures in mind that Milner later proudly declared: 'My numerous pupils will remember that when the late revolution in the science of chymistry took place, I used to address them on the nature of a discrete analysis and inductions in chymical inquiries' (M. Milner, 1842: 543). It was indeed a comment on Milner's close interest in the subject that, within five years of Lavoisier's full-scale attack on the phlogiston theory in 1783, Milner had incorporated such developments into his Cambridge lectures. Milner was also particularly preoccupied with the problem of the nature of heat and he drew heavily on the work of Joseph Black, a manuscript copy of whose lectures he possessed (I. Milner, 1813: 224). Like Watson, Milner was something of a hypochondriac (though both men lived to a ripe old

---

[5] Queens' College, Cambridge, Conclusion book, 1734–87: 81. I owe this reference to Dr John Twigg, who also kindly permitted me to consult his history of Queens' College while it was in manuscript.

age) and in 1790 he ceased his chemical lectures on the grounds that the experiments were undermining his health.

When Milner finally resigned the Jacksonian chair in 1792 he was succeeded by Francis John Hyde Wollaston who continued Milner's practice of lecturing alternately on natural philosophy and chemistry, though he confined himself to chemistry after 1796 when Samuel Vince became Plumian professor and gave regular lectures on experimental natural philosophy. His first lectures were a continuation of Milner's discussion of the nature of heat – a topic which runs through his lectures and accounts for his interest in such recent scientific publications as Count Rumford's experiments designed to show that heat should be considered a form of motion rather than, as was commonly thought, a fluid. Like those of Milner, Wollaston's lectures reflect the uncertainties occasioned by the revolution in chemistry which Lavoisier's work had produced. At first he attempted to introduce his students to both the old and new chemical paradigms 'being unwilling either immediately to discard the old opinions & language of Chemistry, or much more to reject a Theory [what he had earlier called 'the antiphlogistic system of M. Lavoisier'] which by its simplicity & accordance with facts is daily gaining ground even among its most strenuous opponents' (CUL, MS Ee.5.35: 109v). However, as this passage suggests, Wollaston's sympathies were plainly with Lavoisier and he later abandoned any pretence of impartiality in the struggle between the phlogistonists and anti-phlogistonists. Thus he spoke of Lavoisier as the man 'who has destroyed Stahl's doctrine of phlogiston';[6] he also stated that 'it has been established beyond a doubt that water does consist of two distinct substances, chemically combined' (Trinity College, Cambridge, R.8.42: 13) – a reference to Lavoisier's contention that water was not an element but a compound of two substances which he called hydrogen and oxygen. Like his predecessors, Wollaston appears to have attracted good audiences to his lectures; the *Cambridge University calendar* of 1802 speaks of his exhibiting 'not less than three hundred experiments annually'. His own published research consisted of three papers in the *Philosophical Transactions* (1790: 43; 1817: 183 and 1820: 293), two of them concerned with the use of a 'thermometrical barometer' for measuring altitude.

Wollaston's more distinguished younger brother, William Hyde Wollaston (MB Caius, 1788), performed experiments in Francis's laboratory, having been introduced to chemistry by Milner. His interest in the science was further stimulated by his fellow medical student, Smithson Tennant (MB Emmanuel, 1788), who had previously studied medicine at

---

[6] From lecture notes taken by Walter Blackett Trevelyan (BA St John's, 1800) which are included in the BL's copy of F. Wollaston, *Plan of a course of chemical lectures* (1794) (1142.h.21).

Edinburgh in 1781 and attended Black's lectures (Gilbert, 1952: 314–15); Tennant was later to act as professor of chemistry at Cambridge from 1813 until his death in 1815. Though a life-fellow of Caius, William Wollaston's scientific work was chiefly conducted in his London laboratory where, with the assistance of Tennant, he devised a way of producing malleable platinum (and, in the process, established the technique of powder metallurgy) which brought him both riches and scientific fame. His researches on platinum also resulted in the discovery of two new metals, palladium and rhodium. William Wollaston's wide scientific interests are reflected in his twenty-nine papers in the *Philosophical Transactions* which cover fields as diverse as physiology, optics, crystallography and acoustics as well as chemistry. He competed for the Jacksonian professorship on his brother's retirement in 1813 but the post went to William Farish of Magdalene.

Farish had become professor of chemistry in 1794 when the sinecurist Isaac Pennington had finally resigned but since Francis Wollaston was lecturing on chemistry Farish decided to create a new niche for himself by offering a course on the 'Arts and Manufactures, More Particularly such as relate to Chemistry'. Though there was some chemical content in those sections of his lectures concerned with the raw materials of manufacture, the bulk of the course was taken up with an examination of the workings of machines – particularly those which were creating the Industrial Revolution which Farish viewed at first hand in his regular travels around the industrial areas of England. Farish was, in effect, offering a course in mechanical engineering and his lectures, as Hilken writes in his history of Cambridge engineering, were probably 'the first serious attempt in any British university to study the industrial implications of a rapidly developing technology' (1967: 40). Farish's object, as he put it in the *University calendar*, was 'to excite the attention of persons already acquainted with the principles of mathematics, philosophy and chemistry to REAL PRACTICE' (*ibid.*: 42). His course, which he continued after he became Jacksonian professor in 1813, was the most popular set of professorial lectures in the university; John Wright (BA Trinity, 1819) reported attending his 'excellent lectures' and being 'greatly edified'. 'There is scarcely a piece of machinery', he added, 'in the United Kingdom which he does not exhibit on a small scale in actual operation' (Wright, 1827, II: 129).

In their chemical lectures Watson, Milner and Farish all paid some attention to the chemical properties of minerals; indeed, Watson claimed in his *Essay on the subjects of chemistry* (Cambridge, 1771) that 'the great outlines and general divisons of mineral productions may most usefully be made from a chemical investigation of their constituent parts' (1793 ed., IV: 126). Though its links with chemistry were strong the subject of mineralogy was beginning to emerge as a separate discipline. Richard Kirwan, himself both a chemist and mineralogist, commented in the preface to his *Elements of mineralogy* (1784) that 'Mineralogy must . . . on the whole, be considered as a branch of Chymistry' (p. xiii). However, he added in the preface to the second (1796) edition that 'In the preceding decennial period from 1774 to 1784, mineralogy may be said to have for the first time assumed its rank among the sciences'[7] – a comment which reflects his strong commitment to the recent development of a chemical approach to mineralogical classification.

The more general subject of geology – of which, in the late eighteenth century, mineralogy formed the best-developed part – was still establishing itself as a recognised science, and its increasing popularity and significance is evident in the way in which the term 'geology' was coming into increasing use in the last quarter of the century (Porter, 1977: 129). Geology was, however, still only gradually separating itself from natural history more generally, those interested in investigating the animal or vegetable kingdoms often extending their activities to include the mineral kingdom. Thus the study of the earth formed part of the more general interest in natural history within Cambridge in the 1760s and 1770s. Christopher Smart's poem *Jubilate agno* (c. 1760) includes, along with many botanical and zoological references, the unlikely plea: 'The Lord increase the Cambridge collection of fossils' (D. J. Greene, 1953: 336). When Thomas Martyn toured Europe in 1778 and 1779 he collected many geological specimens which were further supplemented by gifts from his friend and fellow-student of both the life and earth sciences, John Strange, the British resident in Venice (BL, Add. 33349: 9). These Martyn donated to the university to supplement the Woodwardian geological collection which, he wrote to Strange in 1781, 'has no volcanic fossils, & is very deficient, in many other provinces of the fossil kingdom' (BL, Egerton MS 1970: 63). By 1782 Martyn was 'lecturing upon the subject of Fossils' (*ibid.*: 83) and in the same year sent specimens from Cambridgeshire to the eminent naturalist Da Costa, author of a *Natural history of fossils* (1757) (BL, Add. 28539: 248).

Since 1728 Cambridge had had a Woodwardian professor occupying what eventually became known as a chair of geology though, at its foundation, its scope was rather more vague. John Woodward prescribed that the professor should lecture on the subject matter of his three major works: *Natural history of the earth, Discourse on vegetation* and *State of physick.*

[7] Cited under 'mineralogy' in the *Oxford English Dictionary.*

As Clark and Hughes wrote: 'It is evident that Woodward's primary object in this foundation was the permanent commemoration of his researches without limitation of subject' (1890, 1: 185), though Woodward's accompanying bequest of his geological collection did give the chair something of a bias towards the earth sciences. None of the eighteenth-century incumbents of the chair appear to have lectured with any regularity and, with the conspicuous exception of John Michell (professor, 1762–4), contributed little to any form of scientific enquiry except to increase the Woodwardian collection of fossils.[8] Before taking up the chair in 1762 Michell published his 'Observations upon the phenomena of earthquakes' in the *Philosophical Transactions* (51: 566–634) for 1760, a major work in the history of seismology since it was the first to argue that earthquakes were accompanied by the propagation of waves (Hardin, 1966: 32); Michell here drew on his field work in which he had described the way in which sedimentary rocks were laid down in strata (Geikie, 1905: 378–9). Despite Michell's important work he appears to have done little to promote geology within the university – a situation that remained unchanged until the chair passed to John Hailstone in 1788.

Hailstone was sufficiently interested in the subject to travel to Germany to study under the eminent mineralogist, Professor Werner of Freiberg. On his return to Cambridge Hailstone published *A plan of a course of lectures on mineralogy, to which is prefixed an essay on the different kinds of mineral collections, translated from the German of Professor Werner* (1792). In the preface he referred to his desire to 'excite the attention of the University to a Branch of Knowledge, which although honoured with an establishment in this place for a considerable number of years, has hitherto been suffered to languish in unmerited obscurity' (p. [i]). This neglect he charitably attributed, not so much to the delinquency of his predecessors, as to the fact that 'Till within these few years the general attention of mankind was directed in Natural History to the departments of Botany and Zoology' (Porter, 1977: 129). Hailstone further underlined the links between the emerging science of geology, and natural history more generally, by commenting 'that notwithstanding we have produced some Naturalists of the first rank from the University of Cambridge, yet a taste for Natural History never seems to have been a prevailing one amongst us' (1792: [i]). But Hailstone hoped that 'The rapid progress which has since been made in Mineralogical knowledge' would mean that Cambridge would now make amends for its past neglect of the study of the mineral kingdom, even though he conceded that 'Geognosy, or the knowledge of the Earth's

---

[8] Charles Mason, Woodwardian professor from 1734 to 1762, did travel widely throughout England and recorded his observations on the natural history of different regions, including their rock structures, in his travel diaries (CUL, Add. 7762; Porter, 1977: 119).

internal structure' was 'a Science yet in its infancy' (Clark and Hughes, 1890, I: 195). Hailstone may have taught for a time but he soon followed the well-established Woodwardian tradition of not lecturing, though he did add yet more specimens to the Woodwardian collection and was available for consultation by those who wished to study it; he also undertook field work in Cornwall and Scotland (Porter, 1977: 144). When he resigned in 1818 a university syndicate was appointed to review the Woodwardian bequest and it was insisted that the new appointee should lecture (Clark and Hughes, 1890, I: 197). The post went to Adam Sedgwick who, though untrained in the science, ushered in a new era in Cambridge geology.

Hailstone's neglect of his lecturing duties was to some extent compensated for by the initiative of Edward Daniel Clarke (MA Jesus, 1794) who, having made a large collection of minerals in the course of his extensive travels throughout Europe and the Middle East, delivered public lectures at Cambridge based on this collection from 1807 using his dramatic gas blow-pipe techniques to illustrate the properties of minerals at high temperatures (Oldroyd, 1972: 219). In the following year the honorary title of professor of mineralogy was conferred on him. Clarke attracted two hundred to his first lecture (Porter, 1977: 144) even though, as his biographer commented, 'The subject [of mineralogy] was little known, and less studied, and by no means popular in the University' (Otter, 1824: 556) – a remark that indicates the lack of activity of Hailstone and his Woodwardian predecessors. Clarke's lectures were descriptive rather than theoretical in character and again illustrate the close links between mineralogy and chemistry since he devised his own scheme of classification of minerals based on chemical characteristics (Oldroyd, 1972: 218–19).

Hailstone's lack of success in promoting his subject – like that of Thomas Martyn – was probably not due simply to indolence: both men had to contend with the fact that there was no institutional incentive at Cambridge to study sciences other than those which contributed to success in the mathematically based Senate House examination. Though, as I have suggested earlier, this entrenched dominance of the mathematical sciences can largely be explained in terms of institutional inertia, the university's reluctance to broaden its prescribed scientific curriculum may have owed something to the conservative reaction at the end of the eighteenth century. This discouraged change of any sort and it also meant that subjects like geology and biology which impinged on the biblical account of the creation of the earth and of man were subject to particular scrutiny. On the other hand, a subject like chemistry – which had no relevance to such religious issues – was not viewed with quite the same concern, though even it was regarded with some suspicion by Edmund Burke, largely because of its associations with the political and religious radical, Joseph Priestley. Like other conservatives in the age of the French Revolution, Burke was most sympathetic to those branches of science and, in particular, natural history which were based on collection and classification in contrast to those which sought to develop a body of theory (Crosland, 1987). Later eighteenth-century Cambridge may not have directly discouraged the study of subjects such as geology or botany but the intellectual climate of England after the French Revolution – particularly in clerical institutions such as the universities – was unfavourable to such subjects developing theoretical structures which might challenge established orthodoxies. The new science of geology which, it was soon discovered, impinged on the biblical account of Creation was particularly susceptible to such pressures and largely survived during the revolutionary period by confining itself to a narrowly empirical view of its subject and by eschewing any larger and more controversial claims (Porter, 1977: 202–6). The biological sciences were less affected, both because they were longer-established and because of their traditional associations with the design argument, but, as the increasingly critical reception accorded to Erasmus Darwin's work after 1789 indicates (Garfinkle, 1955), they could meet with opposition if they ventured into the realm of generalised theories. Thus an anti-jacobin pamphleteer of 1792 attacked naturalistic views of man's origin describing those who wished 'to sever *Man from his* God, and reduce him to a level with the brutes' as hostile to both the existing political and religious order (Jacyna, 1983: 324). In 1819, the year of Peterloo, the attempt by the eminent surgeon William Lawrence to explain the workings of the human mind in naturalistic terms led to Thomas Rennell, Cambridge's Hulsean lecturer, attacking his views as 'strik[ing] deep at the heart of all religion' (Goodfield-Toulmin, 1969: 316). In the following year an Oxford pamphleteer, who also equated Lawrence's views with atheistic materialism, was prompted by Lawrence's work to write: 'For who does not know that we must attribute the French Revolution, with all its horrible attendants of anarchy, despotism and murder, to the persuasion that there was no future existence?' (*ibid.*; Mudford, 1968: 435).

Yet without a body of theory it was difficult to establish the biological and earth sciences on a sound pedagogical foundation. As Hailstone remarked apropos of the earlier history of mineralogy (which had hitherto 'consisted of a few scattered unconnected facts incapable of being digested into a system'): 'what is incapable of being reduced to a system cannot be made the subject of public instruction' (Porter, 1977: 129). It was probably no accident that chemistry – the most popular of the extracurricular sciences – was the one with the best-developed theoretical structure. Even if Cambridge had been disposed to allow its mathematical monopoly to be challenged it would have been difficult to incorporate into the undergraduate curriculum subjects such as botany, zoology or geology, the practitioners of which, at the end of the eighteenth century, tended to shy away from the syntheses and systematic treatment which successful undergraduate instruction required. Ultimately, in the more relaxed atmosphere after the Napoleonic wars, clergymen–scientists such as the Cambridge dons Henslow, Sedgwick and Whewell helped to provide the stamp of respectability for such subjects which, after 1851, were institutionalised in the natural sciences tripos.

Mathematics, by contrast, had the merit in the counter-revolutionary period of providing clearly organised subject matter without any challenge to established modes of thought. In a conservative age mathematics – and in particular geometry – had the attraction of being thought to be a largely closed system with little room for change or revision, at least in its essentials. Among the arguments later advanced by Whewell for maintaining the dominant role of mathematics at Cambridge was that the permanent and uncontentious nature of mathematics was less likely to encourage the spirit of dissent than the less certain and more controversial science based on experiment or observation. In countries like France and Germany, he argued, where students were encouraged to study such sciences there was a 'vehement and general hostility' to existing institutions (Whewell, 1837: 52). In the late eighteenth century Bishop Horne maintained that Cambridge's reputation for heterodoxy was due to its emphasis on mathematics which cultivated a rationalistic spirit which was hostile to Revelation, but the few who took such arguments seriously suggested that the problem lay not so much in the nature of mathematics but in Cambridge's failure to provide an adequate training in theology (*GM*, 1793: 693; Ingram, 1792: 20–1).

By the end of the eighteenth century Cambridge could look back with some pride on its success in assimilating Newtonian natural philosophy and mathematics into its curriculum in a century which was generally suspicious of change. The university could also point to the remarkable growth of an examination system which could lay real claims to impartiality and rigour through its close scrutiny of mathematical competence – a system which was to become the model for British examinations more generally when the reformers of the nineteenth century sought to construct alternatives to appointment by patronage (Roach, 1971: 12–13). However, Cambridge's success in implanting and institutionalising its mathematical traditions had its costs. In a university where prestige was reserved for success in the mathematically dominated Senate House examination there was little institutional encouragement for the observational or experimental sciences, though science generally had gained sufficient ascendancy within Cambridge for some instruction in subjects such as experimental physics, chemistry, botany and geology to be available to the more determined undergraduates. Indeed, there was even little institutional encouragement for further mathematical enquiry once the trials of the tripos were thankfully past. The professorial appointments offered some patronage for the study of the non-mathematical sciences but in a university where most teaching was college-based it is not surprising that these posts were often sinecures. In any case it took a particularly able professor to attract large numbers of fee-paying students to a subject which was non-examinable.

One indication of the low level of interest in scientific research in late eighteenth-century Cambridge was the dissolution within two years of its foundation in 1784 of the Cambridge Society for the Promotion of Philosophy and General Literature, despite the initial support of much of the Cambridge professoriate including Milner, Farish, Vince, Harwood, Martyn and Wollaston (Gorham, 1830: 166–7) – a failure that had its parallel in the collapse of a proposed equivalent at Cambridge of the Oxford Philosophical Society as far back as 1685. It was not until the foundation of the Cambridge Philosophical Society in 1819 – largely at the initiative of the botanist Henslow, and the geologist Sedgwick – that the university had an organisation specifically devoted to the promotion of scientific research, or, as the constitution of the society itself put it, 'the advancement of Philosophy' which, at the first meeting, was amended by the addition of 'and Natural Philosophy'. But this body, too, was overshadowed by the Cambridge mathematical tradition (D. B. Wilson, 1985: 14): Sedgwick later commented 'that the first conception of the Society was that of an organisation for the study of natural history; and he somewhat regretted that the overwhelming mathematical bias of Cambridge had, to a great extent, changed the original design' (Clark and Hughes, 1890, 1: 208).

The dominance of mathematics underlines the extent to which the scientific interests of the university were shaped by its system of examinations. In consequence, the broadening of the university's scientific horizons was largely associated with a further evolution of Cambridge's examination machinery. In the early nineteenth century the most successful academic reformers were those like Robert Woodhouse and George Peacock and other former members of the Cambridge Analytical Society who advocated changes which could be accommodated within the structures of the Senate House examination. Despite initial opposition the new mathematical procedures (largely drawn from Continental analysis) which these men advocated had, by 1820, been successfully incorporated into the tripos (Dubbey, 1963: 48). By increasing the range and sophistication of Cambridge mathematics these developments, in turn, helped to broaden the scientific scope of the examination since more aspects of natural philosophy could be dealt with in a mathematical fashion – hence the wave of new Cambridge texts in physics in the 1820s and 1830s (C. Smith, 1976: 23; Crosland and Smith, 1978: 13). The work of men like Henslow and Sedgwick finally bore institutional fruit with the foundation of the natural sciences tripos in 1851 which had as its examiners the professors of medicine, chemistry, anatomy, geology, botany and mineralogy – the precedent for a tripos in subjects other than mathematics having been created with the establishment of the classical tripos in 1824. Despite such competition the traditional prestige associated with the mathematical tripos meant that for the remainder of the nineteenth century it continued to attract the cream of the undergraduates (Becher, 1986: 85; D. B. Wilson, 1982: 365). Thus, although Cambridge's mathematical tradition may have been built on narrow foundations in the eighteenth century, these foundations were durable enough to survive the upheavals the following century had in store. But the apologetical concerns which had initially largely prompted the university to embrace the Newtonian system, out of which its mathematical traditions grew, gradually receded from view until, by the late nineteenth century, Cambridge mathematics had virtually lost all contact with the theological props which had originally helped to sustain it.

Epilogue

The 'holy alliance' between Newtonian natural philosophy and Anglican latitudinarianism had, by the end of the eighteenth century, proved a fruitful marriage. Confident assertions that science and religion were allies remained part of the intellectual landscape in the first half of the nineteenth century and natural theology continued to be one of the most influential vehicles for the dissemination of new scientific theories (Gillispie, 1959: 227). Natural theology also continued to serve the irenical ends which latitudinarians like Wilkins and Tillotson had ascribed to it in the late seventeenth century, drawing together those, like the early members of the British Association for the Advancement of Science (founded 1831), who shared a common interest in God's Revelation through nature even if they disagreed about the nature of his Revelation through Scripture (Morrell and Thackray, 1981: 229). Newton's name continued to be invoked, in almost talisman fashion, as an instance of the happy conformity of the highest reaches of scientific endeavour and religious belief. Thus William Whewell, in one of his university sermons, cited Newton (along with Bacon, another Trinity graduate) as proof 'that the most capacious intellects of the Christian times have found room for the love of knowledge without expelling the love of God' (Todhunter, 1876, I: 324) and Adam Sedgwick in his *Discourse on the studies of the university* (1834) asserted that 'A study of the Newtonian philosophy . . . teaches us to see the finger of God in all things animate and inanimate' (p. 14). So close was this association of Newton with the cause of religion that the anti-clerical radical Richard Carlisle in 1821 bemoaned the fact that Newton (along with Bacon and Locke) were 'claimed as the patrons of superstition' (Yeo, 1985: 285); Carlisle and other artisan radicals such as Malthus Ryall also argued that science and religion were 'natural enemies' but had entered into a 'hollow conspiracy' to preserve the social and political status quo in the 'fashionable reign of the Bridgewater treatises' (Desmond, 1987: 90). Despite such testimony to the enduring strength of the 'holy alliance' there were some signs, even in the late eighteenth century, that it was under some strain – strain that became more apparent as the nineteenth century progressed.

In the first place, far fewer advocates of natural theology rested their beliefs on specifically Newtonian foundations than had done so in the decades following the publication of the *Principia*. In the late eighteenth century Newtonian-based natural theology was increasingly over-shadowed by natural theology based on the biological sciences. This growing diversity of styles of natural theology increased in the nineteenth century as the pace of scientific change quickened and, in particular, as natural theology sought to accommodate itself to the largely new science of geology which brought a historical dimension to theological issues which had hitherto largely been considered in static terms. The increas-ingly heterogeneous character of the differing varieties of natural theology – which mirrored the increasing diversity of science itself together with the increasing religious diversity of early Victorian society – meant that natural theology had lost much of the clarity and clear outline which had earlier helped to make it comprehensible to a larger public. These differing approaches to natural theology could even be contradictory: J. H. Brooke writes of the debate between the astronomically inclined Brewster and the geologically inclined Whewell over the plurality of worlds that it indicates 'that the natural theology which Darwin is supposed to have destroyed was already a house divided against itself' (1977: 222). In his *Of the plurality of worlds* (1853) Whewell made so many qualifications to the traditional argument from design in order to accommodate it to recent scientific findings that his friend, Sir James Stephen, asked: 'if you are really right, is it not simply impossible to adhere to our commonly received natural theology?' (*ibid.*: 284). Natural theology, then, had lost some of its coherence even before the publication of the *Origin of species* in 1859 challenged the whole concept of design in nature by demonstrating that such apparent design could be viewed as being the result of random forces.

Along with its increasing complexity and the tendency to internal contradictions natural theology was also threatened by the increasing emphasis on revealed theology (Gillespie, 1987: 48–9) – a movement which had its roots in the late eighteenth century and which had gathered pace in the period of political and religious reaction which followed the French Revolution. The most obvious example of this was the growing strength of the evangelicals, though they typified a more general trend which affected other wings of the Church. The suspicion that an emphasis on natural theology led to a downplaying of the importance of Revelation underlay the evangelical Rev. Frederick Nolan's attack on the newly formed British Association in 1833 (Morrell and Thackray, 1981: 234).

Nolan also attacked the Oxford Movement but, though the evangelicals
and tractarians disagreed on many things, they shared similar sentiments
about the British Association's espousal of natural theology as a means of
minimising doctrinal disputes among its members: such sentiments,
wrote Newman's friend, John Bowden, were those of a 'rationalising
latitudinarian' (Orange, 1975: 287). Newman himself – whose early
religious formation was influenced by the evangelical movement (Newman, 1970: 581–3) – also spoke of 'the undue exaltation of the reason'
associated with bodies such as the British Association (Morrell and
Thackray, 1981: 231). Elsewhere he criticised the whole genre of natural
theology – or what he called 'physical theology' – describing it as 'no
science at all, for it is ordinarily nothing more than a series of pious or
polemical remarks upon the physical world viewed religiously' (S. F.
Cannon, 1978: 12). For Newman science and revealed theology occupied
separate spheres which should be kept asunder: 'Theology and Physics',
he later wrote, 'cannot touch each other, have no intercommunion, have
no ground of difference or agreement, of jealousy or of sympathy' (*ibid.*:
11). The increasing force of such religiously based objections to the whole
enterprise of natural theology is apparent in the justifications that the
advocates of natural theology thought it necessary to advance. In his
Discourse on the studies of the university (1834) Sedgwick set out to refute the
arguments of those who had 'asserted within these very walls, that there is
no religion of nature, and that we have no knowledge of the attributes of
God or even of his existence, independently of revelation' (p. 18). Plainly,
his target was the teachings of some of the Cambridge evangelicals, since
he attributed such a view to those who 'believe our corruption to be so
entire, that they deny to the natural man, all perception to the beauty of
moral truth – all knowledge of God – and almost shut out from him the
faculty of reason' (p. 124). In the following year Lord Brougham, in his
Discourse of natural theology (1835), also set out to silence the fears of those
who were 'alarmed lest the progress of natural religion should prove
dangerous to the acceptance of revealed', asserting that it was folly 'to
suppose that natural theology is not necessary to the support of revelation'
(J. H. Brooke, 1979: 49–50).

Even among those broad churchmen who actively continued to promote the alliance between science and natural theology there was a
reluctance to accord too much significance to natural theology even if they
did not go quite so far as Coleridge (who exercised considerable influence
over the broad churchmen) who, in 1825, castigated 'the prevailing taste
for books of natural theology': 'Evidences of Christianity! I am weary of
the word. Make a man feel the want of it; rouse him . . . to the self-
knowledge of his need of it, and you may safely trust to its own evidence'

(Garland, 1980: 63). Thus in the dedication to his Bridgewater tract Whewell wrote: 'Yet, I feel most deeply, what I would take this occasion to express, that this, and all that the speculator concerning Natural Theology can do, is utterly insufficient for the great ends of Religion', something which can 'be achieved only by that Revealed Religion of which we are ministers'. In his introduction he further emphasised the point by remarking on 'the necessarily imperfect and scanty character of Natural Religion' (1862 ed.: vi). Sedgwick, too, at times harped on the inadequacies of natural theology: its conclusions, he wrote, were of 'no small' moral worth but should be kept 'in their proper place, and in subordination to truths of a higher kind'; the Christian did not look to natural theology to supply the foundations of his faith but was drawn to it 'because he believes' (J. H. Brooke, 1979: 42).

Such misgivings about the role of natural theology, together with their determined opposition to utilitarianism (Garland, 1980: 68–9), set the broad churchmen apart from the eighteenth-century latitudinarians with whom they otherwise had much in common. Both movements were largely Cambridge-based and both would have agreed with the goals attributed to the broad churchmen by William Conybeare, a former fellow of Trinity, in his 1853 *Edinburgh Review* article: 'they believe the superficial differences between Christians are as nothing in comparison with their essential agreement; and they are willing that the portals of the church should be flung as widely open as the gates of Heaven' (p. 330) – though Hoadly and his followers would have dissented from his remark that the Church was 'a society divinely instituted for the purpose of manifesting God's presence, and bearing witness to his attributes' (p. 331). As Conybeare noted, even the term 'latitudinarian' was sometimes applied to the broad churchmen by their enemies. However, it is difficult to discern clear links between the eighteenth-century latitudinarians and the nineteenth-century broad churchmen even though their shared goals and common institutional background indicate some connection. Significantly, Conybeare in the course of his article remarked that in 'the last century, the comprehensive Christianity of Tillotson and Burnet degenerated into the worldliness of the Sadducean Hoadly'; he also castigated the views of 'the unbelieving petitioners of the Feathers Tavern' (pp. 335–6). In the eighteenth century the latitudinarians lacked any formal party structure but were to some extent linked by patterns of patronage and education, particularly those associated with Hoadly, Clarke, Edmund Law and Watson. Such associations were broken in the era of the French Revolution when the influence of the latitudinarians waned; consequently, Cambridge broad churchmen like Sedgwick or Whewell do not appear to have been directly influenced by representatives of the eighteenth-century latitudinarian tradition. One indication of the eclipse of eighteenth-century latitudinarianism is the virtual disappearance within early nineteenth-century Cambridge of Socinianism, a mutant form of latitudinarianism; as Sedgwick wrote in 1834: 'There are no avowed Socinians now at Cambridge. During the latter half of the last century there was a considerable number of this party in the University; a few of them were left after I came up to College [in 1804] . . . But they are all gone, and have not left one apostle of their opinions' (Smyth, 1940: 123).

Another indication of the passing of latitudinarianism of the eighteenth-century variety was the increasing emphasis placed on the theological education of trainee clergy. For the eighteenth-century latitudinarians theological essentials could be derived from the study of nature and a largely untutored reading of the Scriptures, but, as the nineteenth century progressed, more was demanded of trainee clergy who were often expected to be familiar with the new perspectives which historical and linguistic studies were bringing to bear on the Scriptures and the traditions of the Church. By the mid-nineteenth century the increasing rigour of theological training made it difficult to find the time to master both divinity and one of the fast-growing sciences (Yule, 1976: 366). More was also expected of the clergy in their pastoral role and fewer and fewer Victorian clergy would have agreed with Paley that 'Amongst the clergy of the Church of England many, without doubt, are very much at their ease' (M. L. Clarke, 1974: 119). Sidney Smith summed up the growing divide between the clerical standards of the eighteenth century and those of the Victorians with his remark to Gladstone in 1835: 'Whenever you meet a clergyman of my age [Smith was then sixty-four] you may be quite sure he is a bad clergyman' (Smyth, 1943: 171). The increasing demands of the clerical profession made nineteenth-century clergymen–scientists vulnerable to the charge that their preoccupation with scientific enquiries involved a neglect of the primary responsibilities of their calling. Critics accused the clerical geologist William Buckland of knowing all the 'ologies' except theology (Chadwick, 1970, I: 565). Sedgwick, another clerical geologist, was taken to task for not spending enough time on the preparation of his sermons (Clark and Hughes, 1890, I: 496).

Scientists, too, grew more assertive about their professional standing and many of them became increasingly resentful of traditions which suggested that their work should be justified by reference to other than scientific goals, such as the further embellishment of the argument from design (F. M. Turner, 1978: 301); some of them also aspired 'to displace the ecclesiastical hegemony' over British educational and intellectual life 'with a scientific one' (Russell, 1983: 258). Just as some clergy saw the scientist–divines as negligent of their clerical duties some scientists regarded them as neglecting their obligations to science. Joseph Hooker spoke slightingly of 'scientifical-geological-theologians' who resembled 'asses between bundles of hay, distorting their consciences to meet the double-call of their public profession' (F. M. Turner, 1978.: 365). Such pressures from both their fellow-clergy and their fellow-scientists help to explain why there were so few successors to such prominent early Victorian clerical scientists as Sedgwick, Henslow, Whewell, Buckland and Conybeare. The growing difficulty of keeping a foot in both the scientific and theological camps is also reflected in the declining proportion of clerical FRSs – in 1849 they formed 9.7% of the Society but this had fallen to 3.1% by 1889 (*ibid.*: 367).

The alliance between science and religion, which had been so marked a feature of the English intellectual landscape in the eighteenth century and continued to remain so in the early nineteenth, had owed much to the fact that both the universities were essentially arms of the Church, so that there was a strong institutional imperative for the clergy to come to terms with secular learning and to seek to demonstrate its moral and theological significance (Yeo, 1985: 287). As the nineteenth century progressed, however, the increasing secularisation of the universities weakened this incentive to produce a harmonious amalgam of science and theology. In the first place Oxford and Cambridge's duopoly was challenged after the foundation of University College, London in 1828, the first of a growing number of rivals. Perhaps even more important was the gradual waning of clerical influence within Oxford and Cambridge themselves. Some of the milestones along this slow and reluctant path were the 1854 and 1856 acts of parliament which abolished religious tests for admissions and degrees, the 1871 University Test Act which freed fellowships from religious tests and the 1877 Universities of Oxford and Cambridge Act which diverted some of the colleges' resources to the central university, chiefly for the promotion of secular disciplines. Such legislative changes were accompanied by an erosion of what had traditionally been the universities' primary function: the training of clergy. At Cambridge the best minds were increasingly turning to professions other than the Church: in 1841–3 65.2% of first-class honours graduates were ordained, but this had fallen to 29.5% by 1871–3 and to 18% by 1881–3; the percentages for fellows entering the Church in the same three periods were 62, 27 and 18 (Haig, 1986: 190).

As Haig points out, the growing number of lay fellows meant that a fellowship was no longer generally regarded as an interlude between graduation and the taking up of a clerical living, particularly after fellows were permitted to marry in 1882 – hence the growing pressure for some form of career-structure which would make a fellowship an acceptable lifetime career. A fellowship, wrote a late eighteenth-century fellow of Lincoln College, Oxford, 'is an excellent breakfast, an indifferent dinner, and a most miserable supper' (Porter, 1982: 178); by the late nineteenth century there was an increasing number of fellows staying for all three meals who had to be offered more inviting fare. What was slowly emerging, then, was the concept of an academic profession as distinct from the clergy (Engel, 1983; Rothblatt, 1968: 227) which, in turn, was linked with a growing emphasis on academic specialisation and research. Such developments further undermined the emphasis on the unity of knowledge and its subordination to ethical and theological ends which had been implicit in the traditional alliance between science and religion.

The slow secularisation of the universities reflected in miniature the weakening of the bonds linking Church and State. Admission of the dissenters and Roman Catholics to the universities was a natural (albeit belated) consequence of the repeal of the Test and Corporation Acts in 1828 and the granting of Catholic Emancipation in 1829 – steps which destroyed the traditional assumption that full membership of the State was predicated on membership of the Established Church. In the eighteenth century the alliance between Church and State had been considered fundamental to the maintenance of the social order. Challenges to this alliance – whether from nonjurors asserting the autonomy of their dispossessed church or from the dissenters – were of major political, as well as ecclesiastical, importance. This close entanglement of the Church with a State which prided itself (however inappropriately) on the rational nature of its political processes was a natural catalyst for systems of theology which emphasised the accord between the secular and the sacred through an illustration of the conformity of natural and revealed theology. Just as Church and State were in partnership so, too, argued the eighteenth-century latitudinarians, were Revelation and human reason. Though both Church and State became more equivocal about the role of reason in the late eighteenth century and, in particular, in the age of the French Revolution, the traditional emphasis on the need to integrate Christianity with secular learning was strong enough to reassert itself in the calmer atmosphere which eventually followed the defeat of the French. But the virtual dismantling of the constitutionally privileged position of the Established Church meant that ecclesiastical affairs were no longer of such great concern to statesmen and the Church's theology no longer carried so heavy a political load. If churchmen wished to assert the autonomy of the Church in the manner of the Oxford Movement then this was no longer a threat to public order in the way that similar claims by the nonjurors (whom the tractarians greatly admired) had been in the eighteenth century. Another indication of the declining political volatility of religious issues was the re-assertion of some degree of control by the clergy over their own affairs with the re-establishment of Convocation in 1852 – a body that had been suspended in 1717 by royal decree because of its politically unsettling behaviour.

As the links between Church and State weakened there was less pressure to demonstrate the conformity between natural and revealed knowledge in the manner of the eighteenth-century clerical defenders of the Hanoverian order. Theologians increasingly asserted not only greater autonomy for the Church as an institution but also for theology as a discipline. It was not only the evangelicals and tractarians who played down the importance of secular learning for theology. *Avant-garde* theologians like Baden Powell (Savilian professor of geometry, Oxford, 1827–60) denied that it was possible to reconcile the Scriptures with science since the two occupied separate realms. Failure to recognise this, he wrote in 1855, had resulted 'either in a lamentable antagonism and hostility, or in futile attempts to combine them in incongruous union, upon fallacious principles' (Young, 1980: 87). Henry Mansel (tutor of St John's College, Oxford) argued in his Bampton lectures of 1858, *The limits of religious thought*, that God's transcendence necessarily implied that He was incomprehensible to human reason (Reardon, 1971: 223) – a view which Whewell, who had devoted his life to demonstrating the conformity of sacred and secular learning, vehemently rejected 'not because it makes Natural Theology impossible, but because it makes Revealed Theology equally impossible' (Todhunter, 1876, I: 341; Yeo, 1979: 512–14). It was the controversy that followed the publication of the theologically adventurous *Essays and reviews* (1860) (which included a contribution from Baden Powell) rather than the appearance of the *Origin of species* in 1859 which prompted the 'scientists' declaration' of 1864–5. This manifesto signed by 65 fellows of the Royal Society and 652 other scientists attempted to re-establish that confidence in the conformity between scientific and religious truth which had, for so long, been a feature of English intellectual life. Against the claims of theologians like Baden Powell the signatories declared that 'We conceive that it is impossible for the Word of God, as written in the book of nature, and God's Word written in Holy Scripture, to contradict one another, however much they may appear to differ.' In a final paragraph (which was later deleted) the document called on the members of Convocation to 'do all in their power to maintain a harmonious alliance between Physical Science and Religion' (Brock and MacLeod, 1976: 41).

Just as the Church was less and less important for the needs of the State so, too, theology became less important as a focus for intellectual activity.

Moreover, as the pace of social and political change gathered momentum the traditional analogy, which underlay the mental world of natural theology, between a divinely ordained static natural order and a largely unchanging social order carried less conviction (C. Brooke, 1985: 69–70). Theology (and, in particular, natural theology) which, in early Victorian times, had continued to provide a 'common context' (Young, 1980) for intellectual life generally had, by the end of the century, become itself but one among a number of other disciplines. One institutional reflection of this was the establishment at Cambridge in 1874 of a separate theological tripos in competition with other triposes in mathematics, classics, moral sciences, natural sciences, law and (after 1875) history, Semitic languages, Indian languages (to list only the pre-1886 foundations). The confidence that all fields of learning could be integrated by reference to common religious or ethical ends was undermined by the ever-growing barriers of expertise and formal qualifications which separated one discipline from another. There was no longer one truth but many truths, no longer one common intellectual language but a veritable tower of Babel (S. F. Cannon, 1978: 280). Natural theology had helped nurture the infant sciences, but by the late nineteenth century they were full-grown adults beholden to no one and determined to go their separate ways.

Bibliography

A. MANUSCRIPT SOURCES

CAMBRIDGE

University Archives
Lett. 13, 14, 17 Official university correspondence
Guardbook 39.19 (Papers concerning the Norrisian chair)

University Library
Additional Manuscripts
    4 Correspondence of John Strype
    20 Life of Symon Patrick by Dr Knight
    589 Lucasian lectures of William Saunderson
    697–9 Divinity exercises of Joseph Beaumont
    2615 fol. 112 Letter concerning the death of John Gay, 1745
    4251 folios 544, 565, 1011 Pitt–Newcastle correspondence, 1763
    5047 Lectures on natural philosophy (probably by Gervase Holmes)
    5803 Lectures of John Symonds, Regius professor of history, 1771–1807
    6958 fol. 207 Richard Watson to William Pitt, 18 February 1797
    7113 Correspondence of Samuel Clarke
    7762 Travel diaries of Charles Mason, Woodwardian professor, 1734–62
    7886–7 Correspondence of William Frend
    7896 fol. 28 Account of Richard Laughton's actions after the Sacheverell trial
    8134 Papers of George Horne

Dd.14.9 Sermons of John Moore
Ee.5.35 Jacksonian lectures of Isaac Milner and Francis Wollaston
Kk.3.1 Divinity lectures of Joseph Beaumont
Mm.1.45; Mm.1.48 Collections of Thomas Baker
Mm.6.50 Selections from the correspondence of John Covel
Oo.6.111 folios 6–8 Oration by Richard Laughton

Christ's College
MS 26 Lectures on natural philosophy (probably by Gervase Holmes)

Clare College
Bursary
    Tutorial accounts of Samuel Blythe (3 vols.)

Fellows' Library

G.3.14 Charles Morgan's mathematical and scientific notes including copies of Cotes's mathematical papers

G.3.21 'The principles of natural religion establish'd' and 'Exposition of the articles of our church' by Richard Laughton

G.6.14 *Principia* with annotations by Richard Laughton

Kk.5.14 'De motu corporum liber' and 'De natura acidorum' by Isaac Newton

N1.2.9 Copies of mathematical papers by Newton and Cotes

P.5.16 Newton's *Lectiones opticae*

College Letterbook

Morgan's Library Catalogue

Corpus Christi College

Hartshorne MSS An extensive collection of eighteenth-century correspondence chiefly relating to clerical and scholarly matters

Emmanuel College

3.1.29 Commonplace book of William Bennet

179 Joshua Barnes's revision of Richard Holdsworth's 'Directions for a student at the universities'

193–5 Lectures on natural philosophy by Henry Hubbard

269 Letterbook of William Burdon

Fitzwilliam Museum

Banks MSS Includes letter of Thomas Green to Joseph Banks, 14 April 1776 (not folioed)

Gonville and Caius College

619/342 Chemical lectures of John Mickleburgh

King's College

Keynes MS 130 Collections of John Conduitt for a life of Isaac Newton

Magdalene College

Correspondence of Daniel Waterland

Queens' College

Conclusion book 1734–87

St John's College

Admonition book

545 'System of morality' by Thomas Balguy

O.84 'Lectures on experimental philosophy' by William Powell

O.85 'A course of mechanical lectures' by Henry Wrigley

U.19 Commonplace book of Brook Taylor

Sidney Sussex College

10.20.1. 11–21 Lectures on morality by John Hey (9 vols.)

Trinity College
Add. a 150 Library catalogue of James Duport
R.1.50–1 Chemical lectures of John Hadley
R.1.54–8 Undergraduate notes of Edward King
R.2.42 Correspondence of Stephen Hales *et al.*
R.8.42 Papers concerning the Jacksonian professorship (including chemical lectures by Francis Wollaston)

OXFORD

Bodleian Library
Aubrey MS 10 'The idea of the education of young gentlemen' by John Aubrey
Autob.d.20 fol. 85 Thomas Hardy to William Frend, March 1831
Ballard 23 folios 114–16 Voting list for the election of the Cambridge University burgesses, 1705
MS Clarendon dep.c.347 Correspondence of Lord Clarendon
Eng. Hist. b.114–15 (R) Petition from Cambridge concerning the 1689 oath of allegiance
Eng. Misc. c.113 fol. 140 Robert Danny to William Stukeley, 1725
Lister MS 35 Correspondence of Martin Lister
Rawlinson C.146 fol. 37 Cambridge's vice-chancellor's prohibition against keeping acts based on Descartes
Rawlinson D.1232 fol. 7 Includes reflections on the Revolution of 1688 by Simon Patrick, Sir Robert Sawyer and William Wotton
Tanner 28 Collection of letters and papers during the year 1688
Tanner 35 Correspondence of William Sancroft
Tanner 155, 158 Collection of letters and papers relating to the University of Cambridge
MS Wilberforce.c.3 Correspondence of William Wilberforce

Christ Church
Evelyn Correspondence no. 79. John Beale to John Evelyn, 2 January 1669

LONDON

British Library
Additional MSS
4224 Biographical collections of Thomas Birch
4251 Notebooks of Thomas Birch
4295 Papers of John Toland
5803, 5811, 5817, 5821–3, 5828, 5831–4, 5841–2, 5846, 5852, 5863, 5865–6, 5870, 5873, 5875, 5877–8, 5880, 5882, 5886 Collections of William Cole (chiefly relating to Cambridge)
22560 Diaries of Rev. John Thomlinson
22908 Correspondence of John Colbatch
22910 Correspondence of John Covel
28539 Correspondence of Emmanuel Mendez da Costa
29546 Collections of George Harbin on ecclesiastical history
29584 Hatton–Finch correspondence
32457–8 Correspondence of Conyers Middleton

32514 Life of the Hon. John North by Roger North

32601 Life of John Wallis

32696, 32710, 32716–19, 32900, 32906–7, 32939, 32942, 32953, 32963, 32977, 32979, 32988 Official correspondence of Thomas Pelham, duke of Newcastle

33349 Correspondence of John Strange with Thomas Martyn

35377, 35585, 35626, 35628, 35640, 35657–8 Papers of Philip Yorke, earl of Hardwicke

Egerton MSS

1970 Correspondence of John Strange

2400 Correspondence of Thomas Gray

Harleian MSS

3784–5 Correspondence of William Sancroft

7030, 7045 Collections of Thomas Baker (chiefly relating to Cambridge)

Landsdowne MSS

1024 Collections of White Kennett

Loan MSS

29/167 Papers of Lord Harley

Stowe MSS

750, 799 Papers of Thomas Parker concerning the universities

British Museum of Natural History

Banksian MS 105 Correspondence of Thomas Martyn

Dr Williams's Library

12.44, 12.57 Correspondence of Theophilus Lindsey

12.45, 12.52 Correspondence of Francis Blackburne

24.168–70 Lectures on the Greek New Testament by John Jebb

28.165 (4) Life of John Disney

Lambeth Palace Library

942 Correspondence of Thomas Tenison

1741 Correspondence of Edmund Gibson

1743 'Proposals for reformation in the church' by Bishop Stillingfleet

Public Record Office

State Papers 35/15 Peter Needham to Thomas Parker, February 1719

Royal Society

MS 82 Correspondence of Brook Taylor

OTHER LOCATIONS

Leeds Public Library

Robinson papers (includes the correspondence of Metcalf Robinson, an undergraduate at Cambridge at the beginning of the eighteenth century)

Leicestershire Record Office

MSS Finch Lit.pap.10 Correspondence of the earl of Nottingham with Daniel Waterland

Manchester Central Library
MS 922.3 N21 Diary of Henry Newcome

Northamptonshire Record Office
MS Dryden (Canons Ashby) 354 Letter of Frederick Leigh on the universities, 1704

Nottingham University Library
Mellish MS 155/94 James Baker to Daniel Finch, 1728

Royal Greenwich Observatory, Herstmonceux
RGO 4 (Maskelyne papers) folios 236–59 Mathematical papers of Israel Lyons

Sheffield City Library
RI 1377 Richard Watson to marquis of Rockingham, 11 May 1771
RI 2105 Richard Watson to marquis of Rockingham, 4 June 1782

Suffolk Record Office
423 Correspondence of Augustus Fitzroy, duke of Grafton
MS 2785 'Herbations chiefly in the neighbourhood of Cambridge' by Michael Tyson

B. PRINTED SOURCES
(place of publication is London unless otherwise stated)

Abbey, C. J. 1887. *The English church and its bishops 1700–1800*. 2 vols.
'Academicus', 1882. *A letter to the reverend Christopher Wordsworth . . . relative to the proposed changes in the examination for the degree of bachelor of arts, in that university*. Cambridge
Ackermann, R. 1815. *A history of the University of Cambridge*. 2 vols.
Albury, W. R. 1978. Halley's ode on the *Principia* of Newton and the Epicurean revival in England. *Journal of the History of Ideas*, 39: 24–43
Allan, D. G. C. and Schofield, R. E. 1980. *Stephen Hales: scientist and philanthropist*
Allen, D. E. 1978. *The naturalist in Britain. A social history*
Anon., 1718. *The church-anatomy . . .*
Anon., 1727. *A copy of the poll taken at the election of members of parliament for the University of Cambridge . . .*
Anon., 1733. *Life of Woolston*
Anon., 1748. *Memoirs of the life, family and character of Charles Seymour, duke of Somerset . . .*
Anon., 1788. *Remarks on the enormous expense in the education of young men in the University of Cambridge . . .*
Anon., 1842. *Recollections of the life of the reverend A. J. Scott*
Anson, W. (ed.) 1898. *Autobiography and political correspondence of Augustus Henry, third duke of Grafton*
Arnold, M. 1962. *Lectures and essays in criticism*. Ann Arbor, Mich.
Aubrey, J. 1898. *Brief lives . . .*, ed. A. Clark. 2 vols. Oxford
Axtell, J. L. 1965. The mechanics of opposition: Restoration Cambridge v. Daniel Scargill. *Bulletin of the Institute of Historical Research*, 38: 102–11
    (ed.) 1968. *The educational writings of John Locke*. Cambridge

Baesel, D. R. 1974. Natural history and British periodicals in the eighteenth century. Unpublished Ph.D. thesis, Ohio State University

Bahlman, D. W. R. 1957. *The moral revolution of 1688.* New Haven, Conn.

Bailyn, B. 1967. *The ideological origins of the American Revolution.* Cambridge, Mass.

Baker, T. 1727. *Reflections on learning*
  1879. *History of the college of St. John's . . . Cambridge,* ed. J. E. B. Mayor. 2 vols. Cambridge

Ball, W. W. R. 1889. *A history of the study of mathematics at Cambridge.* Cambridge
  1893. *An essay on Newton's 'Principia'*

Ball, W. W. R. and Venn, J. A. 1913–16. *Admissions to Trinity College, Cambridge.* 5 vols.

Balleine, G. R. 1951. *A history of the evangelical party in the Church of England*

Barker, E. 1828–9. *Parriana, or notices of the rev. Samuel Parr . . .* 2 vols.
  1948. *Traditions of civility.* Cambridge

Barne, M. 1685. *The authority of church guides asserted*

Barnes, D. G. 1934. The duke of Newcastle, ecclesiastical minister, 1724–54. *Pacific History Review,* 3: 164–91

Baxter, R. 1931. *The autobiography* [An abridgement of *Reliquiae Baxterianae,* 1696.]

Beaumont, J. 1665. *Some observations upon the apologie of Dr. Henry More for his Mystery of Godliness.* Cambridge

Becher, H. W. 1986. Voluntary science in nineteenth-century Cambridge University to the 1850s. *British Journal for the History of Science,* 19: 57–88

Beckett, J. V. 1986. *The aristocracy in England 1660–1914*

Beddard, R. 1965. William Sancroft as archbishop of Canterbury. Unpublished D.Phil. thesis. University of Oxford
  1967. The commission for ecclesiastical promotions, 1681–1684: an instrument of tory reaction. *Historical Journal,* 10: 11–40

Belsham, T. 1789. *Essays, philosophical, historical, and literary.* 2 vols.
  1812, 1873. *Memoirs of the late reverend Theophilus Lindsey*

Benham, W. (ed.) 1889. *Prose works of Thomas Ken*

Bennett, G. V. 1966. King William III and the episcopate. In *Essays in modern church history,* ed. G. V. Bennett and J. Walsh, pp. 104–31
  1971/2. The patristic tradition in Anglican thought, 1600–1900. *Oecumenica* (Strasbourg), 63–85
  1975. *The tory crisis in church and state 1688–1730: the career of Francis Atterbury, bishop of Rochester.* Oxford

Best, G. F. A. 1964. *Temporal pillars: Queen Anne's bounty, the ecclesiastical commissioners and the Church of England.* Cambridge

[Beverley, J.] 1784. *Poll* [at the election for the university of Cambridge burgesses]. Cambridge

Beverley, J. 1793. *The trial of William Frend . . . in the vice-chancellor's court for writing and publishing a pamphlet intitled 'Peace and union recommended'.* Cambridge

Birch, T. 1752. *Life of the most reverend Dr. John Tillotson*
  (ed.) 1772. *The works of Robert Boyle.* 6 vols.

Black, E. C. 1963. *The association. British extraparliamentary political organization 1769–1793.* Cambridge, Mass.

Black, M. H. 1984. *Cambridge University Press 1584–1984.* Cambridge

Blackburne, F. 1804. *The works of Francis Blackburne.* 7 vols.

Bligh, R. 1781. *Letters which passed between the reverend Reginald Bligh and others on account of his being rejected as a fellow of Queens' College . . .*

Bloxam, J. R. (ed.) 1886. *Magdalen College and King James II, 1686–1689* (Oxford Historical Society, vol. 6). Oxford

Bonwick, C. 1977. *English radicals and the American Revolution.* Chapel Hill, N.C.

[Borlase, G.] 1800. *Cantabrigienses graduati . . . ab anno 1659, usque ad annum 1800 . . .* Cambridge

Bosher, R. S. 1951. *The making of the Restoration settlement: the influence of the Laudians 1649–1662.* New York

Bowles, G. 1974. Physical, human and divine attraction in the life and thought of George Cheyne. *Annals of Science,* 31: 473–88

Bradley, I. 1976. *The call to seriousness. The evangelical impact on the Victorians*

Brewster, D. 1855. *Memoirs of the life, writings and discoveries of Sir Isaac Newton.* 2 vols. Edinburgh

Bristed, C. A. 1852. *Five years in an English university.* 2 vols.

Brock, W. H. and MacLeod, R. M. 1976. The Scientists' Declaration: reflections on science and belief in the wake of *Essays and reviews* 1864–5. *British Journal for the History of Science,* 9: 39–76

Brockliss, L. W. B. 1987. *French higher education in the seventeenth and eighteenth centuries. A cultural history.* Oxford

Brooke, C. 1985. *A history of Gonville and Caius College.* Woodbridge, Suffolk

Brooke, J. H. 1977. Natural theology and the plurality of worlds: observations on the Brewster–Whewell debate. *Annals of Science,* 34: 221–86

    1979. The natural theology of the geologists: some theological strata. In *Images of the earth: essays in the history of the environmental sciences,* ed. L. J. Jordanova and R. S. Porter (*British Society for the History of Science Monographs,* no. 1), pp. 39–64

    1985. The relation between Darwin's science and his religion. In *Darwinism and divinity. Essays on evolution and religious belief,* ed. J. Durant, pp. 40–75. Oxford

Brown, A. W. 1863. *Recollections of the conversation parties of the reverend Charles Simeon . . .*

Brown, F. K. 1961. *Fathers of the Victorians.* Cambridge

Brown, T. M. 1974. From mechanism to vitalism in eighteenth-century English physiology. *Journal of the History of Biology,* 8: 179–216

Browning, R. 1975. *The duke of Newcastle.* New Haven, Conn.

    1982. *Political and constitutional ideas of the court whigs.* Baton Rouge, La.

Brunet, P. 1931. *L'introduction des théories de Newton en France au XVIIIe siècle.* Paris

Burdon, W. 1795. *Three letters addressed to the bishop of Llandaff.* Cambridge

    1803. *Unanimity recommended.* Newcastle-upon-Tyne

Burnet, G. 1839. *History of my own time*

    1897–1900. *History of my own time,* ed. O. Airy. 2 vols. Oxford

Burnet, T. 1965. *The sacred theory of the earth.*

Burtt, E. A. (ed.) 1939. *The English philosophers from Bacon to Mill.* New York

Cajori, F. 1919. *A history of the conceptions of limits and fluxions in Great Britain from Newton to Woodhouse.* Chicago

The Cambridge University calendar, for the year 1796 – [And subsequent years.]

Cameron, H. C. 1966. *Sir Joseph Banks.* Sydney

Campbell, T. Q. 1986. John Wesley, Conyers Middleton and divine intervention in history. *Church History,* 55: 39–59

Caner, H. 1972. *Letterbook of the reverend Henry Caner.* Hartford, Conn.

Cannon, J. 1984. *Aristocratic century. The peerage of eighteenth-century England.* Cambridge

Cannon, S. F. 1978. *Science in culture: the early Victorian period.* New York

Cantor, G. N. (ed.) 1981. *Conceptions of ether. Studies in the history of ether theories 1740–1900.* Cambridge

1983. *Optics after Newton. Theories of light in Britain and Ireland, 1704–1840.* Manchester

Carlyon, C. 1856. *Early years and late reflections.* 3 vols.

Carpenter, E. 1948. *Thomas Tenison, archbishop of Canterbury: his life and times*

Cartwright, F. D. 1826. *The life and correspondence of Major Cartwright.* 2 vols.

Carus, W. 1847. *Memoirs of the life of the reverend Charles Simeon*

Chadwick, O. 1970. *The Victorian Church.* 2 vols.

Chipman, R. A. 1954. An unpublished letter of Stephen Gray on electrical experiments, 1707–8. *Isis*, 45: 33–40

Churchill, E. F. 1922. The dispensing power of the crown in ecclesiastical affairs. *The Law Quarterly Review*, 38: 297–316, 420–34

Clark, J. C. D. 1985. *English society 1688–1832.* Cambridge

1986. *Revolution and rebellion. State and society in the seventeenth and eighteenth centuries.* Cambridge

Clark, J. W. and Hughes, T. M. 1890. *The life and letters of the reverend Adam Sedgwick.* 2 vols. Cambridge

Clark-Kennedy, A. E. 1929. *Stephen Hales, D.D., F.R.S.* Cambridge

Clarke, J. 1720. *An enquiry into the cause and origin of evil*

1972 [1st ed. 1730]. *A demonstration of some of the principal sections of Sir Isaac Newton's 'Principles of natural philosophy'.* With a preface by I. B. Cohen. New York

Clarke, M. L. 1974. *Paley: Evidences for the man*

Clarke, S. 1742. *The sermons.* 2 vols.

Clarke, T. E. S. and Foxcroft, H. C. 1907. *A life of Gilbert Burnet, bishop of Salisbury.* Cambridge

Clarkson, T. 1786. *An essay on the slavery and commerce of the human species . . .*

1808. *The history of the abolition of the slave-trade.* 2 vols.

Clay, C. 1980. 'The greed of whig bishops'? Church landlords and their lessees, 1660–1760. *Past and Present*, 87: 128–57

Cobbett, W. (ed.) 1806–20. *Parliamentary history of England.* 36 vols.

Cohen, I. B. 1956. *Franklin and Newton.* Philadelphia

1971. *Introduction to Newton's 'Principia'.* Cambridge

Coleby, L. M. J. 1952a. John Francis Vigani, first professor of chemistry in the University of Cambridge. *Annals of Science*, 8: 46–60

1952b. John Mickleburgh . . . 1718–56. *Annals of Science*, 8: 165–74

1952c. John Hadley, fourth professor of chemistry in the University of Cambridge. *Annals of Science*, 8: 293–301

1953. Richard Watson, professor of chemistry in the University of Cambridge, 1764–71. *Annals of Science*, 9: 101–23

1954. Isaac Milner and the Jacksonian chair of natural philosophy. *Annals of Science*, 10: 234–57

Colley, L. 1982. *In defiance of oligarchy. The tory party 1714–60.* Cambridge

Collignon, C. 1763. *Tyrocinium anatomicum: or, an introduction to anatomy.* Cambridge

Cook, D. 1935. Representative history of the county, town and University of Cambridge. Unpublished Ph.D. thesis, University of London

Cookson, J. E. 1982. *The friends of peace*. Cambridge
Cooper, C. H. 1842–1908. *Annals of Cambridge*. 5 vols. Cambridge
Cooper, S. 1791. *The first principles of civil and ecclesiastical government delineated* . . .
Cope, J. I. 1954. The Cupri-cosmits: Glanvill on latitudinarian anti-enthusiasm. *Huntington Library Quarterly*, 17: 269–86
Cotes, R. 1738. *Hydrostatical and pneumatical lectures*. Cambridge
Coulthurst, H. W. 1796. *The evils of disobedience and luxury*. Cambridge
Cragg, G. R. 1964. *Reason and authority in the eighteenth century*. Cambridge
Craig, J. 1964. Craig's rules of historical evidence. *History and Theory*, 4: 1–31
Crane, R. S. 1934. Anglican apologetics and the idea of progress. *Modern Philology*, 31: 273–306; 349–82
Cressy, D. 1973. Education and literacy in London and East Anglia, 1580–1700. Unpublished Ph.D. thesis, University of Cambridge
Crosland, M. 1987. The image of science as a threat: Burke versus Priestley and the 'philosophic revolution'. *British Journal for the History of Science*, 20: 287–318
Crosland, M. and Smith C. 1978. The transmission of physics from France to Britain 1800–40. *Historical Studies in the Physical Sciences*, 9: 1–62
Crossley, J. and Christie, R. C. 1847–55. *The diary and correspondence of Dr. John Worthington, master of Jesus College, Cambridge*. 3 vols. (Chetham Society Publications, vols. 13, 36, 114.) Manchester
Cudworth, R. 1678. *The true intellectual system of the universe*
Curtis, M. 1959. *Oxford and Cambridge in transition, 1558–1642*. Oxford
[Davies, R.] 1740. *The life and character of Professor Saunderson*
Davies, R. 1759. *The general state of education in the universities* . . . Bath
Davy, C. 1794. *The necessary limitation of the right of private judgment, on controverted points of theology*
De la Pryme, A. 1870. *Diary* (Surtees Society Publications, vol. 54). Durham
Derham, W. (ed.) 1718. *Philosophical letters between the late learned Mr. Ray and several of his ingenious correspondents*
Desmond, A. 1987. Artisan resistance and evolution in Britain. *Osiris*, 2nd ser., 3: 77–110
Dickinson, H. T. 1977. *Liberty and property*
Disney, J. 1785. *Memoirs of the life and writings of Arthur Ashley Sykes* (ed.) 1787. *The works of John Jebb*. 3 vols.
Douglas, D. C. 1939. *English scholars 1660–1730*
D'Oyly, G. 1821. *The life of William Sancroft, archbishop of Canterbury*. 2 vols.
Dubbey, J. M. 1963. The introduction of the differential notation to Great Britain. *Annals of Science*, 19: 37–48
Duffy, E. 1976. 'Whiston's Affair': the trials of a primitive Christian 1709–14. *Journal of Ecclesiastical History*, 27: 129–50
Dyce, A. (ed.) 1836–8. *The works of Richard Bentley*. 3 vols.
Dyer, G. 1796. *Memoirs of the life and writings of Robert Robinson*
1814. *A history of the university and colleges of Cambridge*. 2 vols.
1818. *Four letters on the English constitution*
1824. *The privileges of the University of Cambridge* . . . 2 vols.
Eagles, C. M. 1977. David Gregory and Newtonian science. *British Journal for the History of Science*, 10: 216–25
Ecton, J. 1742. *Thesaurus rerum ecclesiasticarum* . . .
Edleston, J. (ed.) 1850. *Correspondence of Sir Isaac Newton and Professor Cotes* . . .
Edwards, J. 1714. *New discoveries of the uncertainty, deficiency, and corruptions of human knowledge and learning*

Ehrman, J. 1969. *The younger Pitt*. Vol. 1

Emerson, R. 1977. Scottish universities in the eighteenth century. *Studies on Voltaire and the Eighteenth Century*, 167: 453–74

Engel, A. J. 1983. *From clergyman to don: the rise of the academic profession in nineteenth-century Oxford*. Oxford

Enros, P. 1979. The Analytical Society: mathematics at Cambridge University in the early nineteenth century. Unpublished Ph.D. thesis, University of Toronto

'Eubulus', 1822. *Thoughts on the present system of academic education in the University of Cambridge*

Evans, E. J. 1985. *Political parties in Britain 1783–1867*

Every, G. 1956. *The high church party 1688–1718*

Farrell, M. 1973. The life and work of William Whiston. Unpublished Ph.D. thesis, University of Manchester, Institute of Science and Technology

Feingold, M. 1984. *The mathematicians' apprenticeship. Science, universities and society in England, 1560–1640*. Cambridge

Ferguson, J. 1976. *An eighteenth-century heretic, Dr. Samuel Clarke*. Kineton, Warwick

Field, W. 1828. *Memoirs of the life, writings and opinions of Samuel Parr*

Findon, J. C. 1979. The nonjurors and the Church of England, 1689–1716. Unpublished D.Phil. thesis, University of Oxford

Firth, C. H. 1917. Modern history in Oxford, 1724–1841. *English Historical Review*, 32: 1–21

Flower, B. 1796. *National sins considered, in two letters to the Rev. T. Robinson . . .* Cambridge

Force, J. E. 1985. *William Whiston: honest Newtonian*. New York

Fowler, E. 1670. *The principles and practices of certain moderate divines of the Church of England, abusively called latitudinarians . . .*

Fowler, L. and H. (eds.) 1984. *Cambridge commemorated*. Cambridge

Fox-Bourne, H. R. 1876. *The life of John Locke*. 2 vols.

Foxcroft, H. C. 1902. *Supplement to Burnet's 'History of my own time'*. Oxford

Frank, R. G. 1973. Science, medicine and the universities of early modern England: background and sources. *History of Science*, 11: 194–216, 239–69

    1979. The physician as virtuoso in seventeenth-century England. In *English scientific virtuosi in the 16th and 17th centuries*, ed. B. Shapiro and R. G. Frank, pp. 59–114. Los Angeles, Calif.

    1980. *Harvey and the Oxford physiologists*. Berkeley, Calif.

[Frend, W.] 1787. *Considerations on the oaths required at the time of taking degrees*

Frend, W. 1789. *Thoughts on subscription to religious tests particularly that required by the University of Cambridge of candidates for the degree of bachelor of arts, in a letter to the reverend H. W. Coulthurst . . .*

    1793a. *Peace and union recommended to the associated bodies of republicans and anti-republicans*. St Ives

    1793b. *An account of the proceedings in the University of Cambridge, against W. Frend . . . for publishing a pamphlet, intituled 'Peace and Union' . . .* Cambridge

    1795. *A sequel to the account of the proceedings in the University of Cambridge, against the author of a pamphlet entitled 'Peace and Union' . . .* Cambridge

Fuller, T. 1840. *The history of the University of Cambridge*, ed. J. Nichols

Gabbey, A. 1982. Philosophia Cartesiana triumphata: Henry More (1646–1671).

In *Problems of Cartesianism*, ed. J. Lennon *et al.*, pp. 171–250. Kingston and Montreal

Garfinkle, N. 1955. Science and religion in England, 1790–1800: the critical response to the work of Erasmus Darwin. *Journal of the History of Ideas*, 16: 376–88

Garland, M. 1980. *Cambridge before Darwin. The ideal of a liberal education, 1800–60.* Cambridge

Gascoigne, J. 1984a. Mathematics and meritocracy: the emergence of the Cambridge mathematical tripos. *Social Studies of Science*, 14: 547–84

   1984b. Politics, patronage and Newtonianism: the Cambridge example. *Historical Journal*, 27: 1–24

   1985. The universities and the Scientific Revolution: the case of Newton and Restoration Cambridge. *History of Science*, 23: 391–434

   1986. Anglican latitudinarianism and political radicalism in the late eighteenth century. *History*, 71: 22–38

   1988. From Bentley to the Victorians: the rise and fall of Newtonian natural theology. *Science in Context*, 2

   1989a. A reappraisal of the role of the universities in the Scientific Revolution. In *Reappraisals of the Scientific Revolution*, ed. D. Lindberg and R. Westman. New York

   1989b. Church and state allied: the failure of parliamentary reform of the English universities. In *The first modern society: Essays in English history in honour of Lawrence Stone*, ed. L. Beier, D. Cannadine and J. Rosenheim, pp. 401–29. Cambridge

   forthcoming. Barrow's academic milieu. In *Before Newton: the life and times of Isaac Barrow*, ed. M. Feingold. New York

Gay, P. 1970. *The Enlightenment. An interpretation.* 2 vols.

Geikie, A. 1905. *The founders of geology*

   1918. *Memoir of John Michell.* Cambridge

Gilbert, L. F. 1952. W. H. Wollaston manuscripts at Cambridge. *Notes and Records of the Royal Society*, 9: 311–32

Gillespie, N. C. 1987. Natural history, natural theology, and social order: John Ray and the 'Newtonian Ideology'. *Journal of the History of Biology*, 20: 1–50

Gilley, S. 1981. Christianity and enlightenment: an historical survey. *History of European Ideas*, 1: 103–21

Gillispie, C. C. 1959. *Genesis and geology. The impact of scientific discoveries upon religious beliefs in the decades before Darwin.* New York

Gisborne, T. 1789. *The principles of moral philosophy investigated . . .*

Gjertsen, C. 1986. *The Newton handbook*

Goodfield-Toulmin, J. 1969. Some aspects of English physiology: 1780–1840. *Journal of the History of Biology*, 2: 288–320

Gordon, J. 1771. *The causes and consequences of evil speaking against government considered . . .* Cambridge

Gorham, G. C. 1830. *Memoir of John Martyn and Thomas Martyn*

Gowing, R. 1983. *Roger Cotes – natural philosopher.* Cambridge

Grafton, third duke of (Augustus Henry Fitzroy). 1789. *Hints submitted to the serious attention of the clergy, nobility and gentry, by a layman*

Green, I. M. 1978. *The re-establishment of the Church of England 1660–1663.* Oxford

Green, J. 1749. *Commencement sermon.* Cambridge

[Green, J.] 1760. *The principles and practices of the Methodists considered . . .* Cambridge

[Green, J.] 1761. *The principles and practices of the Methodists further considered; in a letter to the reverend Mr. George Whitefield.* Cambridge

1763. *A sermon preached before the lords spiritual and temporal . . .*

Green, V. H. H. 1964. *Religion at Oxford and Cambridge*

Greene, D. J. 1953. Smart, Berkeley, the scientists and the poets. A note on eighteenth-century anti-Newtonianism. *Journal of the History of Ideas,* 14: 327–52

Greene, R. 1707. *Encyclopaedia, or method of instructing pupils.* Cambridge

1711. *A demonstration of the truth and divinity of the Christian religion . . .* Cambridge

1712. *The principles of natural philosophy . . .* Cambridge

1727. *The principles of the philosophy of the expansive and contractive forces . . .* Cambridge

Grove, R. 1676. *Vindication of the conforming clergy . . .* (Second edition.)

Guerlac, H. 1977. *Essays and papers in the history of modern science.* Baltimore

Guerlac, H. and Jacob, M. C. 1969. Bentley, Newton and Providence. *Journal of the History of Ideas,* 30: 307–18

Guerrini, A. 1985. John Keill, George Cheyne and Newtonian physiology 1690–1740. *Journal of the History of Biology,* 18: 247–66

1986. The tory Newtonians: Gregory, Pitcairne and their circle. *Journal of British Studies,* 25: 288–311

1987. Archibald Pitcairne and Newtonian medicine. *Medical History,* 31: 70–83

Gunn, J. A. W. 1983. *Beyond liberty and property. The process of self-recognition in eighteenth-century political thought.* Kingston and Montreal

Gunning, H. 1855. *Reminiscences of the university, town and county of Cambridge.* 2 vols.

Gunther, R. W. T. (ed.) 1928. *John Ray: further correspondence*

Guttridge, G. H. 1966. *English whiggism and the American Revolution.* Berkeley, Calif.

Haig, A. G. L. 1980. The Church of England as a profession in Victorian England. Unpublished Ph.D. thesis, Australian National University

1986. The church, the universities and learning in later Victorian England. *Historical Journal,* 29: 187–201

Hailstone, J. 1792. *A plan of a course of lectures on mineralogy, to which is prefixed an essay on the different kinds of mineral collections, translated from the German of Professor Werner.* Cambridge

Hales, S. 1733. *Statical essays*

1961 [1st ed. 1727]. *Vegetable staticks.* With preface by M. A. Hoskin

Hall, A. R. and Hall, M. B. (eds.) 1965–86. *The correspondence of Henry Oldenburg.* 13 vols. Madison, Wisc.

Hallifax, S. 1768. *Two sermons preached before the University of Cambridge in the year 1768.* Cambridge

1769. *Sermon preached before the honourable House of Commons . . . Jan 30, 1769, appointed to be observed as the martyrdom of King Charles I.* Cambridge

1772. *Three sermons preached before the university on the attempt to abolish subscription to the thirty-nine articles of religion.* Cambridge

Hankins, T. L. 1985. *Science and the Enlightenment.* Cambridge

Hans, N. A. 1951. *New trends in education in the eighteenth century*

Hardin, C. L. 1966. The scientific work of the reverend John Michell. *Annals of Science*, 22: 27–47

Harrison, W. J. 1958. *Life in Clare Hall, Cambridge 1658–1713.* Cambridge

Hartley, D. 1749. *Observations on man*

Hartshorne, A. (ed.) 1905. *Memoirs of a royal chaplain, 1729–1763: the correspondence of Edmund Pyle . . . with Samuel Kerrick*

Hayter, T. 1754. *An essay on the liberty of the press*

Hazard, P. 1965. *European thought in the eighteenth century.* Harmondsworth

Hearne, T. 1885–1921. *Remarks and collections.* 11 vols. Oxford
  1966. *The remains.* Fontwell

Heathcote, R. 1756. *The use of reason asserted in matters of religion: or, natural religion the foundation of revealed*

[Heberden, W.] 1792. *Strictures upon the discipline of the University of Cambridge . . .*

Heeney, B. 1976. *A different kind of gentleman.* Hampden, Conn.

Heimann, P. M. and McGuire, J. E. 1971. Newtonian forces and Lockean powers: concepts of matter in eighteenth-century thought. *Historical Studies in the Physical Sciences*, 3: 255–61

Henning, B. D. 1983. *The House of Commons 1660–1690.* 3 vols.

Henslow, J. 1835. *Address to the reformers of the town of Cambridge.* Derby

Herne, T. 1719. *An essay on imposing and subscribing articles of religion*

Hervey, T. 1881. *Life of the reverend Samuel Settle.* Colmer

Hey, J. 1841 [1st ed. 1796]. *Lectures in divinity . . .* 2 vols. Cambridge

Hilken, T. J. 1967. *Engineering at Cambridge University 1783–1965.* Cambridge

Hill, B. W. 1976. *The growth of parliamentary parties 1689–1742*
  1985. *British parliamentary parties 1742–1832*

Hill, C. 1961. *The century of revolution 1603–1714.* Edinburgh

Hirschberg, D. R. 1980. The government and church patronage in England, 1660–1760. *Journal of British Studies*, 20: 109–39

Hiscock, W. G. (ed.) 1937. *David Gregory, Isaac Newton and their circle.* Oxford

Historical Manuscript Commission Reports:
  1. *The manuscripts of the earl of Egmont.* 3 vols. 1920–3
  2. *The manuscripts of his grace the duke of Portland; preserved at Welbeck Abbey.* 10 vols. 1891–1931
  3. *The manuscripts of the earl of Buckinghamshire, earl of Lindsey, earl of Onslow, Lord Emily, Theodore J. Hare esq., and James Round esq., M.P.* 1895
  4. *The manuscripts of the Marquess Townshend.* 1885
  5. *The manuscripts of the earl of Westmorland, Captain Stewart, Lord Stafford, Lord Muncaster, and others.* 1885

Hoadly, B. 1710. *The origin and institution of civil government . . .*
  (ed.) 1738. *The works of Samuel Clarke.* 4 vols.

Hoadly, J. (ed.) 1773. *The works of Benjamin Hoadly.* 3 vols.

Hobhouse, S. (ed.) 1948. *Selected mystical writings of William Law*

Hodgson, R. 1811. *Life of the right reverend Beilby Porteus*

Holmes, G. 1967. *British politics in the reign of Anne*
  1982. *Augustan England. Professions, state and society, 1680–1730*

Horne, G. 1756. *An apology for certain gentlemen in the University of Oxford . . .* Oxford

Horsley, S. 1813. *The speeches in parliament of Samuel Horsley.* Dundee
  1816. *Sermons.* 3 vols.

Hoskin, M. A. 1961. 'Mining all within': Clarke's notes to Rohault's *Traité de physique. The Thomist*, 24: 353–63

Howard, H. F. 1935. *An account of the finances of the College of St John the Evangelist, 1511–1926.* Cambridge

Howell, T. 1816–26. *A complete collection of state trials.* 34 vols.

Hubbard, H. 1750. *A sermon preached before the governors of the charity for the relief of the poor widows and orphans of clergymen* . . .

Hudson, C. W. 1975. The English deists. Unpublished MA thesis, University of Sydney

Hughes, E. 1952. *North country life in the eighteenth century.* Vol. 1. Oxford

Hughes, J. J. 1977. The missing 'last words' of Gilbert Burnet in July 1687. *Historical Journal,* 20: 221–7

Hunt, J. 1870–3. *Religious thought in England from the Reformation* . . . 3 vols.

Hunter, M. 1975. The origins of the Oxford University Press. *The Book Collector,* 24: 511–34

   1981. *Science and society in Restoration England.* Cambridge

   1982a. Ancients, moderns, philologists and scientists. *Annals of Science,* 39: 187–92

   1982b. *The Royal Society and its fellows 1660–1700 (British Society for the History of Science Monographs,* no. 4)

Hyman, A. 1982. *Charles Babbage, pioneer of the computer.* Princeton

Ingram, R. A. 1792. *The necessity of introducing divinity into the regular course of academical studies considered.* Colchester

   1807. *The causes of the increase of methodism and dissension, and of the popularity of what is called evangelical preaching* . . .

Isaacs, T. 1982. The Anglican hierarchy and the Reformation of Manners 1688–1738. *Journal of Ecclesiastical History,* 33: 391–411

Jackson, J. 1718. *The grounds of civil and ecclesiastical government* . . .

Jacob, M. C. 1976. *The Newtonians and the English revolution.* Hassocks, Sussex

   1981. *The radical enlightenment: pantheists, freemasons and republicans*

Jacob, M. C. and Lockwood, W. A. 1972. Political millenarianism and Burnet's *Sacred theory. Science Studies,* 2: 265–79

Jacyna, L. S. 1983. Imminence and transcendence: theories of life and organisation in Britain, 1790–1835. *Isis,* 74: 311–29

Jenkin, R. 1700. *The reasonableness and certainty of the Christian religion.* 2 vols.

   1709. *Remarks on some books lately published, viz. Basnage's History of the Jews, Whiston's Eight Sermons, Locke's Paraphrase and notes on St Paul's epistles, Le Clerc's Bibliothèque choisie*

Jenkins, H. and Jones, D. C. 1950. Social class of Cambridge University alumni of the 18th and 19th centuries. *British Journal of Sociology,* 1: 93–116

Jenyns, L. 1862. *Memoir of the reverend John Stevens Henslow*

Johnson, T. 1735. *Quaestiones philosophiae.* Cambridge

Jones, R. F. 1965. *Ancients and moderns.* Berkeley, Calif.

Jones, W. 1787. *Essay on the Church.* Gloucester

   1795. *Memoirs of the life, studies and writings of George Horne* . . .

   1834. *Memoirs of the life, ministry, and writings of the reverend Rowland Hill* . . .

Jones, W. H. S. 1936. *A history of St Catharine's College, Cambridge.* Cambridge

Jones, W. P. 1937. The vogue of natural history in England, 1750–1770. *Annals of Science,* 2: 345–52

   1961. The idea of the limitations of science from Prior to Blake. *Studies in English Literature,* 1: 97–114

   1965. *Thomas Gray, scholar.* New York

   1966. *The rhetoric of science*

Jortin, J. 1846 [1st ed., 1751–4]. *Remarks on ecclesiastical history*. 2 vols.

Judd, G. P. 1955. *Members of parliament, 1734–1832*. New Haven, Conn.

[Jurin, J.] 1734. [Author given as 'Philalethes Cantabrigiensis'.] *Geometry no friend to infidelity; or a defence of Sir Isaac Newton and the British mathematicians . . .*
    1735. *The minute mathematician; or the free-thinker no just-thinker*

Kassler, J. C. 1979. *The science of music in Britain, 1714–1830*. 2 vols.

Kearney, H. 1970. *Scholars and gentlemen. Universities and society in pre-industrial Britain 1500–1700*

Kendrick, T. F. J. 1968. Sir Robert Walpole, the old whigs and the bishops, 1733–1736: a study in eighteenth-century parliamentary politics. *Historical Journal*, 11: 421–45

Kenyon, J. 1977. *Revolution principles. The politics of party 1688–1720*. Cambridge

Kipling, T. 1802. *The articles of the Church of England proved not to be Calvinistic*. Cambridge

Kirwan, R. 1784. *Elements of mineralogy*

Knight, D. M. 1972. *Natural science books in English 1600–1900*

Knight, F. 1971. *University rebel: the life of William Frend 1757–1841*

Knox, V. 1824. *The works, with a biographical preface*. 7 vols.

Korsten, F. 1985. Thomas Baker and his books. *Transactions of the Cambridge Bibliographical Society*, 8: 491–513

Kramnick, I. 1986. Eighteenth-century science and radical social theory: the case of Joseph Priestley's scientific liberalism. *Journal of British Studies* 25: 1–30

Kubrin, D. 1967. Newton and the cyclical cosmos: Providence and the mechanical philosophy. *Journal of the History of Ideas*, 28: 325–46
    1968. Providence and the mechanical philosophy: the creation and dissolution of the world in Newtonian thought. Unpublished Ph.D. thesis, Cornell University

Kuhn, A. J. 1974. Nature spiritualised: aspects of anti-Newtonianism. *English Literary History*, 41: 400–12

Langdon-Brown, W. 1946. *Some chapters in Cambridge medical history*. Cambridge

Latham, R. and Matthews, W. (eds.) 1970–83. *The diary of Samuel Pepys*. 10 vols.

[Law, E.] 1774. *Considerations on the propriety of requiring a subscription to articles of faith*

Law, E. 1776. *Reflections on the life and character of Christ*
    1820. *Considerations on the state of the world, with regard to the theory of religion*

Law, G. 1804. *The limits to our enquiries, with respect to the nature and attributes of the deity*

Lee, H. 1702. *Anti-scepticism, or notes upon each chapter of Locke's Essay . . .*

Leedham-Green, E. 1986. *Books in Cambridge inventories*. Cambridge

Legg, J. W. 1914. *English church life from the Restoration to the tractarian movement*

Leigh, A. A. 1899. *King's College*

Le Mahieu, D. L. 1976. *The mind of William Paley. A philosopher and his age*. Lincoln, Nebraska

Lloyd Jukes, H. A. 1964. Peter Gunning, 1613–84: scholar, churchman, controversialist. *Studies in church history*, ed. G. W. Dugmore and C. Duggan, 1: 222–32

Loane, M. 1952. *Cambridge and the evangelical succession*

Locke, J. 1708. *Some familiar letters between Mr. Locke and several of his friends*
    1975 ed. *An essay concerning human understanding*, ed. P. Nidditch. Oxford

Long, R. 1742. *Astronomy, in five books*. 2 vols.

Lucas, P. 1974. A collective biography of students and barristers of Lincoln's Inn, 1680–1804: a study in the 'aristocratic resurgence' of the eighteenth century. *Journal of Modern History*, 46: 227–61

Lukis, W. C. (ed.) 1882–7. *The family memoirs of the reverend William Stukeley M.D.* . . . (Surtees Society Publications, vols. 73, 76, 80). Durham

Lunn, J. R. 1883. *Memoir of Caleb Parnham* (Cambridge Antiquarian Society Publications, vol. 31). Cambridge

Lynam, R. (ed.) 1825. *The complete works of William Paley*. 4 vols.

Lyons, I. 1758. *A treatise on fluxions*. Cambridge

McAdoo, H. R. 1965. *The spirit of Anglicanism: a survey of Anglican theological method in the seventeenth century*

McCormmach, R. 1968. John Michell and Henry Cavendish: weighing the stars. *British Journal for the History of Science*, 4: 126–55

    1969. Henry Cavendish: a study of rational empiricism in eighteenth-century natural philosophy. *Isis*, 60: 293–306

McDowell, R. B. and Webb, D. A. 1982. *Trinity College Dublin 1592–1952. An academic history*

McGuire, J. E. and Tamny, M. (eds.) 1983. *Certain philosophical questions: Newton's Trinity notebook*. Cambridge

McKelvey, J. L. 1973. *George III and Lord Bute*. Durham, N.C.

McKenzie, D. F. 1976. Richard Bentley's design for the Cambridge University Press, c. 1696. *Transactions of the Cambridge Bibliographical Society*, 6: 322–7

McKitterick, D. 1986. *Cambridge university library. A history*. Vol. II: *The eighteenth and nineteenth centuries*. Cambridge

McLachlan, H. 1920. *Letters of Theophilus Lindsey*. Manchester

    1931. *English education under the test acts*. Manchester

Malden, H. E. 1902. *Trinity Hall*

Manuel, F. 1963. *Isaac Newton historian*. Cambridge, Mass.

    1968. *A portrait of Isaac Newton*. Cambridge, Mass.

    1974. *The religion of Isaac Newton*. Oxford

Marsh, H. 1792. *An essay on the usefulness and necessity of theological learning, to those who are designed for holy orders* . . . Cambridge

[Marsh, H.] 1808. *Memoir of the late reverend Thomas Jones*. Cambridge

Marsh, H. 1813. *A letter to the reverend Charles Simeon* . . . Cambridge

[Marsh, H.] 'Philograntus', 1822. *A letter to the right reverend John [Kaye], Lord Bishop of Bristol* . . .

Marsh, R. 1699. *The vanity and danger of modern theories*. Cambridge

Martyn, T. 1764. *Heads of a course of lectures in botany, read at Cambridge*

Mason, J. E. 1935. *Gentlefolk in the making: the history of English courtesy literature from 1531 to 1774*. Philadelphia

Mason, W. (ed.) 1807. *The works of Thomas Gray*. 2 vols.

Masson, D. 1859–94. *The life of Milton* . . . 6 vols. Cambridge

Masters, R. 1831 [1st ed. 1753]. *History of the College of Corpus Christi* . . . *Cambridge*, ed. J. Lamb

Mather, F. C. 1985. Georgian churchmanship reconsidered. *Journal of Ecclesiastical History*, 36: 255–83

Matthews, A. G. 1934. *Calamy revised* . . . Oxford

    1947. *Walker revised* . . . Oxford

Mayo, C. H. 1922. The social status of the clergy in the seventeenth and eighteenth centuries. *English Historical Review*, 37: 258–66

Meadley, G. 1810. *Memoirs of William Paley*. Edinburgh

Metzger, H. 1938. *Attraction universelle et religion naturelle chez quelques commentateurs anglais de Newton*. Paris

Middleton, E. 1786. *Biographia evangelica*. 4 vols.

Miller, D. P. 1981. Sir Joseph Banks: an historical perspective. *History of Science*, 19: 284–92

Miller, E. 1961. *Portrait of a college. A history of the college of St John the Evangelist*. Cambridge

Milner, I. 1813. *Strictures on some of the publications of the reverend Herbert Marsh, D.D.*
1820. *Sermons*. 2 vols.

Milner, J. 1781. *Gibbon's account of Christianity considered: together with some strictures on Hume's 'Dialogues concerning natural religion'*. York

Milner, M. 1842. *Life of Isaac Milner*

Monk, J. H. 1822. *The duty of attention to the original objects of academical institutions*. Cambridge
1826. *Memoir of James Duport*. Cambridge
1830–3. *Life of Richard Bentley*. 2 vols.

Moore, C. 1885. *John Moore*

Moore, J. 1715. *Sermons on several subjects*

More, L. T. 1934. *Isaac Newton, 1642–1727: a biography*. New York

Morrell, J. B. 1971. The University of Edinburgh in the late eighteenth century: its scientific eminence and academic structure. *Isis*, 62: 158–71

Morrell, J. B. and Thackray, A. 1981. *Gentlemen of science: the early years of the British Association for the Advancement of Science*. Oxford

Moule, C. H. 1892. *Charles Simeon*

Mudford, P. 1968. William Lawrence and the natural history of man. *Journal of the History of Ideas*, 29: 430–6

Mullinger, J. B. 1873–1911. *A history of the university of Cambridge*. 3 vols. Cambridge
1901. *St. John's College*

Murphy, M. J. 1977. *Cambridge newspapers and opinion 1780–1850*. Cambridge

Murray, N. V. 1975. The influence of the French Revolution on the Church of England and its rivals, 1789–1802. Unpublished D.Phil. thesis, University of Oxford

Namier, L. and Brooke, J. 1964. *The House of Commons 1754–90*. 3 vols.

Napier, A. (ed.) 1859. *The theological works of Isaac Barrow, D.D.* 9 vols. Cambridge

Newman, J. H. 1970. *Prose and poetry*, ed. G. Tillotson. Cambridge, Mass.

Newton, I. 1974. *Mathematical principles of natural philosophy*. Translated A. Motte, 1729; ed. F. Cajori. Berkeley, Calif.

Nichols, J. 1812–15. *Literary anecdotes of the eighteenth century*. 9 vols.
1817–58. *Illustrations of the literary history of the eighteenth century*. 8 vols.

Nicolson, M. H. 1929a. Christ's College and the latitude-men. *Modern Philology*, 27: 35–53
1929b. Early stages of Cartesianism in England. *Studies in Philology*, 36: 356–74
(ed.) 1930. *Conway letters: the correspondence of Anne, Viscountess Conway, Henry More, and their friends 1642–1684*. New Haven, Conn.

Norman, E. R. 1976. *Church and state in England 1770–1970*. Oxford

North, R. 1890. *The lives of the Norths*, ed. A. Jessopp. 3 vols.

O'Day, R. 1982. *Education and society 1500–1800. The social foundations of education in early modern Britain*

Ogden, H. V. S. 1940. The state of nature and the decline of Lockian political theory in England, 1760–1800. *American Historical Review*, 46: 21–44

O'Gorman, G. 1982. *The emergence of the British two-party system 1760–1832*

Oldmixon, J. 1730–9. *The critical history of England*. 2 vols.

Oldroyd, D. 1972. Edward Daniel Clarke, 1769–1822, and his role in the history of the blow-pipe. *Annals of Science*, 29: 213–35

Oldroyd, D. R. and Hutchins, D. W. 1979. The chemical lectures at Oxford (1822–54) of Charles Daubeny. *Notes and Records of the Royal Society*, 33: 217–59

Olson, R. 1983. Tory–high church opposition to science and scientism in the eighteenth century: the works of John Arbuthnot, Jonathan Swift, and Samuel Johnson. In *The uses of science in the age of Newton*, ed. J. G. Burke, pp. 171–204. Berkeley, Calif.

Open University, 1974. *New interactions between theology and natural science*. Milton Keynes

Orange, A. D. 1975. The idols of the theatre: the British Association and its early critics. *Annals of Science*, 32: 277–94

Osmond, P. 1944. *Isaac Barrow: his life and times*

Otter, W. 1824. *The life and remains of the reverend Edward Daniel Clarke* . . .

Overton, J. 1802. *The true churchmen ascertained* . . . York

Overton, J. H. 1885. *Life in the English church, 1660–1714*

Owen, J. 1794. *The retrospector: reflections on the state of religion and politics in FRANCE AND GREAT BRITAIN*

Packer, J. W. 1969. *The transformation of Anglicanism 1643–1660*. Manchester.

Paley, W. 1800. *The life of Edmund Law*
   1845. *The works; to which is prefixed the life of the author, complete in one volume*. Edinburgh

Palmer, R. R. 1976. Turgot: paragon of the Continental Enlightenment. *Journal of Law and Economics*, 19: 607–19

Parkinson, R. (ed.) 1854–7. *The private journal and literary remains of John Byrom*. 3 vols. (Chetham Society Publications, vols. 32, 34, 40). Manchester

Parr, S. 1801. *A spital sermon preached . . . upon Easter Tuesday, April 15, 1800. To which are added notes*

Patrick, S. 1662. *A brief account of the new sect of latitude-men*

Peacock, D. M. 1794. *Considerations on the structure of the House of Commons, and on the plans of parliamentary reform agitated at the present day*

Pearson, E. 1810. *Cautions to the hearers and readers of the reverend Mr. Simeon's sermon* . . . Cambridge

Peckard, P. 1759. *Observations on Mr. Fleming's Survey* . . .

[Peckard, P.] 1776. *Subscription or historical extracts*

Peckard, P. 1783. *The nature and extent of civil and religious liberty*. Cambridge

Peile, J. 1900. *Christ's College*
   1913. *Biographical register of Christ's College, Cambridge*. Vol. II: *1666–1905*. Cambridge

Perry, C. 1841. *Clerical education, considered with an especial reference to the universities*

Phelps Brown, E. H. and Hopkins, S. V. 1956. Seven centuries of the prices of consumables, compared with builders' wage-rates. *Economica*, n.s., 23: 296–314

Piggott, S. 1950. *William Stukeley*. Oxford

Plumb, J. H. 1969. *The growth of political stability in England 1675–1725*

Pocock, J. G. A. 1950–2. Robert Brady, 1626–1700. A Cambridge historian of the Restoration. *Cambridge Historical Journal*, 10: 186–204

1985a. Clergy and commerce. The conservative Enlightenment in England. In *L'età dei lumi. Studi storici sul settecento Europeo in onore di Franco Venturi*, vol. 1, pp. 523–62

1985b. *Virtue, commerce, and history.* Cambridge

Pollard, A. and Hennell, M. (eds.) 1959. *Charles Simeon*

Popkin, R. H. 1971. The philosophy of Bishop Stillingfleet. *Journal of the History of Philosophy*, 9: 303–19

Popple, M. 1793. *Considerations on reform . . .*

Porter, R. S. 1977. *The making of geology. Earth science in Britain 1660–1815.* Cambridge

1980. Science, provincial culture and public opinion in Enlightenment England. *British Journal for Eighteenth-Century Studies*, 3: 20–46

1981. The Enlightenment in England. In *The Enlightenment in national context*, ed. R. S. Porter and M. Teich, pp. 1–18. Cambridge

1982. *English society in the eighteenth century*

Porteus, B. 1767. *Commencement sermon.* Cambridge

Powell, W. S. 1746. *Heads of lectures in experimental philosophy.* Cambridge

1758. *A defence of the subscriptions required in the Church of England*

1774. *An observation on the design of establishing annual examinations.* Cambridge

Price, D. J. 1952. The early observatory instruments of Trinity College, Cambridge. *Annals of Science*, 1: 1–12

Pryme, G. 1870. *Autobiographical recollections*

Ramsden, R. 1800. *The alliance between the church and the state*

Rattansi, P. M. 1962. The literary attack on science in the late seventeenth and eighteenth centuries. Unpublished Ph.D. thesis, University of London

Raven, C. 1950. *John Ray, naturalist.* Cambridge

Ravitch, N. 1966. *Sword and mitre. Government and episcopate in France and England in the age of aristocracy.* The Hague

Reardon, B. M. G. 1971. *From Coleridge to Gore. A century of religious thought in Britain*

Redwood, J. 1976. *Reason, ridicule and religion: the age of enlightenment in England, 1660–1750*

Reedy, G. 1985. *The Bible and reason. Anglicans and Scripture in late seventeenth-century England.* Philadelphia

Rennell, T. 1799. *Ignorance productive of atheism, faction and superstition.* Dublin

Richardson, C. 1928. *English preachers and preaching 1640 to 1670: a secular study.* New York

Roach, J. 1971. *Public examinations in England 1850–1900.* Cambridge

Robb-Smith, A. H. T. 1974. Cambridge medicine. In *Medicine in seventeenth-century England*, ed. A. G. Debus, pp. 327–69. Berkeley, Calif.

Robbins, C. 1959. *The eighteenth-century commonwealthsman . . .* Cambridge, Mass.

Roberts, P. 1796. *Observations on the principles of Christian morality and the apostolic character: occasioned by Dr. Paley's view of the evidences of Christianity*

Robinson, R. 1807. *Miscellaneous works.* 4 vols. Cambridge

Rook, A. 1969a. Medicine at Cambridge, 1660–1760. *Medical History*, 13: 107–22

1969b. Robert Glynn (1719–1806), physician at Cambridge. *Medical History*, 13: 251–61

(ed.) 1971. *Cambridge and its contribution to medicine*

1979. Charles Collignon (1725–1785): Cambridge physician, anatomist and moralist. *Medical History*, 23: 339–45

Ross, J. 1756. *Commencement sermon*. Cambridge

Rothblatt, S. 1968. *The revolution of the dons. Cambridge and society in Victorian England*

Rowbottom, M. 1968. The teaching of experimental philosophy in England, 1700–1730. *Actes du XIe Congrès International d'Histoire des Sciences*, 4: 46–63. Warsaw

Rowden, A. W. 1916. *The primates of the four Georges*

Rowning, J. 1735. *A compendious system of natural philosophy*. Cambridge

Rupp, G. 1986. *Religion in England 1688–1791*. Oxford

Russell, C. A. 1983. *Science and social change 1700–1900*

Rutherforth, T. 1744. *An essay on the nature and obligations of virtue*

1748. *A system of natural philosophy, being a course of lectures on mechanics, optics, hydrostatics, and astronomy* . . . 2 vols. Cambridge

Rutt, J. (ed.) 1831. *Memoirs and correspondence of Joseph Priestley*. 2 vols.

Ryle, J. C. 1978. *Christian leaders of the eighteenth century*. Edinburgh.

Salzman, L. F. *et al.* 1938–78. *The Victoria history of the County of Cambridge and the Isle of Ely*. 6 vols.

Sanderson, M. (ed.) 1975. *The universities in the nineteenth century*

Sangster, P. E. 1964. The life of the reverend Rowland Hill (1777–1833) and his position in the evangelical revival. Unpublished D.Phil. thesis, University of Oxford

Sargent, J. 1833. *The life of the reverend T. T. Thomason*

Schneider, B. R. 1957. *Wordsworth's Cambridge education*. Cambridge

Schofield, R. E. 1970. *Mechanism and materialism. British natural philosophy in the age of reason*. Princeton

1978. An evolutionary taxonomy of eighteenth-century Newtonianisms. *Studies in Eighteenth Century Culture*, 7: 175–92

Schofield, T. P. 1986. Conservative political thought in Britain in response to the French Revolution. *Historical Journal*, 29: 601–22

Scott, R. F. 1903. *Admissions to the College of St. John the Evangelist, Cambridge, Part III*. Cambridge

Sedgwick, A. 1834. *A discourse on the studies of the university*. Cambridge

Sedgwick, R. (ed.) 1970. *The history of parliament: the House of Commons, 1715–1754*. 2 vols.

Selby-Biggs, L. A. (ed.) 1879. *British moralists*. 2 vols. Oxford

Shaftesbury, the earl of 1716. *Letters to a student at the university*

Shapin, S. 1981. Of gods and kings: natural philosophy and politics in the Leibniz–Clarke disputes. *Isis*, 72: 187–215

Shapin, S. and Schaffer, S. 1985. *Leviathan and the air-pump. Hobbes, Boyle and the experimental life*. Princeton

Shapiro, B. J. 1969. *John Wilkins 1614–1672. An intellectual biography*. Berkeley, Calif.

Sharp, T. 1825. *The life of John Sharp, D.D.* . . . 2 vols.

Sharpe, W. 1817. *A course of sermons* . . . *before the University of Cambridge during* . . . *April 1816*. [1st ed. 1816; 2nd ed. with an appendix 1817.] Cambridge

Sher, R. B. 1985. *Church and university in the Scottish Enlightenment*. Edinburgh

Sidney, E. 1844. *The life of the reverend Rowland Hill*

Smith, C. 1976. 'Mechanical philosophy' and the emergence of physics in Britain: 1800–50. *Annals of Science*, 33: 21–9

Smith, C. U. M. 1987. David Hartley's Newtonian neuropsychology. *Journal of the History of the Behavioural Sciences*, 23: 123–36

Smith, G. 1755. *Remarks upon the life of the most reverend Dr. John Tillotson compiled by Thomas Birch*

Smith, R. 1738. *A compleat system of optics* . . . 2 vols. Cambridge
    1749. *Harmonics.* Cambridge

Smyth, C. H. E. 1940. *Charles Simeon and church order.* Cambridge
    1943. The evangelical movement in perspective. *Cambridge Historical Journal*, 7: 160–74

Snapp, H. 1973. Church and state relations in early eighteenth-century England. *Journal of Church and State*, 15: 83–96

Soloway, R. A. 1969. *Prelates and people. Ecclesiastical social thought in England 1783–1852*

Somervell, D. C. 1965. *English thought in the nineteenth century.* New York

Spears, M. K. 1948. Matthew Prior's attitude towards natural science. *Proceedings of the Modern Language Association*, 63: 485–507

Spiller, M. R. G. 1980. *'Concerning natural experimental philosophie': Meric Casaubon and the Royal Society.* The Hague

Spurr, J. 1985. Anglican apologetic and the Restoration church. Unpublished D.Phil. thesis, University of Oxford

Squire, S. 1748. *An historical essay upon the ballance of civil power in England, from its first conquest by the Anglo-Saxons to the time of the revolution*
    1753. *An enquiry into the foundation of the English constitution; or, an historical essay upon the Anglo Saxon government*
    1762. *A sermon preached before the lords spiritual and temporal . . . Jan. 30, 1762, being the anniversary of the martyrdom of King Charles I*

Standish, J. 1676. *A sermon preached before the king at Whitehall, September the 26th 1675*

Steffens, H. J. 1977. *The development of Newtonian optics in England.* New York

Stephen, L. 1962. *History of English thought in the eighteenth century.* 2 vols.

[Stevens, W.] 1777. *Strictures on a sermon entitled 'the Principles of the Revolution vindicated . . .' by R. Watson*

Stewart, L. 1978. Whigs and heretics. Unpublished Ph.D. thesis, University of Toronto
    1981. Samuel Clarke, Newtonianism and the factions of post-revolutionary England. *Journal of the History of Ideas*, 42: 53–72

Stillingfleet, E. 1707–10. *The works . . . together with his life and character.* 6 vols.

Stone, L. 1964. The educational revolution in England, 1560–1640. *Past and Present*, 28: 14–28
    1974. The size and composition of the Oxford student body. In *The university in society*, ed. L. Stone, vol. 1, pp. 3–110. Princeton
    1980. The results of the English revolutions of the seventeenth century. In *Three British revolutions 1641, 1688, 1776*, ed. J. G. A. Pocock, pp. 23–108. Princeton

Stone, L. and Stone, J. C. F. 1984. *An open elite? England 1540–1880.* Oxford

Straka, G. 1962. The final phase of divine right theory in England, 1688–1712. *English Historical Review*, 77: 638–58

Stratton, F. J. M. 1949. *The history of the Cambridge observatories.* Cambridge

Stromberg, R. N. 1954. *Religious liberalism in eighteenth-century England.* Oxford

Strong, E. W. 1957. Newtonian explications of natural philosophy. *Journal of the History of Ideas*, 18: 49–83

Sullivan, R. E. 1982. *John Toland and the deist controversy*. Cambridge, Mass.

Sutherland, L. S. and Mitchell, L. G. 1986. *The history of the university of Oxford*. Vol. v: *The eighteenth century*. Oxford

Syfert, R. H. 1950a. Some early reactions to the Royal Society. *Notes and Records of the Royal Society*, 7: 207–58

1950b. Some early critics of the Royal Society. *Notes and Records of the Royal Society*, 8: 20–64

Sykes, A. A. 1740. *The principles and connexion of natural and revealed religion*

Sykes, N. 1926. *Edmund Gibson, bishop of London*. Oxford

1928. Benjamin Hoadly. In *The social and political ideas of some English thinkers of the Augustan age AD 1650–1750*, ed. F. J. C. Hearnshaw, pp. 112–56

1934. *Church and state in England in the eighteenth century*. Cambridge

1935. Queen Anne and the episcopate. *English Historical Review*, 50: 433–64

1955. The sermons of Tillotson. *Theology*, 58: 297–302

1959. *From Sheldon to Secker: aspects of English church history 1660–1768*. Cambridge

Symonds, J. 1778. *Remarks upon an essay entitled, The history of the colonisation of the free states of antiquity, applied to the present contest between Great Britain and her American colonies*

Talon, H. (ed.) 1950. *Selections from the journals and papers of John Byrom*

Tanner, J. (ed.) 1917. *The historical register of the University of Cambridge . . . to the year 1910*. Cambridge

Taylor, A. (ed.) 1858. *The works of Symon Patrick, D.D. . . .* 9 vols.

Taylor, S. 1985. Sir Robert Walpole, the Church of England, and the Quakers tithe bill of 1736. *Historical Journal*, 28: 51–77

Thackray, A. 1970. *Atoms and powers: an essay on Newtonian matter-theory and the development of chemistry*. Cambridge, Mass.

1972. *Dalton: critical assessments of his life and science*. Cambridge, Mass.

Thayer, H. S. (ed.) 1974. *Newton's philosophy of nature: selections from his writings*. New York

Thomas, R. 1961. The seven bishops and their petition, 18 May 1688. *Journal of Ecclesiastical History*, 12: 56–70

Thorne, R. (ed.) 1986. *The House of Commons, 1790–1820*. 5 vols.

Todhunter, I. 1876. *William Whewell, D.D.* 2 vols.

Torrey, N. 1930. *Voltaire and the English deists*. New Haven, Conn.

Toynbee, P. 1927. Horace Walpole's 'Delenda est Oxonia'. *English Historical Review*, 42: 95–108

Tunstall, J. 1765. *Lectures on natural and revealed religion . . .*

Turnbull, H. W. *et al.* (eds.) 1959–77. *The correspondence of Sir Isaac Newton*. 7 vols. Cambridge

Turner, F. M. 1978. The Victorian conflict between science and religion: a professional dimension. *Isis*, 69: 356–76

Turner, J. 1685. *A discourse concerning the Messias, to which is prefixed a large preface, ascertaining and explaining the Blessed Trinity, against the late writer of The intellectual system*

Tweddell, R. 1816. *Remains of the late John Tweddell*

Twigg, J. D. 1983a. The parliamentary visitation of the University of Cambridge, 1644–1645. *English Historical Review*, 97: 513–28

1983b. The University of Cambridge and the English Revolution, 1625–1688. Unpublished Ph.D. thesis, University of Cambridge

1987. *A history of Queens' College, Cambridge.* Woodbridge, Suffolk
Ure, P. (ed.) 1958. *Mr. Hobbes's state of nature considered,* by J. Eachard. Liverpool
Valadez, F. M. and O'Malley, C. D. 1971. James Keill of Northampton, physician, anatomist and physiologist. *Medical History,* 15: 317–35
Van Mildert, W. (ed.) 1823. *The works of Daniel Waterland.* 11 vols. in 12. Oxford
Vellacott, P. C. 1924. The struggle of James II with the University of Cambridge. In *In memoriam: A. W. Ward,* pp. 81–101. Cambridge
Venn, H. [n.d.] *The complete duty of man.* With a preface by J. Venn
Venn, J. 1834. *The life and a selection from the letters of the late reverend Henry Venn* 1901. *Caius College.* Cambridge
Venn, J. A. 1908. Matriculations at Oxford and Cambridge, 1544–1906. *Oxford and Cambridge Review,* pp. 48–66
Vince, S. 1806. *Observations on the hypotheses which have been assumed to account for the cause of gravitation from mechanical principles.* Cambridge
1807. *Confutation of atheism from the laws and constitution of the heavenly bodies.* Cambridge
Vincent, W. 1780. *A letter to the reverend Dr. R. Watson . . .* [on the political opinions advanced in his Fast sermon . . .]
Vincent, W. A. L. 1950. *The state and school education 1640–1660*
Wakefield, G. 1792. *Memoirs of the life of Gilbert Wakefield, written by himself*
1798. *A letter to Sir John Scott, his Majesty's attorney-general, on the subject of a late trial [the King v. Wakefield, for libel]* at the Guildhall
1813. *Correspondence of the late Gilbert Wakefield with the late right honourable Charles James Fox . . .*
Walker, A. K. 1973. *William Law: his life and thought*
Walpole, H. 1845. *Memoirs of the reign of King George III.* 4 vols.
Walsh, J. D. 1958. The Magdalene evangelicals. *Church Quarterly Review,* 159: 499–511
1959. Joseph Milner's evangelical church history. *Journal of Ecclesiastical History,* 10: 174–87
Walters, S. M. 1981. *The shaping of Cambridge botany.* Cambridge
Ward, R. 1710. *The life of . . . Dr. Henry More . . .*
Ward, W. R. 1958. *Georgian Oxford.* Oxford
Wardale, J. R. 1899. *Clare College*
(ed.) 1903. *Clare College, letters and documents.* Cambridge
[Watson, R.] 1772. *A letter to the members of the honourable House of Commons; respecting the petition for relief in the matter of subscription*
Watson, R. 1776. *The principles of the revolution vindicated.* Cambridge
1780. *A sermon preached before the University of Cambridge, Feb. 4 1780, being the day appointed for a general fast.* Cambridge
(ed.) 1791. *A collection of theological tracts.* 6 vols.
1793 [1st ed. 1781–7]. *Chemical essays.* 5 vols.
1798. *An address to the people of Great Britain*
1817. *Anecdotes of the life of . . .*
Webster, C. 1969. Henry More and Descartes: some new sources. *British Journal for the History of Science,* 4: 359–77
1975. *The great instauration. Science, medicine and reform, 1626–1660*
Westfall, R. 1975. The role of alchemy in Newton's career. In *Reason, experiment and mysticism in the Scientific Revolution,* ed. M. L. Righini Bonelli and W. R. Shea, pp. 189–232

1980. *Never at rest. A biography of Isaac Newton.* Cambridge

Weston, W. 1739. *Some kinds of superstition worse than atheism. Two university sermons with an account of the author's usage by the deputy vice-chancellor*

Whewell, W. 1837. *On the principles of English liberal education*
1862. *Lectures on the history of moral philosophy.* Cambridge
1862 ed. [1st ed. 1833]. *Astronomy and general physics considered with reference to natural theology*

Whiston, W. 1708 [1st ed. 1696]. *New theory of the earth*
1730. *Historical memoirs of the life of . . . Samuel Clarke*
1753. *Memoirs of the life and writings of Mr. William Whiston . . .*
1972 ed. [1st ed. 1716]. *Sir Isaac Newton's mathematical philosophy more easily demonstrated,* ed. I. B. Cohen. New York

White, J. 1746. *Third and last letter to a gentleman dissenting from the Church of England . . .*

Whiteside, D. T. (ed.) 1967–81. *The mathematical papers of Isaac Newton.* 8 vols. Cambridge

Whittingham, R. (ed.) 1838. *The work of the reverend John Berridge*

Wigmore-Beddoes, D. G. 1971. *Yesterday's radicals. A study of the affinity between Unitarianism and broad church Anglicanism in the nineteenth century.* Cambridge

Wilberforce, R. I. and S. 1838. *The life of William Wilberforce.* 5 vols.

Wilberforce, W. 1958 [1st ed. 1797]. *A practical view of the prevailing religious system of professed Christians in the higher and middle classes in this country contrasted with real Christianity*

Wilde, C. 1980. Hutchinsonianism, natural philosophy and religious controversy in eighteenth-century Britain. *History of Science,* 18: 1–24

Williams, B. 1932. *Stanhope. A study in eighteenth-century war and diplomacy.* Oxford

Williams, E. N. 1960. *The eighteenth-century constitution.* Cambridge

Wilson, A. M. 1983. The Enlightenment came first to England. In *England's rise to greatness 1660–1783,* ed. S. B. Baxter, pp. 1–28. Berkeley, Calif.

Wilson, D. B. 1982. Experimentalists among the mathematicians: physics in the Cambridge natural sciences tripos, 1851–1900. *Historical Studies in the Physical Sciences,* 12: 325–71
1985. The educational matrix: physics education at early Victorian Cambridge, Edinburgh and Glasgow universities. In *Wranglers and physicists,* ed. P. H. Harman. Manchester

Winstanley, D. A. 1922. *The University of Cambridge in the eighteenth century.* Cambridge
1935. *Unreformed Cambridge.* Cambridge
1940. *Early Victorian Cambridge.* Cambridge

Wood, A. 1813–20 [1st ed. 1691–2]. *Athenae Oxonienses . . .,* ed. P. Bliss. 5 vols.

Woolston, T. 1729–30. *Discourses on the miracles of our Saviour*

Wordsworth, C. (ed.) 1842. *The correspondence of Richard Bentley . . .* 2 vols.
1874. *Social life at the English universities in the eighteenth century.* Cambridge
1877. *Scholae academicae.* Cambridge

Wormhoudt, A. 1949. Newton's natural philosophy in the Behmenistic works of William Law. *Journal of the History of Ideas,* 10: 411–29

Wratislaw, A. H. 1850. *Observations on the Cambridge system . . .* Cambridge

Wright, J. M. F. 1827. *Alma mater, or seven years at the University of Cambridge . . .* 2 vols.

Bibliography

Wyvill, C. 1771. *Thoughts on our articles of religion, with respect to their supposed utility to the state*
    1794–1806. *Political papers . . .* 6 vols. York
Yeo, R. 1979. William Whewell, natural theology and the philosophy of science in mid-nineteenth-century Britain. *Annals of Science*, 36: 493–516
    1984. Science and intellectual authority in mid-nineteenth-century Britain: Robert Chambers and *Vestiges of the natural history of creation*. *Victorian Studies*, 28: 5–31
    1985. An idol of the market-place: Baconianism in nineteenth-century Britain. *History of Science*, 23: 251–98
Yolton, J. W. 1956. *John Locke and the way of ideas*. Oxford
Young, R. M. 1980. Natural theology, Victorian periodicals and the fragmentation of a common context. In *Darwin to Einstein. Historical studies on science and belief*, ed. C. Chant and J. Fauvel, pp. 69–106
Yule, J. D. 1976. The impact of science on British religious thought in the second quarter of the nineteenth century. Unpublished Ph.D. thesis, University of Cambridge

Index

compiled by Janet D. Hine
in consultation with the author